T0328302

Funding the Greek Crisis

Funding the Greek Crisis

The European Union, Cohesion Policies, and the Great Recession

Constantinos Ikonomou

**Ph.D. University of Cambridge,
Adjunct Lecturer, National and Kapodistrian
University of Athens, Department of Economics
Professor-Consultant, Hellenic Open University
Member of the Board, Supreme Council for Civil
Personnel Selection (Greece)**

ACADEMIC PRESS

An imprint of Elsevier

Academic Press is an imprint of Elsevier
125 London Wall, London EC2Y 5AS, United Kingdom
525 B Street, Suite 1650, San Diego, CA 92101, United States
50 Hampshire Street, 5th Floor, Cambridge, MA 02139, United States
The Boulevard, Langford Lane, Kidlington, Oxford OX5 1GB, United Kingdom

Notices
Knowledge and best practice in this field are constantly changing. As new research and experience broaden our
understanding, changes in research methods, professional practices, or medical treatment may become
necessary.

Practitioners and researchers must always rely on their own experience and knowledge in evaluating and using
any information, methods, compounds, or experiments described herein. In using such information or methods
they should be mindful of their own safety and the safety of others, including parties for whom they have a
professional responsibility.

To the fullest extent of the law, neither the Publisher nor the authors, contributors, or editors, assume any
liability for any injury and/or damage to persons or property as a matter of products liability, negligence or
otherwise, or from any use or operation of any methods, products, instructions, or ideas contained in the
material herein.

Library of Congress Cataloging-in-Publication Data
A catalog record for this book is available from the Library of Congress

British Library Cataloguing-in-Publication Data
A catalogue record for this book is available from the British Library

ISBN: 978-0-12-814566-1

For Information on all Academic Press publications
visit our website at https://www.elsevier.com/books-and-journals

Working together
to grow libraries in
developing countries

www.elsevier.com • www.bookaid.org

Publisher: Janco Candice
Acquisition Editor: Scott Bentley
Editorial Project Manager: Michael Lutz
Production Project Manager: Anusha Sambamoorthy
Cover Designer: Matthew Limbert

Typeset by MPS Limited, Chennai, India

To my parents

On fait la science avec des faits, comme on fait une maison avec des pierres; mais une accumulation de faits n' est pas plus une science qu' un tas de pierres n' est une maison.

H. Poincaré

Contents

Foreword   ix
Acknowledgments   xiii
Introduction   xv

1 **The great Greek crisis**   1
   1.1 The country of Greece: a fragmented territory   1
   1.2 Basic facts and figures on the Greek crisis   2
        1.2.1 The Greek case: a significant component in a chain of events   3
   1.3 Debts, interest rates and the resulting financial support   8
   1.4 The three different periods of debt-to-GDP ratio   11
   1.5 Explanations of the Greek crisis   21
        1.5.1 Structural and policy-oriented explanations   21
        1.5.2 A brief historical assessment in welfare terms
               of Greece's choice to integrate in the European Communities   28
        1.5.3 Explaining the Greek crisis by looking at the mirror of the
               European institutional responses   32
        1.5.4 Policy-oriented and on-crisis policy explanations   37
        1.5.5 IMF policies and its mistakes   62
   1.6 Debt per GDP: the denominator of the fraction   69

2 **Theoretical underpinnings**   73
   2.1 Introduction   73
        2.1.1 Resource allocation   73
        2.1.2 Investment theory: choice, programming, strategy   74
        2.1.3 Emphasizing infrastructure investment for development
               purposes   77
        2.1.4 A useful distinction for economic growth and development
               studies: autonomous versus induced investment   81
        2.1.5 Implications from emphasizing autonomous
               investment: a few points from theory   84
        2.1.6 On the theory and policy of competitiveness   102
        2.1.7 Investment under EU Cohesion and Agricultural Policy   109
        2.1.8 A few comments on EU Cohesion Policy, management,
               and organizational learning: a reference to Senge's theory   114

3   Analysis of the deeper causes of the Greek crisis   117
3.   The allocation of EU Funds in Greece   117
 3.1   Amounts and levels of invested expenditure   117
 3.2   Funding allocation and priorities   120
  3.2.1   An imbalanced allocation of EU funds   120
  3.2.2   Other priorities funded   123
  3.2.3   Human capital policies   124
  3.2.4   Agriculture as a principal funding priority 126
  3.2.5   Private investments   129
 3.3   Comparing the allocation of funds in Greece
   and other Cohesion countries   147
 3.4   The programming of Cohesion policy in Greece   151
 3.5   Regulation and competition   192
 3.6   Critical issues: the use and absorption of funds
   and programming failures   192
 3.7   Output produced   222
 3.8   Greece's Balance with the EU: A country progressively
   assuming its responsibilities   222
 3.9   Long-term effects and implications from the
   imbalanced allocation of funds   232
  *3.9.1   Effects upon manufacturing and industrial
   restructuring*   232
  *3.9.2   Effects on competitiveness, exports, and the
   balance of payment: Greece's suffocating problem* 239
 3.10   Tracing the prospect of convergence; wishful thinking and
   reality   254
 3.11   Public sector expenses   264
 3.12   The turning of an economy to consumption-based   267

4   Conclusions   269
 4.1   Conclusions and final thoughts   269
  4.1.1   Projecting few conclusions in growth theory and
   macroeconomics   280

References   287
Appendix: Additional theoretical implications   305
Index   309

Foreword

The Greek crisis—its origins, management, and effects—has been at the center stage of public debate ever since it erupted in 2010. Was it expected? Could it have been prevented? Could it have been managed differently so that the ensuing profound recession and the dramatic rise in unemployment and poverty could be avoided? What are the policy lessons that can be drawn from the crisis that could mitigate the incidence and costs of future crises in Eurozone member-countries? What are the implications for European policy making and for cohesion policy in particular?

The book at hand by Dr. Ikonomou, provides credible answers to most of these questions based on insightful theoretical arguments and thorough empirical research. In the process, it highlights the failures of policy making at both national and European Union levels, thus providing important and timely recommendations for the future.

According to the author, the Greek crisis of 2010 erupted as a consequence of a growing competitiveness gap that was allowed to widen unabated for two decades (1989–2010). By 2009, the trade deficit in goods and services had reached almost 13% of GDP. Despite considerable transfers from Community Structural Funds, the current account deficit, financed mostly by external sovereign borrowing, exceeded 10% of GDP throughout the period. The accumulation of debt, which rose from 80% of GDP in 1990 to 127% in 2009, was perceived to be unsustainable by private market participants and speculators. They proceeded to bet against Greek sovereign bonds and the euro in the early months of 2010. The unprecedented rise in interest rates that ensued barred the country from accessing international financial markets to cover mounting financial needs, forcing it to seek assistance from its EU partners.

The rest is history: the Greek government signed in May 2010 the first Financial Assistance Program (FAP) with the European Commission and the IMF receiving a loan of 110 billion euros; this was followed by two additional FAPs in 2011 and 2015 amounting to additional loans of 165 billion and 86 billion euros. The provision of loans was accompanied by harsh conditionality conditions included in three consecutive Memoranda of Understanding. Austerity measures included severe cuts in fiscal expenditures, wages, and pensions, coupled with increased taxes, a severe squeeze in liquidity, and an ambitious program of labor market liberalization. These measures resulted in a sharp drop in disposable incomes and a deep recession. The country lost a quarter of its Gross Domestic Product in the course of 7 years, while the unemployment rate more than doubled from 10% in 2009 to 21% in 2017. Around 250,000 small and medium size companies (SMEs) shut down and poverty levels increased. From a longer-term perspective, the economic meltdown and increased uncertainty resulted in a large increase in nonperforming loans and private sector indebtedness, a sharp decline in investment activity and productivity and a brain drain, as a large number of young people and professionals left the country in search of better opportunities abroad.

The author adopts an innovative structural approach to present and explain the origins of the crisis. Focusing on the composition of investment expenditures following Greece's entry into the EU in 1981, he argues convincingly that the development paradigm adopted by consecutive Greek governments proved to be unsustainable. In their efforts to make Greece one of the first countries to join the newly formed Economic and Monetary Union (EMU)—Greece joined the EMU in 2001—policy makers put increased emphasis on nominal convergence at the detriment of real convergence. Rapid nominal growth, regardless of its source, was expected to raise tax receipts and lower the debt to GDP ratio, thus helping the country satisfy the Maastricht criteria for entry; clever asset swaps were also used to mask the external debt exposure of the country. To spur growth, investments in transportation, telecommunications, energy, health care, and education were given high priority. Economic and social infrastructure development, supported by EU structural funds over a number of programmatic periods, induced high rates of consumption and growth but discouraged productive private sector investment and innovation. Continuous resource misallocation in support of nontradable goods and services ended up in producing a growing competitiveness gap that eventually gave rise to a debt crisis. The appreciation of the real exchange rate in the absence of investment- promoting structural reforms prevented economic, environmental, and technological transformations from taking place, thus eroding the country's comparative advantage in rapidly globalizing markets.

Therefore, according to Ikonomou, the Greek debt crisis was the outcome of a competitiveness-eroding process that was systematically disregarded by policy makers both at the national and European levels.[1]

His insightful analysis deepens our understanding of the Greek crisis and sheds light on the origins of financial crises, especially in developing countries and emerging economies. High growth performance over a short period of time does not prevent financial crises from eventually occurring. All depends on the sources of growth and a country's ability to continuously upgrade its productivity and international competitiveness. Insufficient attention to economic and technological transformation by countries which rely on external borrowing from private financial markets to cover mounting trade deficits, make these countries vulnerable to speculative attacks in international financial markets.

According to Ikonomou, the same myopia has characterized the design and implementation of EU cohesion policies over the past years. EU policy makers were not sufficiently alarmed by the low levels of absorption of the 2000−2006 Competitiveness Program that aimed at promoting productive restructuring. Their

---

[1] It should be pointed out that the dangers ahead were highlighted by a few forward looking politicians and academics as early as 2002; see G Arsenis.

excessive preoccupation with the overall level of absorption and efficient use of available funding under the 3rd Community Support Framework, led them to allow the reallocation of resources towards increased infrastructural investment as well as institutional capacity building. Despite the shared responsibility of EU institutions in the implementation of cohesion policies, the effectiveness of policies adopted by member states to actually promote cohesion was largely neglected. The importance of competitiveness-enhancing measures for the EU integration process itself and for the financial stability of the Eurozone was downplayed. This is an important point raised by Ikonomou that should be seriously considered as the Community is about to revamp its cohesion policy during the next programmatic period. Structural and institutional reforms to enhance productive investment, innovation, and entrepreneurship should be given high priority. Appropriate incentives and disincentives, structured around smart conditionality criteria, should be used to promote productive and cohesive restructuring, which is a prerequisite for sustainable development. As has been pointed out by other authors, "one-size fits all policies," such as misguided investments, income-support transfers, or massive public employment programs, often result in "protected, assisted and sheltered economies," which "prove to be increasingly incapable of mobilizing their true economic potential."[2] Ikonomou extends this argument further by linking such policies with systemic financial crises and EU-wide financial instability. EU cohesion policy therefore needs to become much more place-sensitive and transformative.

These conclusions, derived from his extensive analysis of the Greek case, lead the author to revisit and criticize the theoretical underpinnings of growth theory. By not paying adequate attention to the composition of investment for the sustainability of growth, standard theoretical models cannot adequately explain economic cycles and debt dynamics.

The book at hand is thus useful and interesting for both theorists and policy makers. By making a strong case in favor of productive investments and cohesion policies as catalysts for sustainable development and financial stability, Ikonomou makes a noteworthy contribution to the development literature and the policy debate on how to attain the sustainable development goals.

Prof. Louka T. Katseli
Department of Economics, National and Kapodistrian University of Athens, Ex Minister of Economy, Competitiveness and Shipping, Athens, Greece

---

[2] Fratesi, U and Rodriguez-Pose A., 2016, "The crisis and regional employment in Europe: what role for sheltered economies?" Cambridge Journal of Regions, Economy and Society. 2018;11:189–209.

Acknowledgments

This book is the result of many years of work. It started with my PhD studies on the Greek economy at the University of Cambridge that helped me to study several aspects of the Greek economy and the application of EU Cohesion Policy in Greece. It continued with my work at ELIAMEP, ever since I returned from Cambridge, on a rather ambitious project assessing the effects of EU Cohesion Policy, commissioned by the Prime Minister's office.[1] The major part of this work was written more recently, over the last 2 years.

I would like to thank professors and lecturers at the Department of Economics of the National and Kapodistrian University of Athens, where I have shared my concerns about the Greek economy and its crisis for many years and discussed this rather neglected angle of Greek economic policies on the influence exercised upon the economy from policies co-funded by the EU. Being privileged enough to offer room for many different views in economics, the Department's environment has helped me to find my own way in explaining the main arguments of the present text. I would like to thank mostly the Associate Professors and Professors at the Sector of International Economics and Development, in particular Lina Kosteletou and Louka Katseli who have always found some time to listen to me and share some of my scientific views. My student, Alexandros Kordas, has been very helpful in producing most of the Tables and Figures of the present work, during the last part of this research and I would like to thank him very much for his voluntary support.

I would also like to thank the editorial team of Elsevier who have worked to produce this outcome and especially the executive editor Scott Bentley who believed in this work, and decided to embrace it with trust and confidence.

Constantinos Ikonomou
Ph.D. University of Cambridge

[1] The report, produced by the Think Tank ELIAMEP (Hellenic Foundation for European and Foreign Policy), was a meticulous assessment conducted for the Greek Central Bank of Greece, on behalf of the then Greek Prime Minister.

Introduction

The recent global crisis had strong consequences upon the Greek economy and society. The overall shrinking of the Greek GDP from 2008 to 2016 reached unprecedented levels, despite numerous policies scheduled and applied in collaboration with the IMF, the EU authorities, and EU partners. In real terms, it has exceeded the respective levels of cumulative shrinking after the 1929 crisis in the US economy.

Greece joined the European Economic Community as a tenth member, in 1981. It was one of the earliest EU member-states and a founding member of its monetary zone. Historically committed to European unification and the enlargement process, it has welcomed and worked hard for deepening integration and the participation of new member-states on equal bases. Thus, any policy lessons drawn from the case study of a state eager to further integrate have a more general interest and value, at least for every new member-state joining the EU. From this perspective, it is interesting to investigate if some particular mistakes have impeded the combined efforts of Greece and EU authorities to cofund the development priorities set during several consecutive decades and to identify the actual allocation of investments that had been promoted by EU policies. This knowledge could help to understand how to deal with economies that could be described as peripheral European, small and less advanced, at least in terms of allocation of the funds devoted to their support.

Following the recent crisis, the Greek authorities and all political and economic leaders were accused of having failed to implement numerous policies that have been scheduled, implemented, and assessed over the decades and had been cofunded by the EU. Within few years, hundreds of critical articles, books, and other texts were written on Greece's incapacity to grow and develop, without considering the extent and breadth of policies implemented after Greece joined the EEC.

However, significant efforts had been undertaken by EU authorities during the last decades to help this nation-state with its own development choices and requirements, through the EU Cohesion and Regional policy. The latter promotes investments for development purposes in less advanced states and regions across Europe. Its focus is mostly geographical, regional, and local but it also advances national-level aims and targets. In those areas, it occupies fully the country's administrative system. Hence, it is interesting to investigate its long-term implementation in Greece, and at the national level.

The present book starts by offering a few basic elements and figures of this great Greek crisis that help to realize that it stands among the two worst crises in the history of nation-states. Even today, this conclusion is not very clear for some economists. An analysis is provided of the principal causes and explanations of the Greek crisis, which are distinguished as structural and policy-oriented. The particular policy errors made after 2008 are given attention. Several of the problems and weak points of IMF policies are briefly discussed, before reaching the main point raised through this book: that the Greek crisis is primarily the outcome of a wrong model of growth.

Then, after following a necessary review in the relevant literature, the focus is given on studying the development priorities set by the Greek state and the allocation of EU funds directed to the Greek economy over the three and a half decades of Greece's membership, namely from 1981 to 2016. During this period, and especially after 1989, extended amounts were directed to Greek regions through "regional operational programmes" and to the state as a whole, through consecutive "sectoral operational programmes" aiming at strengthening the economy, by focusing on competitiveness, education, energy, health, and the other main social and economic activities and policy priorities.

Evidence is provided on the Greek economy's competitiveness, structure of exports and imports, balance of payments and trade, either for Greece only or in comparison to other states. A few important conclusions are reached on the effects of EU Cohesion policies and their medium- to long-term impact, mostly at the state level. Greece's hidden problem of competitiveness, that has emerged over the decades and has been further accentuated by its long-term development policies and priorities, is illustrated.

The analysis is based on the actual documents of economic development and planning, and on several of the ex-ante and ex-post evaluation studies and assessments conducted by the Greek state and various Greek institutions. Emphasis is given on a relatively recent relevant study conducted by ELIAMEP, which has focused on key aspects of policies cofunded by the EU.

A principal conclusion reached is that, over the years and in agreement with the EU Commission authorities, Greece has applied a series of development policies that overemphasized infrastructure and autonomous rather than induced investments. It overspent money in this direction and overlooked the promotion of other priorities, significant for development purposes, especially those related to the private sector. In this way, it has put at risk the developmental efforts historically made under the aegis of EU Cohesion Policy and the Greek state.

This unbalanced type of investment is argued to be a development mistake that can seriously harm any economy if extended in time, not just the Greek; one that brings many economic, financial, social, political, and other implications and upheavals. Several of these implications lie at the root of the Greek problem and their change should be prioritized for most Greek observers, economists, or other social scientists (by changing culture, behavior, institutions etc.). On the contrary, the present book argues that an economy can be trapped on a path that promotes a certain type of investment that does not favor sustainable, long-term growth. The expectations created out of such investment policies in Greece, by economic, social, and political interests, and the rise of administrative weaknesses and bureaucracy have brought negligence for the reforms required and left room for the expression of economic problems that impeded growth. It is Greece's own policies, cofunded and supported by EU authorities that have nurtured the crisis before its appearance and paved the way for the strong cyclical fluctuation of the Greek economy. Such policies were based on theoretical guidance espoused—if not promoted—by EU authorities, via EU Cohesion policy.

The historically extended in time, overemphasis placed on infrastructure and social goods and not on the private sector is a finding that first appeared in the study by ELIAMEP and a main reason why I decided to start writing the present book. I realized its significance in economic theory and economic policy-making, while working as a researcher at the project conducted by ELIAMEP that assessed the effects of EU Cohesion Policy on Greece.

I then thought to investigate the theory of investment and realized further the significance of distinguishing between autonomous and induced investment. Thus, I went a step further to investigate economic growth models and realized that the negligence of the type of investment promoted is a handicap in these models. My concerns about the significance and relevance of this finding for growth theory, and my doubts as to where we actually stand in terms of economic theory and modeling have grown. Do we actually prefer using growth models that ignore the type of investment promoted, even though they investigate all other factors for their significant contribution in economic growth, including the (increasing) returns? These growth factors, for example knowledge, innovation, research, and technology are certainly important for growth but investment and the type of investment is also quite significant.

The literature review is composed from main points made from investment studies, economic planning, economic growth theory, and growth modeling, several of the most significant aspects of a rather growing literature on infrastructure and a short but concise review of the theory of competitiveness. Less informed readers will get a brief overview of some of the most important aspects and developments of economic theory. The reference to numerous economic theories makes the present book an interesting introductory text in economic theory, its application, and several of its debates in practice. More knowledgeable readers are asked to actively engage in studying most of them, in the light of the present findings.

One can describe economic theory like a pyramid whose bases are more significant to mention than its top. Digging in the past of economic theory to select its most useful bases is not so easy as it seems, as disciplinary developments often impede our paths of investigation, shedding light on new paths and directions. More and more economists study increasing rather than decreasing or constant returns, imperfect and monopolistic competition rather than perfect competition, and secondary growth factors, such as knowledge, rather than the key growth factors, like the type and proportional allocation of investment in capital. This has not prevented me from rethinking the discussion held in the past on the acceleration coefficient, the distinction between autonomous and induced investments, and from investigating Solow's model rather than the other growth models, most studied in these days. Despite its critics, it remains a robust tool, whose analysis and conclusions can be transferred at the AK and other growth models. Other economists, more knowledgeable and capable to better highlight and pickup the most appropriate elements from the wide range of growth theories, may wish to take the relevant discussion a step further. The famous Cambridge controversy that focused on the problem of calculating capital and, through this, of the aggregate functions of output may help to shift the theoretical interest of the present book to other directions.

With the present book, I have sought to give some answers to questions about the Greek crisis, by first providing most of the existing explanations. Then, I have stressed what I believe would be an interesting, additional direction to investigate in the study of the Greek crisis, as well as other economic crises.

If the 1929 crisis in the United States was a reason for the development of macroeconomics, the post-2008 crisis in Greece should become a reason to reconsider certain of our very firm conclusions about economic theory. Of course, it is a spatially located crisis but Greece belongs in the Eurozone and some common elements with other economies in the Eurozone can be identified, both in relation to the economy and to the policies cofunded by the EU.

All that economists can do most of the time (or offered the opportunity to do) is to question the validity of some assumptions and suggestions made and leave the rest of their colleagues to think whether they are right or wrong in their own views. Suggesting that motives, culture, or economic and social behavior only are more important than the type of policies pursued in explaining a whole crisis is a single-sided view of the crisis. The present book leaves enough room for these critical approaches, presented in the first chapter. It highlights though more the need to promote a better balance in the typology of investments for development and economic transformation purposes. One of its main purposes is to show that the theory of investment and the type of investment promoted has to come closer to the study of economic growth theory and models.

Despite the claims of eminent macroeconomists that economic fluctuations had disappeared (mostly in the US and due to the policies applied there), the strong cyclical fluctuation of the Greek economy provides substantial evidence for their presence, spatially located in the Eurozone. Many doubts are raised as to whether real business cycle theory suffices to predict economic fluctuation and growth, as pertained by some of its proponents.

It would have been interesting, in the light of the present major explanation of the Greek crisis, to investigate further the causes of the 1929 crisis, and more generally of crises derived from the US economy, which, acting as a major inhibitor of global crises, affects the rest of economies. Whichever are the explanatory paths followed in the discipline, economic problems will remain and economics will keep developing, since it is an imperfect discipline, as imperfect as human nature.

When a crisis erupts, lessons from the past should be realized, taught, and learned. A crisis requires a clear-sighted judgment about it. In Greek, the word crisis means judgment. The present text aims to explain why the Greek economy has not managed to react appropriately and to cope with the negative effects of the recent crisis and lagged behind the rest of its EU partners, because of the development path and choices historically followed.

Finally, it is important to stress that Greece, hoping that problems will be resolved inside the European Union, has remained in the common currency despite all the difficulties encountered.

Constantinos Ikonomou
Ph.D. University of Cambridge
National and Kapodistrian University of Athens, Athens, Greece

The great Greek crisis

1

1.1 The country of Greece: a fragmented territory

Greece is a country of almost 11 million people. Approximately three-quarters of its territory is covered by sea and approximately three-quarters of its mainland is covered by mountains. It is one of the two European countries[1] that comprises a whole archipelago, containing more than 250 populated islands at the east, west, and south of its mainland and, in total, more than 10,000 islands of any size and shape. It is no exaggeration to say that the country's coastal zone is comparable to that of a continent. Greece's mountainous part comprises also hundreds of scattered little villages. This fragmented physical landscape has historically nurtured strong centripetal forces in spaces of urban agglomeration. While their expression was prevented in the past by physical barriers and the absence of physical infrastructure, they were strengthened after the late 1950s by rising economic forces, the country's progressive steps to development, and the increase of its rural exodus and depopulation. Even today, after the application of many policies for regional development and cohesion, almost 4 million people reside in the region of Attiki, Athens and its suburbs, while the broader regions of the two main cities, Athens and Thessaloniki, are home to almost half of the Greek population.[2]

Greece's populated islands and little villages require autonomous economic and social infrastructure, for example, in electricity, water, sewage, telecommunication, transport, and to cover many other social needs, such as in primary education, health care, etc. With the country's progressive rise of growth levels, the costs for building new or renewing the old infrastructure has risen too. Domestic land prices have also increased, especially after the country's decision to join the monetary zone, and in places of physical beauty that are permanent tourist attractions, influenced both by the local and the international demand.

Since the 1970s, Greece has faced naturally many of the challenges that most developed countries face, in terms of urbanization and agglomeration costs, side-effects of spatial imbalances, and infrastructure needed. The rising levels of growth and development made the policies pursued to cover these costs more expensive. Furthermore, distributing equally across its space those benefits resulting from joining the EU and from enhancing the growth process has always been an important

---

[1] Together with Croatia. Finland too contains many lakes.

[2] Distances measured in time are also very extended. Until very recently, commuting from one side of Greece, Rhodes, to the other, Corfu, required 14 h by boat to Athens plus 8 h by car and boat from Athens to Corfu. The development of tourism and tourist infrastructure brings a lowering of time distance by air and sea.

Funding the Greek Crisis. DOI: https://doi.org/10.1016/B978-0-12-814566-1.00001-X

aspect to consider in policies, especially for its least accessible and most vulnerable and weakened regions and localities. The democratic system of representation, for a presidential parliamentary democracy established in 1974 with the third Hellenic Republic, has helped towards this direction.

1.2 Basic facts and figures on the Greek crisis

The crisis in Greece started in the year 2008 and it lasts until today. In the year 2016, Greece's real GDP contraction became the worst in the history of mankind for the last hundred years and the most prolonged in duration, exceeding that of the United States in the 1929 crisis (contraction levels have reached 26.42% as opposed to 26.4%, respectively). In terms of nominal GDP change, Greece is still in the second worse historical position, after the 1929 crisis of the US economy. This is seen in Fig. 1.1[3] that illustrates the nominal GDP contraction for the most well-known crises in modern economic history of nation-states (excluding the cases of some states in crises where real GDP contraction was calculated to be zero or positive in nominal terms). By taking into account only GDP contraction, real or nominal, one can hardly argue that policies to support the Greek economy, developed by the IMF and Greece's European partners, have been successful, despite the intentions.

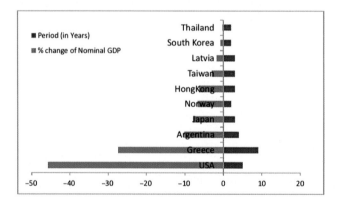

Figure 1.1 Crises in history, nominal change of GDP.
Source: US Department of Agriculture, Economic Research Service, data accessed 29/12/2017. Data from the Economic Research Service used were real 2010 GDP (B$) and GDP deflators (2010 = 100). Data on USA were accessed from the website www.balance.com. *Note:* Data for Greece include 2016, a year of 0.0 I growth rate. The periods of crises acknowledged are the 1929 global crisis for USA (1929–1933), the 1998–2001 crisis of Argentina, Hong Kong (1998), South Korea (1998), and the recent global post-2008 crisis for Greece (ongoing), Norway (2008–2009), Japan (2007–2009), Thailand (2007–2009), and Latvia (2008–2010).

---

[3] Four more crises were considered: the early 1990s crisis for Sweden (1990–93), the 1998–99 crisis for Colombia, and the 1997–98 crisis for Malaysia and Philippines.

Furthermore, the extent of the crisis in Greece is remarkably prolonged, the only such extent in the modern history of nation-states (Fig. 1.1). Even states that took part in the first and second World War took less time to recover, if one includes the years of war. The comparison with war years is not without any relevance. Millions of Greeks live now below the average poverty level and thousands eat from the garbage or are still queuing to get a piece of food whenever this is offered for free.

What is more, it is not still certain that the crisis in Greece has finished nor that economic recovery will return as fast as it has returned in the crises occurring in other states. Table 1.1 shows that all countries that were found in crises (in their most significant crisis in history) had managed to recover in GDP terms within a five-year period, starting from the year that their contraction was over (with the exception of Hong Kong, whose net recovery is negative and the ratio of recovery to contraction is high but its contraction was not high in nominal GDP terms). The evidence shows that even the economy of the United States, facing the most studied and influential economic crisis in history, managed to recover and gain the GDP lost within five years. Similarly, five years were more than enough for a strong recovery by the Argentinian economy.

The strong recession and depression in the Greek economy is seen in Table 1.2 and Fig. 1.2. Fig. 1.2 in particular, illustrating those macroeconomic accounts and figures for which results are deteriorating, helps to show that the Greek economy is undergoing a depression phase. During the period from 2008 to 2016, the Greek GDP fell by 28%, private consumption by 25.3%, public consumption by 29.7%, and unemployment rose by almost 200%. On the other hand side, exports and the balance of current transactions have much improved.

In economics and social studies the counterfactual question is usually asked of what would have happened in the absence of policy. It is worth asking where exactly would Greece have been without the policies for her support? Would it be in a better position or worse, enhancing its growth contraction? Clearly for a country that appears to take the lead as the most significant case of a financially harmed economy in the history of nation-states to consider after a crisis, it is hard to imagine a worst case scenario.

1.2.1 The Greek case: a significant component in a chain of events

Greece drew the international attention for several consecutive years after the 2008 global crisis erupted, due to its mounting debt and what was diagnosed as a sovereign external debt crisis of the Greek state. The beginning of the global crisis is generally considered to originate in the malfunctioning of the subprime mortgage market in the United States. In the first semester of 2007, house prices fall for the first time after 1991. In April 2007, the New Century Financial Corporation ceases its operation, in May 2007 UBS announces that it shuts down its Dillon Read Capital Management (a fund associated to investments in housing) and in August 9, 2007, BNP Paribas ceases the operation of three funds investing in financial

Table 1.1 GDP contraction vs GDP recovery (five-year period after the crisis)

Country	Nominal GDP contraction (%)	Period (years)	Years	Five-year recovery	Net recovery	Ratio of recovery to contraction (n. GDP)	Real GDP contraction (%)
Greece	− 27.3	9	2008 onwards	?	?	?	− 26.42
United States	− 45.7	5	1929–1933	52.6	6.9	− 0.87	− 26.40
Argentina	− 10.1	4	1998–2001	166.4	156.3	− 0.06	− 18.4
Japan	− 7.9	3	2007–2009	8.4	0.5	− 0.94	− 6.5
Hong Kong	− 6.3	3	1997–1999	2.4	− 3.9	− 4.67	− 5.9
Latvia	− 1.7	3	2008–2010	35.6	138.1	− 0.05	− 20.6
South Korea	− 0.8	2	1997–1998	54.6	53.8	− 0.01	− 5.5
Thailand	− 0.2	2	1997–1998	34.4	18.1	− 0.01	− 10.2
Sweden	6.9	4	1990–1993	36.9	43.9	0.19	− 4.3
Colombia	7.9	2	1998–1999	103.1	110.9	0.08	− 4.2
Philippines	21.7	2	1998	54	75.7	0.40	− 0.6

Note 1: Five-year recovery is measured as a change of GDP for a five-year period after the end of the crisis. Net recovery is measured in percentage as the nominal GDP change from the initial year of the crisis to the final year of the five-year, post-contraction period.

Note 2: The ratio of recovery to contraction is a fraction of the nominal GDP recovery in the five-year post-crisis period, divided by the nominal GDP contraction of the crisis period. The smaller is the fraction, the higher is the recovery. The closer is the fraction to unity, the more the recovery approaches the size of contraction. The higher than unity is the fraction, the more prolonged in time is the effect of contraction (see the case of Hong-Kong). The negative sign shows a shift from a (negative) contraction to a (positive) recovery. Absolute values could be employed.

Note 3: Real GDP contraction refers to real GDP changes (expressed in percentages). The period of real GDP contraction differs in some cases and includes an initial or final year. In some cases of crises, contraction was present only in real GDP terms (Sweden, Colombia and Philippines).

Note 4: Question marks for Greece indicate that there is neither five-year period of recovery nor net recovery so far, hence the ratio cannot be calculated and it is uncertain how much it is going to be.

Source: As in Fig. 1.1 above, all countries included.

Table 1.2 Contraction results (change in basic macroeconomic accounts during the crisis)

	Real GDP	Private consumption	Public consumption	Exports of goods	Net Exports of goods and services	Balance of current transactions	Unemployment
2008	242.0	163.0	50.1	24.7	− 30.5	− 38.3	7.8
2016	174.2	121.7	35.2	28.3	− 1.3	− 1.0	23.6
% change 08-16	− 28.0	− 25.3	− 29.7	14.5	95.9	97.5	202.6
Absolute change	− 67.8	− 41.3	− 14.9	3.6	29.2	37.4	15.8

Source: AMECO (variables used are GDP, gross domestic product at current prices (UVGD); private consumption, private final consumption expenditure at current prices (UCPH); public consumption, final consumption expenditure of general government at current prices (UCTG); exports of goods, exports of goods at current prices (UXGN); net exports of goods and services, net exports of goods and services at current prices (UBGS); balance of current transactions, balance on current transactions with the rest of the world (UBCA); unemployment, unemployment rate: total—member states, definition EUROSTAT (ZUTN). *Note:* Inflation in Eurozone is relatively low.

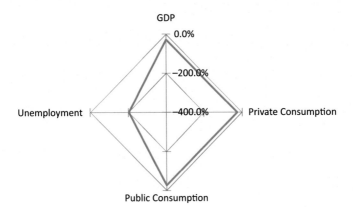

Figure 1.2 Contraction and depression in the Greek economy: percentage changes of GDP, unemployment, private and public consumption.
Source: AMECO series, as presented in Table 1.2. *Note*: For illustration purposes unemployment change is depicted by the use of a negative sign.

instruments in the same market. Many other cases of banking institutions appear that are associated with the housing market in USA and face similar financial problems. Following the nationalization of Fannie Mae and Freddie Mac in September 7, 2007, the acquisition of Merill Lynch by the Bank of America on September 14, 2007, the bankruptcy of Lehman Brothers on September 15, 2008, the nationalization of Northern Rock by the British Government on February 17, 2008 and the accumulated debts in other international banks and companies, Greece became the first case of a nation-state that faced most seriously the prospect of bankruptcy after the global crisis. This prospect was postponed by the particular action taken by its Eurozone and European partners—mostly that of France and Germany—the international influence exercised by the government of the United States, other careful political and economic analysts from this country, and the discreet role played by other nation-states, especially those participating in the funding of the Greek state through the International Monetary Fund (IMF).

A sovereign external debt crisis erupts when a country owes a large amount of external debt (measured as a percentage of its GDP) to foreign borrowers and the measures available to guarantee its repayment do not suffice to guarantee it. In the Greek case, printing money, a main available measure to cope with crises in an economy, has been abandoned since Greece has joined the currency union and transferred the relevant policies to the discretion of the European Central Bank. Furthermore, the state's capacity to raise taxes, which is another available measure, has been historically limited.

Such was the significance of the Greek case that those eleven million people that were producing less than 250 billion of GDP annually by 2008, had become for a certain period the most significant component in the chain of events of the global crisis, during which it became almost synonymous with the "Greek crisis."

International funds and investors have seen behind the Greek case a weakness, a hole in the whole edifice of the Eurozone, which is the most advanced stage of integration attained by the European states. They had assessed that the debt of Greece was no longer sustainable and suddenly became unwilling to lend additional funds to the Greek state, its domestic banks, or its businesses. Some of these international investors went a step further, by speculating in favor of the prospect of Greece's bankruptcy, its capacity to remain a member of the Eurozone, and that of the common currency's viability and longevity, as a whole.

The Greek case has become a major reason why the international interest in the global crisis shifted from the operation of the US subprime mortgage market and that of mostly US banks and businesses to the Eurozone. It revealed several weaknesses in the operation of the common monetary union, as put in place at the beginning of the 2000s, the absence of substantial components necessary for its operation, and a lack of efficacy to respond in international crises, exogenously derived.

The US economy, benefiting from the long-standing presence of mechanisms, prior experience to handle crises, and an experienced policy-making personnel, took relatively early its first substantial policy responses to the crisis on November 25, 2008, when its central bank—the FED—announced its program of quantitative easing and its commitment to buy assets of a value up to US$600 billion. Few weeks after, on December 15, 2008, the TARP had approved a loan of US$13.4 billion for General Motors and Chrysler, and on February17, 2009, another US$787 billion financial package was approved for strengthening the US economy.

On the European side though, it was realized that several components were missing from the most advanced stage of the European integration process, its common currency union: (i) the fiscal side and aspects of the integration edifice were rather limited, if not built at all; (ii) stability features at state level—such as the national exchange rate mechanism—were abandoned, not given sufficient attention, and not replaced by new stability mechanism of a similar kind at the common currency level; while (iii) the European Central Bank (ECB) lacked the mechanisms and tools to support financially Eurozone states, and its only commitment to keep inflation low surpassed any other targets that a central bank can use to stabilize an economy.

Starting from the Greek case, which acted as a catalyst for investigating the missing elements and components of the most advanced stage of integration attained in Europe that were considered as "design failures," the prospect of further integration in Europe was envisaged (De Grauwe, 2013; De Grauwe and Ji, 2014). Having a high deficit in the year 2009 that could increase its explosive debt even further and that had limited its capacity to borrow, Greece had become a conscious carrier of the message that had to be transmitted to Eurozone decision-makers that more needed to be done in the currency zone for the benefit of Greece, and in order to safeguard stability and protect all states participating in this particular common currency union. It also helped at the time that the Greek political personnel had the responsibility to handle this matter as a common European matter. The first SBA plan gave enough time for the Eurozone to build a "firewall" to protect Greece and other member-states (IMF, 2013).

The Greek case had also highlighted concerns about the health of the financial sector in most European countries, including the United Kingdom. It acted as a precedent for responding in crises expressed in other Eurozone countries. It revealed a discussion on the necessity of closer integration, on the promotion of new forms of governance and it brought tensions among European partners and between the United States and some European partners (Nelson et al., 2011).

The ongoing developments of the Greek crisis brought a realization of the ties developed between the Greek economy and the economy of the United States, mainly through revealing the relation and underlying ties between the economies of the EU and the United States. The prospect of European slow growth that would have caused the common currency's devaluation and affected US exports and competitiveness, the substantial exposure of US banks in the Greek economy but mostly in the Spanish and Italian economy that would face similar problems, and the role of United States in IMF, have all brought a broader international realization that the Greek case should be treated as a common European matter and problem (Nelson et al., 2011). This is also reflected in the rejection of the US House of Senate legislation suggesting voting against the active involvement of IMF in more advanced states in June 2011, which would include Greece (Nelson et al., 2011).

1.3 Debts, interest rates and the resulting financial support

In 2009, Greece's debt reached 127% of its GDP. This was far beyond the rest of the Eurozone and European states that all had levels below 100%, apart from Italy (see Fig. 1.3). In Fig. 1.3, it appears that Greece belonged to a group of states, along with Italy and Belgium, whose central government debt was already above 100% of its GDP in the second half of the 1990s, clearly separated from another group of states, whose debt was below 60% of GDP. This is the most common group of states, as the 60% of GDP threshold was placed by the Maastricht Treaty as a criterion and precondition for organizing and joining the common currency union. While Italy and mostly Belgium had managed to reduce the debt as a proportion of

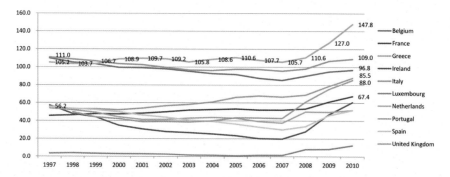

Figure 1.3 Central government debt, % of GDP, Greece and selected Eurozone countries and the United Kingdom.
Source: OECD database.

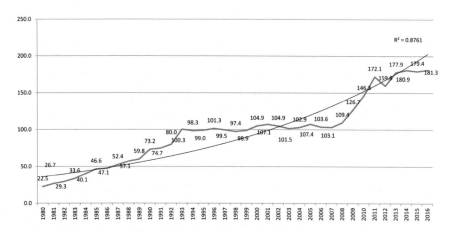

Figure 1.4 Central government gross debt, % of GDP, Greece.
Source: Federal Reserve Bank of St Louis, Economic Research Division, Greece: general government gross debt, % of GDP, annual, not seasonally adjusted.

their GDP until 2007, Greece, along with Portugal, envisaged the prospect of its early destabilization. After 2008, the increasing trend had become more general.

Fig. 1.4 illustrates the long-term picture of Greece's central government gross debt, measured as percentage of its GDP. Starting from 22.5% in 1980, it has managed to stabilize for approximately 15 years, from 1993 to almost 2007, at average levels of approximately 102%. Then it rose again, reaching a record high at 180.9% in 2014 and 181.3% in 2016. Even if for the aforementioned period (from 1993 to 2007) the debt has remained a constant proportion of GDP, Greece's debt-to-GDP has actually risen exponentially, if measured from 1981, its joining year in the European Communities (since the exponential line fits at R^2 levels equal to 0.8761).

As seen in Fig. 1.5, the long-term, 10-year, government bond yields started to rise in the second semester of 2009. It was then realized that the Greek government would no longer be able to pay back its loans, because of its mounting debt (as percentage of GDP). The rising yields of the long-term Greek bonds in 2009 were due to a prior signal sent in international markets that it will be no longer possible to pay the entire amount of Greek bonds. In general, a bond yield, i.e., the amount an investor realizes on a bond, is a function of its price. If the price of a bond is 100 at a certain year and it yields 10%, and the next year falls at 50 Euros, then its yield shall go up at 20%. As bond prices increase, bond yields fall (and the lower the price of a bond, the higher is its yield). In other words, when the yields rise, the prices of bonds fall and vice versa. Bond prices depend on the assessment of whether they will be finally paid (their entire amount).

It took less than two years for the levels of long-term government bond yields to almost quintuple. Starting from 6.02 on January 1, 2010, a first peak was reached at 29.24 on February 1, 2011 and another one at 27.82, six months later, on June 1, 2011.

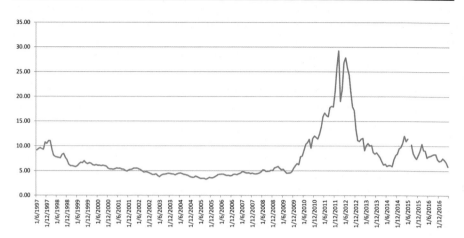

Figure 1.5 Long-term government bond yields: 10-year, Greece.
Source: Federal Reserve Bank of St Louis, Economic Research Division, long-term
government bond yields: 10-year: main (incuding benchmark) for Greece, percent, monthly,
not seasonally adjusted.

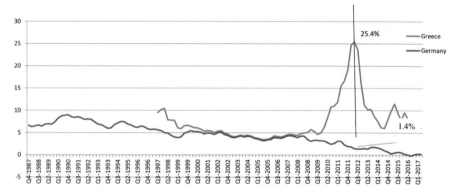

Figure 1.6 Long-term interest rates in Greece, comparison with those of Germany.
Source: IMF (original), collected from OECD database.

In May 2010, the month during which the Greek state agreed to sign a three-year
agreement for the stabilization of the economy under its first Memorandum of
Understanding, yields were at almost 8%.

At the same time, the long-term interest rates started to rise from the third quarter of 2009 up to the third quarter of 2012, reaching, within three years a record
high of 25.4% and a spread differential of 24%, in comparison to the German long-
term interest rates (Fig. 1.6).

Greece has signed two international package bailout programs with the IMF,
first in 2010 and then in 2012. The first was a Stand-By Arrangement with the

IMF, signed on May 9, 2010, and scheduled to last for three years. The IMF's involvement was organized in association with the European Commission and the European Central Bank ("the troika"). Such SBA arrangements are designed to help short-term problems in the balance of payments. The IMF's SBA represented 13.56% of the Greek GDP (IEO of the IMF, 2016: 1). The IMF loans comprised an amount of €30 billion, while the contribution offered by Euro area partners was at €80 billion[4]. This agreement was cancelled on March 14, 2012.[5] It was then replaced by a new program, implemented under the Extended Fund Facility (EFF), signed for a four-year period and placed in operation on March 15, 2012. The EFF arrangements were planned to envisage the challenges and face the long-term problems in the balance of payments that require economic reforms.[6] The Greek EFF arrangement comprised €28 billion from the IMF and €144.7 billion from European partners. It represented 14.64% of Greece's GDP and lasted until January 15, 2016 (IEO of the IMF, 2016: 1). To face the challenges of its sovereign external debt crisis, Greece has signed an additional ESF program of €86 billion in 2015, without the IMF's financial contribution but only from its European partners. The total amount committed for Greece was at 331.7 billion Euros and those already disbursed by February 2018 were 267.2 billion Euros.

1.4 The three different periods of debt-to-GDP ratio

The first remarkable period of the rise of Greece's debt, proportional to its GDP, was in the 1980s. This is a period of a constant rise. Starting from 22.5% of GDP in 1980, when most European states had higher levels, it reached a level of 100.3% in 1993. During this period, the private sector in some utilities owned by the Greek state (in electricity, telecommunications, water, sewage, and others) was rather underdeveloped.

During the 1980s, the Greek state was spending significant amounts on wages, funding public companies, and other public expenses. It provided significant loans to state-owned companies, while it increased pensions both in numbers and as a total, and to provide income in various minorities, especially of low- and middle-income classes, not necessarily belonging to the groups of the socially excluded, distressed, and the least privileged (Kazakos, 2001; Xafa, 2017; Papadopoulos, 2016; Romaios, 2012). In 1982, a political decision was taken to increase the minimum salaries and wages by 40%, in a single day (Kazakos, 2001). This decision reflected the more general willingness of the socialist government that held power

---

[4] This amount was reduced by 2.8bn because Slovakia did not participate and Ireland and Portugal required assistance for themselves

[5] when €53 billion were absorbed out of the total (Venizelos, 2017).

[6] Similar, though shorter in time EFFs (for three years) were signed by Ireland and Portugal on December 16, 2010 and May 20, 2011, respectively, representing 13.62% and 14.87% of their GDP, respectively. These had used €22.5 billion and €26 billion of IMF loans and €45 billion and €52 billion of European funds, respectively (IEO of the IMF, 2016).

at the time, after joining the European Communities, in 1981, to support lower income citizens and cope with the negative effects on the society from the rising competition from abroad. A range of studies refer to the more than doubling of employees in the public sector during the 1980s (see Papadopoulos, 2016). Romaios (2012: 349) refers to a 32% increase in their numbers from 1980 to the end of the first political period of the new socialist government (in 1985). He also refers to a state-provider, who did not exercise the necessary controls in the productiveness, the effectiveness of employees, and in the development policies pursued. Several observers appear to agree (including Romaios, 2012; Kazakos, 2001; Papadopoulos, 2016) that it is in this period that the country enters a vicious circle.

A significant reason why such increases in minimum wages occurred is because of high levels of inflation during the late 1970s and the 1980s. While in the 1970s, when two petroleum shocks occurred, average inflation was at 12%; in the 1980s it rose at levels just below 20% (Papadopoulos, 2016). A successful effort was made to reduce it from 24.9% in 1980 to 20.5% in 1983. Substantial income losses caused by inflation were compensated by an automatic adjustment of salaries to inflation, while, as Dracatos (1988) explains, two-thirds of price rises were transferred into the current account deficit that was significantly widened. Furthermore, in the early 1980s and after Greece had joined the European Communities, prices started to increase in tradable goods, followed by a rise in wages and salaries (Dracatos, 1988). Most likely price rises were transferred from tradables to nontradables, putting in operation a certain Balassa—Samuelson effect (something that has been observed in several other cases of states joining the EU).

The 1980s witnessed also a strong rise in consumption and the rate of consumption (Dracatos, 1988). With the benefit of hindsight, one can now better realize that the Greek economy entered into a path of consumption-based development as a way to compensate for substantial losses of income and the price rises that had started in the 1970s and continued during the 1980s. Facing the challenges of deindustrialization, organizational restructuring, and global competition, the socialist government placed at the epicenter of its policies the target of full employment, sacrificing other macroeconomic targets and fiscal stability and viability.

In 1983, the Greek drachma was devaluated by 15.5%, to compensate for losses in competitiveness. At the time, the role of the public sector in boosting exports was considered indispensable (Kazakos et al., 2016). Several institutions were created towards this direction: a general agency to support exports, an institution to guarantee exports, and a new organization for standardization and packaging. Import protection measures for certain industries were also decided (Kazakos et al., 2016). The existing deficit and the fall in the flows of net private funds made the borrowing of the state necessary (Kazakos et al., 2016).

At the same period of time, the interest rates of all credit institutions were very high and their levels had not allowed investment and the promotion of production. As Dracatos (1988) pointed out, the role of credit policy in activating production was insufficient and could not tackle a problem of liquidity, already present in 1982.

In February 1982, the Greek state submitted a memorandum with its positions with regards to its relation with the European Communities, in order to cope with several of its economic problems. The memorandum, while it acknowledged Greece's long-term structural and macroeconomic imbalances and problems, also diagnosed the strength of competition received by the European Communities and the state's difficulty to cope with it at the time, given the extremely limited transfer of funds through the common European budget[7] (Kazakos, 2001).

Evidence of Greece's difficulty as an early member-state to cope with competition from the EC is found in the extended analysis provided by Giannitsis (1988). By reference to the 1981−86 period, Giannitsis (1988) has identified shifts of market shares, the fall of competitiveness, and the associated lowering in growth rates. He suggested the incapacity of the traditional industrial pole of Greek manufacturing, which developed after the War, to cope with competition from its EC partners. This part was distinguished from another part undergoing transformation. He found limited integration of the Greek manufacturing in international markets and the sustaining of protection (even if lowered). Giannitsis (1988: 422) also referred to a certain negative positioning of the Commission against all those elements that would have been crucial tools for a development-oriented manufacturing policy. He mentioned the rejection of infant industry protection, "the silent rejection of financing of large manufacturing investments in the context of the Memorandum, the appeal to the European Court and the coercion in adjustment in all industries of state subsidy, of capital movement, of the protection of underdeveloped manufacturing activities (agricultural machines, cars, pharmaceuticals, etc.), and especially, the imposition of the Single Market in 1992, even with few opportunities of deviation" (Giannitsis, 1988: 422),[8] which all formed partial actions of "a broader perception, whose central target was the maintaining of a status quo and of the intra-European division of labor in the participation in benefits from manufacturing specialization, and the power balances between European 'North' and 'South'" (Giannitsis, 1988: 422).

In 1985, as soon as the Greek socialist government took power for the second time (a four-year electoral circle), it envisaged seriously the prospect of implementing a stability program to reverse the trend observed through the current account imbalances. This stability program was finally decided and, as an exchange, the Greek government borrowed a loan by the Community, of US$1750 million. The alternative offered by Community authorities to the Greek government would have been to address the International Monetary Fund (Kazakos, 2001). The Greek government had also decided not to request funds from international markets, because the timing was critical and the borrowing interest rates would have been much higher than the loan of the Community. The program of the Greek government targeted

---

[7] The memorandum was published in the Review of European Communities (3/2, 1982: 187−207), as referred in Kazakos (2001). This text can be considered to be one first seed for the need of common European policies through the reallocation of funds from the common budget, to support the most weakened economies and in particular of the Mediterranean Integrated Plans, a predecessor of the EU Cohesion Policy. This text was requesting specific support for development plans in sectors, industries and regions and time to cope with divergence from competition rules applied in the European Community.

[8] Translated by the author.

the immediate improvement of the competitiveness of the Greek economy, the slow-down of inflation, and the empowerment and modernization of productive structures (Kazakos, 2001). An instant 15% depreciation of the Greek drachma helped the immediate implementation of the program and the promotion of a policy of strong currency ("strong drachma"). The state decided not to sacrifice but keep public investments intact (Kazakos, 2001).

Two additional conditions had favored the choice of this policy (to get a loan by the E.C.). Firstly, the Community allowed Greece not to abolish certain privileges (such as export supports and the monopoly in petroleum). And secondly, "the dramatic fall in petrol prices that contributed in the improvement of the balance of payments and the fall of international interest rates that reduced the burden of the state's budget from payments of interests" for existing accumulated debts (Kazakos, 2001: 381).

Despite these conditions, the program lasted only for two years. Kazakos (2001) attributes this short duration to the following reasons: (i) the main burden of the program was carried by salaried employees, and especially some categories out of them; (ii) a problem of credibility: the policies that had to be implemented after the stability program were far from pre-electoral promesses and the expectations created in the electoral body. The latter was given the promises of "even better days"[9] (Kazakos, 2001: 381−382). The Greek prime minister, a highly recognized economist, was clear enough and insisted in informing the Greek citizens that the economy required such a policy shift, to stand on its two feet rather than on "glassware feet"[10]; (iii) the program was single-sided and did not have a developmental orientation. Thus, while it reduced real wages by 13.4% within two years, it left the sources of fiscal deficits intact and had not touched upon the problem of cutting public spending (ibid: 387). As an "involuntary byproduct", it led to the creation of a policy of "strong drachma". The Commission had calculated that the drachma appreciated by 27% from 1988 to 1996 (ibid: 387).[11] Arsenis (2016) suggests that policies for strong drachma have been rather unsuccessful.

Xafa (2017) explains that a substantial rise on the debt-to-GDP ratio from 1992 to 1993, came as a result of the government's decision to record the unrecorded past debts of the agricultural cooperations and businesses, of the Greek Agricultural Bank (ATE), of the Greek Bank of Industrial Development ("ETBA") that had owned several businesses, and of other state-owned banks, as well as of the guaranteed and nonguaranteed debts of state-owned businesses and organizations during the 1980s. The Greek Organization for the Restructuring of Businesses ("OAE") was launched in 1981, as an outcome of the two petroleum shocks, of deindustrialization and the rising international competition. Its target was the restructuring of key-player firms and of the Greek industry. This target has not been achieved and

---

[9] A historical phrase of the Greek prime minister, at the time.

[10] Another historical phrase of the Greek prime minister. Arsenis (2016) considers that he had rather "conservative" views about the problem of debt and had expressed his concerns and fears about its high levels.

[11] The reference offered by Kazakos for these calculations is the following: Commission of the EU: Report on Convergence in the European Union in 1996, Brussels, 6.11.1996, COM (96) 560 final (at a time when the German Marc has appreciated only by 4%).

the accumulated debt of 43 enterprises that amounted to 172 billion drachmas was finally tripled before the Greek government decided to privatize these firms, in 1990 (Xafa, 2017). In 1992, the Greek government issued state bonds to pay all unrecorded loans, which increased public debt by 21.6% of GDP (Xafa, 2017). The abrupt rise of debt-to-GDP ratio at the time was also due to Greece's decision to join the currency union, which presupposed the neutrality of the Greek central bank from the state. The state had to assume the debt burden of three major accounts of the Greek central bank: its loans for petroleum imports, its exchange rate differences, and the financing of deficits. These were accumulated over the decades in the accounts of the Greek central bank and their size was at 3.1 billion drachmas, representing at the time 22.3% of Greece's GDP. At the time, the Greek state used IMF support to organize this part of the debt by issuing international bonds. Xafa (2017) points out that the result of this regulation was that the public debt rose from 87.8% in 1992 to 110.1% in 1993.

It is noteworthy that a decade before the Treaty of Maastricht, the Greek state had fulfilled the 60% debt-to-GDP ratio (that was established as a necessary precondition for joining the common currency union, after the Treaty of Maastricht, in 1993). However during a period of several consecutive years, both before and after it joined the common currency, Greece had failed to fulfill this particular criterion. This is indicative of the tendency formed in the Greek economy during its EC membership.

A separate period of debt-to-GDP ratio is the one that starts from 1993 and reaches up to 2008, just before the advent of the crisis. This is an extended time period, during which the debt-to-GDP ratio stabilized at levels approximately a little higher than 100%. One should make a significant distinction between the first phase of this period, when all amounts are calculated in Greek Drachmas and the second period, after 2001, when the Euro replaces the Drachma. In terms of EU Cohesion policy programming, this period comprises also two separate policy programming periods of the Greek state, the first lasting from 1994 to 1999 and the second lasting from 2000 up to 2006 (see chapters 2 and 3).

The most important aspect of this period is that while the debt, measured as a percentage of GDP, remains rather stable, it continues to rise significantly in nominal terms. Fig. 1.7 shows the annual levels of Greece's GDP consolidated gross debt. While it was at €100.8 billion in 1995, it grew at €136.5 billion in 1999 and at €163 billion in 2001. The biggest part of the gross consolidated debt of the Greek state was accumulated after 2001. From 2001 to 2008, the debt rises from €163 billion to an unprecedented at the time (for the whole history of the Greek state) amount of €264.8 billion. Within this short period, the debt rises by almost €101.8 billion and more than doubles in comparison to 1998, mostly produced after its entry into the Eurozone. This, one can argue, is a principal reason why markets reacted, as it appeared that Greece was envisaging some sort of discrepancy or malfunctioning in operation. €51.1 billion of debt was accumulated from 2000 to 2004, in the early phase of the 2000−7 policy programming period and €65.5 billion in the 2004−8 period. If measured from 2004 to 2009, a period that includes 2009, the year of change of government, the debt increases—again—by €101.8 billion.

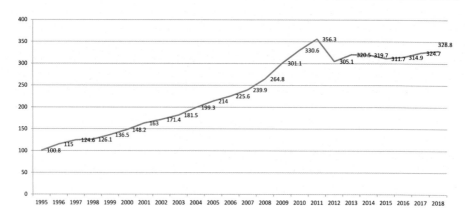

Figure 1.7 General government consolidated gross debt of Greece, in € billions.
Source: General government consolidate gross debt: excessive deficit procedure (based on ESA 2010), Variable of AMECO series: UDGG. *Note*: Estimates for 2017 and 2018.

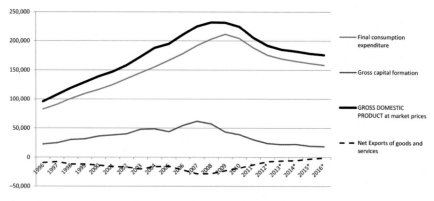

Figure 1.8 GDP and its components (expenditure approach).
Source: Hellenic Statistical Services, available on-line since 17/10/2017. *Note*: The GDP is calculated by adding Final Consumption Expenditure (FCE), Gross Capital Formation and the difference between Exports of Goods and Services and Imports of Goods and Services. GDP measured in market prices. Data have been reviewed using as a base year 2010, according to EC regulation 549/2013 (ESA 2010). Estimates for the 2011−16 period (in asterisk).

Fig. 1.8 breaks down GDP to its components, namely final consumption expenditure, gross capital formation, and net exports of goods and services. It thus helps to make a closer inspection of the aforementioned rising trend of the GDP for the 2001−9 period. It appears from Fig. 1.8 that this rising trend of GDP is associated mostly with a rising trend in final consumption expenditure (since 1996) rather than with the rising trend of the gross capital formation. The latter is less evident in comparison to the former, which is much steeper. Furthermore, it is obvious that with respect

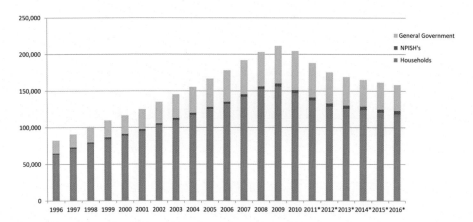

Figure 1.9 Breakdown of consumption expenditure, 1996—2016.
Source: Hellenic Statistical Services, available on-line since 17/10/2017. *Note*: Final Consumption Expenditure (FCE) is the sum of Consumption of the General Government, the consumption by the NPISH's (Non-profit institutions serving households) and the consumption by households. Data have been reviewed using as a base year 2010, according to EC regulation 549/2013 (ESA 2010). Estimates for the 2011—16 period (in asterisk).

to the third component of GDP, the net exports of goods and services (exports minus imports of goods and services) are negative and their trend deteriorates until the year of the crisis and the advent of IMF adjustment policies. In other words, the Greek economy is characterized by a strong rise of consumption in comparison to a more limited capacity to form fixed capital. The outcome is such that more imports than exports of goods and services take place.

Fig. 1.9 unveils the structure of the final consumption expenditure. It makes evident that it is not only the consumption of households that is much higher, proportional to the general government's consumption (and of course that of the nonprofit institutions serving households—NPISH) but also that there is a substantial rising trend in the consumption of households that could be characterized as a major growth component. It is worth mentioning that the proportional allocation of consumption does not significantly change after 2009. Thus, one can reach a significant conclusion that the formation of fixed capital in Greece had not sufficed to push exports and the country's development (expressed through the rise of its GDP in the pre-entry period of the Eurozone and after it has joined) was due mostly to consumption. It is this precise growth pattern that is associated with rising levels of debt.[12]

In the year 2008 and thereafter, the debt continues to rise, but that part of its rise can be attributed to the outburst of the crisis, apart from the reasons producing the aforementioned evident and significant rising trend.

One cannot give a reliable prediction as to whether the rising trend would have continued in the event that the crisis had not appeared. But the two, the rising trend

---

[12] More evidence on the consumption-based development is provided later.

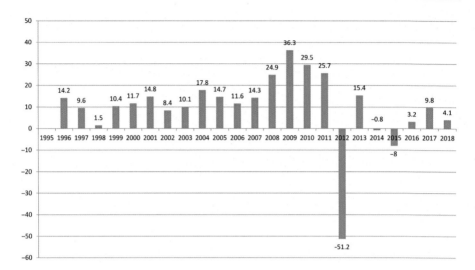

Figure 1.10 Annual Change of General goverment consolidated debt, in € billions.
Source: AMECO series, UDGG. *Note*: Estimates for 2017 and 2018. Calculations by the author.

and the crisis advent, could be seen as two—instead of a unique—separate causes, bringing the same outcome (after 2008).

Straight after 2008, the rise of the consolidated debt is so sharp that reaches €356.3 billion in 2011.

As seen in Fig. 1.10, the change on annual consolidated gross debt was €14.8 billion in 2001 (from 2000 to 2001), €17.8 billion in 2004, and €14.7 billion in 2005.

The change in the General Government's consolidated debt was reduced in the period after 2004, as soon as the government changed (Fig. 1.10).[13] This trend of falling central government consolidated debt is similar to that observed in the 1996—98 period, during the first phase of that period. If seen together, they reveal political efforts to stabilize fiscally the economy. In 2004, the year when the Olympic Games were held in Athens, the change was at €17.8 billion, an extra of €7.7 billion since 2003 (when the change was at €10.1 billion).

Figs. 1.7 and 1.10 show that in all years but for 2012 (when the PSI - Private Sector Involvement- was imposed), the Greek debt was increasing in net terms, either at a high or low rate. This is not evidenced in the trend of the debt per GDP. The reason obviously is that the denominator of the fraction increases too.

---

[13] It is the purpose of this book to discuss and observe from a distance, as objectively as possible, the macroeconomic figures and results of the Greek state, as a whole. Therefore political arguments are generally not considered or treated except indirectly, unless supported by evidence. In this particular case, political observers often raise a point of dichotomy in the middle of the second phase of that period, by associating changes after 2004 and before 2009 with the change in the government and the advent of the right-wing party (see Simitis, 2005). Such a dichotomy is not evident and it is more reliable to refer to the presence of a rising trend that starts as soon as the country joins the Eurozone.

Table 1.3 **Projection of the growth trend of annual government gross consolidated debt for the period 2008–11**

	Consolidated debt (officially recorded figures)	Debt figures projections after 2008	Debt figures projections after 2008
		Projections made by using the average growth rate (7.5%) for the 2001–8 period, imposed each year after 2008	Projections made by using the average growth rate (7.5%) for the 2001–8 period only upon the debt level recorded each year (2009–11)
2000	148.2		
2001	163		
2002	171.4		
2003	181.5		
2004	199.3		
2005	214		
2006	225.6		
2007	239.9		
2008	264.8		
2009	301.1	284.8	284.8
2010	330.6	307.5	323.8
2011	356.3	332.4	355.5
2012	305.1	359.3	
2013	320.5	382.3	
2014	319.7	406.5	

Source: Data on gross capital consolidated gross debt—excessive deficit procedure based on ESA 2010, (UDGG), AMECO.

The third and last period starts with the advent of the global crisis in 2009 and continues until today.

As discussed, as soon as the global crisis bursts, a second reason is added to the growing trend of the crisis. However, both reasons culminate in achieving the same result, the reproduction of the same trend. This is seen in the following evidence. From 2001 to 2008 (the year just before the advent of the crisis), the annual average growth rate of Greece's consolidated debt is at 7.5% (Table 1.3). In the second column of Table 1.3, the same average growth rate (7.5%) is projected first at the officially recorded figure of debt for the year 2008, then for the result reached for 2009, then for the result reached for 2010 and so on. In the last column, this average growth is projected only upon the actual figures of consolidated debt recorded each year after 2008, up to 2011.[14]

[14] The picture is changed in the next year, due to the P.S.I. ("haircut" of the Greek debt), implemented in 2012.

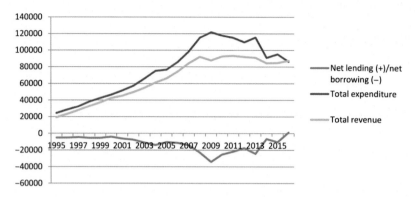

Figure 1.11 Total expenditure, total revenue and the net borrowing of the General Government.
Source: Hellenic Statistical Authority, Data changed to constant prices by the use of Harmonized Consumer Price Index, AMECO series (ZCPIH), In € millions.

Table 1.3 shows that if we impose the same average growth trend on the actual debt level each year (in the last column), the debt would have reached similar levels by 2011 with those finally (officially) recorded. Furthermore, by isolating and using this 2001−8 growth trend only (second column) and by starting after 2008, the hypothetical levels of consolidated debt reached in year 2012 are almost similar to those that have been reached in reality (those in the first column). This outcome for the year 2011 is reached despite the fact that a number of active IMF policies were pursued. Out of this projection, one can reach the conclusion that the IMF policies had not succeeded in withdrawing the macroeconomic imbalance and the rising trend of Greece's debt up to that point in the early 2010−11 period.[15]

Fig. 1.11 illustrates the total revenue, total expenditure, and net lending of the general government from 1995 to 2016. The general government comprises the central government, the local government, and the social security funds. Both total expenditure and total revenues rise. The increase in net borrowing is owed in the growth of total expenditure above the levels of total revenue, especially after 2002 and after 2007. If the political choice/willingness was such that total revenues had exceeded total expenditure, net borrowing would have been reduced.

In comparison to other Eurozone partners, Greece's net borrowing as percentage of its GDP starts deteriorating after 1995, when the country's efforts to join the Eurozone intensify and during its early participation at the Eurozone (2001−9) (Fig. 1.12).

---

[15] One should note that in 1995 a significant amendment takes place in the calculation of all macroeconomic accounts in Greece, as it is obliged to abandon the OECD method of calculation macroeconomic amounts and use the ESA95 methodology, common for all EC states.

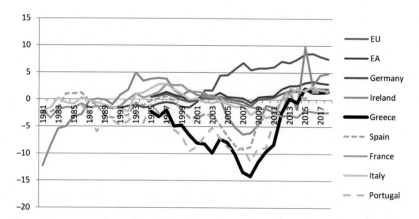

Figure 1.12 Net lending (+) or borrowing (−), as % of GDP.
Source: AMECO series, UBLA (Net lending (+) or net borrowing (−): total economy).

The credit rating of the Greek economy, as provided by several credit rating companies, does not follow the same or respective distinction made for the three periods of time. In various measurements used by different credit rating companies (Fig. 1.13), Greece's credit rating reached its peak in the 1998−2008 period, as soon as the country improved its macroeconomic figures and especially after it had joined the Eurozone, reaching levels as high as Aa2. It then substantially fell from 2008 to 2011, as soon as the Greek crisis burst, reaching levels of credit rating of actual very limited significance (at Ca or C).[16]

1.5 Explanations of the Greek crisis

1.5.1 Structural and policy-oriented explanations

Various explanations of the Greek crisis have been suggested. A main distinction can be made between structural explanations and those related to policy-orientation or policy-errors.[17] The former refer to the structural causes, which can be identified to be: (i) structural elements of the Greek economy and society before the crisis; (ii) the operation of the European Monetary Union and that of the EU economy as a whole; (iii) the intensification of globalization and the operation of the global economy as a whole (its overfinancialization, its de-regulated environment, its associated speculative attack without any limits against national economies and currencies); (iv) the systemic and structural operation and enforcement of core−periphery relations in the Eurozone, where

[16] Having been strongly criticized on the role in the global crisis and their lack of objectivity, the rating companies had changed their assessments to be much more austere and secured.
[17] A similar distinction is provided in the work of Mavroudeas (2015).

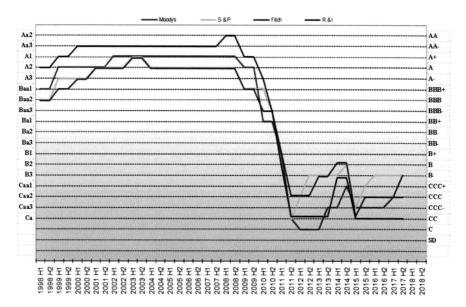

Figure 1.13 Credit ratings of the Greek economy.
Source: Public Debt Management Authority, Greece.

Greece has participated since 2001; (v) systemic causes that relate to crises; and
(vi) Greece's constant "destiny" to default.

Policy-oriented explanations refer to policy errors and to policy decisions and
paths pursued by the Greek state. Two periods of application of policy are significant to consider: the whole period of Greece's membership at the EU starting in
1981 and a shorter period that extends from the years just before the crisis, to the
critical two-year period of the bursting of the Greek crisis (2009–10) and the following years. Policy errors relate to such aspects as: (i) the tolerance for decades
of a greater than required public debt, primarily in net terms but also proportionally to the Greek GDP; (ii) the continuous borrowing of the economy, in order to
fund particular needs and political decisions associated with it; (iii) the mismanagement of public finance; (iv) the overemphasis placed on consumption rather
than on savings or the boosting of competitiveness; (v) the particular political
choices made in borrowing funds from the IMF (see section 1.5.5 below); (vi) the
mishandling or blurring of Greece's financial state from a statistical point of view
by its Statistical Authority; as well as (vii) "gross policy errors" made by the
EMU authorities in preventing and handling the Greek crisis. For analytical purposes, one can distinguish between long-term policy errors derived from the policy paths and orientation taken and pursued since 1981 and policy errors during
the relatively narrow historical span of the years of the explosion of the Greek crisis. For simplicity purposes the terms *policy orientation* and *on-crisis* policy
errors will be used in the remainder of this text to account for these two different
explanations.

There is a difference between structural and policy-oriented explanations.[18] Structural explanations have a more deterministic character. The main idea behind deterministic explanations is that it would have not been possible for Greece to face its problems anyway. For example, the common currency problems were problems that Greece could not resolve by itself, despite its intense efforts to do so in 2009 and the years that have followed.[19]

Policy-oriented explanations on the other hand are open to all possible outcomes. For possibilism, a philosophical stream, actions or inaction of people affect their results in their economies or societies, thus placing human activity at the epicenter of analysis. Hence, economic policies and actions taken by the economies of nation-states are responsible for the amount and type of challenges, difficulties, and other financial and economic problems and barriers encountered. Possible outcomes may differ from one period to another, from one country to another, etc., and policies are indispensable for handling economic and financial problems.

A main structural explanation refers to the operation of the European Monetary Union and that of the EU economy as a whole. From this perspective, it is suggested that the opening of European borders and in particular the implementation of the common currency has created several "bubbles," which were further fueled by the very fast transfer of EU funds inside the EMU. Followers of this view also suggest that the unification process has favored the consumption by the European South of the particular production of Northern European countries, and has had as an effect the turning of the economies in the European South towards being more consumption-based and the formation or sustaining of core—periphery relations among European and mostly Eurozone partners.[20] The setting-up of the EMU has reinforced booms in the South, which became busts when the crisis erupted (De Grauwe, 2013). This view is reinforced by the Walters critic, which pertains that a monetary union is more likely to be an unstable system and that as soon as inflation rates differ, they will tend to increasingly diverge.

This view is favored by the absence of stabilizers in the economy of the common currency. Some significant stabilizers for national economies were neutralized when the common currency area was put in place and they were neither replaced by others nor was any emphasis given on their significance. Such stabilizers were the exchange rate mechanism that was transferred at common currency level and not replaced by some strong mechanism of an equal—among partners—distribution of benefits from the common currency exchange mechanism. Mostly one could argue that the common currency's exchange rate mechanism is affected by the

---

[18] Another possible way to distinguish is between domestic and external to Greece's factors (Nelson et al., 2010, 2011). In this section most of the structural explanations are external and all policy explanations are domestic.

[19] Mainly by the prime minister George Papandreou, whose active initiatives have helped to spur a relevant discussion in the political debates held in Europe and then by his successors, Lucas Papademos, Antonis Samaras, and Alexis Tsipras.

[20] In this context lies the identification of peripheral Cohesion-four states by the use of the slang term "PIGS" (the initials from Portugal, Ireland, Greece, and Spain), which largely ignores the substantial efforts undertaken by European partners to support growth and development in these countries.

larger in size, more significant economies. Other stabilizers that were neglected were progressive taxation (not considered in some states), and unemployment benefits and schemes. Most importantly, one could suggest that the absence of a common fiscal policy among Eurozone states was another problem acting against the stabilization of national economies, and in particular that of Greece. According to the fundamentals of macroeconomic theory, fiscal policy should be employed in association with monetary policy to achieve stabilizing effects. Since the prospect of fiscal harmonization, if not that of a fiscal union, was disregarded and separated from the monetary policy, a sharp line of stability was withdrawn. Seen from the perspective of a common economy, allied in terms of common institutional and policy aspects, the common currency economy has disregarded, if not neglected, the full range of instruments that concerned fiscal integration. This is the main reason why "design failures" of the Eurozone were considered to exist, whose effects were spread across European economies that were associated with trade, financial, political, and other ties (see also further analysis in section 1.5.3).

Another structural explanation refers to the outburst of the recent crisis in relation to the structure of the global capitalism. As soon as the crisis erupted, overfinancialisation, the generation of substantial amounts of funds by the use of financial engineering techniques—that did not reflect some production capacity—and the free movement of capital, had to be limited and the prospect of limited investment opportunities was revealed. Substantial amounts of nonactive funds were unleashed to speculate against the common currency in particular, viewing behind the Greek case a grandiose opportunity for obtaining "profits" similar or even larger to those acquired from those funds that speculated in favor of the crisis outburst. What is more, such funds were actively convinced by the energetic response of the government of the United States against the crisis that did not leave room to gamble against its own currency. The Greek case came as an organic part of a series of events, where mostly large-scale corporations and banks were the victims, testing the underdeveloped capacity of the Eurozone to cope with—exogenous—crises.

A further structural explanation is that of core—periphery relations strengthened in the Eurozone. Myrdal's theory of cumulative causation suffices to remind how a negative change in the periphery causes a cumulative causation mechanism that progressively deteriorates the economic and financial state of a periphery. Similarly, this appears to be the conclusion of a series of theories that explain the formation of core—periphery imbalances and the presence of a transmission mechanism of economic malaise across peripheries.

This explanation should be seen in association with the theory of economic cycles, according to which macroeconomic imbalances are an intrinsic characteristic of capitalism and their expression is expected to take place (Box 1.1 discusses extensively the old theory of business cycles). This explanation is placed within the context of destabilization effects brought after an asymmetric shock and after a crisis taking place. It is also associated with the abovementioned loss of monetary autonomy by the Greek state. Some economists believe that macroeconomic imbalances have become a derelict of the past, but—even if such a view could ever

Box 1.1 A few significant points from existing theories on debt

The public debt of a state is, in practice, a form of state financing. A government finances its needs through taxes, compulsory contributions to social security funds, private sector activity, shares that it may hold in public or semipublic companies, from privatization and profits of its central bank. These needs can also be financed through borrowing funds.

Public borrowing is created by borrowing from private agents and banks, by taking compulsory loans, issuing new money, through external or internal borrowing, through productive or consumption loans, through short-term or long-term loans (Kazakos et al., 2016).

Public loans are distinguished into various categories. In terms of their way of funding, they are separated into compulsory or noncompulsory; in terms of the sources of their funding, in domestic or external (from another country); in terms of the needs they cover, in production or consumption loans (Kazakos et al., 2016). They are also distinguished into negotiable and nonnegotiable and in constant or floating interest rate. Finally they are distinguished in terms of the currency issued.

There are three different theoretical perspectives on public sector borrowing and debt accumulation, discussing the effects of borrowing. These are also meaningful to consider in explaining the causes of debt accumulation, in such cases where it is continuous and such effects turn also to causes.

According to the traditional IS-LM analysis, the replacement of taxes by debt (ceteris paribus for the level of public expenditure), increases available income, reduces total savings, boosts total effective demand, increases the interest rate, crowds-out private investments, and reduces the percentage of unemployment (Kazakos et al., 2016). All these effects were found to hold in the Greek case (as discussed in section 1.5.4). For interest rates in particular, one could suggest that they were rising up to the mid-1990s, and after that efforts to reduce inflation were intensified in order to join the monetary union. One can identify a similar trend only behind the rise of spreads, after the global crisis erupts.

Borrowing is considered as a way to replace taxes and satisfy the need to immediately raise tax rates and/or impose new taxes and/or strengthen tax collection mechanisms, in order to draw more income out of taxes that will be used to pay back existing loans.

Proponents of this side suggest that people do not understand that their current decision(s) to borrow will affect their future choices, through raising taxes in future (Kazakos et al., 2016). In the neoclassical approach, where consumption behavior is based on expected lifetime, state deficits reduce a certain tax burden that has to be undertaken by the present generation, against future generations. From this perspective, a government that reduces taxes increases future taxes and its decision is similar to borrowing funds, as if consumers were burdened by loans (Kazakos et al., 2016).

(Continued)

Box 1.1   (cont'd)

As explained later (section 1.5.4), the borrowed funds in the Greek case were mostly used for consumption purposes and people had not realized that a time will arrive when taxes will have to be raised to pay back the loans, or had considered that if such a time arrives, they will not be held responsible or they will avoid suffering the collective consequences of their choice. During the period of extensive borrowing, savings were reduced and people had created an illusionary vision of their own wealth. They had thought that the funds borrowed were part of their own wealth rather than part of an effort to sustain the same growth model, undermining its sustainability and the wealth of future generations. In practice extensive borrowing causes a wealth illusion effect.

On the other hand lies a view based on the Ricardian equilibrium, according to which rational consumers realize that borrowing will affect their future consumption and restrict their current consumption behavior and patterns, to support the welfare of future generations (Barro, 1974). This view is likely to find an application at the individual level of a rational consumer than at the aggregate level of a whole society, where the entity that borrows funds (the state), differs from the collective entity that consumes these funds, i.e., the society, the users of public goods, and more precisely those individuals who obtain part of these borrowed funds through wages and salaries and use them for present consumption purposes. Their myopic behavior and the incapacity of some people to leave a legacy in future generations may be some of the reasons that neutralize the Ricardian equilibrium (Abel et al., 2010).

Finally another view, held by Keynesians and especially post-Keynesians, is that public debt increases net wealth of households but inflation reduces such increases upon their real wealth (Kazakos et al., 2016).

hold—the Greek case helps to accept that macroeconomic imbalances can take place and be exacerbated when monetary autonomy is lost. In this respect, the Greek crisis is a case to test the views held on the capacity of policy-makers to erase macroeconomic imbalances (the belief of achieving a period of "great" moderation in the United States) and the presence of such imbalances at a regional context, in particular in regional spaces of the common monetary currency. If in environments of lost monetary autonomy macroeconomic imbalances are exacerbated, and the strength of causal mechanisms put in operation is such that great economic imbalances are produced and reproduced, then the Greek case is worth considering and studying for an extra reason.

A structural logic may be found in the view that financial crises tend to exacerbate sharp economic downturns, lower government revenues, widen government deficits, and bring higher levels of debt, pushing many economies into default (as presented in Nelson et al., 2010: 1). In this perspective, there is some circular sequence of events in the event that a crisis appears.

The twin deficit hypothesis is another explanation that could also be considered as structural. According to this hypothesis, there is a strong link of association between the government budget deficits and the current account deficits in an economy. This is proposed after the macroeconomic equation:

$$CA \ (NX) = (Savings - Investments) + (Tax - Government \ Expenditure),$$

An increase in the government budget deficit will increase the deficit of the current account balance if the former reduces also the desired national savings (Abel et al., 2010). The persistence of twin deficits should normally require addressing the problem by devaluing the currency. The twin deficit hypothesis results in the policy suggestion to sell off domestic properties to international investors (by privatizing them), so as to raise the income obtained from abroad (Abel et al., 2010).

The relation between fiscal deficits and debts has been described as a snowball effect. Debt stabilization passes through the reduction of fiscal deficits and the creation of fiscal surpluses, something that reveals the significance of deficits in the production and sustaining of large debts.

Another relevant hypothesis is that the debt creates debt. According to this hypothesis, countries that owe significant amounts will finally end up borrowing even more to repay past loans, entering a vicious circle of debt creation and rising.

In their seminal work on debt crises all over the world and in various historical settings, Reinhart and Rogoff (2009) differentiate between external and domestic default crisis. They identify banking crises as a main cause of external default crises and provide evidence on strong association of defaults to inflation. These two causes appear to be somehow structurally related to defaults. They also trace patterns of cycles of sovereign default and external debt. The term "odious debt" is used for lending money to a suspiciously kleptomaniac and corrupt government (Reinhart and Rogoff, 2009: 63). Several observers have considered the Greek debt to be odious but from dissimilar perspectives (Manopoulos, 2012; HP Debt Truth Committee, 2015).

Finally, another significant cause lies in the 1999–2000 Athens stock market crash. This however is not only a structural problem but also related to policy guidance. The rise of the stock market's shares and values was affected by policies and has followed a general trend of rising values and prices all over Greece (in real estate, land, prices of goods and services, etc.) observed after the mid-1990s, and as soon as Greece's firm decision to join the monetary zone was announced. This trend was further boosted by the Olympic Games and the related construction projects. What is worth considering though is that substantial funds vanished in the stock market crash, just before the country's entry into the Eurozone and caused liquidity constraints in the markets, which have influenced the investment pattern and behavior of many incomers and business owners. Investment behavior was distorted, precisely at the time when it had to be offered new paths and alternatives, and when Greeks had to be taught and given some good examples on how to invest their own private funds.

One of the key structural explanations of the Greek crisis refers to the structural weaknesses and problems of the Greek economy that have increased over the years its appetite for external borrowing. Some of these structural weaknesses are explained by discussing policy-oriented explanations later on. These structural causes should be seen as reasons for not espousing, if not fully rejecting, the following of a parsimonious macroeconomic trajectory in the Greek economy and for the continuous over the years ostracism of those energetic and active forces of the Greek economy that merited better conditions for work, professional development, and for undertaking risks and initiatives and succeeding.

1.5.2   A brief historical assessment in welfare terms of Greece's choice to integrate in the European Communities

Greece is one of the states that has not benefited much from the European integration process. It has considered the significance of the prospect of its membership since the very early steps of the unification process and has managed to join the EC as its 10th member-state. Even if a range of Cohesion policies were applied over the years, the welfare effects from the application of the Single Market have not been fully materialized in Greece.

Table 1.4 shows that, in terms of GDP per head, measured in purchasing power parities, Luxembourg and Ireland are the two states mostly benefiting out of the EU integration process. Luxembourg has gained almost 61,000 PPP units since 1971, while Ireland gained almost 46,000 since 1973 (within 42 years of EU membership). Their annual welfare gain is twice that of states like Germany, Netherlands, or Belgium. Sweden, without being a Eurozone member, has improved by an annual 1145 within 20 years of EU membership, almost double that of its Scandinavian Eurozone partner, Finland. This is far better than its annual performance since 1971 (521 only), indicating the substantial welfare effects for Sweden since its joining year. Greece in particular, hit by the crisis and the strong economic and monetary cycle, has gained only 126 PPP units annually since 1981, its joining year. Since this is approximately ten times less than Luxembourg, Sweden, or even Ireland and is comparable to only South Africa's similar performance from the rest of OECD states, one can argue without doubt that Greece's actual welfare benefits from joining the EC and those accrued from Eurozone membership are strongly limited, if not negative. This is getting even worse if seen in comparison to non-EU members. Such results for Greece are remarkable, because according to the basics of integration theory and its original developments, the economic integration amongst states aims primarily at increasing their welfare (see Glencross, 2014).

The three larger in size European states that have worked hard to prepare the unification process, France, Germany and the UK, are not amongst those benefiting mostly in welfare terms. Some of the explanations can relate to the rise of immigration and demographic pressure exercised across all of them, while other may differ for each state. For instance the German unification may be a reason

Table 1.4 GDP per head and change of GDP per head, European OECD and selected OECD states

Country name	GDP change since joining year (no of years)	Annually (annually since 1971)	1971–2015	1971	1981	1991	2001	2011	2015
Austria	10,179 (20)	504 (556)	24,456	18,343	24,613	31,079	38,035	42,954	42,798
Belgium	22,091 (44)[a]	502 (502)	22,091	18,885	24,778	30,418	36,575	40,544	40,977
Denmark	19,755 (42)	470 (485)	21,358	23,191	26,828	33,459	41,662	43,484	44,549
Finland	11,094 (20)	555 (504)	22,194	15,779	21,742	26,345	34,778	39,626	37,973
France	18,337 (44)[a]	417 (417)	18,337	18,591	24,069	29,147	34,534	36,626	36,928
Germany	23,546 (44)[a]	535 (535)	23,546	18,975	24,580	31,722	36,619	41,462	42,522
Greece	4287 (34)	126 (199)	8744	14,912	19,369	20,622	25,262	25,665	23,656
Ireland	45,932 (42)	1094 (1065)	46,841	11,275	15,468	21,266	40,350	43,043	58,117
Italy	15,675 (44)[a]	356 (356)	15,675	17,504	24,092	30,608	36,004	34,818	33,180
Luxembourg	60,909 (44)[a]	1384 (1384)	60,909	28,237	33,091	55,323	77,327	85,845	89,147
Netherlands	23,495 (44)[a]	534 (534)	23,495	21,923	26,249	31,945	41,423	45,117	45,419
Portugal	10,854 (29)	374 (349)	15,376	11,291	15,004	21,178	26,437	26,901	26,668
Spain	12,432 (29)	429 (394)	17,321	14,404	17,780	23,641	30,516	31,556	31,726
Sweden	30,155 (20)	1145 (521)	22,908	21,230	24,964	29,471	36,222	42,456	44,138
United Kingdom	19,247 (42)	458 (478)	21,033	17,002	19,951	26,050	33,310	35,983	38,036
EU28	—	291[b]	4007[b]			—	30,637	33,805	34,714
EU15	—	453 (453)	19,927	17,733	22,564	28,570	34,749	37,077	37,660
OECD—Total	—	474 (474)	20,850	16,721	21,015	26,385	32,309	35,788	37,572
Norway	—	838 (838)	36,863	22,411	32,526	40,924	54,929	57,804	59,274
Switzerland	—	416 (416)	18,283	35,577	38,787	44,031	48,004	53,295	53,860
Iceland	—	582 (582)	25,607	16,624	25,312	28,399	34,563	39,055	42,230
China	—	291 (291)	12,783	480	734	1602	3886	10,149	13,263
Costa Rica	—	281[b]	6736[b]	—	—	7808	9944	13,155	14,544

(Continued)

Table 1.4 (Continued)

Country name	GDP change since joining year (no of years)	Annually (annually since 1971)	1971–2015	1971	1981	1991	2001	2011	2015
United States	–	632 (632)	27,821	23,772	29,123	35,726	45,007	48,704	51,592
Japan	–	500 (500)	21,983	15,085	20,681	30,656	33,217	35,021	37,068
South Africa	–	114[b]	2610[b]	–	–	9572	9811	12,043	12,182

[a]For EC-6 countries, the calculated period starts from 1971.
[b]Calculations for available study period. Data for South Africa available until 2014. Except for United Kingdom, United States, and Norway all values are estimated for years 1971, 1981 (expect further for France and Finland), and 1991 (except further for France, Finland, Canada, Germany, Costa Rica, and South Africa). All OECD totals are estimates. For 2015 data are provisional for France, Greece, Netherlands, Portugal, Spain, EU28, EU15, and OECD total.

Source: OECD database, constant purchasing power parities per head, constant prices, $, OECD base year (US Dollar, 2010).

Table 1.5 Yearly average annual growth rate of GDP and cumulative GDP change in different integration periods: 1981–91, 1991–2001, 2001–08, 2008–16

	1981–1991	1991–2001	2001–2008	2008–2016	2001–2016	2011–2016
Austria	2.4	2.5	2.14	0.7	1.4	0.97
Belgium	2.0	2.1	1.97	0.8	1.4	0.88
Czech Rep.	–	0.8	4.35	1.2	2.7	1.49
Denmark	2.0	2.5	1.37	0.4	0.9	1.01
Estonia	–	-0.2	6.01	0.1	3.4	2.74
Finland	2.3	2.4	2.87	-0.3	1.2	0.20
France	2.4	2.1	1.65	0.6	1.1	0.85
Germany	2.6	2.0	1.36	1.0	1.2	1.40
Greece	0.9	2.6	3.51	-3.3	-0.1	-2.79
Hungary	–	-0.3	3.34	0.7	2.0	1.63
Ireland	3.5	7.1	4.14	3.7	4.4	5.70
Italy	2.3	1.7	0.89	-0.8	0.1	-0.31
Latvia	–	-0.3	7.41	-0.2	3.8	2.83
Lithuania	–	0.9	7.40	2.0	4.2	2.99
Luxembourg	5.3	5.2	3.38	2.1	3.0	2.86
Netherlands	2.3	3.2	1.95	0.6	1.2	0.85
Poland	–	3.6	4.12	3.2	3.6	2.55
Portugal	3.4	2.8	1.08	-0.4	0.3	-0.44
Slovak Rep	–	0.2	6.27	2.3	4.1	2.24
Slovenia	–	2.0	4.24	0.2	2.0	0.68
Spain	2.9	2.9	3.25	0.0	1.5	0.31
Sweden	1.9	2.1	2.59	1.5	2.2	1.95
United Kingdom	2.6	2.4	2.32	1.0	1.7	1.69
EU28	–	0.3	2.04	0.5	1.3	1.03
EU15	2.4	2.3	1.87	1.0	1.2	0.89
OECD total	3.1	2.7	2.16	1.1	1.7	1.58
Norway	2.6	3.5	2.09	1.3	1.6	1.32
Switzerland	1.9	1.2	1.9	4.8	1.7	1.25
Iceland	2.5	2.7	2.5	1.3	3.0	2.98
China	9.3	10.3	9.3	3.6	9.1	5.62
Costa Rica	–	4.5	4.91	1.6	3.9	2.82
USA	3.0	3.2	3.0	0.6	1.8	2.86
Japan	4.5	1.3	0.99	0.4	0.8	0.85
South Africa	1.3	1.9	1.3	1.5	2.8	1.31

Note: Data for former CEE countries were not available during the 1980s. For Estonia data were available from 1994, for Latvia from 1995, for Lithuania from 1996, for EU28 from 1996, for South Africa from 1996, for Costa Rica from 1992. For all these states or group of states the calculations are made using the abovementioned initial year. In 1999, Austria, Belgium, Finland, France, Germany, Ireland, Italy, Luxembourg, Netherlands, Portugal, and Spain had met the Euro-convergence criteria. Greece joined in 2001, Slovenia in 2007 (Malta and Cyprus in 2008), the Slovak Republic in 2009, Estonia in 2011, Latvia in 2014, and Lithuania in 2015. Except Greece, the rest joined the EU in May 2004.
Source: Data extracted from OECD database.

explaining Germany's performance in per capita terms. The UK case merits more attention. While the UK has focused historically on financial services, Switzerland a non-European member has outperformed it in welfare terms. What is more, surrounded by states that either have benefited much more out of the integration process, such as Ireland and Sweden, or remained neutral and far from the unification process but benefited more in welfare terms, such as Norway or Iceland, the UK had more reasons than initially suggested (in various debates held on Brexit) to consider exiting the EU. The dilemma posed was either to abandon the integration process or join the currency zone, with all its problems and weaknesses (see section 1.5.3). Not to mention that the crisis has unveiled that despite its contribution to the EU budget and EU policies, as member of the Economic Union, the expected results of such policies were not finally reached. Table 1.5 shows that Greece's limited growth is achieved despite her high growth rates, achieved during the 1990s and the early period of its Eurozone membership (that were higher in comparison to those of most European states and the EU15 average).

1.5.3 Explaining the Greek crisis by looking at the mirror of the European institutional responses

One can understand many things about the Greek crisis by looking at the mirror of the EU-wide institutional responses that it has brought. The Greek state was the first in the chain of states that were affected by the crisis in the Eurozone. These were Portugal, Spain, Ireland, and Cyprus, all of them peripheral in the EU. As a result of the pressure exercised by the markets in Greece and in other Eurozone states, new institutions have been formed and new policies improvised in the Eurozone over the last few years. Such is the extent of the amendments and changes taking place in the Eurozone after the Greek crisis that the period resembles the post-1929 period in the United States, when numerous institutions and the whole subdiscipline of macroeconomics were created to overcome economic and financial problems.

This process of institutional building is characteristic of the response of European states in times of hardship. The very creation of the European Communities in 1958 took place after the creation of dozens of institutions, such as the Council of Europe (1949), OEEC (in 1948 that later changed to OECD), the Western European Union (1954), the European Coal and Steel Committee (1951), the European Atomic Energy Committee (EURATOM), and the European Economic Community (in 1957).

It took only but a few years of crisis to realize that: (i) there were ample limitations in the ECB's available tools, their extent and scope; (ii) a significant institutional gap existed for EMU's own institutions; and (iii) the unification process had to be completed by taking macroeconomic theory more carefully into account. It was realized that reaching a stage of integration that is based only on a monetary unification was not sufficient and that a monetary union is more solidly built and its rationale and scope better promoted if it is combined with a union in banking matters as well as in fiscal, political, and/or legal matters (see Ioannou et al., 2015; Verdum, 2017).

In order to advance a banking union, three main pillars were placed in operation: bank resolution, bank supervision, and bank regulation. These are advanced through the single supervisory mechanism (SSM) that supervises principal banks, the Single Resolution Mechanism (SRM) that resolves problems of failing banks, the SRF (Single Resolution Fund), and the European Deposit Insurance Scheme (EDIS). The Banking Union is also based on the Capital Requirements Directive (CRD), the Bank Recovery and Resolution Directive (BRRD), and the Capital Requirements Regulation (CRR), based on Basel III principles.

The banking crisis helped to realize that countries are exposed to insolvency risks when they cannot print out money, and that the central bank of the Eurozone, the ECB, was not acting as a lender of last resort (LOLR) for sovereign borrowers and for governments that have to borrow to bail out banks. The ECB overemphasized price stability instead of financial stability as a whole, which requires attention and action against credit bubbles. According to economic theory, a state should have the capacity to monetize its deficit to some degree, i.e., to be able to finance its deficit by issuing some bonds that will be purchased by its central bank. On the contrary, since the inception of the common currency, the Eurozone partners had agreed that the ECB cannot schedule some particular programme to purchase bonds and provide credit to central governments, agencies, and institutions. Its prior efforts towards this direction were stuck in the TFEU, which prohibited legally the monetary financing by the ECB and bailouts.[21] An effort was made to overcome this problem progressively; firstly by using the Covered Bond Purchase Programme (CBPP), launched in 2009, followed by the Securities Markets Programme in May 2010, which helped to purchase sovereign bonds on secondary markets and a second CBPP2, in November 2011. The ECB had then finally acted progressively as a lender of last resort in the government bond markets by launching its outright monetary transactions program (EP, 2015). This policy was continued through a third CBPP3 and the launch of an Asset-Backed Securities Purchase Programme (ABS PP), which in January 2015 was followed by an expanded Asset Purchase Programme (EAPP), known as QE, since the ECB creates money to purchase financial assets from private investors, such as banks, pension funds, and insurance companies (EP, 2015).

While a central authority, the ECB, was created for monetary purposes, fiscal matters had remained highly decentralized (Cœuré, 2016). Originally, it was thought that country-specific shocks would reduce simply by the commitment of states to fiscal soundness and that financial linkages would not affect the spreading of a shock, in the absence of mechanisms to deal with such shocks and the general lack of preparedness (Allard et al., 2013). What is more, the EU has disregarded the basic knowledge of economic theory on combining monetary with fiscal policies to promote stabilization, precisely in the way this takes place for single currencies.

[21] In Articles 123 and 125.

Proponents of fiscal centralization argued that delegating authority at common currency level is required if the effects from domestic fiscal policies spread across the currency zone, and that effectiveness will rise if considerable externalities will be reduced (Viera at al., 2003; Collignon, 2001). Since its inception, the Eurozone partners had agreed to set-up the Broad Economic Guidelines, as the main coordination instruments among domestic fiscal policies (Collignon, 2001). Instead of taking the wiser decision to improve stability features that would replace those in operation of single currencies, they had decided to interfere with domestic fiscal autonomy by imposing fiscal constraints upon public deficit and debts (in the Maastricht Treaty, the Stability and Growth Pact, and through the penalties of the Excessive Deficit Procedure). Even if penalizing countries should be the outcome of automatic rules rather than of discretionary choices (Uhlig, 2002, quoted in Viera et al., 2003), in the absence of other economic "cushions," independent fiscal reactions were thought crucial for domestic policy-making (Viera et al., 2003).

The policy vacuum in fiscal matters has opened new debates on the need for sound fiscal policy and balancing growth. New fiscal institutions and policies were launched in the Eurozone in a few years, such as the European Financial Stability Facility, the European Stability Mechanism, the European Semester, the "six-pack" and the "two-pack" legislation, the Fiscal Compact, and independent national fiscal councils. These have helped to strengthen fiscal governance promoted through the SGP (Ioannou et al., 2015).

The independent national fiscal councils would monitor fiscal rules and allow moving from rule-based to institutionally-based fiscal policy in the Eurozone (Cœuré, 2016). Both "packs" operated in parallel with the Treaty on Stability, Coordination, and Governance (TSCG), which aimed at further complementing the SGP and at contributing to bringing stability to the monetary union, mainly through its Fiscal Compact. The six-pack legislation also created the Macroeconomic Imbalance Procedure and several Macro Financial Assistance Facilities were placed in operation (EFSF, ESM, EFSM, BoP Assistance[22]) (Emerson and Giovannini, 2013). More recently, the seed of "debt brakes" was introduced to replace the SGP, which was espoused as a "Golden Rule."

Fiscal balance was thought to take place by organizing more effective prevention of "gross policy errors" (by introducing expenditure benchmarks), by focusing not only on deficit but on debt developments (on sufficiently diminishing debt ratio), and through better rule enforcement (and the expansion of sanctions), based on prevention and correction of macro imbalances, macroprudential supervision, regulation and supervision of financial systems (see Feddersen, unknown year). A better rule enforcement and even stricter rules and penalties were thought to be the remedy for correcting macroimbalances, instead of realizing that the absence of stability features causes problems of macroeconomic instability.

A series of additional fiscal measures and instruments are currently being considered to promote further fiscal integration and absorb cyclical shocks. These

---

[22] The European Financial Stability Facility, the European Stability Mechanism, the European Financial Stabilization Mechanism. The Balance of Payment Assistance addresses non-Eurozone members.

comprise automatic or semiautomatic measures for insurance, such as a European unemployment insurance scheme and an unemployment reinsurance fund (EU Parliament, 2016). They also comprise the promotion of a common public investment strategy, building upon the current EFSI (European Fund for Strategic Investment), subject to the European Stability Mechanism (ESM) or its potential transformation to a "European Monetary Fund."

Overall, one could refer to an overemphasis placed on monetary matters in the EMU rather than on broader aspects of economic policy before the Greek crisis, the absence of a coherent multiperspective policy framework that ought to have been put in place before the creation of the Eurozone, policy misconceptions, policy misdiagnoses as soon as the crisis occurred, and a more general lack of preparedness from the side of the Eurozone and the EU, in terms of institutions and policies (Box 1.2).

Box 1.2 About economic cycles and their explanations

In the last decades, most economists had considered that economic cycles are a derelict of economic theory from the past. Before the advent of the global crisis, many are those, for example, who believed that the economy of the United States had managed to undergo a period of "great moderation" of economic cycles and that such examples of economic cycles had disappeared for good. The crisis questioned such views and brought a refreshing look at macroeconomics as a discipline, whose principal target has been the understanding and policies required to reduce economic cycles as a phenomenon. The view that cycles remain present and that economic policies do not suffice, is gaining more and more ground in economic policy circles. It is worth reviewing some of the main points of economic and business cycle theory, from the past.

Harbeler (1968) distinguishes between long waves and business cycles. The former may extend to periods of 50 or 60 years, while short-cycles, for which the term "business or trade cycle" is used, refers to shorter periods of time, which are superimposed on the long waves.

Cycles are considered to be "serially correlated, "cyclical movements in real output," and co-movements of aggregate variables that deviate from their own trend (Lucas, 1975: 1113). They are composed of several phases (of dissimilar expansion or contraction), which, though not periodic, have dissimilar length and amplitude (Duarte, 2015). A cycle is a "cumulative, self-reinforcing process of expansion and contraction" (Harbeler, 1968: 276), formed by an upswing (prosperity), an upper turning-point (crisis), a downswing (depression), and a lower turning-point (revival) (Harbeler, 1968). Cycles can be viewed as a combination of "ceilings" and "floors" attained by macroeconomic variables. Their basic characteristic is their pervasiveness, as

(Continued)

Box 1.2   (cont'd)

they affect all phases of economic life and are reflected in all measures of economic activity (Harbeler, 1968).

In the various explanations for cycles, there is a search for the dominant or "causally relevant" factor, and all other factors are considered secondary and their importance is undermined.

A distinction has been made between passive and active factors causing cycles, between controllable and uncontrollable factors, between endogenous and exogenous factors (though as Harbeler claims there can be no pure endogenous or exogenous factors). Another distinction made is between causes and conditions of the cycles and between conditions *per quam* and *since qua non* (Harbeler, 1968). Though it is difficult to draw a sharp line between passive and active factors, the institutional factors can be considered as passive, while changes in demand or inventions can be considered as active (Harbeler, 1968).

Any cause is expressed at a particular institutional environment (Harbeler, 1968). If one or more significant aspects of an institutional environment were changed and if some active forces were missing (such as demand changes or inventions) a business cycle may have not occurred (Harbeler, 1968). A cycle is possibly associated to the rigidity of an economic system or its financial and monetary organization (Harbeler, 1968).

Business cycles, especially in the long run, have been studied extensively. Many different theories and explanations have been offered. One of these is capital investment theory, which traces the cause of long-waves in massive overinvestments of capital goods, such as railroads or factories (Harbeler, 1968).

These cause an upswing that is bound to be followed by a downswing, when capital depreciation takes place (Harbeler, 1968). The overinvestment theory has been contrasted to overconsumption theory.

Harbeler points out that apart from the main explanatory factors of business cycles there is "an endless variety of changes in the sphere of economic and social life, which, without being essential features of the cycle, are more or less regular concomitants of its progress" (Harbeler, 1968: 275). "Most of these changes do not appear regularly in all cycles" (Harbeler, 1968: 275).

The presence of several irregularities and far-reaching differences between the characteristics of each cycle, make each cycle an individual phenomenon, embedded in a particular socio-economic structure (Harbeler, 1968: 275). As Harbeler proceeds: "Technological knowledge, methods of production, degree of capital-intensity, number, quality and age-distribution of the population, habits and preferences of consumers, social institutions in the widest sense including the legal framework of society, practice in the matter of interventions of the State and other public bodies in the economic sphere, habits of payment, banking practices and so forth—all these factors change

(Continued)

Box 1.2   (cont'd)

continuously—and are not exactly the same in any two cases" (Harbeler, 1968: 275). He then suggests that this is a reason why dissimilarities are found in the cycles occurring in different states, in different periods of time.

Harbeler (1968) does not associate economic cycles to different social and economic conditions that will produce dissimilar theories of the business cycle but suggests "that a very general theory of the most important aspects of the cycle can be evolved," with "a very wide field of application."

Two main features of the cycles appear to be that production and employment move in parallel with money value and that fluctuations are particularly stronger for producer's goods rather than for consumers (Harbeler, 1968).

A range of theories discuss economic and business cycles. Capitalist crisis theory argues that long-waves are inherent in capitalism and are an expression of its self-destruction. War-theory argues that long-waves are closely associated with wars (Harbeler, 1968). The monetary theory associates cycles with the quantity of money and its velocity (Harbeler, 1968). When the quantity of money reduces, demand falls, stocks accumulate, production falls, losses incur, and unemployment rises (Harbeler, 1968). Wage and other incomes will have to fall to restore equilibrium (Harbeler, 1968). Finally, innovation theory claims that innovation causes an upswing, since it offers good returns. However as each innovation prevails against others, no room is left for their expression and, thereafter, a downswing is caused. The latter can be overcome through new innovations (Harbeler, 1968).

Cycles are also caused by random shocks or by apparently random shocks (in such factors as investment or business expectations) that may act to pull output up in times of prosperity or pull it down in times of depression (Sherman, 1964).

1.5.4   Policy-oriented and on-crisis policy explanations

Several policy-oriented explanations have already been suggested. The analysis of previous historical periods and records of indebtedness of the modern Greek state relates indebtedness to the role exercised by international interests and international policies. In a collection of his analyses about the previous indebtednesses, Toussaint (2017) provides an account of several causes that remind of the prior experience of indebtedness of the Greek state, after its overburdening from loans. Even if one may argue that "this time is different," because Greece is an equal member of the EU and the Eurozone, having reached the most advanced stage of integration, prior experience reminds of the suffering of the Greek state and its impediments to grow. Greece came to a state of a debt default on several occasions —in 1826, 1843, 1893, and 1933—and, in all these occasions, international creditors ceased their agreed financing in the Greek economy after an international crisis had burst (Toussaint, 2017). For instance, the 1825–1826 crisis in international markets made London's bankers unwilling to pay the agreed loans.

In 1833, the newly formed Greek state had to face the consequences of the 1825–26 international crisis. A "troika" of three states, France, Great Britain, and Russia, decided to intervene and ask a French bank to lend new funds to Greece. Having acted as guarantors, they decided as an exchange -as Toussaint (2017) explains- to bring a king in Greece, by amending the Constitution. In 1843, the country declared its indebtedness, because it was unable to pay back the interest rates and very severe measures and conditions of austerity were imposed for the economy (which comprised laying-off one-third of its employees) (Toussaint, 2017). Similarly, hard conditions were imposed on the Greek state in 1898, by the International Financial Commission, since it was asked to pay more than 40% of its income in order to pay back its loans (ibid). The massive influx of Greek immigrants from Minor Asia in 1922 and the additional war loans offered to Greece for the First World War had increased Greece's debt as a proportion of its GDP and made it difficult to cope with it (Toussaint, 2017). Of course the Greek state would have not been formed in 1821 without the intervention of the three great powers at the time, France, Great Britain, and Russia. Similarly, after the Second World War, in a period when most states were making substantial steps of development, Greece was facing the civil war and its consequences.

Dertilis (2016) traces a spiral of wars, civil wars, and bankruptcies in the modern Greek state. He argues that since its independence in 1821, the Greek state has suffered from four civil wars and was involved in seven external wars. In these two centuries, the Greek state went bankrupt seven times, has dived into crises, and has lived only in the most recent period without an international control (Dertilis, 2016). He pertains that in all the bankruptcies and wars of the Greek state, there is a sequence of causes and effects that he suggests is composed by the reckless military expenses, indebtedness, and inefficient tax collection. These are connected in a vicious circle. It is the axis of war–bankruptcy that brings always an international control and restructuring of the debt (Dertilis, 2016).[23]

An additional historical explanations relates to the historical timing of the global crisis. In late November 2009, following the aforementioned problems with Lehman Brothers and international banks, several doubts were raised as to whether Dubai World, a state-owned corporation in Dubai, would default on its debt. This fact raised fears across international markets concerning the prospect of a possible cascade of sovereign defaults of governments that were facing difficult circumstances after the crisis and were incapable of repaying back their debt (Belkin et al., 2010: 3). From this perspective Greece was found to be in the middle of a storm in the ocean, without a "lifejacket". The funds seeking to draw as much as possible from cases of default had just realized the prospect of their potential losses, as well as that of collecting strong prospect of collecting great amounts out of such cases of sovereign debt defaults, in particular by speculating against the common

---

[23] Dertilis, a historian himself believes that history rarely teaches but is never repeated but considers the case of the history of the modern Greek state to be an exception to that rule (Dertilis, 2016).

European currency, a newly formed currency espoused by many states that appeared to be more fragile and unprotected than originally thought. At the same time, the strong criticism raised on the role of international credit institutions that were rating the financial credibility of other institutions and nation-states (such as Moody's and Standard and Poor's) made these companies the hardest critics and much more inelastic in their assessments about state economies, keen on removing from their own shoulders the responsibility of not sending (once again) an early warning.

This historical timing has matched with allegations at the time that Greece was attempting to obscure its true debt statistics (Nelson et al., 2010). What was an internal and, at best, intra-Eurozone issue—the way the Greek deficit was measured and the different possibilities offered for its measurement—had become a matter of global concern, as it was thought that behind these efforts to amend its statistics lied a more general effort to sweep problems of the Greek economy under the carpet.

A historical accounting of the Greek crisis is important before considering further policy-oriented and on-crisis policy-error explanations. According to a special chronicle of the Greek crisis, presented by the central Bank of Greece (2014) (that has been integrated in the European Central Banking system since 2001), Greece had managed to join the Euro in 2001 as an outcome of its efforts to achieve nominal convergence, even if macroeconomic imbalances had not been resolved on a permanent basis. This is due to: (i) the great fiscal adjustment achieved, reflected in the fall of the general government deficit from 13.6% of GDP in 1993 to 3.1% in 1999, and the increase of its primary surplus from 2.7% of GDP in 1994 to 4.3% in 1999; (ii) the increase of economic activity from 2% in 1994 to 3.4% in 1999; (iii) the limitation of inflation rate from two-digit figures before 1993 to 6.8% average in the 1994−1999 period, and the significant fall of interest rates; and (iv) the reduction of debt dynamics, which fell from 110.1% of GDP in 1993 to 105.5% of GDP in 1998 and 104.6% in 1999 (Bank of Greece, 2014). Inflation in that period was at historically low levels: it was on average 1.5% below the average of Eurozone states, with a constant loss of competitiveness of the Greek economy. While the Greek economy was growing at 4.2% in the 2000−7 period (or 3.6% in the 2001−8 period), this growth was based on domestic demand that rose by 4.5%, mainly due to the rise in private consumption, which, due to the rise in incomes, the development of consumer credit, and the borrowing of the economy, grew at 4.2%, almost as much as the GDP (see Table 1.6) (Bank of Greece, 2014: 15). The growth of investments in construction and real estate has also contributed to growth performance (Bank of Greece, 2014: 15). The chronicle of the Bank of Greece highlights that imports were increased to compensate for the lack of capacity of domestic production to respond to developments in domestic demand (imports of goods and services expanded by an average rate of 4.5% in the 2001−7 period). As a result of their increase, the deficit of the current account balance also increased (from an average 3% of GDP in the 1994−1999 period to an average 8.5% in 2000−7), which exceeded 10% in 2007 and reached 14.9% of GDP in 2008. Imports were funded by access to cheap capital borrowing, both private and public sector (Bank of Greece, 2014: 17). Had Greece not been a member of the

Table 1.6 **Some significant variables of the Greek economy**

Year	Annual percentage changes in real effective exchange rate (on the basis of relative consumer prices/on the basis of relative unit labor costs)	Current account balance	Trade balance	Credit to households by domestic MFIs (consumer credit)	Credit to nonfinancial corporations by domestic MFIs	General government revenue	General government expenditure	General government net borrowing (deficit)	Public debt
2001	1.1/0.7	− 7.2	− 14.8	5.4	34.3	40.9	45.4	− 4.4	103.7
2002	2.6/4.0	− 6.5	− 14.5	6.2	35.1	40.3	45.1	− 4.8	101.7
2003	5.5/4.0	− 6.5	− 13.1	7.2	35.4	39.0	44.7	− 5.7	97.4
2004	1.9/4.3	− 5.8	− 13.7	9.2	38.6	38.1	45.5	− 7.4	98.6
2005	− 0.1/0.5	− 7.6	− 14.3	11.3	42.0	39.0	44.6	− 5.6	100.0
2006	0.8/0.8	− 11.4	− 16.9	12.7	44.9	39.2	45.3	− 6.0	106.1
2007	1.6/1.6	− 14.6	− 18.6	14.3	49.9	40.7	47.5	− 6.8	107.4
2008	2.5/7.1	− 14.9	− 18.9	15.6	56.8	40.7	50.6	− 9.9	112.9
Average annual percentage of GDP (or rate of change):									
2001−2007	1.9*/2.5*	9.1	− 15.5	10.1	41.2	39.6	45.5	− 5.8	102.2
2001−2008	2.0*/3.1*	− 9.8	− 15.9	10.8	43.2	39.7	46.1	− 6.3	103.5

*Cumulative change in the 8-year period 2001−2008: 16.9% (on the basis of relative consumer prices), 27.7% (on the basis of relative unit labour costs).

Source: Bank of Greece, 2014: 16. Data collected by ELSTAT and the Bank of Greece.

Eurozone, the national currency would have been devalued and high inflation would have occurred (Bank of Greece, 2014: 16−17). The rise of private consumption brought the widening of the contribution of trade in total added value, from 14.1% in 2000 to 17.4% in 2007 (Bank of Greece, 2014: 17). A great part of trade activity concerned imported consumer and durable consumer goods. It is indicative that the 148,100 cars purchased on average from 1990 to 1998, became 270,200 on average in the 1998−2008 period.

A view that is gaining a growing number of supporters after the crisis is the overemphasis that the Greek economy placed on consumption-based development rather than on production, competitiveness, and exports as a policy problem that was extended in time (see IMF, 2012; Bank of Greece, 2014).

Fig. 1.14 shows that Greece's average final private consumption for the 1993−2016 as a whole, is far greater than that of other Mediterranean and Scandinavian countries and EU averages. Greece exceeds even the two Balkan countries that bear more resemblance to this peculiar consumption pattern. On the contrary, its final public consumption (general government) is one of the lowest, as opposed to the example of the Scandinavian countries.

The emphasis that the economy has placed on consumption in comparison to investment is seen in Table 1.7. Over the decades, consumption is more and more emphasized and reaches a level close to 85% of GDP in the 1990−2009 period.

The main problem with a demand-driven path of development is that if it turns out to be a long-term choice then any consumption-based solution is rendered inappropriate when a crisis arrives, i.e., at a period when boosting growth through consumption will be mostly required to recover from an economic shock. The Bank of Greece chronicle does not go as far as to explain why production, exports, and competitiveness were not sufficiently promoted by the Greek state, an issue which lies

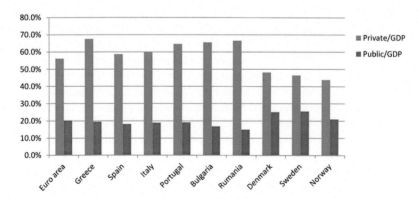

Figure 1.14 Average private and public consumption expenditure, 1993−2016.
Source: AMECO series, private final consumption expenditure at current prices (UCPH) and final consumption expenditure of general government at current prices (UCTG) and Gross domestic Product (UVGD). *Note*: Average is measured as the sum of public or private consumption for the period as a percentage of GDP, divided by the number of years, current prices.

Table 1.7 **Consumption and Investment as percentage of GDP, Greece, selected periods**

	Consumption as % of GDP	Investment as % of GDP
1970–1979	70.7	30.7[a]
1980–1989	79	24.9[a]
1990–1999	84.5	20.6[a]
2000–2009	86	23
2010–2016	91.02	14.71[b]

[a]Estimated.
[b]Provisional.
Note: Investment as % of GDP (*Source*: OECD) and consumption as % of GDP (*Source*: AMECO Database).

at the "heart" of the Greek problem. As if some automatic mechanism exists that replaces consumption needs by the necessary exports.[24]

Tsoukalas (2013: 80) highlights the problem that it is not that the Greek economy was growing but that this particular growth was owed to the rise of private consumption at a time when most of its organizational and productive forces remained stable or even weakened. This could be named as a state of illusion for the Greek society, which allowed the outburst of the great crisis on its shoulders. Another way to put it is that the Greeks were not producing as much as they thought that they really were and certainly not as much as they were consuming.

The IMF itself has made clear that the principal difference between the first and the second programme co-funded by the IMF lies in the interest that the second programme had put in the matters of production, competitiveness, and exports (IMF, 2012). According to the IMF (2012), the debt will not be reduced simply by following the range of reforms suggested, but requires an emphasis to be given to these particular aspects of reforms (IMF, 2012). One has to note that such views came with a certain—though substantial—delay and the problem of the limited contribution of production and exports in GDP growth was not realized and envisaged as a priority in IMF and EU policies.

Since 1981 and for an extended period of time, Greece's public debt has raised its real interest rates and the cost of capital, causing higher exchange rates for the Greek national currency, and an environment especially adverse for the SMEs (Pitelis, 2013). Early in the 1990s, the shrinking of Greek manufacturing was thought to result from limited investments, and was attributed to two main factors: the rising interest rates and the fall in capital efficiency in manufacturing. The latter was considered to result from currency appreciations, the rising cost of energy and petrol and the redistribution policies applied since the 1980s (Oikonomou, 1992: 156). All these aspects had to be tackled. In the early 1990s, there was a widespread belief among Greek economists, the political elite, and the society that the problems of Greek manufacturing and production would have been resolved through a

---

[24] What the Bank of Greece chronicle does not discuss is why exceeding the deficit in 2008 and 2009 had brought such an unprecedented outcome.

strategy built around the country's access to the currency union. As competitiveness was progressively deteriorated, despite decisions taken on the appreciation of the Greek drachma and policies conducive to growth, the emphasis was placed on stabilizing the macroeconomic environment and on the achievement of high standards of living, similar to those of the EU's most advanced and integrated states. During the 1990s and after the decision to join the common currency zone, the Greek state has focused on the improvement of a series of macroeconomic indexes. The targets were to reduce inflation, interest rates, public sector deficits and advance growth rates that would help to achieve "nominal convergence" with the rest of common currency states (Oikonomou, 1992). Indeed, Greece has finally managed to achieve remarkable nominal convergence, after three decades of high inflation, of monetary, exchange rate, and public sector instability, and of low growth rates, if compared to those achieved during the 1950s and 1960s (Stournaras, 2008: 53).

Some economists blame the Greek government's decision in the late 1990s to use what is termed as "creative accounting" before its entry into the Eurozone for its government debt issued in yen and dollar, which was swapped to Euro. These swaps (which were created by Goldman Sachs) were offered at off-market prices (at a weaker rate between Euro and yen and dollar). While this was a disguise for actual debt statistics that helped the Greek economy the years before entering the crisis, it also brought an extra credit of $1 billion expenses and the need to pay back this swap transaction, thus increasing the debt (Bazli, 2010; Armitage and Chu, 2015). Greece's decision to use swaps as a means to marginally reduce the debt and enter the currency zone was one that profited both Greece and Goldman Sachs, who gained substantial profits out of this transaction. It became more visible in the Commission, as a similar method was used by several other states (Armitage and Chu, 2015). What one however does not take into account in this critique is the dynamics of the intense workload of the Greek government in the late 1990s to improve all macroeconomic indexes and remain within the strict requirements and deadlines for joining the currency zone, despite the substantial difficulties and impasses raised on the way, for a certain debt burden that represented a proportionally low part of its overall debt, and for a problem that might have been resolved after Greece had joined the currency, by the use of a more judicious policy on expenditure and deficit management.

A general agreement appears to have been reached in the broad literature that relates to the Greek crisis that in the 2002−8 period, when Greece had become a full member of the Eurozone, it failed to use properly its access to cheap credit in order to repay back its loans (Xafa, 2017; Bank of Greece, 2014; Nelson et al., 2011). So, an opportunity to reduce the debt-to-GDP ratio was lost by not conducting the appropriate policies. Such a historical opportunity is significant, not only due to its implications on the Greek debt but also because it would have triggered much earlier a better reaction against necessary reforms in the Greek economy and helped the Greek society to accustom to the necessity of changes required.

On-crisis policy explanations relate to the particular actions taken or the inaction in 2009 and the years that have followed, starting from 2010 and the agreement with the IMF.

One of the most significant on-crisis policy errors relates to the lack of a firm decision to control the levels of deficit during 2009. When the new government came into power in September 2009, it was already informed by the Governor of the Bank of Greece that the deficit was beyond targets and had exceeded the levels needed to keep the debt at sustainable levels. In presenting the Interim Report of the Bank of Greece, the Governor informed the Greek Parliament and the Cabinet of ministers on "pre-existing large macroeconomic imbalances and structural weaknesses of the Greek economy, the most important manifestations of which are the large 'twin' deficits (the budgetary deficit and the current account deficit) and debts (public debt and external debt)" (BoG, 2009: 4). The Interim report highlighted that during the nine-month period from January to September "the deficit reached 9.9% of annual GDP (compared with 4.9% of GDP in the same period last year). The general government debt was also projected to rise significantly this year (from 99.2% of GDP in 2008 and 95.6% of GDP in 2007), as it already stood at 111.5% of annual GDP at end-June" (BoG, 2009: 4). It called for a plan of reforms both by restructuring public expenditure and through implementing structural reforms (BoG, 2009). It also informed that according to estimates of the Greek statistical authority, the growth rate of the Greek economy was at zero percent the first half of 2009, while in 2008 it was at 2%, and in 2007 at 4.5%.

Instead of taking the decisions that would reduce the deficit simply by cutting expenditure and increasing the government's revenues, the newly elected (in October 2009) government took the opposite direction. According to the annual report of the Court of Audit of the Greek Republic for the year 2009, the deficit of the Greek government reached 12.18% of GDP instead of 3.5% that was initially calculated in the Budget, amounting in total €28.926 billion (Court of Audit, 2011: 38) (Table 1.8).

A similar mistake though was made by the previous government that had taken the decision in 2008 to support the Greek banks in their efforts to fund firms and to enhance liquidity in the market. The government's support package for the banks—whose implementation started in the year 2009—was organized to face the problems of a rather strong, for the Greek entrepreneurs, common currency (Papathanasiou, 2017). In times of crisis, people's panic becomes dangerous for the banks and their liquidity may not suffice to cope with excessive demand for money (as panicked customers en masse seek to withdraw money from the banks or transfer it abroad) (Spartiotis and Stournaras, 2010). The liquidity of a bank is necessary and its absence may turn even a financially healthy credit institution to noncredible, leading the bank to bankruptcy. Two other reasons that may raise the danger of lack of liquidity (apart from panic) are the noncredible guarantees of bank deposits and the doubts of customers that the government or a central bank is not ready to support the bank in a state of emergency (Antzoulatos, 2017). All these reasons were attempted to be managed by the programme for the provision of bank liquidity.

The programme was based on the decision taken in the European Summit of Euro area leaders who acknowledged the need to enhance banking liquidity in all Euro area countries. Greece was one of the very first members of the Eurozone to prepare and vote a law (Law 3723/2008) for its implementation. The Law introduced three main

Table 1.8 Extra payments in the year 2009 by the new government elected in excess of the budget, not provided in the bill or amounts of expenditure that was abolished

Type of expenditure	Amount, M€	Note
Payment of various services		
Doctors extra hour payment	70.111	Excess of budget amount
Payments for people employed in the elections	132.687	No provision in the budget
Payments of law 3758/2009	71.878	No provision in the budget
Special allowance for mechanics, geologists, geo-technical professions by the 2430/1996 law	105.940	No provision in the budget
Civil servants pensions	143.614	Excess of budget amount
Payment of benefits and allowance for special accounts abolished by the 3697/2008 law	245.626	Payment of abolished expenditure
Income transfers	**Amount, M€**	**Note**
Payment of expenditure for local authorities abolished (prefectures) in partial employment, health care and social care allowance and benefits, student transportation, oil production protection, control of outdoor markets and trade, and other reasons of expenditure of prefectures	339.201	Payment of abolished expenditure
Subsidies for nursing institutions and hospitals	1,481.169	Excess of budget amount
Extra payments towards the social security organization "IKA-ETAM"	1,500.000	Excess of budget amount
Extra payments towards self-employment workers insurance organization	871.074	Excess of budget amount
Excess payments for various other organizations of the public sector (KEΔ, ΑΠΕ, ΟΠΕ, ΕΡΤ, political parties, etc.)	88.342	Excess of budget amount
Excess payments for organizations of the public sector in social policy (ΟΑΕΔ, ΕΦΕΤ, ΟΑΣΠ, etc.)	173.835	Excess of budget amount

Source: Based on Anagnostou (2017).

axes for the banking liquidity package: (i) Public Sector's participation in the share capital of Greek Banks, up to €5 billion; (ii) Public Sector's guarantees for credit institutions for loans, up to €15 billion (of short to medium term); and (iii) Special bonds

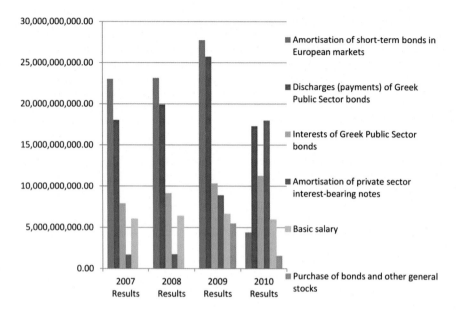

Figure 1.15 The six largest amounts for items of 2009 expenses, in descending order for 2009.
Source: General National Account Department, Ministry of Finance, Greece. *Note*: The "amortization of short-term bonds in European markets" is an accounting figure.

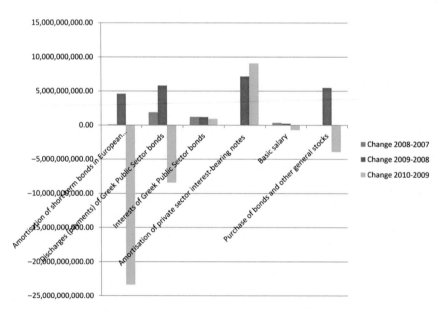

Figure 1.16 Changes of the six highest amounts of items, from 2007−8, 2008−9, and 2009−10.
Source: General National Account Department, Ministry of Finance, Greece.

by the Public Sector that were to be used by the Greek Banks (€8 billion)—(Articles 1, 2, and 3, respectively, of Law 3723/2008). All these measures had to be implemented until December 31, 2009. However, the precautionary character of policies in support of banking liquidity was not associated with the need to cut down expenditure and compensate for the additional expenses that a support package would entail.[25]

Fig. 1.15 provides information from four consecutive Government's reports (for 2007–10) on the six principal items of expenses, placed in descending order for the year 2009.

Fig. 1.16 provides the change of these items, from 2007 to 2008, 2008 to 2009 and 2009 to 2010. According to Fig. 1.16, the most significant changes in items for 2009 were (in descending order): (1) the "amortization of private sector interest-bearing notes"; (2) the "purchase of bonds and other general stocks"; (3) the "discharges (payments) of Greek Public Sector bonds"; (4) the "amortization of short-term bonds in European markets" that expired in the year 2009; (5) the "interests of Greek Public Sector bonds" and; finally (6) the provision of "basic salary."[26] The second in order, change of item is due to the abovementioned policies for enhancing banking liquidity, decided a year before. These policies appear to have raised the expenses for the budget much more than any other suggested by Anagnostou (2017) and those referred in Papathanasiou (2017). Only this second item of expenses, which was due to the Greek policy to resolve problems in banking liquidity that raised substantially the expenses for the year 2009, represented almost 20% of the total Budget deviation for the year 2009 (of €28.926 billion). Such policies raised the expenses for the year 2009 more than those advanced after the election of the new government, in the last quarter of the year. Thus, one should refer primarily as an origin of the Greek crisis that once the Greek state had decided to enhance banking liquidity it had not realized the need to cut expenditure for this purpose. And that such cutting of expenditure was not implemented by three consecutive Ministers of Finance.

Furthermore, the item on the "amortization of short-term bonds in European markets" that was the highest amongst all from 2007 to 2009 had increased in the year 2009 because of the announcement of the rise in the deficit that created additional borrowing needs during the year.

From Fig. 1.16 it is also evident that the most significant item that has changed from 2008 to 2009 was the "amortization of private sector interest-bearing notes," a great part of which was due to expire in the year 2009.

In the series of reasons why expenses in the Greek Budget remained high in the year 2009, one should add the decision to turn 33,500 employees that were working part-time (though covering permanent needs) to permanent employees (following the application of a 1999 European directive). This decision was taken after 2004 (though postponed for a long time by the previous government that did not want to

---

[25] Neither was this realized to be a potential problem in the policy document of the Euro area leaders that had rather called for a uniform policy across the European space, irrespective of its effects upon national debt.

[26] When the minister of Finance was George Alogoskoufis. The sequence of ministers of Finance was Prof. Christodoulakis, Prof. Alogoskoufis, Papathanasiou, and Dr. Papakonstantinou (in 2009).

undertake the fiscal burden). Had the government had the chance not to renew the contracts of all these part-time employees, it might have had enough flexibility and an immediate action at its discretion to cut expenditure, in times of crisis.

Rapanos (2008) acknowledges that the Budget voted each year by the Greek Parliament has been violated every year. He also explains that the way of structuring the Budget is subject to issues of transparency, a great degree of concentration in decision-making, multiple nonessential controls, absence of accountability, no assessment if the expenditure made brings the actual results, as well as organizational weaknesses (Rapanos, 2008: 176). He suggests that the presence of such issues, as well as middle-term Budget frameworks, logical and judicious hypotheses for macroeconomic changes and bottom-up techniques for budget calculation, are all necessary for fiscal and public-sector progress (Rapanos, 2008: 175).

One could trace a sequence of events that starts with the decision to join the common currency, the intense macroeconomic—though mostly nominal—adjustment policies, the stock market crash, Greece's entry into the Eurozone and the imposition of strong liquidity constraints, efforts to resolve liquidity problems and policies for the provision of banking liquidity, and the persistence of policies that had not allowed reducing the debt further, proportionately to GDP.

In its report prepared for the US Congress, the US Congressional Research Service had acknowledged that Greece suffered from "high government spending, structural rigidities, tax evasion, and corruption" (Nelson et al., 2010: 4). It referred to the view held by "observers" of the presence of a large and inefficient public administration, overstaffing, poor productivity, costly pension and healthcare systems, and the general "absence of the will to maintain fiscal discipline" (Nelson et al., 2010: 5). It also acknowledged the role of the adoption of the Euro and the lax enforcement of EU rules.

In policy-oriented explanations, the main focus is given on the operation of Greece's economy and the mismanagement of its public finance which comprises also European funds, i.e., of its public expenditure and of the sources of public income that have caused over the years the growth of its public debt. High government deficits are thought to lie at the epicenter of all causes for Greece's default and derive from costly pension systems, tax evasion, weak revenue collection, and "the absence of the will to maintain fiscal discipline" (Nelson et al., 2010). The absence of controls on behalf of the Greek state has helped towards this direction.

Many reasons can be identified that explain the mismanagement of public resources. One could refer to several thousands of cases of professionals and businesses—among which the largest ones—Greek and European—have preferred to follow an extended tax evasion during an extended period of time (Manolopoulos, 2012). Or the more general behavior and malpractice of businesses and people holding political and societal power, from the whole spectrum of political parties and the society. One should be fair against the Greek society, as against any other society, and underline that the greatest part of the Greek society had tried to remain within the lines of decent and honest economic behavior. But such malpractices are always easier to spread from top to bottom. The view that there was a "conspiracy among all Greeks" (Manolopoulos, 2012) creates the illusionary picture of a devilish nation rather than one where each citizen is influenced by the economic and social behavior of the other that is being tolerated and not punished. One should be careful before projecting such generalities.[27] For many years, whoever attempted to break the silent rules of tolerance was treated as a "snitch" in many forms of social life, where compliance was needed. And over the decades there have been several thousands—if not hundreds of thousands—of Greeks, from the full range of society that had tried to do so but had tragically failed and had not the power to continue. As Christakis and Fowler (2009) explain, such malpractices and other common societal behaviors can spread in the society through various networks of people formed. Networking and the association of people in networks have been a distinctive element of the Greek society during the study period and one had to be quite powerful to go against it.[28] One cannot accuse a whole society that has been the victim for actions taken on its behalf or for its victimization.[29] Neither it can accuse societies for developing self-serviced networks and establishing relationships.

In terms of the particular expenses made by the Greek state, one could refer to several cases of mishandling apart from wages and salaries. One of the most significant among them is the case of expenses for defense, in what was one of the most prolonged periods of peace for the modern Greek state. Manolopoulos (2011) uses data from the Stockholm International Peace Research Institute for the 2004−9 period to show that Greece was one of the major international importers of defense equipment (the second) during this, critical for the Greek state, period, both per head and proportionally to its GDP. At the same time, on the annual report by SIPRI in 2010, Greece represented the second main client of Germany's exports in weapons, after Turkey (13% and 14%, respectively) (Manolopoulos, 2011), in practice being the victim of an idiosyncratic competition for military expenses between the two countries. Manolopoulos (2011: 158) refers to the circular direction of borrowed funds that while funded by western banks in France or Germany, these same loans were also used to pay for military and defense material produced by French and German companies.

The overindebtedness of the Greek state is not just due to the mismanagement and overspending of public funds but also to the more general aspirations of the Greek society (not just polity) for producing a social state that supports all activities. In other terms, the failure of a model of socially supportive economic development and growth.

The view that political clientelism lies at the core of all other explanations of the Greek case has also been espoused on several occasions (e.g., Pappas, 2012;

---

[27] A similar argument was developed by the former minister Pagkalos "we all ate them, together" (Pagkalos, 2012) and received strong criticism from Greek society. As if the tax-evasion culture is not spread easier from top to bottom.

[28] One should remind here the infamous phrase used by the former Greek prime Minister Konstantinos Mitsotakis on the "collusion of (economic, political, and social) interests" («διαπλεκόμενα») in the Greek economic and political life, which identified and accused their presence and role in shaping politics and ignoring democratically elected governments.

[29] Economics and social studies would not make sense in such a world.

Tsoukalas, 2013; and many others). In the mid-1990s, in order to keep average wages low in the public sector, the practice of introducing bonuses rather than raising wages was spread (as a means to avoid paying more for pensions after retirement), culminating in the overuse and overspending of public funds for such bonuses, for a state that has never monitored their use and allocation, at least per person. In the absence of a proper organization and the general view held in the Greek society that the state should not abolish rights and privileges, thousands of cases of early retirement, of pensions to people who have passed away, and increased expenses, often of irrational character, of public spending towards state-funded organizations, such as hospitals, were left not surveilled, harming the character of public spending that should be fair and supportive to common rather than individual causes. Despite that, such incidents started to spread as soon as the country joined the EC in 1981 and refer to several thousands of people (for a state of approximately ten millions on average for the period studied); they are indicative of the absence of the state's willingness and lack of competence to impose a judicious management of public sources and enhance accountability. This is a principal reason why some commentators have spoken of the "enemy from within."[30]

Another reason could be that the actions and initiatives taken by the Greek private sector had never managed to create a sense of confidence and trust in both employees and employers, even after the EU umbrella came in. Certainly, a part of this problem relates to the strong skepticism, if not hostility, with which the private sector has been envisaged over a long period of time (Manolopoulos, 2012). Private investors and entrepreneurs were considered to be exploitative and manipulators. A source of this hostility may be ideological but another source stems from the reality.

During the 1980s, the Greek society envisaged entrepreneurs as hostile to the Greek culture of equalization and the same opportunities for all that was being promoted at the time, as they would gain and share more profits than the rest of the society. This was a period when two strong ideological sides were opposing each other in the Greek society: the ideology that everyone is the same[31], which was considered to be a democratic right, advanced by the relatively recent parliamentary democracy, and, on the other hand, a view emphasizing the freedom of choice, freedom of expression, of capital and its movement, which were not taken as granted at the time.[32] The latter was considered to be a fierce and aggressive expression of "neoliberalism" rather than a mature basis upon which democratic societies manage to build their long-term conditions for sustainable growth and development. This

---

[30] Christodoulakis (1998: 29−30) traces the origins of public mismanagement in the government prior to the socialist government taking power in 1981. He suggests that in the political period preceding the 1981 elections, the government has used fiscal policy to sustain the provisions offered to a nucleus of its voters, satisfy the accumulated needs of its supporters and undermine the capacity of the socialist political party that was about to come into power. It is hard to give much credit to such views with evidence provided in Fig. 1.4, because the debt proportionally to GDP was at very low levels at the period before 1981.

[31] Same but not necessarily equal.

[32] It is worth mentioning that only in 1987 was the first free radio station created, by Athens municipality.

dividing line has never been crossed in the Greek society, at least by parties at the center-left political spectrum, for reasons that relate to its political exploitation and manipulation (apart from ideological reasons).[33] It is in the period after the fall of communism that the Greek society starts to look at freedom of choice and capital with more concern.

It is worth being reminded that the Greek state had lied near the "iron curtain" and had faced a civil war as soon as the second World War was over, driven by ideological motives. The political results of the civil war should be seen as lasting at least over two generations and an insightful and careful analyst of the Greek case might go as far as to explain how it has affected the—acceptable by the society—model of political power and its exercise during the second half of the 20th century. The historical memory of a country that has suffered from strong inequalities over the past two centuries has certainly influenced the choices of the society and the claims for same opportunities for all.

In the early 1980s, the political decision taken to avoid the bankruptcy of large-scale enterprises and to support them through launching a specific Organization for the Restructuring of Businesses had its roots not only in socialist ideological and political views but on the more general economic environment that was character-ized by the rise of international competition, the relaxation of domestic demand in a series of industries, the reduction of protectionism, the inefficiency of organiza-tional and administrative practices in the top management of these large enterprises, and mistaken investment choices (Kazakos, 2001: 359). As Kazakos (2001) explains, credit policy and the levels of interest rates were not allowing large-scale firms to cope with international competition and implement the necessary corporate restructuring. Perhaps in the Greek entrepreneur of the 1980s and 1990s, the cun-ning, the smart, the virtuose, one could find the force that destroys rather than builds the whole society, despite the efforts of the rest. A self-harming, self-damaging entrepreneurship capital that could not recycle its own numerous healthy forces, in the absence of policies supporting entrepreneurship.

Clearly, ever since the 1980s the Greek society has chosen a path that had put a blame or anathema on the private sector. It has tolerated acts of violence and dis-ruptions against the private sector and several of the efforts conducted by the state for privatizing public sector corporations (for instance in the early 1990s), which were privatized a few years after. A part of this behavior could be explained by political ideology and fanatical political behavior. But the coin has two sides and another, significant explanation could relate to the absence of respect by Greek employers towards employees, many incidents of exploitation of employees by employers, the nonpayment of salaries and social security contributions, and the breeding—historically—of a certain character of employers that were doing busi-ness in a short-term, opportunistic manner. Their arrogant and reckless behavior

---

[33] Even today, the Greek prime minister of a political party that sits comfortably on the left side of the political spectrum, accuses the right-wing party of being neoliberal, while the left party implements policies that could be considered by political commentators as strongly neoliberal, at least in compari-son to the past.

against employees, opportunism and the showing-off of their wealth during this period of time, all helped in this direction. Perhaps the rising of a middle class in the 1980s also created numerous misbehaving employers. Besides, the academic debates on building and creating healthy entrepreneurship have arrived with a long delay in the Greek scientific community. More recently, based on the Global Entrepreneurship Monitor, the main obstacles of entrepreneurship were identified to be: (i) the lack of entrepreneurship opportunities; (ii) the "swallow" character of entrepreneurship; (iii) the family-based financing of entrepreneurship; and (iv) fear of failure (Ioannides, 2008).

Furthermore, the immature, if not absent in many cases, labor market[34] and its strong fragmentation, at least geographically, that was not helping to promote labor migration, has also contributed to how people envisaged the prospect of job opportunities and getting a more permanent job that enhanced pressure to find a job in the public sector.

A critical point to consider is that in the early 1980s, the Greek state had to face new conditions formed in its labor market. From 1981 to 1990, a net influx of Greek immigrants (333,800, mostly from Northern Europe) and the rise of the figure of women participating in the labor market had created demographic pressures on the Greek labor market (Korres and Chionis, 2003: 237). As a result the numbers of newly introduced unemployed in the Greek labor market increased. They were at 45.2% in 1988 and increased to 54% in 1991 (Korres and Chionis, 2003: 237). Youth unemployment has also been high in Greece ever since 1981. Young unemployed (14−29 years old) represented 60% of the total in 1993 (Korres and Chionis, 2003: 237). Thus, during the 1980s and early 1990s, the Greek labor market and economy was envisaging the prospect of its growth in numbers, which did not reflect its actual growth in size and economic activity.

Petrakis (2011: 358) refers to the "long-term social choice" to absorb the surplus of the labor force by widening the size of the public sector that he acknowledges as one of the "deeper causes of the Greek economic and social problem." Tzanatos (2016) argues that from 1970 to 2016, employment rose by 31% in the private sector and by 150% in the public sector. He refers to a rise in wages by 30% in the public sector, from Greece's entry into the Eurozone to 2009. While Petrakis (2011) provides evidence for the years 2006, 2008, and the whole 1998−2009 period that shows the very large numbers of permanent and temporary employees that are a part of the public sector, in some form of relation, Tsampra and Chatzimichalidou (2014) refer to evidence that sustains the argument that the Greek public sector was not oversized in the 2000−10 period, holding a middle position in comparison to other OECD partners. They refer to an overall stabilization trend of the numbers of employees in the public sector, in the 1999−2008 period. Tsampra and Chatzimichalidou (2014) explain that it is wages and salaries in the public sector that were high—in other terms the high labor costs. They refer to evidence that the performance and efficiency of the Greek public sector, based on the Public Sector

---

[34] For decades, jobs were not properly advertized and the largest part of the society investigated their job prospects through their personal acquaintances.

Performance (PSP) and Public Sector Efficiency (PSE) indexes, was found to lie below OECD standards.[35] The size, organization of public services, and their performance are three separate aspects that are worth considering separately.

While, from a comparative perspective, the Spanish state has chosen, in a similar period for its economy, to cope with high levels of unemployment after joining the EC, the Greek government took the strategic decision as soon as it joined the EC to organize its economic policies around the general policy target to advance full employment. This strategic choice has never been actually amended over the whole study-period, to the extent that it was a feasible outcome and the by-product of the macroeconomic policies pursued.[36] Perhaps in this point lies one of the most significant reasons why the Greek economy had not managed to undergo the necessary corporate and business sector restructuring and why it had to face—after all these human capital and labor policies applied—the very same result: the absence of jobs. One should be more skeptical and consider that point within the context of global changes, shifts in the global capital and globalization that has brought substantial changes in most European economies facing similar challenges. Of course in the Greek case in particular, low levels of unemployment during the 1980s and early 1990s combined with high levels of inflation.

Christodoulakis (1998: 61) referred to the saturation of mechanisms of employment to the public sector 15 years after the socialist government first came into power. He also diagnosed problems in job matching, information, the need to introduce new technologies in traditional sectors that require radical changes, the rise of employment because of women participation, immigrants' legalization and search for urban jobs, and the appearance of new, multiple categories of unemployed (Christodoulakis, 1998).

While a policy centered around full employment (as promoted by the socialist government in the early 1980s and espoused by consecutive socialist governments and the right-wing party) deserves less criticism for its economic essence and value, one should consider that it does not allow domestic politics and policies to appreciate and understand on time the actual problems of the private sector—the absence of good and sustainable jobs in the labor market (that would derive from internationally competitive markets)—and, in particular, its needs in terms of research and development, required to restructure and face continuous challenges from international competitors. Besides, it is recognized that a great part of unemployment is owed to technological changes and globalization. Giannitsis (2008b) provides evidence on the lack of capacity to integrate new technologies in Greek products and exports. Komninos (2008) referred to scattered research and development policies across sectors, agents, and teams of small size, with introvert public institutions, of limited response to economic and social needs and requirements, weak intermediate mechanisms of technology transmission, qualitative and quantitative inefficiency of mediators (Komninos, 2008). He also traces incompatibility between labor

---

[35] With evidence provided by Afonso, A., Schuknecht, L., Tanzi, V., 2005. public sector efficiency: an international comparison, Public Choice 123 (3—4), 321—347.

[36] This is reflected in the second section of this work on the amounts devoted to human capital policies and the labor market.

supply and demand in the chain of research-technology-innovation that results from the intense social demand for tertiary education, with new scientists not absorbed in the production processes in the country (Komninos, 2008: 460). Indeed, rather than turning to research and knowledge production, their promotion and diffusion in the private sector as key policy priorities—such as in countries like South Korea or Finland and Ireland in Europe—Greece witnessed a formidable lack of exploitation over the decades of its human potential and resources. The most recent substantial "brain drain," observed after the crisis erupted, should be seen as a culmination of the phenomenon of the oversupply of scientists that never really matched their demand in the Greek labor market (for a unique analysis on brain drain see Lamprianidis, 2011). Finally, Komninos (2008: 461) also refers to a lack of entrepreneurial spirit in research matters and a bureaucratic, time-consuming model of management of research, centered around ex-ante assessments rather than substantial evaluation of research results.

A divide was created between the public sector and entrepreneurs of the private sector. Doxiadis (2015) refers to an "unseen rupture," progressively created in the Greek economy and society between, on the one hand, the public sector and those entrepreneurs that had sought protection and support by the Greek state, by seeking to doing business with it, and, on the other hand, a minority group of entrepreneurs that had sought to become or remain exporting and internationally competitive, refraining from the state and its business. The group of the latter had been shrinking over the years.[37]

In the 1980s, the Greek economy was influenced by a protective ideological direction that viewed a significant part of its productive powers as guilty, and eroded their efforts to sustain and enhance the means through which to cope with an international environment that raised barriers in the promotion of exports and limited their capacity to compete. Certainly in the mid-1990s, this policy-making line was crossed. A general belief came into the society that it should espouse the powers of the private sector and allow its expression in the Greek economy, even if, in such cases, one could argue that it was somehow still manipulated towards certain policy directions, those created and provided by the policies pursued by state and government. Yet, as Christodoulakis (1998: 71–72) explains, economic policy-making (of the government in power) had to differentiate from other perspectives across some distinct lines: the view that the state has to keep the ownership of the means of production, the view that markets should be regulated because market failures occur, and the financing of the social state.

At the time, the funding from European policies helped the state to become a very powerful player in the domestic market created, by launching projects of ten or even more times larger than those of the private sector. It thus acted as a magnet for many private firms that sought to enhance their prospects of doing business with the state and abandoned many other opportunities in the market. Despite its tolerance and concern about aspects of the private sector, the public sector kept for itself a great part of economic activity and what the domestic market created, and it was, in some cases, the major supplier or customer (e.g., in the health or the

---

[37] If seen from this perspective, the group of the former should comprise foreign businesses too, not only domestic Greek. This is seen with the aforementioned example of military expenses.

education sector). We could draw the picture of an economy that for an extended period of time has been overbased on the public sector, rather than standing on its own two feet, the public and the private, and helping the former to challenge the latter and vice versa. A more effective role would lie in becoming the catalyst for the provisions of the necessary conditions for the production of such goods, public or private, in low cost and good quality.

The case of Ireland, where the debt burden was enhanced in the private rather than the public sector, makes this argument on the public sector burdening look rather uncertain as a primary cause for the burst of the crisis. One could argue that the crisis might have exploded anyway, had the debt burden been more equally shared among the public and the private sector.

Central planning and public spending had displaced private initiative and entrepreneurship. Rapanos (2008) explains that the Greek economy and society had realized in practice the distance that exists between on the one hand a theoretical perception of central programming that considers the central planner as wise, knowledgeable, unselfish, one that can maintain a distance from information and yet benefit from full and perfect information, fully efficient and goal-oriented, and, on the other, public policy in practice that is quite different. He refers to several attempts made after 1981 for fiscal stabilization and the decisiveness with which they were taken (especially after the mid-1990s), which however had only a short-term impact and reckons that, at the very end, factors exogenous to the Greek society have been more helpful towards imposing such fiscal stabilisation (Rapanos, 2008: 166).

A strongly associated policy-relevant reason is bureaucracy and red tape. Bureaucracy comes as the natural effect of the overconcentration of economic and political power in a state that since the 1980s favored and promoted the general view that the state should be in charge and could resolve all economic problems, starting from setting up the necessary conditions at the macroeconomic environment, instead of undertaking a more discreet role and acting as a catalyst. Several substantial and crucial efforts and innovations were made to overcome the Lernaean Hydra of bureaucracy (some of which were successful, e.g., the creation of the National System of Health in its early period of operation during the 1980s, the creation of the Citizens' Service Centres ("ΚΕΠ"), and that of the Supreme Council for Civil Personnel Selection ("ΑΣΕΠ")) but it was hard to overcome all problems arising from the size, organization, and policies of the public sector and the funds required to support it. Red tape may be the outcome of excessive regulation both from domestic policies and promoted through the need to comply with EU regulations and laws, over the decades.

In his analysis of the Greek crisis that places the rise of populism at the epicenter of all problems, Pappas (2014) reckons that populism started to rise in the 1980s, as soon as the socialist party took power. Even today, a part of the Greek society espouses this view and considers valid the view held by Pappas (2014) that promises given in the late 1970s and during the 1980s had to be satisfied by particular political actions that were to satisfy the needs of millions of people that believed in socialism. Here the argument is that of strong political expectations. Pappas (2014) refers to the agility of a particular political leader and widely recognized by the

Greek society charismatic figure, Andreas Papandreou, who, at a certain time of history, managed to introduce a convincing for the masses story that stood inbetween the wishes of the Greek people for getting more access to decisions taken about their lives from a political elites, and their understanding that the Greek state was not acting as an independent one, as sovereign power was exercised upon it by foreign powers. Pappas (2014: 61) also refers to the distortion of values of freedom, as a strategic means for imposing the values of socialism, to the benefit of "people's sovereignty." Christodoulakis (1998: 166) refers to a shift from the claim for equality to the imposition of equalization. Populism has been viewed as guilty for creating networks that replaced competition (Kazakos, 2001: 346). One way or another there has to be some political explanation for the quadrupling of the debt as a percentage of GDP, though the most important implication of the views held by Pappas (2014) is that even if the debt-to-GDP ratio was not as high as the decades that followed, it is the breeding of a certain political culture and ethos and of a certain short-term behavior of citizenship that has contributed to this end, and which made citizens accustomed to request rather than respect rights and privileges. It is this particular behavior that has remained powerful for at least two decades after.

Many economists, political scientists, and other observers often refer to the influential role the public sector syndicates have exercised since the early 1980s, when they envisaged their rights for claiming better labor conditions as universal but also as rights for causing several disruptions in economic and social life. Dertilis (2016) refers to the relationship formed between social groups and leadership, and the patronizing relations of leaders with their supporters, leading the former to tolerate tax evasion and high expenditure for hiring and wages in the public sector. He places such relations as driving forces of his aforementioned spiral of war and military expenses, indebtednesses, and insufficient tax resources (Dertilis, 2016).

Political party enmity and culture (Kazakos, 2011), polar bipartisanship of extreme polarization (Pappas, 2014), political prejudices and stereotypes (Pappas, 2014; Papoulias, 2008), an older in age political personnel, incapable of assimilating changes taking place in the international scene or of looking forward, one that has tolerated for years behaviors from the past and tax evasion in economic and social life (Nelson et al., 2011; Pappas, 2014), incapable of considering the necessity of reaching agreements and compromises in the political and economic sphere, but, at the same time, ready to fully undermine and directly destroy or—at best— amend past policies, decisions, and their various formulations rather than building upon them, have also contributed and prolonged the causes of the crisis. This has even been worsened by the low quality of political institutions that have been measured through a series of indexes in international records to have worsened from 1996 to 2008, and the absence of institutional safety valves (the "checks and balances") that would allow the control and proper operation of political institutions (Petrakis, 2011; Kaufman et al., 2009, quoted in Petrakis, 2011). Kazakos et al. (2016) share the broader perspective held by Acemoglu, Johnson and Robinson (in a series of publications) on the absence of participative mechanisms. They believe if such mechanisms were present in the Greek open society, they could have undermined and challenged the status of political and societal relations and balances.

Giannitsis (2005) refers to the traumatic triangle formed among socialism, the economy, and the state. He emphasizes that a general policy for social protection and reduction of inequalities was based on income redistribution, reorientation of public spending towards weaker social strata, a relaxing of income policy that has brought wage raises, and the pursuit of external and internal borrowing (Giannitsis, 2013: 69).

Kazakos et al. (2016) also acknowledge problems with the political business cycle, present in the calculations of the political system and elite. They suggest a lack of concern for long-term effects and characterize the Greek society as a rent-seeking society (Kazakos et al., 2016: 301−306). Finally, they refer to the speech delivered by George Papandreou to his political party, according to whom, the Greek society and its political elites have reached a state where scandalous favor was baptized many times as "justice," the privileges of the few and of some professionals were considered as "acquis", provoking others was thought to be a right, becoming the new rich to be a token of civilization, searching for easy enrichment as a healthy enterprise, competitive production turned to a hunting for a state or a European subsidy, and tax evasion had become an expression of smartness (Papandreou, 2010; quoted in Kazakos et al., 2016).[38]

Kazakos et al. (2016) also refer to circumstantial reasons that have brought the Greek crisis for the particular period 2008−9. However, they consider the particular behavior, the actions or inaction of those people acting in the years of the crisis as subject to formal or informal rules, present over the decades, and to particular values, thus viewing their policy mistakes as systemic rather than circumstantial (Kazakos et al., 2016: 299).

Giannitsis (2013) refers to the great systemic political, moral, and development problem of Greece.[39] He deconstructs the view of the odious debt by suggesting that it is the persistence of a particular square that has caused the Greek debt, which he identifies to be composed of the "high tax evasion in higher incomes and extended in lower income scales, deep corruption and arbitrariness of the whole system (starting from the political system, the public administration, the local government and reaching to segment across the whole spectrum of the society), a system of state clienteles of the public sector and, coherent to the aforementioned, fundamental issue of equality against the law and social justice"[40] (Giannitsis, 2013: 90−91).

One of the most important policy problems is the weak collection of resources, which is considered to have contributed to Greece's consecutive budget deficits (Nelson et al., 2010). A series of economic and social reasons can be found to explain the extended tax evasion and the size of the informal, unofficial sector of the Greek economy that was calculated in 2001 to be at least 35% of the Greek GDP (Tsatsos, 2001). Among these, one has to note the rooted perception in the Greek society that it is the state's obligation to provide a series of public services

---

[38] Translated by the author.

[39] One should acknowledge his more general contribution to the study of the Greek development problem with at least five of his individual works and edited volumes, since 2008, two of which were written before the crisis erupted.

[40] Translated by the author.

and the absence of both an assimilation by the society that such a provision requires the necessary funds and a sense of responsibility and tax consciousness. One cannot ignore that this is a matter of business interests and businessmen who exercise their political pressure to keep tax rates low and not pay their taxes (Toussaint, 2017).

Table 1.9 reveals that the main problem in revenues for both 2008 and 2009 was found in the total of tax and nontax revenues, which represented in 2009 77.9% of their predictions, due to problems in the collection of revenues, in all categories and totally.

Corruption is a reason for not paying taxes. Corruption in Greece has many explanations. One relates to the organization of the state and its lack of capacity to exercise control and use its judiciary system to implement the laws. Another refers to social relations and the absence of consciousness from a part of the society and the citizens that they should undertake the cost of a certain amount of social services and infrastructure that they deserve to use and benefit from. Tsoukas (2015) refers to the Greek case as an illustrative example of the "tragedy of commons", where the problem of free-riding of public goods has harmed the economy. He suggests that tolerance of free riders at the "game" of public goods "played", has loosened progressively the values that sustained that "game" and ended up at "a tragedy of commons". He borrows the term from Hardy's (1968) analysis on the "tragedy of commons" to refer to a society where each member and group of interest has been looking to satisfy its own individual interests, a situation where the exploitation of the common "field" of interests (and the negative externalities produced by it) harm the common interest for the society (Tsoukas, 2015). The word tragedy emphasizes a moral failure and the lack of success (Tsoukas, 2015).

In close association, Petrakis (2011) refers to the cultural values and background of the Greek society, its stereotypes and human behavior. In organizational terms, he draws from the landmark analyses initiated by Hofstede (2001) and GLOBE (Koopman et al., 1999) that assess Greece as part of a more general Mediterranean group of countries. As far as the social capital is concerned, Petrakis (2011) refers to the results of the European Value Survey, as analyzed by Van Oorschot et al. (2006) that revealed a general problem of trust and to the 2002 European Social Survey (2002), as analyzed by Paraskevopoulos (2007), on the limited social capital in Greece, in terms of the generalized trust and participation in groups.

As Papoulias (2008) explains, public policies, changes, and reforms in Greece are always measured on political terms. There is a lack of quantified targets and uncertainty in the environment. Such an uncertainty brings continuous institutional changes and amendments to cope with the uncertainty, convictions, and prejudices, as North (2005; quoted in Papoulias, 2008) explains. There is an absence of institutional memory, while political prejudices and stereotypes do not allow the state and public administration to exploit previous experience and the competent human force (Papoulias, 2008).

Pagoulatos (2008) refers to three main pillars, necessary for reform policies that had to be considered and used properly or placed in action: (i) the pull factors from a domestic policy sphere that historically has not managed to bring such reforms, as the two main parties were trapped in a prisoners' dilemma that results in extending

Table 1.9 **Predictions and realized payments for 2008 and 2009 (% for 2009)**

	Predictions 2008	Realized Payments 2008	Predictions 2009	Realized payments 2009	Percentage of realized payments against predictions (2009)
Direct taxes	20,755,000,000	19,148,178,018.49	25,482,000,000.00	19,315,143,451.36	75%
Indirect taxes	31,350,000,000	28,304,076,603.24	32,147,000,000.00	25,482,728,785.63	79.27%
Total tax revenues	52,105,000,000	47,452,254,621.73	57,629,000,000.00	44,797,872,236.99	77.74%
Property revenues and entrepreneurial activity of state	1,750,000,000	1,751,017,971.57	2,078,000,000.00	1,393,621,535.27	67.06%
Rest of nontax revenues	1,122,000,000	1,898,140,311.76	2,160,000,000.00	2,035,125,774.96	94.21%
Total nontax revenues	2,872,000,000	3,649,158,283.33	4,238,000,000.00	3,428,747,310.23	80.91%
Total of tax and nontax revenues	54,977,000,000	51,101,412,905.06	61,867,000,000.00	48,226,619,547.22	77.95%
Transfers from EU, Member-states and other revenues	543,000,000	578,750,562.19	405,000,000.00	264,326,941.60	65.26%
Total of regular revenues	55,520,000,000	51,680,163,467.25	62,272,000,000.00	48,490,946,488.82	77.87%
Credit revenues	34,562,000,000	65,070,158,712.57	35,639,000,000.00	97,984,561,070.00	274.94%
Total of regular and credit revenues	90,082,000,000	116,750,322,179.82	97,911,000,000.00	146,475,507,558.82	149.60%
Various specific nontax revenues	1,006,000,000	553,703,152.16	1,455,000,000.00	55,296,802.38	3.80%
Revenues from public investment	240,000,000	349,877,686.11	200,000,000.00	182,788,079.30	91.50%
(Income) support and other transfers	4,292,000,000	4,668,299,461.64	3,500,000,000.00	1,857,554,365.09	53.07%
Credit revenues programme of public investments	4,768,000,000	4,590,493,093.86	5,100,000,000.00	7,271,649,275.56	142.58%
General total	100,388,000,000	126,912,695,573.59	108,166,000,000.00	155,842,796,081.15	144.08%

Source: Court of Audit, 2011.

their differences and promoting strategies of clashes rather than cooperation; (ii) the push factors, always present from an external environment, such as the Olympic Games held in Athens in 2004; and (iii) a political−administrative mechanism that for years was subject to various pathologies, such as the overscattering of local administrative units, "not in my backyard" policy perceptions, and legal formalism. The latter requires poles of institutional stability and continuity, with authorities that exercise regulatory and surveillance policies but that can share the burden of nonpopular decisions (Pagoulatos, 2008: 217−218).

Immigration is one aspect that is not well studied for its effects upon public policy, the handling of policy funds, and the rise of expenses, as well as for its side-effects on nurturing the shadow economy and promoting aspects of illegal economic activity. For a number of reasons, including ideological views and perceptions, such effects of immigration are totally ignored and discussed only on subjective bases. Yet, immigration in Greece has been rising significantly ever since the early 1990s, turning the country from a migration sender to a migration host over the second half of the study period. The first wave of immigrants, composed of Albanians, has remained the most significant since the 1990s, even if a large proportion of them are now Greek citizens, with full rights. In 2001, out of the 797,000 of legal immigrants that represented 7% of the Greek population, 438,000 were Albanians (Gropas and Triantafyllidou, 2005).[41] In the official population census of 2011, a total of 912,000 immigrant stock, composed of 713,000 of third-country nationals and 199,000 of EU non-Greek citizens, represented approximately 8.5% of the population, of which 52.72% were Albanians. Bulgarians and Romanians, two of the EU member-states in the Balkans, represented another 13.42%, as the second and third largest immigration community, respectively, and their rising figures reflect an intra-European mobility trend, after the borders were opened (Triantafyllidou, 2014).

Kazakos et al. (2016) distinguish between the conventional economic approach, policy mistakes and problems in institutions and values, which explain the Greek crisis endogenously and its exogenous causes that relate to the architecture of the Euro. According to the former the crisis is attributed to constantly deficient fiscal management that covered consumption purposes in periods of development, debt accumulation that marked the model of growth, the expansion of the state and tax-evasion, rapidly growing private consumption, beyond normal growth of construction, low interest rates, increase of real wages especially in the public sector that affected those of the private, constant reduction of national savings, supply of goods and services that characterized inefficient use of resource, and the country's international specialization that constantly deteriorated its competitiveness (Kazakos, et al., 2016: 298−299). They consider the large demand surplus over the decades as the outcome of fiscal deficits, public sector borrowing and their conveniently covering by easy private borrowing (Kazakos, et al., 2016: 299). A broader picture

---

[41] In the calculations about the Greek debt no one counts that Greece has been so supportive to a whole other state, Albania, one of the poorest states in Europe that has experienced conditions of dramatic poverty after the fall of communism. It would have been worth considering the net effects (expenses minus income received) of this particular category of immigrants, for future reference.

would explain the Greek crisis as a mixture of various causes, such as accumulated macroeconomic imbalances, a large public sector, external imbalances, weakened competitiveness, nonsustainable pension and social security schemes, and low performance of labor markets (Tzannatos, 2016).

One of the most significant policy errors relates to the particular political decision taken by the newly elected Greek government in September 2009 to change the methodology of the calculation of the deficit and increase it. Since the higher the deficit, the more debt accumulates in an economy and the more unlikely it becomes to be repaid, the problem with amendments in the calculations of the deficit is that they can lead to adverse effects and raise the deficit in the long run. In the Greek case, it is probably the first time that while the deficit was already high by the middle of year 2009, the new government, taking power after the Greek elections, took a series of decisions to recalculate the deficit that increased it, even if it was already high enough and higher than expected. The European Statistical Authority has left room for flexibility through its ESA-95 direction, being aware that such flexibility could be used for political purposes and always to the benefit of the state. In the Greek case though, for the first time a state decided to change the methodology of deficit calculation (therefore of the debt too, as the former adds up to the latter) and include in the deficit expenses that increase rather than decrease the deficit. Flexibility in this case was used by the state that took the decision to recalculate the deficit and both the European statistical authorities and—mostly—the European Commission accepted such a negative deficit recording for the Greek case, as opposed to the calculation of deficit for other European states. Therefore, one important policy error possibly lies in the flexible treatment of the calculation of deficits of nation-states that allows them to be treated on dissimilar terms and, on the basis of this treatment, to be considered even as indebted. It appears that in the Greek case at least, somehow the principle of equality and equal treatment among European member-states was overthrown by the principle of flexibility.

Last but not least, a different perspective on the actual causes of the Greek crisis emphasizes the significance of the external imbalance in economies. Galenianos (2015) considers flawless an explanation solely based on fiscal imbalances. Its arguments could be summarized as follows. Fiscal imbalances are the symptom of the prolonged absence of external balances. Negative external balances are a reason why economies have to borrow from abroad, thereby increasing their deficits and their overall debt, if such deficits are increased for an extended period of time. In the Greek case, external balance deficits were produced by current account deficits, in particular the trade balance deficit. Consumption has increased and the domestic population has raised consumption for imports rather than exports, which has raised the trade deficit and deteriorated the current account deficit.

As Galenianos (2015) explains, external balance is the capacity of the state in the long run to accumulate capitals abroad. If capitals are accumulated abroad, consumption is below its productive capacity. On the contrary, if it accumulates debt (negative capital), its consumption is above its productive capacity. External balance is considered to be attained by a country when its current account balance is neither deeply in deficit nor at a strong surplus. Internal balance on the other hand is about achieving full employment of resources and price stability. The more a state is competitive and can produce products that will be sold in international markets, the more it can improve its trade account, thereby improving its current account and attaining an external balance (Galenianos, 2015). Galienanos (2015) in particular provides a comparison that juxtaposes the case of Greece and Portugal against that of Spain and Ireland. These are all countries that had undertaken a memorandum of understanding and were assessed by the international investors and markets to face serious problems and challenges. He thus questions the debt-to-GDP ratio cause and raises an issue as to why Italy and Belgium had not become the object of the crisis themselves (Galenianos, 2015). Is this a matter of good international relations or of the more general macroeconomic picture and the fundamentals of these two countries? One however does not have a clear indication of why the cases of Greece and Ireland, both members of the Eurozone and the EU, should be exactly the same and considered under the same prism and perspective. Based on the abovementioned analysis, such a view would entail that the two countries have followed similar historical paths of economic accumulation and social choices.

Finally, as far as political responsibility is concerned, one should add into the list of causes of the crisis the more general ignorance for the risk taken by exceeding the GDP-to-debt ratio threshold. For decades, the political personnel had viewed the Greek economy as much more safe and secure underneath the common currency umbrella. Besides, the safety of the common currency was a principal reason for deciding to join it.

1.5.5   IMF policies and its mistakes

The global crisis has revealed the problems of the Greek economy and the crisis of Greece's model of growth.

After the Greek crisis erupted, additional causes prolonged its duration, up until today. Various causes have influenced the outcome of policies exercised and suggested by the IMF, such as political crises, inconsistent policies, insufficient reforms, fears about the prospect of "Grexit" (exiting the Eurozone and possibly the EU, as there was no clause from exiting the monetary union only), low business confidence, and the weakened Greek banks (Blanchard, 2015). The limited political willingness to promote numerous reforms should be viewed within the context of the fierce adjustment requested from the Greek society, and the social and political turmoil and tensions raised against it. The list of additional causes can be extended and specified even further. Greece has considered on several occasions the prospect of Grexit, due to the harshness of economic and social conditions and the role of political forces and movements (see Varoufakis, 2017). But one could argue with certainty that what kept it inside the common currency edifice is its willingness to be a part of the European family of nations.[42] With the benefit of hindsight, one could go as far as to review the aforementioned list of structural or policy-oriented

---

[42] It is reminded that Greece was the seventh state that applied to become member of the EEC, a prospect that was postponed, after the dictatorship was imposed. It joined as the tenth member and remains until today a dedicated supporter of the European edifice, despite all the difficulties encountered.

reasons that have caused the Greek crisis and claim their partial significance, by reference to all these additional causes emerging after the crisis erupted.

It is however noteworthy to refer to the mistakes of policies conducted by the IMF, since reform programs were scheduled and initiated by the IMF and there is now a literature suggesting that its involvement in the case of Greece was not made without mistakes (e.g. in Nelson, 2017; Christodoulakis, 2014). It appears that the IMF had not realized directly the problems of the Greek economy and has made several mistakes on its assessments that have brought a limited success of programs advanced.

One problem with the application of IMF policies is that it could not devalue the currency. As opposed to the rest of the cases in which it is involved across the world, where, as soon as it takes in charge, it aims at imposing a severe adjustment program by using the tool of currency devaluation, in Greece the currency could not have been devalued, because it was the common currency. The quest for devaluation was a common European matter for the Board and president of the ECB to decide; they were unwilling to undertake a cost that was not reflecting the state of other Eurozone economies. Thus the social and economic effect of IMF policies was much stronger and more difficult to assimilate.

Furthermore, the second important mistake, if not conscious, is that it has postponed the debt restructuring that was not implemented in 2010, when the SBA was signed. The Fund went a step even further and amended its own clause to participate only in programs of countries whose debt is sustainable. The reason for postponing debt restructuring is that most of the larger international creditors of Greece were European Banks (mostly French, German, but also Italian) and it would have caused them significant damages. These European Banks were given ample time to sell their bonds in the ECB. By the time debt restructuring was undertaken, through the PSI[43] (the "haircut") in 2012, the ECB had purchased the Greek loans and avoided the contagion of the crisis. Varoufakis (2017) explains that the French Banks were trapped because they no longer had available their national central bank to support them, for instance by issuing money and helping them to avoid their substantial losses in the event that the Greek loans were not paid back (similarly this applies to the German and other European banks that were exposed in the Greek debt). What is more, they were facing a similar prospect in the case that their loans provided to Spain, Portugal, and Italy were not paid back. It is therefore no exaggeration to argue that it was decided, both by Greece and its partners, to sacrifice the Greek economy—like a modern Iphigeneia—in order not to allow the contagion of the Greek crisis in the EU and to allow the rest of the European banking system to remain sustainable; a sacrifice however that did not go as far as the Grexit. What was decided by Greece, its European partners and international agents (IMF and its members) was the sharing of support of the Greek economy by the IMF members (that includes mostly the United States but also various countries across the world, some of which are poorer than Greece) and by EU and Eurozone partners that were asked to rescue the Greek economy by providing bilateral loans to Greece (Varoufakis, 2017).

[43] Initials for Private Sector Involvement.

A principal reason for delaying debt restructuring was the fear of contagion (since the case of Lehman Brothers was still at the time fresh in memory) and the absence of "firewalls" and stability mechanisms that would have avoided contagion (Blanchard, 2015; Nelson, 2017). The reaction of the president of the ECB against debt restructuring was negative,[44] as he remained overattached to the Central Bank's principal role to ensure stability (Venizelos 2017). Certainly this decision was not that of the IMF alone. As Blanchard (2015) puts it "the risks were perceived to be too high to proceed with (debt) restructuring" (Blanchard, 2015). He suggests that the delay of debt restructuring has had as an effect, at least partially, a proportionally high part of the use of the first program to replace private debt by official debt (Blanchard, 2015). Behind the lines, one could draw the conclusion that Greece was the object of a policy whose subject was other countries and the strong Eurozone interests at stake. Perhaps, from the perspective of a nation-state this is one of the most severe critiques one can exercise to the IMF and its policies.[45]

This critique should be seen in the light of the IMF's role and mission to secure, guarantee, and restore, if necessary, monetary and financial stability in the international monetary system. This comprises issues of monetary and financial stability in the Eurozone and globally that, one way or another, had to become central to its policy.[46] Also one should be fair and agree that the IMF had no prior experience in dealing with currency zones, in particular one formed by some of the most advanced states of the world. In other words, international monetary stability was placed above concerns for the Greek economy and society. Finally, it is worth considering that the PSI, the first debt restructuring effort, was the largest in economic history so far. As Venizelos (2017: 112) reports, the debt restructuring intervention in 2012 comprised a nominal haircut of €126 billion and an additional restructuring with a fall of interest rates and greater period of debt repayment. The total amount of these interventions has been calculated to be at €180 billion, an amount equal to Greece's current GDP figures (Venizelos, 2017).

As one can see in Figs. 1.17 and 1.18, the weighted average cost of Greece's debt (its average interest rate) rose from 3.4% in 2003 to 4.6% in 2008 and 4.3% in 2010, the first two years after the crisis, when it was most difficult to borrow. Then it has started to fall, due to the policies followed for reducing the debt burden annually by the IMF and the EU and the access given to Greece in ESF loans. Furthermore, the weighted average maturity of Greece's debt (the average duration of the debt) was at 7.7 years in 2003 and increased to 14.1 years in 2007. It fell significantly to 5.6 and 3.8 years in 2009 and 2010, respectively, when no one wanted to lend to Greece in the long term. As a result of support to Greece's debt relief and growth promotion policies, the weighted average maturity was at 13.1 years in 2016, while the cost of the debt was at 2.9%.

---

[44] Jean-Claude Trichet at the time, though names do not mean something more than policies in this case, some of which, as explained, had to be taken in a policy vacuum and the absence of "firewalls."

[45] Before considering such a critique, one should calculate carefully who has benefited out of the Greek loans and by how much.

[46] Somehow the IMF suggests and implements policies that reduce the negative effects of structural and policy causes that lead to crises.

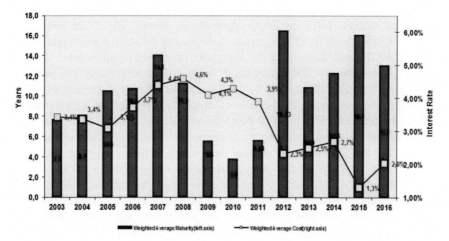

Figure 1.17 Weighted and average cost/maturity of annual funding.
Source: Public Debt Management Authority, Greece. The reprofiling of Greece's debt has brought the following picture for Greece's debt maturity starting from 1 September 2017). One can see that the repayment of Greece's loans is spread across time, following the policy of smoothing the repayment of EFSF loans.

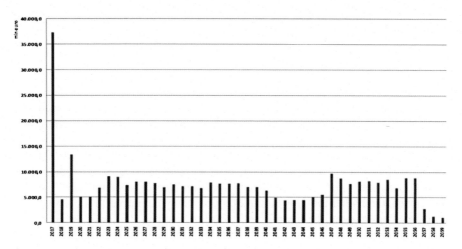

Figure 1.18 Repayment of Greece's loans for each year (2017−59).
Source: Public Debt Management Authority, Greece.

One of the most significant problems was the optimism placed by the IMF on achieving its targets in the initial SBA plan (that started in May 2010). According to the basic scenario, Greece's public debt would have reached its peak at 149% in 2013 and progressively reduced to 120% in 2020. The scenario also predicted growth levels at 2.75% after 2015 (Ignatiou, 2015). Similar of course were the projections of the European Commission, who presented a scenario in support of the

IMF policies on the PSI, according to which the Greek debt following the PSI would have reached 120% by 2020 (European Economy, 2012; Christodoulakis, 2014). As Christodoulakis (2014) explains, the reason behind the misdiagnosis was that the IMF ignored the impact the depression would have upon debt. Even the European Commission's 2013 scenario of annual debt projections (according to which the debt would fall to 116% by 2020) were not realistic (European Economy, 2013). The only exception to the rule of misleading projections came from the OECD, for a level of 157% by 2020 (see Christodoulakis, 2014).

A significant problem was the miscalculation of fiscal multipliers of the Greek economy by the IMF (see Blanchard and Leigh, 2013). For instance in its September 2010 Report, the IMF suggested that the Greek economy would grow at 4.6% in the period 2012−13, a period when GDP contraction exceeded 12% (Christodoulakis, 2014). This is a problem because such a miscalculation affects the denominator of the debt-to-GDP fraction, and reduces the significance and impact of the changes implemented that affect the nominator (see Box 1.3).

Other problems with the IMF policies are the scheduling and application of the front-loaded program, the belated emphasis on problems of competitiveness,

---

Box 1.3 Debt to GDP and its components

The following equation shows how the government debt-to-GDP ratio changes.

$$b_t = b_{t-1}(1 + r_t - g_t) - \text{pbal}_t,$$

where, b_t are the debt-to-GDP ratio, in different times, t (b_{t-1} is the debt-to-GDP in time $t-1$); t is subscript for time; r is the average nominal effective interest rate on debt; pbal is the primary budge balance to GDP ratio; and g is the nominal GDP growth rate.

The equation shows that the debt-to-GDP ratio in time t (b_t) depends on the debt-to-GDP ratio at a previous year, $t-1$ (b_{t-1}). The latter is multiplied by the component $(1 + r_t - g_t)$ and then the primary balance is subtracted.

Hence, the higher the growth rate of an economy compared to the effective interest rate on debt, the more b_t falls. On the contrary, the lower the growth rate of the economy compared to the effective interest rate on debt, the more b_t rises.

In Greece, despite the relatively low effective rate on debt (achieved through the "troika's" loans), the fierce fiscal adjustment that the Greek economy had to undergo, had led it into deep recession resulting in extended in size, negative growth rates in real GDP, and consequently nominal GDP. This is one of the reasons explaining why the central government debt as a proportion of the GDP (b_t) skyrocketed from 126.7% (in 2009) to 181.3% (in 2016), as opposed to the IMF's predictions and expectations.

entrepreneurship, and production, and the lack of understanding for a reform fatigue and the roof of tax-raising policies. The following Figure is indicative of IMF's own critical approach on his own findings and suggestions (Fig. 1.19).

In his blog on the IMF, Blanchard (2015) refers to the following four critiques on the Greek program:

    i) The 2010 program only served to raise debt and demanded excessive fiscal adjustment.

    ii) The financing to Greece was used to repay foreign banks.

    iii) Growth-killing structural reforms, together with fiscal austerity, have led to an economic depression.

    iv) Creditors have learned nothing and keep repeating the same mistakes (Blanchard's answers in such critiques are provided in his blog).

It is unfortunate that evidence such as that presented in the earlier section of this book (on the basic facts and figures of the Greek crisis) does not appear in the IMF's investigations on Greece. Of course, such evidence shows that IMF policies have succeeded in restoring the balance of current transactions and export-orientation but they also reveal the overconcentration of policies on fiscal and balance of payment policies rather than on growth.

It has also been considered that in its early understanding and dealing with the Greek crisis, the IMF viewed the Greek crisis as a liquidity crisis and not as a solvency crisis (Dullen et al., 2016). The difference between illiquidity and insolvency is significant. The former is a case where a country has a short-term funding problem, while the second is where it is unable and/or unwilling to pay its debts indefinitely (Reinhart and Rogoff, 2009: 59). This is also evidenced through the policy shift made from the first to the second programme.

All these reasons, related to the action or inaction of the IMF, could be additional for understanding why the Greek crisis has extended in time but they are not explanations for the appearance of the crisis at the first instance. Furthermore, one should underline that these are placed on one side of the balance, whereas on the other side, one could put the IMF's work for the rescue of the Greek economy.

One should also be careful before exercising a critique to IMF policies, most of which were conditional on specific, prespecified reforms (the conditionality clause, agreed through each Memorandum of Understanding). Many of these reforms were reasonable and necessary preconditions for restoring financial and debt sustainability. Others though had a long-term character and aimed at better organizing the administration and the information for decision-making purposes. A key priority was the privatization of various public goods (in which the state has invested billions of funds, as seen in the last chapter of this book), especially through the 2012 EFF arrangement.

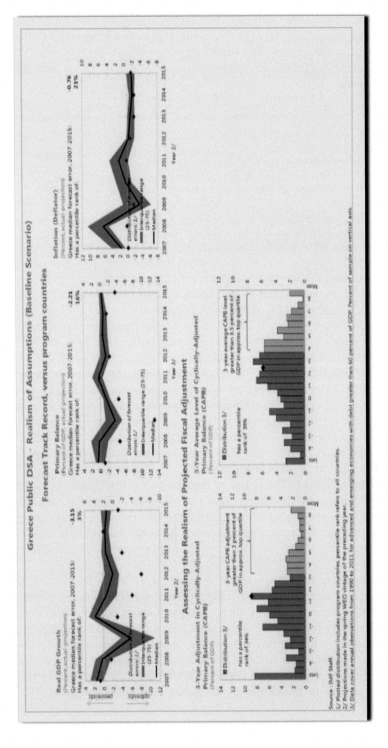

Figure 1.19 Mistakes in predictions as assessed by the IMF.
Source: IMF (2017).

The first SBA included reforms on fiscal consolidation (such as tight supervision of expenditure commitments by the government departments, and effective tax collection and a series of tax-raising measures and a privatization plan), structural fiscal reforms (a pension reform, the strengthening of tax administration through various measures including an audit system to defeat tax-evasion and the organization of a large tax-payer unit, the strengthening of the General Accounting Office), labor market reforms (such as measures to promote part-time work and temporary contracts), public sector modernization (in planning, organization and control operations, in public procurement, the implementation and usefulness of social programmers, the introduction of a system of a local administration reform, the modernization of the health system) and the strengthening of competition (by opening markets and liberalization of restricted professions, organizing the provision of e-services, conducting a business plan for the railway sector, actions that simplify procedures for businesses and investment licensing, remove rigidities, administrative and regulatory constraints and foster a business friendly environment, actions to privatize energy and promote innovation), and reforms in the domain of Justice (a new Code of Civil Procedure, reduction of case backlog in courts, promote anti-corruption legislation) (IMF, 2010, 2014).

Several of these reforms though crossed too far over the lines of social stamina, turning the society against their implementation. For example the pension reform eliminated by more than 50% the pensions of most categories of pensioners that had contributed for decades in the Greek pension system as employees. Consecutive IMF programs had created a spiral of expectations that were easily disproved due to the austerity measures imposed, and were bypassed by creating new programs and setting new targets. The IMF had chosen to follow a rather convenient method to reschedule its claims, on consecutive rounds, in order to achieve its goals.

1.6 Debt per GDP: the denominator of the fraction

All the above-mentioned explanations of the Greek crisis are significant to consider, as they are key explanations and reasons why the debt has risen in nominal terms. However, if one considers the debt in proportion to GDP, there is another category of explanations to focus upon: one that relates to the denominator of the fraction of the debt, which is expressed in terms of GDP.

One can hardly claim that the growth model of the Greek state throughout the decades was based on boosting investments and promoting private sector activity. It is true that over the years, the Greek state has launched numerous policies to support private sector activity, of theoretical origin, which have been applied in other countries. Many of these policies were not continued over the years and knowledge on their promotion was not accumulated. The principle of using negative conclusions from unsuccessful attempts and policy failures was never followed. Consecutive Greek governments had not created over the decades the image of a state that treats with skepticism various policy suggestions and assesses extensively all possible sides of the effects and the impact of each new policy that is about to be launched. Hundreds of new policy ideas and initiatives, were thought worth-implementing in the Greek conditions, irrespective of where and how exactly they were applied in other places. The economic and political elites have a role in forming this situation. Policy assessment has remained in many cases an empty letter, an unfinished and incomplete work to be completed by future governments, elected representatives, and policy-makers. Various policy indexes are missing, in a full range of policies, including the absence of credible macroeconomic accounts for certain periods of time. Thematic policies had been launched only for a limited number of policies, always in the subjective manner that would promote amendments rather than assess conclusions.

Before the 1980s, the Greek government had its own programming units, was building its own, well-defined capacity in terms of personnel and processes to complete results and reach outcomes, based on a sense of hierarchy, credibility of the public sector, accountability, control, and the formation of skills. As opposed to this administrative model, the period of governance of the state inaugurated after the 1980s and mostly in the 1990s and onwards has brought a serious loss in capacity building of the state, of its institutional memory and capacity to reach conclusions and outcomes. The latter were transferred mostly into the hands of various consultancies that have replaced the actual programming units of the state itself, the general directories, sections, and departments of the state and the role of university institutions. The diffusion of a model of state's governance that had to consider and satisfy a myriad of short-term interests and views on economic policies, had blurred the picture of mainstream economic knowledge and thinking that was much more evident and clear in the past and was not well produced in Greek universities. Production of goods and its needs had not become a policy priority. The state's actual sovereign power was lost much before the sovereign debt crisis has erupted.

A characteristic example of the absence of assessments of policies conducted by the state is the Greek development law, a special law applied to support investments, mostly from the private sector. The law has been changed over the years several times by all Greek governments (including the incumbent) but these changes were never really based on any particular assessments but on more general views and economic thinking. In general, the assessment of policies as conducted by various consultancies over the years on behalf of the Greek state had lacked objectivity, conclusions about how to economize resources and where not to spend, how to save money, time, processes etc., how to multiply effects, bring leverage, promote interaction, spur positive side-effects, and open paths. In brief, one could hardly find a critical assessment of the policies implemented, and if there were any, they would have been considered as the by-product of political reactions against policies, lack of understanding about mainstream policy thinking, and an act of opposition against a government, rather than a voice of a critic, aiming at improvements. The universities themselves were not left to undertake such a role, as the state has systematically espoused a policy that would offer millions of Euros from European funds to consultancies, often politically associated and remarkably fewer bits and pieces to proper scientific work. Poor assessments is also the case with EU authorities that, for example, have been using the European model QUEST II to predict the effects of projects implemented in Greece in the 2000–6 period that strongly diverted from the original conclusions of this particular model. Perhaps one should trace here the more general direction in regulated policy-making exceeding the borders of the Greek state to comprise European authorities too, according to which everything goes well and is placed in order, as long as funds are provided for.

Economic assessments without macroeconomic models, predictions, experiments to find the most appropriate methods of assessment, proper quantifications and indexes are unlikely to lead to final outcomes. Competitiveness programs had never clearly defined their targets and their potential effect on growth, nor were they associated with macroeconomic indexes and their improvement. Importantly though, the microeconomics of implementing competitiveness has never been critically thought and considered.

Many of the institutions built had lacked for years the personnel and required more time to operate and advance their targets, while in many cases their work was not fully respected. The complexity of projects has undermined the scope of assessment of effects.

And most of all, the Greek state has overemphasized and prioritized infrastructure investment and hard policy building rather than soft policies that require a different type of policy-making philosophy. By overemphasizing the provision of public goods and services, the Greek state has not envisaged its role as a catalyst in the private sector initiative.

Since growth would have come from the private sector, domestic or foreign, and its investments have not been raised over the years, one should consider why such investments had not occurred and whether a problem in the promoted growth model is likely to have occurred.

Theoretical underpinnings

2

2.1 Introduction

A principal policy option for a developing country, part of its economic strategy, is to follow a path of economic integration with other, more advanced, states (Balassa and Stoutjesdijk, 1975). The scope of integration is not only to increase competition and identify new opportunities due to economies of scale and market size expansion but also to lessen the power of special interests, compensate changes in various industries, and reduce investment requirements (Balassa and Stoutjesdijk, 1975: 41). The integration process is likely to lead to unequal distribution of costs and benefits, especially if states from dissimilar levels of development attempt to integrate (Balassa and Stoutjesdijk, 1975: 43). One way to evidence such integration imbalances is by examining intra-area and state-level trade imbalances (Balassa and Stoutjesdijk, 1975: 44). To reduce their intensity, a policy of investments is required. A high degree of competitiveness should be gained in countries that choose to integrate in the same common space. Their steps forward in economic growth terms should be assessed.

2.1.1 Resource allocation

The *primary goal* of *every economy* is to maximize wealth by allocating more efficiently its resources and capital in the long run. This is difficult since every country's economy is unique, with its own allocation plan, not only financially bound but also socially, politically, historically, and spatially.

Optimal allocation[1] requires a choice between public and private goods. Public goods are nonrival and nonexcludable. They are justified when markets fail and goods are unlikely to be produced otherwise (Stiglitz, 2000). Excludability allows forming an economic system where goods and services satisfy people's needs, at least in cost terms (Case, 2008). While private goods are produced through the price system, public goods are chosen through voting and representation. In each country, different equilibria are formed in the production of public and private goods to improve the well-being of citizens (Stiglitz, 2000). Market failures and great income imbalances push government intervention and emphasis toward public goods production, to maximize social welfare. Producing solely public goods though entails two main problems or risks: The difficulty to reveal the actual preferences of citizens, especially when choices have to be made between two different public goods, and to add these preferences correctly, in order to find out collective

---

[1] One of the three main functions of the public sector, along with, distribution, and macroeconomic stability according to Musgrave (1959).

Funding the Greek Crisis. DOI: https://doi.org/10.1016/B978-0-12-814566-1.00002-1

preferences by using all available information (Stiglitz, 2000). Thus, excessive emphasis on public goods production means that actual preferences are overlooked and public goods are rather imposed.

In such cases, optimal allocation would require the presence of a ubiquitous planner to combine all individual preferences and account for what a society is willing to pay, at each level of public good (Case, 2008). This hypothetical central planner would not be influenced by interest groups, political parties, ideologies, or agencies. Prudently and unselfishly, he would introduce and implement policies, being fully aware of all factors that can have a market impact. Without competition, pricing public goods and services may create production surpluses and price rising.

Economists acknowledge that the demand for active government intervention derives from imperfect competition, public goods, externalities, imperfect markets, and imperfect information (Stiglitz, 2000). The demand for public provision of goods and services, such as education or health, does not necessarily mean their insufficiency in markets (Stiglitz, 2000). Furthermore, the consequences of a public sector program depend directly on how expensive it is. Governments may impose payment at market prices to provide a good, may charge the good in prices reaching production cost (e.g., in electricity) or much below the production costs, may offer the good for free (e.g., elementary or secondary education), or distribute it in a way corresponding to the needs and benefits of the country (Stiglitz, 2000). Substitution effects are likely to occur when the provision of a good or service takes place, as consumers prefer to consume more from this good (Stiglitz, 2000).

2.1.2   Investment theory: choice, programming, strategy

To optimize resource allocation through active government intervention, while advancing economic change and growth, any economy requires the *supply of investment opportunities*. Economic theory stresses that investments are necessary to address the needs and deficiencies in capital, labor, and other important long-term growth factors. The latter include research and technology, innovation, social, institutional, and cultural capital, and various provisions of the welfare state.

The concept of investment is used to refer to tangible or intangible assets produced, their finance, as well as to processes used in their production and implementation. A narrow definition focuses only on stock of capital changes, usually in the medium to long term. The broad asset-based definition covers all mobile and immobile property, as well as shares, stocks, debentures, interests, money claims, intellectual property rights, and business concessions by law or contract (UNCTAD, 2011). An even broader definition would expand to comprise changes advanced in labor and other factors of production. Investments can be considered to impart specificity to resources (Youngson, 1956).

Despite its importance, there is *no comprehensive theory on investment* so far. This is critical to the economic policy associated with the variety and scope of economic theory. The most widely accepted neoclassical theory of investment cannot adequately answer the question of whether economic development should emphasize infrastructure development, infant industries, innovation and the expansion of domestic demand or invest in the long-term restructuring of SMEs. Would economic competitiveness be boosted simply by raising the levels of domestic investment, as emphasized on development studies for commodity-dependent economies converting natural resources (UNCTAD, 2015b) or by focusing on foreign direct investments (UNCTAD, 2015a and 2014)?

In the long run, policies aiming at raising investment ratios do not suffice to increase productivity too (Erdős, 1973). Technological advancement and the increase of modernization rate should be targeted too. Modernization occurs when investments in manufacturing or imports of more modern equipment increase the productive capacity, even if productivity remains below world standards (Erdős, 1973). Modernization reflects technical change, not technological development in the economy. If the manufacturing of productive equipment in a country is low, technical development may not occur. The modernization of an economy may derive from investments in imports and not in manufacturing products, as long as these imports raise the productivity of domestic firms. In this case, modernization in productive equipment may be a basis for technological development on a national scale, but it is not technological development per se (Erdős, 1973). Raising productivity on the other hand associates with other factors apart from technological development and the modernization rate, such as changes in skills, application of management principles, various organizational amendments, quality controls, etc.

When capital stock and output increases take place through labor expansion but without technical progress, capital widening occurs. When technology also improves, capital deepening occurs.

Prioritizing investments, creating the right hierarchy and making the most rational choices about them, increasing investment sizes, deciding on their planning and pursuing it effectively and consistently, especially for longer periods of time, are all difficult to advance, not only for states but also for supranational authorities supervising their development, such as that of the EU. While private investments simply have to follow market and profit opportunities and interests, public and semipublic investments are more difficult to plan. The latter, while they seek to provide public goods that meet various social needs and requirements, responding to the variety of social claims, they may also support, directly or indirectly, private sector needs, their gearing and leverage, by expanding the range of goods and services produced and upgrading their quality. Or, on the contrary, they may lead to their crowding out and extend the free rider problem.

The *choice of investments* presupposes economic *programming and strategy*. Economic programming starts with analyzing an economy's domestic and external environment and prioritizing the needs in its sectors and its territory, through forecasting and identifying problems, risks, and alternatives. Then setting goals and formulating targets in various programs and subprograms is required, the creation of appropriate budgets and allocation of funds, and their proper coordination and assessment. It also requires decision-making that incorporates a certain degree of flexibility.

Various *tools and incentives* are used to promote investment planning and *attract investments*. These include new investment laws, national enterprise support regimes, and are implemented through specific investment and development agencies and the organization of national institutional, legal, and tax environments for each state (UNCTAD, 2015a). Market liberalization reforms are combined with regulatory environments. Most states apply restrictions and choose a regulatory framework that promotes, supervises, monitors, and controls investments from a national security, environmental, or other perspective, aiming at their implementation according to initial plans and at limiting harmful effects and consequences (UNCTAD, 2015a). Exceptional forms and tools are also sometimes selected, e.g., the creation of specific economic zones (UNCTAD, 2015a).

Investment strategy on the other hand is a broader concept that refers to the series of coherent and consecutive choices that remain aligned to one or more goals set in advance. The term also refers to the choice of products and services that should be produced and offered.

An important part of investment strategy relates to the creation and operation of appropriate institutions. Institutions have been considered a principal factor affecting economic development and the distribution of resources (Acemoglu et al., 2005). Being endogenous, they influence and are influenced by power distribution, which is also endogenous. Political institutions are more important, influencing economic institutions and their outcome (Acemoglu et al., 2004). Creating and promoting a different selection of institutions leads to dissimilar economic performance (Acemoglu et al., 2004, 2005). Institutions are necessary to define and promulgate property rights of private and public resources, their use, exploitation, and allocation. They offer exclusivity in the use of resources, the rights to use and exchange them, that affect their value. They influence delegation, rent, or selling of a property. They also influence the efficiency of resource allocation by limiting expropriation and facilitating market transactions (Besley and Ghatak, 2010). They help to guide incentives and internalize the externalities associated with resources, both benefits and costs. Respecting and accepting property rights are necessary for development. In the public choice perspective, the nonefficient operation of institutions may be promoted by decision-makers not seeking to maximize social welfare but their private interests.

Institutions may help to avoid strong political pressure and influence exercised upon programs and processes. Political and democratic decision-making processes are bound to affect programs and the resulting decisions for laws and regulations implementing them, given that alternative policies exist that may be selected (Stiglitz, 2000). What is more, several interest groups are formed, aiming at influencing the paths and trajectories of resource and capital allocation, and claiming the necessity of various programs and public goods and services for their own benefit. Every economy is composed from interest groups but some particular interest groups may make use of all sort of political and social power, direct or indirect, to promote their own interests, at the expense of others, ignoring whole economic industries or areas. They may seek to take advantage of various flows and deficiencies, in different stages of the development process, from programming to final completion of programs, benefiting from constant outsourcing of programming work that reduces its academic merits and criteria and from lowering the standards or even eliminating its evaluation and control.

2.1.3 Emphasizing infrastructure investment for development purposes

Infrastructure is promoted for economic development and social purposes, all over the world. A distinction is usually made between economic and social infrastructure. Economic infrastructure includes transportation assets, such as roads, highways, bridges, tunnels, railroads, seaports, and airports; electricity assets, such as power generation stations, gas networks and electricity transmission lines, oil pipelines, fuel storage facilities and renewable energy systems; water infrastructure assets, such as water distribution systems, wastewater collection, and processing systems; communication infrastructure assets, such as radio and television broadcast towers, wireless and cellular communication towers, transmission systems, cable systems and satellite networks, etc. Social infrastructure assets are schools, hospitals and other healthcare facilities, subsidized housing, prisons, stadiums, athletic and recreation assets, etc.

In less advanced states, regions, or localities, the design, financing, building, and operation of more elementary forms of infrastructure may have to take place from scratch. This is termed "greenfield" or "growth infrastructure." Infrastructure is argued to massively reduce poverty, within a time horizon of two to three decades (IPRCC and OECD, 2010). Building the professions, institutions, processes, and analytical and managerial tools for infrastructure development is a complex and time-consuming process (IPRCC and OECD, 2010). Infrastructure has an impact on people's lives and opportunities, and can help to integrate extended regional parts of an economy and their natural and human sources (IPRCC and OECD, 2010). The significance of infrastructure is greater and absolutely necessary, in the early stages of economic development.

As economies advance, existing infrastructure that has already been built in the past requires its renewal and less frequently its building from scratch. In more advanced states and regions, existing forms of infrastructure have to be renewed. This is termed "brownfield" or "mature infrastructure" (Russ et al., 2010).

For Russ et al. (2010: 2), greenfield assets have higher risk/higher returns profile, while brownfield assets have lower risk and lower returns. They suggest that a number of factors, such as the maturity of target projects, the extent of geographical diversification, sector diversification, and asset-specific factors, may have an impact (Russ et al., 2010).

The significance of infrastructure is such that it is considered to be the second pillar and criterion for ranking countries in terms of competitiveness (World Economic Forum), 2016: 35).

A great potential demand for infrastructure investments is identified all over the world (OECD, 2014). The levels of infrastructure funds that are assessed to be required in the near future are estimated to accumulate to several trillions of US dollars (OECD, 2007a; Inderst, 2009). According to a recent report prepared by Preqin (2017), record fundraising levels for infrastructure were reached globally in 2016. The report refers to a tendency for concentration in a smaller group of managers that, at European level, stem mostly from the United Kingdom, Germany, and

France (Preqin, 2017). Even the most advanced states initiate massive infrastructure plans; this is the case of the 2012 National Infrastructure Plan in the United Kingdom that amounts to B£375 billion of public and private investment (HM Treasury, 2014). At EU level, the EU Cohesion Policy emphasized infrastructure investments (Crescezni and Posé-Rodriguez, 2012; EIB, 2010). The private sector is increasingly involved in infrastructure investments (proportionately to GDP), mostly in utility and private companies, using schemes of public—private partnerships (OECD, 2013). International institutions initiate data collection and the analysis of risk and return for potential infrastructure investments (OECD, 2015).

Infrastructure investments are argued to be significant not only at global and national scale but also at regional and local levels. Global problems, such as climatic change, raise the interest for particular infrastructure projects, e.g., in renewable energy (UBS, unknown year). The infrastructure needs of many metropoles and large cities have also been identified, as urban growth and continuous sprawl create infrastructure needs and raise debates on the necessity of renewal of existing and old infrastructure (GLA, 2014). Regional and local authorities in particular face the challenges to borrow funds and/or attract national or international (European) grants that could be used to promote new or existing and incomplete infrastructure projects, placed within the context of a post-crisis recessionary period (O'Brien and Pike, 2015). Austerity imposed at national scale requires financial solutions from abroad, at the global level, turning, from this perspective, infrastructure financing in bigger cities to a local phenomenon.

Selecting infrastructure projects among a series of alternatives is an important investment decision. The United Kingdom selects which infrastructure projects to finance on the basis of their national significance for projects that must also enhance quality, sustainability, and capacity, on their contribution to economic growth or capacity to attract private sector investment, and on their meeting strategic governmental objectives (House of Commons, 2017).

To cope with the drain of public resources, several countries already seek to attract private sector contribution in infrastructure investment to undertake the funding, use, operation, and management of infrastructure, while at the same time ensuring the delivery of necessary social and private goods (Panayiotou and Medda, 2014).

Specific institutions and banks are created and existing ones expand their financial scope and reach, such as the European Investment Bank or the Asian Infrastructure Investment Bank, which pursue infrastructure building policies (Callaghan and Hubbard, 2016). Institutional and other investors (mutual funds, sovereign wealth funds, life insurance companies), including large pension funds, choose to invest hundreds of billions of US dollars in infrastructure investments (Croce, 2011). Foreign aid takes often the form of infrastructure investment (Foster et al., 2009). The need to diversify financial sources involved in public infrastructure and to reduce the "infrastructure gap," especially in low- and medium-income countries and many emerging markets and developing economies is given special attention (OECD, 2015).

Such is the penetrating view on the significance of the infrastructure that a special journal has been created that echoes such views (the *Journal of*

Infrastructure Development). A special term, "infrastructure industry," has been used to refer to infrastructure and to emphasize its investment needs (Preqin, 2017). Within a period of almost 20 years, its study from a financial point of view has developed extensively.

Three separate terms are employed in the study of the interplay between infra-structure and finance: funding, financing, and its financialization. Infrastructure funding refers to the source of funds for infrastructure. Infrastructure financing involves the costs for the provision of capital, both of capital itself and the services for the financing arrangements required (O'Brien and Pike, 2015). The financializa-tion of infrastructure refers to the growing significance of finance and of the role of institutional and other intermediaries in infrastructure (O'Brien and Pike, 2015).

The financialization of infrastructure and the transformation of its ownership are increasingly taking place at the global scale (O'Brien and Pike, 2015; PWC and GIIA, 2017). The engagement of the private sector with public infrastructure assets widens and deepens (O'Brien and Pike, 2015). This trend has risen in the United Kingdom since the 1980s and in other European countries since the mid-1990s, and many infrastructure projects have been built. Increasingly, many governments turn to private markets to collect funds (Babson, 2011; House of Commons, 2017). Several vehicles to draw funds have been suggested by several authors as the most suitable. For example Russ et al. (2010) refer to publicly listed funds, private infra-structure funds (General Partnerships), private infrastructure fund of funds, direct investment (traditionally more available to institutional investors), while UBS (unknown year) refers to direct infrastructure investment, unlisted or listed funds investing in direct infrastructure, and/or listed infrastructure companies, listed stocks, and infrastructure funds. Investors propose their own investment portfolios that comprise infrastructure (Owen, 2015). The United Kingdom has organized a special Pensions Infrastructure Platform to fund infrastructure by the use of pension funds (Institute and Faculty of Actuaries, 2015; House of Commons, 2017).

A growing number of views is expressed that infrastructure is a financial asset to invest on, which generates returns, and has distinct financial features. As an asset, infrastructure is argued to be more resilient and generally expected to deliver stable returns over the economic and business cycles, because it offers essential services that are relatively inelastic to a fall in demand. It is considered to offer attractive returns, of relatively limited correlation to those of other assets, with sta-ble, long-term, and predictable cash flows, low default rates, and to be a socially responsible investment (Anikeef, 2014). It is also suggested to offer relatively high-er and less volatile credit quality levels, when compared against other assets (Roberts et al., 2015: 7). It requires large amount of capital and has long life spans that extend, for example, for a 50-year period for roads, bridges, and tunnels, 10 years for telecommunication cables, and up to 60 years for electricity gridlines (Russ et al., 2010: 2; Babson, 2011). The initially high capital investment required raises significant impediments for potential competitors and investors, barriers to entry, and limits the competition. It is also characterized by economies of scale, high fixed, low variable and low operating costs, high target operating margins, and long duration (Anikeef, 2014: 9; Roberts et al., 2015). Its returns are generally assessed to be better than average and several other investment options, reaching low double-digit figures for core infrastructure projects (Morgan, 2009; Babson, 2011). Infrastructure projects have also been assessed to offer protection against inflation (Morgan, 2009).

Taken as an asset, infrastructure is thought to play different possible roles in the portfolio of potential investors, depending on their risk—return targets (Russ et al., 2010).

According to UBS (unknown year) infrastructure is subject to several risks. These are suggested to be operational risks and construction risks for greenfield assets, debt and refinancing risks, which are subject to inflation, credit risks, patronage/demand risk especially in transport assets, and regulatory risks, since they are subject to regulation and contractual arrangements. Inderst (2009: 20—21) refers further to business risks created by technology and the entry of new competitors, legal and ownership risks (e.g. from not granting planning consents, from unknown future litigation or the running out of lease), regulatory risks (e.g., when fee rises fall behind scheduled), environmental risks and hazards, and political and social risks (opposition raised from pressure groups, corruption, change of mind by politicians and political authorities). The safety and security of infrastructure assets poses another risk and challenge (CEC, 2006). According to Morgan (2009), risks in investing in infrastructure differentiate per subsector, stage of development, political and regulatory environment, limitations in liquidity, and the absence of reliable, long-term data, and estimates that suffice to account for comparisons and reliable assessments among infrastructure projects and plans. Core infrastructure projects such as bridges, tunnels, railroads, pipelines, energy transmission and distribution, and water and wastewater systems have lower risk and less return, while more opportunistic infrastructure projects that involve greater risk and returns include satellite networks, merchant power generation, and development projects, especially in non-OECD countries (Morgan, 2009). Airports, seaports, rail links, rapid rail transit, and contracted power generation are classified as value-added infrastructure projects (Morgan, 2009).

Taken as an asset, infrastructure is thought to play different possible roles in the portfolio of potential investors, depending on their risk—return targets (Russ et al., 2010).

Several observers go a step further and base their assessment on infrastructure on a number of recently developed indices that track the performance of infrastructure-related investments (Idzorek and Armstrong, 2009). Such indices are the Dow Jones Brookfield Global Infrastructure Index, the Macquarie Global Infrastructure Index, the MSCI All Country World (ACWI), the Infrastructure Sector Capped Index, the S&P Infrastructure Index, the UBS Global Infrastructure and Utilities Index (Izdorek and Armstrong, 2009).

The OECD emphasizes the need to employ various tools and incentives for attracting and promoting infrastructure investments, and centers its policy recommendations around financing infrastructure, engaging more pension funds, improving the regulatory and institutional framework, strengthening governance and strategic planning for infrastructure, integrating technology, and using a toolkit for monitoring, decision-making, and analyzing interdisciplinary infrastructure issues (OECD, 2007). In parallel with infrastructure financing, the need to strengthen the SME sector is also acknowledged (World Bank et al., 2015).

The growing involvement of pension funds in infrastructure funding schemes raises further concerns about its risk, viability, and use. Diversifying investment portfolios across industries and areas is used as a way to reduce and manage risk. Financial and risk management indexes, such as return ratios, are employed to secure infrastructure investment. These need to take into account political and social risks resulting from economic and political conditions. It is thus necessary to look at the long-term implications of infrastructure investments, especially the deficits and debts they can cause.

Munnell (1990) emphasized that investing in infrastructure does not provide robust results on the generation of private investment. Besides, little evidence was found for the "Aschauer hypothesis" (according to which differences in stocks of infrastructure account for different levels of productivity, output, and growth) and Ford and Poret (1991) emphasized its more cautious interpretation.[2] Furthermore, transport infrastructure was suggested to be a poor predictor for growth (Crescezni and Posé-Rodriguez, 2012). Such results are not hard to accept, given that, as discussed, infrastructure is characterized by monopolistic qualities, entry barriers, captive customer earnings, low volatility of cash flows, long asset life, and large investment scale (Peng and Newell, 2007) as well as inelastic demand. Furthermore, there are many examples of European infrastructure projects that are ill-conceived, badly implemented, and where funds are overspent (Subacchi et al., 2014).

Negative implications from investing in infrastructure are suggested in New Economic Geography readings. For example, in their model of two regions (southern and northern), two factors (workers and capital), and two final good sectors (Manufactures M and a homogenous good A), Baldwin et al. (2002: 17−7) suggest that—investing in—"infrastructure that facilitates intra-regional trade in the south lowers spatial concentration, decreases growth in the whole economy and increases nominal income inequality between north and south and between workers and capital owners."

2.1.4 A useful distinction for economic growth and development studies: autonomous versus induced investment

2.1.4.1 Induced investment, acceleration, and the cost of capital

It is generally believed that the expansion of capital stock through investments also increases income. Youngson (1956) suggested that when studying economic growth, the focus should be given on the nature of decisions giving rise to capital creation rather than on the nature of capital created.

---

[2] Since Aschauer's original associations may also indicate that governments tend to spend more on infrastructure whenever productivity growth is high and income rises.

A useful distinction, not given sufficient attention in economic literature, has already been made between *autonomous* and *induced* investment (see in Hamberg and Schultze, 1961). Various forms of government spending, such as roads, highways, and airports, water and sewage works, hydroelectric projects, and others, are autonomous of income (Hamberg and Schultze, 1961). They are provided for reasons relating to equity and social choice and are made accessible to all citizens, as social goods. In societies of long-standing imbalances, such investments appear as a rather natural path to follow in the long run. Governments undertake them well before their demand appears, due to indivisibilities in social capital, time lags in the growth of demand, and because of their contribution in structural changes taking place in the expanding economy (Hamberg and Schultze, 1961: 55). Research on their necessity is not always a prerequisite. Autonomous investments are also the residential construction investments as well as the innovative investments undertaken either to lower costs at prevailing levels of output or to introduce new products that displace substitute products in consumer budgets (Hamberg and Schultze, 1961: 55).

For induced investments, anticipated profitability is consistent with current income levels. Induced investment increases the stock of capital, offering greater productive capacity (Hamberg and Schultze, 1961: 54). It takes place in existent, "old" types of products, in response to pressures to expand existing productive capacity and emanates from "high marginal costs, strain on existing staff and capital stock, bottlenecks and delays" (Hamberg and Schultze, 1961: 54). Thus, it depends on existing levels of income.[3]

Induced investment accelerates economic growth, as the interaction between the multiplier and the acceleration coefficient increases growth rates (Hicks, 1950). In Hicks' model, after reaching a full employment ceiling, a downswing process starts (of a dormant accelerator), constrained by rising trends in autonomous investments and growing needs for replacement investments (Arndt, 1951).

The acceleration principle itself is based on the assumption that there is a constant ratio of capital to product α, for which $K_t = \alpha Y_t$. For a previous period, $t - 1$, $K_{t-1} = \alpha Y_{t-1}$. Therefore, by subtracting we get $K_t - K_{t-1} = \alpha(Y_t - Y_{t-1})$. Denoting the change in capital as $\Delta K = K_t - K_{t-1} = I_t^N$, where I_t^N denotes net investments, we get $I_t^N = \alpha(Y_t - Y_{t-1})$. According to this equation, net investments are the constant ratio of capital to product, multiplied by the change in the product.

Adding depreciation D, we get $I_t^N = \alpha(Y_t - Y_{t-1}) + D$.

If part of the net investments are independent of changes in the levels of output, then such an autonomous part of investment, I_0, can be added, to separate from the non-autonomou part.

$$I_t^N = \alpha(Y_t - Y_{t-1}) + D + I_0 \quad \text{or} \quad I_t^N = I_0 + \alpha \Delta Y + D$$

---

[3] In a macroeconomic context, autonomous and induced investment are added to provide full investments, i.e., $I = I_o + I_a (Y)$. However, one cannot treat the autonomous part of investment as the innovational part of investments, as Sordi (2003: 292) does. The two concepts, autonomous and induced investments are much richer and cannot be distinguished by drawing the line of innovation.

Two important points are raised with respect to investments. The first is to focus on the decision of desired stock of capital, i.e., the stock that firms wish to have in the long run. The other is to emphasize the decision of desired investment, i.e., the level of investment we wish to have in the long run (as Keynes did), which is an important aspect of growth (Milios et al., 2000). The desired level of capital is for some economists the most important aspect of growth that should influence investment decisions (see Milios et al., 2000).

Though criticized as being simplistic and unable to sufficiently explain trade and economic cycles (Kaldor, 1951), the acceleration principle could help to explain why some economies grow faster than other. Even for Kaldor (1951: 840), the accelerationist approach is useful if a series of partial acceleration coefficients are considered for different consecutive periods. While he criticized Hicks' model as being too static, treating fluctuations as movements around a stationary equilibrium (Kaldor, 1951: 834), he suggested that an equilibrium will remain dynamically (as well as statically) stable. This means that following a disturbance, the economy will take a path leading to a "smoothly converging movement toward an equilibrium position" (Kaldor, 1951: 834). The difficulty of causing induced investment is so high that Kaldor went on to assume that investment associates negatively to capital stock because firms with highly accumulated capital stock will not invest further.[4]

The acceleration principle was modified to incorporate stock adjustments,[5] and is now referred as *stock adjustment principle*. This principle captures the difference between the desired and achieved stock of capital for each period. Enterprises do not adjust their capital stock to the desired stock instantaneously; time is needed to order new machines, construct new lines, buildings, units, or factories, etc. The rate at which firms adjust their existing capital stock to that desired, defines the distribution of their expenditure for capital stock increases (Dornbush and Fisher, 1990).

A simple expression of stock adjustment principle is the following:

$$\Delta K_{t+j} = g\alpha(Y_t - Y_{t-1})$$

where g shows the way firms adjust their capital after a change in their demand, and j represents the time required to adjust capital stock.

If firms have unused capacity, instead of the change in product between periods $t-1$ and t, one can employ the deviation of product from a normal level. If we symbolize this normal level with Y_t^N, then we can assume $\Delta K_{t+j} = g\alpha(Y_t - Y_t^N)$,

And if: $Y_t^N = K_t/\alpha$

It turns out that $\Delta K_{t+j} = g\alpha Y_t - gK_t = g(\alpha Y_t - K_t)$ where αY_t is the desired cost of capital and K_t the existing. According to this equation, net investments in period $t+j$ are a proportion of the difference between a desired and existing capital stock.

---

[4] In modifying the acceleration model originally assumed in Hicks and Samuelson cycle theory, $I_t = I_o + v(Y_t - Y_{t-1})$, Kaldor rewrote the equation of investment as: $I_t = I_o + v(Y_t - Y_{t-1}) - jK$, to indicate the negative association of capital stock K.

[5] See Chenery, H.B., 1952.

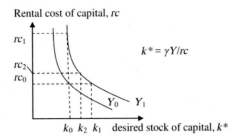

Figure 2.1 Graphical illustration of the relationship between the rental cost of capital and the stock of capital, for different income levels.
Source: Dornbusch, R., Fischer, S., 1990. Macroeconomics. McGraw-Hill, New York.

Dornbusch and Fischer (1990) explain that the desired stock of capital, denoted as k^*, equals the product, Y, divided by the rental cost (rc) of capital ($k^* = \gamma Y/rc$). The product may rise without changes in the desired stock. As illustrated in Fig. 2.1, if the desired stock of capital remains unaltered (e.g., in k_0), when the product rises (e.g., from Y_0 to Y_1) the cost of capital (rc) rises too (from rc_0 to rc_1). This is the case when economic policy overemphasizes autonomous investments and the desired stock of capital does not change. Even for partial increases in the desired stock of capital (due to induced investments satisfying part of the full amount of increases in the desired stock needed), as the product rises the cost of capital will rise too and could become relatively more expensive. In both cases, the rising cost of capital raises barriers to economic growth process and deteriorates domestic economic prospects.

Autonomous investment generating productive capacity may be competitive with productive capacity created by induced investment. Thus, the overall capital is likely to be depressed and some capital stock rendered idle, due to a shift in consumer preferences from one bundle of consumption to another (Hamberg and Schultze, 1961). In such cases, the acceleration effect is reduced.

Autonomous investment can be viewed as an absorber of savings, since it reduces the amount that has to be absorbed by acceleration-induced investment and it lowers the equilibrium growth rate that associates with the acceleration coefficient (Hamberg and Schultze, 1961: 53). Thus, in a neoclassical analysis, it will affect the steady state. A fall in the steady state may also result from limited technological advancement.

2.1.5 Implications from emphasizing autonomous investment: a few points from theory

2.1.5.1 Implications on the rise of public expenditure

When governments intervene by providing autonomous investments and generally promote them as a type of investment, they seek to better organize economic activity, so as to fulfill their two main goals, efficiency and equity. Overemphasizing autonomous investment, without putting some controls and at the expense of induced investment should be expected to raise a state's expenditure.

According to public economics, a state's public expenditure increases for a number of reasons, in several ways. According to "Wagner's law," a state's expenditure has always a rising trend, due to the increase of administrative services, the increase of complexity, urbanization, rising externalities, and the public sector's strong interest to control monopolies created out of the growth and development process. This law was proved in some cases but questioned when cross-sectional and other econometric studies were explored (Georgakopoulos, 1997; Magazzino et al., 2015).

Another suggestion for the increase of state's expenditure was made by Peacock and Wiseman (1961). They had argued that it follows a noncontinuous step-like pattern, influenced by political factors, the level of taxation and citizens' choice, expressed through voting. They referred to (1) a "displacement effect,", i.e., a discontinuity in the growth pattern of public expenditure, when people realize the necessity of new expenditure and accept increased levels of taxation (and tax tolerance), (2) the "inspection effect," during wars or social disturbances or political instability, when citizens are forced to resolve important problems and realize the necessity to increase public expenditure, and (3) the "concentration effect," i.e., a concentration tendency that increases the size of government, whenever economic growth takes place.

Another view about the rising pattern of public expenditure is expressed by Baumol (1967). In describing his unbalanced growth model, he suggested that public sector expenditure rises as a proportion of total, if the ratio of private-to-public output remains the same. Baumol had seen behind this rising trend, the gains in productivity for the private sector, which are due to technology. If there is strong political demand, labor will shift to the less productive—public—sector and the level of expenditure in this sector will rise (relative to the private sector).

Bureaucracy, its perpetuation and its increase, is another reason why increasing government investments may accumulate even higher levels of public expenditure. Autonomous investments require the setting up of rules and standardized procedures and processes, often of excessive size and request, giving birth to organizational weaknesses and a Weberian type of bureaucracy. Whichever is the perspective taken, an overemphasis on autonomous investment enhances public expenditure.

2.1.5.2   Implications on the balance of trade

Consider the familiar equation for current account

$$CA = S - I \text{ or } CA = S_p + S_g - I,$$

where S_p = private savings, S_g = government savings, and I = total investments.[6]

Assume that investments are the sum of autonomous, I_o and induced, I_n, $I = I_o + I_n$, then:

---

[6] Deficits and debts are progressively accumulated when S and CA turn to negative.

$$CA = \left\{ \left(S_p + S_g \right) \right\} - \left(I_o + I_n \right) = \left\{ \left(S_p + S_g \right) - I_o \right) \right\} - I_n$$

This equation shows that the more investment and its components (I_o and I_n) increase, and the more savings (S_p and S_g) reduce, the more the CA deficit increases. Thus, when a substantial outflow of private savings toward other countries or offshore companies occurs, the current account deficit rises.

Savings are used to fund investments or state deficits. The more they are used to fund state deficits, the less savings are available to fund investments. A rising CA deficit absorbs more savings and the levels of government expenditure and investment fall. We are aware that the savings are leakages in the economic circular flow of an open economy.

Furthermore, when governments use their savings to excessively fund investments in imported capital goods, their savings will start to fall. The multiplying effect for the domestic economy from boosting investments in imported capital goods reduces, unless the degree of economic integration is high and the economy gains out of its economic interaction with those where the imported goods are coming from.

If a proportion is lost due to induced investments, then we can assume this proportion to be a function k of total savings, $S_p + S_g$.

At the same time:

$$\begin{aligned} CA \quad &= \left\{ \left(S_p + S_g \right) - \left(S_p + S_g \right) k \right\} - \left(I_o + I_n \right) \\ &= \left\{ \left(S_p + S_g \right) \left(1 - k \right) - I_o - I_n \right. \end{aligned}$$

Thus, the current account is no longer reduced only by ($I_o + I_n$) but by a greater component, ($S_p + S_g$)k + ($I_o + I_n$) and is more likely to become negative.

Since total investments is the sum of autonomous and induced, the more government invests in autonomous investment and the provision of public goods, the more public savings are required and absorbed, thereby expanding deficits and, in the long run, debts. Redirecting autonomous investments to reach a better balance with induced investment could offer a way to avoid such problems, placing the burden of savings on the side of the private sector.

Raising autonomous investment and the provision of public goods would require using domestic savings, public and private, in those cases where national public and private sector's contribution is requested (such as in the EU Cohesion Policy, discussed later). If a proportion of savings is required, due to autonomous investments I_o, we can assume this proportion to be a function of autonomous investment, a proportion λ of ($S_p + S_g$).

Thus:

$$\begin{aligned} CA \quad &= \left\{ \left(S_p + S_g \right) - \left(S_p + S_g \right) k - \left(S_p + S_g \right) \lambda \right\} - \left(I_o + I_n \right) = \\ &= \left(S_p + S_g \right) \left(1 - k - \lambda \right) - \left(I_o + I_n \right) = \end{aligned}$$

We are aware that $0 < \lambda < 1$ and $0 < k < 1$.
The greater is λ and k, the lower is ($S_p + S_g$) $(1 - \lambda - k)$.

Hence, the current account should be reduced by an even greater aggregate component, i.e., $(S_p + S_g)(\lambda + k) + (I_o + I_n)$.

Thus, even after starting from a positive current account (CA) balance position, deficits are likely to be created.

Given that $S = I + CA = I + (NX + NFP)$, where NX is net exports and NFP net factor payments from abroad, in order to rebalance current account deficits and keep the balance of payment zero (i.e., $CA + FA + KA = 0$, where KA and FA are the capital and financial account respectively), one has to sell financial and capital account assets (in FA and KA).

This result of course is subject to the interest rate, the exchange rate of the currency, and the levels of public consumption (namely wages and pensions).

Fig. 2.2 illustrates that while investments increase over the years (shifting I_0 from time period t_0 to I_1 in t_1), savings fall from S_0 to S_1 and, as a result, the current account deficit (CA = S − I) expands. The interest rate is assumed to be lower than the equilibrium point of intersection between investment and savings, since we focus on a small open economy, like the Greek (Fig. 2.2). When induced investment (I_{ind}) is considered, investment becomes more inelastic (as illustrated in Fig. 2.2). Thus, in the event of investment expansion that incorporates more induced investment, the levels of deficit are restrained.

In a small open economy, the multiplier is $1/(s + \mu)$, where s is the marginal propensity to save and m the marginal propensity to imports, and lower to the multiplier of a closed economy, $1/s$ $[1/s > 1/(s + \mu)]$.

The saving rate of an economy that emphasizes autonomous investment is likely to reduce, and given that imports of goods from other countries will increase, m shall rise. Thus, in comparison to a closed economy, the multiplier $1/(s + \mu)$ is more likely to fall.

Furthermore, a fiscal expansion is bound to bring trade deficits.

In the familiar analysis from macroeconomics, denoting TB as the trade balance, such that $TB = X - M$, where X are exports and M imports, with imports having an autonomous part, such that $M = M_0 + \mu Y$, we get:

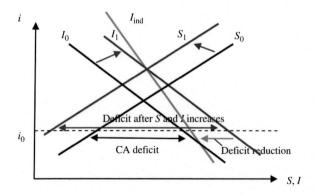

Figure 2.2 Potential influence of induced investment on current account deficit.

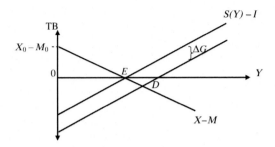

Figure 2.3 Trade deficit and its deterioration when government expenditure rises.

$$TB = X - M = X - M_0 - \mu Y$$

The change in trade balance is:

$$\Delta TB = \Delta X - \Delta M = \Delta X_0 - \Delta M_0 - \mu \Delta Y \Leftrightarrow \Delta TB = -\mu \Delta Y \qquad (2.1)$$

And also considering G to be government expenditure. Since, government expenditure has a multiplier such that:

$$\Delta Y = \left(1/(s + \mu)\right)\Delta G \qquad (2.2)$$

From Eqs. (2.1) and (2.2) we can conclude $\Delta TB = -\mu/(s + \mu)\Delta G < 0$

Thus, a fiscal expansion emphasizing autonomous investments that produce more imports than exports and brings higher levels of marginal propensity to imports (μ), is likely to increase trade deficits.

We can illustrate trade balance TB and income Y on two axes, depicting the two curves, $S(Y) - I$ and $X - M$ (Fig. 2.3). When an increase in government expenditure occurs, the curve $S(Y) - I$ shifts to the right, giving higher income levels but with trade deficit.

2.1.5.3 Implications on growth: Is there a substitution relation between technology and integration?

A firm's product exhibits diminishing returns, i.e., the rate of output growth starts reducing after some point, as production factors rise. This trend is illustrated in the diminishing slope of the production curve in Fig. 2.4, which differentiates between a case where a firm manages to benefit from integration (Q_{integr}) and one that it does not ($Q_{non-integr}$). Similar increases in labor, from L_0 to L_1, offer higher output increases. A firm can produce more at an enlarged, integrated common market. Without integration benefits (also resulting from reaching a stage of market saturation), production can increase through successful technological investments. Producing a new product however contains risks and is less safe than selling existing products in new markets. Thus, integration may provisionally substitute the need for

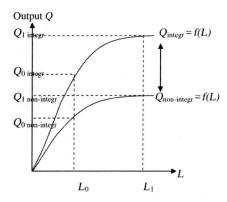

Figure 2.4 Production curves for an integrated and a non-integrated economy.

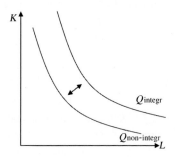

Figure 2.5 Marginal technical rate of substitution for an integrated and a non-integrated economy.

technological advancements (so long as output rises), even for firms that may require technological inventions to address large domestic and saturated markets.

The interrelation between capital and labor is illustrated in Fig. 2.5. Due to the integration process, the rate of substitution of the production factors capital (K) and labor (L), known as marginal technical rate of substitution, may expand (rightward), since more capital and more labor may be employed. Again, in a hypothetically closed economy, such a result is produced only by technical advancements.

2.1.5.4 Implications on growth modeling and theory: the neoclassical model, the AK model, and a reconsideration of its critique

In this section, a reference is made to the basic features primarily of the neoclassical and then of the AK growth model, in order to prepare the discussion on their possible improvements.

Numerous growth models, including the most preeminent among them, Solow's model, assume a variable capital to output ratio, in a continuous production function (contrary to an assumption made in the past of fixed capital−output ratio, as found in Harrod–Domar model). Induced investment could raise the levels of capital and thus the capital to labor ratio (K/L)

Solow's growth model in particular, also known as the neoclassical, is designed to show how capital accumulates in the economy, the relationship among capital, labour and technology, how income is produced in the economy and also to identify the steady state of an economy, i.e., the best possible position for an economy, as well as the "golden rule" level of capital, i.e., the level of capital per worker, where consumption is maximized (measured as the difference between output and depreciation).

As Easterly (2001) points out, one of the surprising outcomes of the Solow's growth model was that investment in buildings or machinery was not as important as capital, labor, or even technology. Of course, investments were treated uniformly. The view that investments are very significant for economic growth has been characterized as "capital fundamentalism" (Easterly, 2001).

The neoclassical model is derived from the most elementary aspects of economic theory, the basic knowledge that product is the sum of consumption and investment, i.e., $Y = C + I$. Dividing both sides by L, we get: $Y/L = C/L + I/L$. This equation claims that per worker product is the sum of consumption per worker and investment per worker. We can rewrite this equation as:

$$F\left[k_{(t)}\right] = \left[C/L\right]_t + \left[I/L\right]_t \tag{a}$$

The ratio of capital to labor $k = K/L$ does not grow and the rate of growth of capital, K, and labor, L, are the same. It rises if the growth rate of capital is higher than that of labor and falls if it is lower. Assume the growth rate of labor of a state or region is 20% per decade and the growth rate of capital to be 15%. In this case the ratio of capital to labor will fall. Let us depict the difference of the growth rate of capital (the derivative of K divided by K) and labor (the derivative of L divided by) as:

$$\frac{\dot{k}}{k} = \frac{\dot{K}}{K} - \frac{\dot{L}}{L} \tag{b}$$

We can illustrate $k' = \dot{k}/k$, $K' = \dot{K}/K$ and $L' = \dot{L}/L$, changing the equation to

$$k' = K' - L' \tag{c}$$

This equation reveals that the rate of growth of capital to labor is the difference between the rate of growth of capital and of the rate of growth of labor.

Consider the rate of growth of labor is constant, n. If n is placed in Eq. (b) and both the sides multiplied by $k = K/L$, then we get:

$$\dot{k} = \frac{\dot{K}}{K}\frac{K}{L} - n\frac{K}{L},$$

which simplified for k gives

$$\dot{k} = \frac{\dot{K}}{L} - nk \Leftrightarrow \frac{\dot{K}}{L} = \dot{k} + nk \tag{d}$$

The derivative of capital, $\dot{K}$, is assumed to be the investment. Thus the first part of Eq. (d) is I/L.

Combining Eqs. (a) and (d), we get $F\left[k_{(t)}\right] = \left[C/L\right]_t + \dot{k} + nk$. According to this equation, the per capital output is a function of consumption per labor, a part of investment that keeps the ratio of labor to capital constant despite that the labor force rises, nk, and a part of $\dot{k}$ that is the part that is rising (Jones, 1975). Capital per labor is divided to per labor consumption, a part of "capital widening" and one of "capital deepening" (that enhances capital).

The neoclassical model assumes constant returns to scale, though it accepts diminishing returns to scale for capital (as explained in Fig. 2.7).

The steady state is an equilibrium point that is stable. If an economy reaches the steady state, its per capita production will be constant and will no longer change. It reflects the maximum level of output per worker that an economy can reach. The economy is considered to return to the steady state, even if investment for example expands further. To find out the steady state of the economy, one should define the ratio of capital to labor as $k = K/L$.

Following Solow's analysis, we can express the growth rate of k (denoted as $\dot{k}$ by the use of a dot) by equation:

$$\dot{k} = sf(k) - (\delta + n)k \tag{2.3}$$

where:
$Y = f(k)$ is a way to rewrite the production function, given that $k = K/L$;
s is the marginal propensity to savings, $0 < s < 1$;
$s(y)$ or $sf(k)$ is the savings function;
n is the growth rate of labor, $n = L_t/L_0$, which grows exogenously at $L_t = L_0 e^{nt}$; population and labour force are assumed to be the same
δ is the depreciation rate of capital.
The difference between income and savings, $Y - sf(k)$, represents consumption.
The economy is at a steady state if:

$$sf(k) - (\delta + n)k = 0 \tag{2.4}$$

i.e., when the difference between $sf(k)$ (which is practically the increment of capital and shows actual investment per unit of labor unit) and $(\delta + n)k$ (which is the increase of labor plus the depreciation rate and represents the breakeven investment necessary to keep k at its existing level) is zero.

In other words, the steady state is found at the contact point between these two parts of the growth equation, and provides stability in the growth path. Following Solow's analysis, Fig. 2.6 illustrates the point of intersection of variables nk and $sf(k)$.

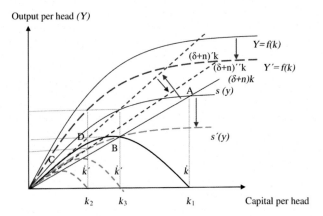

Figure 2.6 Impact of autonomous investments: a fall in income levels, a proportionally higher fall in savings and a rise in population lead to a shift of the steady state and fall of capital per head (or capital to labour ratio) k.

Fig. 2.6 illustrates the curves $f(k)$, $sf(k)$, and $(\delta + n)k$, starting from the point of zero production. The horizontal axis depicts k (capital per head) and the vertical $f(k)$, $sf(k)$, $(\delta + n)k$. The savings function $s(y)$ or $sf(k)$ will be at lower levels than $f(k)$ function. $(\delta + n)k$ is illustrated by a straight line, starting from the beginning of the axes, having as slope $\delta + n$.

In Fig. 2.6 we also illustrate the curve $\dot{k}$ as the difference between $sf(k)$ and $(\delta + n)k$, at every level of the ratio of capital to labor, k. It is $\dot{k} = sf(k)\text{-}(\delta + n)k$.

As discussed, what is known as the "golden rule" helps to find out which level of capital per worker is necessary to maximize consumption. This is the point where $\dot{k}$ (as defined) is maximized. The golden rule is found only at a particular saving rate, for a prespecified function of savings and output. Each economy has to seek for it (given its particular saving and output patterns), and it is not expected to gravitate around it automatically (Mankiw, 2003).

One cannot be absolute about the original predictions of the neoclassical model. For example, when savings fall, a new steady level will appear, at a lower capital per head level. This is seen in Fig. 2.6 of the neoclassical growth model, where savings (a function of y) reduce and the curve of savings shifts from $s(y)$ to $s'(y)$ (while, at the same time, consumption, i.e., the difference between Y and $s(y)$ increases), leading to a new point of intersection of the new savings function with $(\delta + n)k$ line. This is achieved when the curve of $\dot{k}[\dot{k} = sf(k) - (\delta + n)k]$, which represents capital to labor, simultaneously reduces, by shifting to the left, from $\dot{k}$ to $\dot{k}'$.

Cambridge's "capital controversy" has emphasized a limitation in the neoclassical model. It emphasized that there is a problem (a fallacy) in the composition of capital and that the aggregate production function cannot be simply the added sum of the individual production functions of each firm. The economic and technological homogeneity of capital goods was a point hard to accept by Joan Robinson and other proponents of the school of Cambridge (Jones, 1975). This is one of the most important, if not the most important critique exercised on neoclassical theory.

One should acknowledge further that several critiques have been exercised against the neoclassical model, its assumptions and the emphasis laid on technology and multifactor productivity, as opposed to multiple other growth factors, neglected in the model, which are important in the analysis and understanding of growth. "Solow's residual" has generated a prolific discussion against the model that strongly criticized its efficiency as a tool in explaining growth and the steady state. Another significant critique emphasized is that Solow's model is exogenous, as savings are exogenous. It also treated technology as exogenous. Such features pushed towards the creation of endogenous growth models that used microeconomic foundations for introducing the savings function and other features of the model. Furthermore, the life cycle hypothesis has been used to measure consumption, offering another potential explanation for consumption and savings behavior pattern, different from the analyses of marginal propensities of consumption and savings. However, if one wishes to remain within this particular analytical framework, before advancing the analysis in other levels, due to the significance it lays on capital and labor and its capacity to trisect growth across three main growth components, one of the main problems and a possible suggestion concerning the model's capacity and plausibility to accurately reflect economic outcomes may lie within a different path: a more appropriate incorporation of the above-mentioned distinction between induced and autonomous investment.

Going back to Fig. 2.6, the emphasis placed on autonomous investments will bring, apart from the fall in savings, a rise in population (or labor) and a fall in income levels finally attained. The rise in population is due to people's access to cheaper and free social goods, which improve their well-being and consequently affect state's demographics and immigration toward the country. The fall in income takes place as savings fall too. In Fig. 2.6, the rise in population is illustrated by a shift of $(\delta + n)k$ curve to the left (known as "capital widening"), from $(\delta + n)k$ to $(\delta + n)'k$. The fall in income is illustrated by a shift of the Y curve to the bottom. Thus, a new stability point is created that is no longer situated in B (as originally expected) but at C. Furthermore, a new curve that expresses the difference between $sf(k)$ and $(\delta + n)k$ is created, k' (that is no longer k). Note that point C does not guarantee a point of stability (depending on the relative movement/shift of Y, sY [or $sf(k)$] and $(\delta + n)k$ curves). It is hard to trace point C below (inside) the savings function $s'(y)$. To achieve a new level of stability, population should now reduce, due to emigration (illustrated by the shift of $(\delta + n)'k$ curve to $(\delta + n)'k$ (depicted in blue)). In such cases, a stability point is reached, at point D, which is now closer to point D (than C) and a new curve k' is created. Another possibility is, of course, that curve $(\delta + n)'k$ does not shift as much as illustrated in the figure.

The model is useful to understand that, ceteris paribus, economies become wealthier when the saving rate is high, depreciation is low, and productivity is high.

It is not developed for an open economy. For an economy that is progressively integrating in a common space, a fall in savings may result from rising consumption for imported goods that are not produced domestically.

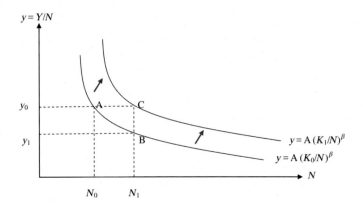

Figure 2.7 Average product of labor.

Assuming the presence of technology (or total factor productivity, TFP), one way to rewrite the neoclassical aggregate production function is in the form:

$$Y(t) = F(A(t), \ K(t), \ N(t))$$

where $K(t)$ is capital, $N(t)$ is labor, and $A(t)$ is considered to be technology (or TFP). Technology is considered to be free, and publicly available as a nonexcludable, nonrival good.[7]

We can also consider another formulation of the standard Solow model, as:

$$Y = z \, F(K, \ N)$$

where K is capital, N is population (or labor force L), and z is TFP.

As discussed, the model assumes CRS for the production function, such that $zY = F(zK, \ zN)$, for any positive number of z. The CRS means that if all inputs increase by a proportional factor, say z, all outputs increase by the same proportion, z. This is not incompatible with the law of diminishing marginal returns, since increasing one input by a positive proportional factor, and keeping another input constant, leads to less than proportional increase in output.

In Fig. 2.7, the average product of labor is depicted as a function of the population workforce (labour). The negative slope is due to diminishing returns, illustrated with a movement along the curve, e.g., from point A to point B. When capital stock rises, the average product of labor shifts up. If capital stock and labor increase in the same proportion, then the average product of labor remains constant (from A to C).

For N, the following equation holds, $N_{t+1} = (1 + t)N_t$

TFP is considered to be neutral in the model.

If we convert all variables to their per worker version, dividing by N we get $Y = z \, F\big(K/N, \ 1\big)$

---

[7] This assumption is very much similar to that used by Solow (1974), also found in Dasgupta and Heal (1974). See also in Baumgartner (2003).

By setting $k = K/N$ and after ignoring 1 (since it is a constant), we can simplify the equation as $y = zf(k)$ [where $f(k) = F(K,1)$].

Thus, dividing the production function by the size of workforce (N), we obtain a new expression, which associates per capital output to the availability of capital per worker.

$y = Y/N$ denotes per capital income and $k = K/N$ is capital to labour ratio.

One can express the original equation $y_t = A\left(Kt/Nt\right)^{\beta} \Leftrightarrow y_t = Ak_t^{\beta}$

Consider that the previously elaborated production function takes the form of a Cobb-Douglas production function:

$$Y = zK^{\alpha}N^{1-\alpha}$$

We assume TFP (depicted with z) to grow at a constant rate of growth γ, such that:

$$A_{t+1} = A_t(1 + \gamma), \quad \text{with} \ 1 < \gamma < 0$$

By assuming TFP to be labor-augmenting, we can also introduce it in the equation (as in Romer's model), turning the equation to:

$$Y = K^{\alpha}(AN)^{1-\alpha}$$

where $z = A^{1-\alpha}$.

This equation with labor-augmenting TFP can be expressed in per worker terms, if we divide both sides by AN

$$\tilde{y} = \frac{Y}{AN} = \frac{F(K, AN)}{AN}$$

Investments are given by equation:

$$I_t = S_t + (T_t - G_t) + NX_t \quad \text{(i)}$$

where

$$\begin{aligned}
S_t &= sY & \text{(ii)} \\
T_t &= T_0 + tY & \text{(iii)} \\
G_t &= G_0 + gY & \text{(iv)} \\
NX_t &= X_t - M_t & \text{(v)}
\end{aligned}$$

where S_t is savings, T_t taxes and G_t government expenses (all in time t), s is the marginal propensity to savings, t and g are the part of taxes and government expenses that associate to income respectively, T_0 and G_0 are the autonomous part of taxes and government expenses respectively, and NX_t are net exports in time t, calculated as the difference between exports, X_t, and imports, M_t.

Furthermore, X_t is a function of foreign income, Y_f, and of the exchange rate, R, while M_t is a function of domestic income, Y, of the exchange rate R, and of the marginal propensity to exports, μ, such that:

$$X_t = h(Y_f,\ Y,\ R) = \pi(Y) + \theta\big(Y_f,\ R\big) \bigg\}$$
$$M_t = M_0 + \mu(Y,\ R) = \xi(Y,\ R)$$

$$NX_t = X_t - M_t = h(Y_f,\ Y,\ R) - \xi(Y,\ R) \Leftrightarrow \bigg\}$$
$$NX_t = \pi(Y) + \theta\big(Y_f,\ R\big) - \{M_0 + \mu(Y,\ R)\}$$

Assuming Y_f, R both constant and letting a constant, C_0, such that $C_0 = \theta(Y_f, R) - M_0$, i.e., $NX_t = \pi Y - \mu Y + C_0$,

By replacing in Eq. (i) for I, and taking into account (ii), (iii), (iv), and (v) we get:

$$I_t = sY + T_0 + tY - G_0 - gY + \pi Y - \{C_0 + \mu Y\}$$

$$I_t = T_0 - G_0 - C_0 + sY + tY - gY + \pi Y - \mu Y$$

$$I_t = \big\{T_0 - (G_0 + C_0)\big\} + \{sY + tY - gY + \pi Y - \mu Y\}$$

$$I_t = \{T_0 - G_0 - C_0\} + \{(s + t + \pi - g - \mu)Y\} = I_0 + \varphi Y$$

By replacing $I_0 = \{T_0 - G_0 - C_0\}$ and $\varphi = s + t + \pi - g - \mu$,

We can then reach out of Eq. (i) the following $I_t = I_0 + \varphi Y$

This equation shows that I_t increases when the autonomous part of investments, I_0, increases and when s, t, and π increase. It decreases when g and μ increase.

So, whenever g, the non-autonomous part of government expenditure increases, income decreases.

Given that $I_t = I_0 + \varphi Y$, the capital accumulation equation (also known as the law of motion of capital), turns now to:

$$K_{t+1} = (1 - \delta)K_t + (I_0 + \varphi Y)$$

which, given that, as assumed, $Y = F(K_t,\ A_t N_t) = K_t^{\alpha}\ (A_t N_t)^{1-\alpha}$, turns to:

$$K_{t+1} = (1 - \delta)K_t + \{I_0 + \varphi\, F(K_t,\ A_t N_t)\}$$

If we convert everything into efficiency units of labor, by dividing by $A_t N_t$ both sides of the equation:

$$\frac{K_{t+1}}{A_t N_t} = (1 - \delta)\frac{K_t}{A_t N_t} + \frac{\{I_0 + \varphi\, F(K_t,\ A_t N_t)\}}{A_t N_t} \Leftrightarrow$$

$$\frac{A_{t+1} N_{t+1}}{A_{t+1} N_{t+1}}\frac{K_{t+1}}{A_t N_t} = (1 - \delta)\frac{K_t}{A_t N_t} + \frac{I_0 + \varphi\, K_t^{\alpha}(A_t N_t)^{1-\alpha}}{A_t N_t} \Leftrightarrow$$

$$\frac{(1+\gamma)A_t(1+n)N_t}{A_{t+1}N_{t+1}}\frac{K_{t+1}}{A_tN_t} = (1-\delta)\frac{K_t}{A_tN_t} + \frac{I_0 + \varphi\, K_t^\alpha(A_tN_t)^{1-\alpha}}{A_tN_t} \Leftrightarrow$$

$$\frac{(1+\gamma)A_t(1+n)N_t}{A_{t+1}N_{t+1}}\frac{K_{t+1}}{A_tN_t} = (1-\delta)\frac{K_t}{A_tN_t} + \frac{I_0}{A_tN_t} + \frac{\varphi\, K_t^\alpha(A_tN_t)^{1-\alpha}}{A_tN_t} \Leftrightarrow$$

$$\frac{(1+\gamma)A_t(1+n)N_t}{A_{t+1}N_{t+1}}\frac{K_{t+1}}{A_tN_t} = (1-\delta)\frac{K_t}{A_tN_t} + \frac{I_0}{A_tN_t} + \varphi\, K_t^\alpha(A_tN_t)^{-\alpha}$$

By setting:

$$\check{k}_t = \frac{K_t}{A_tN_t} \quad \text{and} \quad A_tN_t = \frac{K_t}{\check{k}_t}$$

we get:

$$(1+\gamma)(1+n)\check{k}_{t+1} = (1-\delta)\check{k}_t + \frac{I_0\check{k}_t}{K_t} + \frac{\varphi\, K_t^\alpha}{(A_tN_t)^\alpha} \Leftrightarrow$$

$$(1+\gamma)(1+n)\check{k}_{t+1} = (1-\delta)\check{k}_t + \frac{I_0\check{k}_t}{K_t} + \frac{\varphi\, K_t^\alpha}{\frac{(K_t)^\alpha}{(\check{k}_t)^\alpha}} \Leftrightarrow$$

$$(1+\gamma)(1+n)\check{k}_{t+1} = (1-\delta)\check{k}_t + \frac{I_0\check{k}_t}{K_t} + \varphi\, \check{k}_t^\alpha \Leftrightarrow$$

Subtracting from both sides $(1+\gamma)(1+n)\check{k}_t$ we get:

$$(1+\gamma)(1+n)(\check{k}_{t+1} - \check{k}_t) = \{1 - \delta - (1+\gamma+n+\gamma n)\}\check{k}_t + \varphi\, \check{k}_t^\alpha + \frac{I_0\,\check{k}_t}{K_t} \Leftrightarrow$$

$$(1+\gamma)(1+n)(\check{k}_{t+1} - \check{k}_t) = \varphi\, \check{k}_t^\alpha - \{(\delta+\gamma+n+\gamma n)\}\check{k}_t + \frac{I_0}{K_t}\check{k}_t$$

$$(1+\gamma+n+\gamma n)(\check{k}_{t+1} - \check{k}_t) = \varphi\, \check{k}_t^\alpha - \left(\delta+\gamma+n+\gamma n - \frac{I_0}{K_t}\right)\check{k}_t$$

By replacing $f(\check{k}_t) = \varphi\, \check{k}_t^a = (s + t + \pi - g - \mu)\check{k}_t^\alpha$ and $I_0 = (T_0 - G_0 - C_0)$

$$(1+\gamma+n+\gamma n)(\check{k}_{t+1} - \check{k}_t) = f(\check{k}_t) - \left(\delta+\gamma+n+\gamma n - \frac{I_0}{K_t}\right)\check{k}_t \qquad (2.5)$$

The curve appears to be exponential.

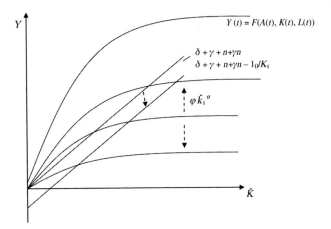

Figure 2.8 A potential investigation of the steady state in Solow's growth model.

For the first part of the right-hand side of Eq. (2.7), $\varphi \, \check{k}_t^{\alpha}$, where $0 < \alpha < 1$
the higher is α, the more the curve $\varphi \, \check{k}_t^{\alpha}$ is shifted upward and vice versa (the lower is α, the more the curve is shifted downward). Thus, the higher is α, the steady state is positioned more to the right, at the intersection of the two curves, in their graphical representation (Fig. 2.8).

But the curve's position also relates to φ. If φ rises, the curve $\varphi \, \check{k}_t^{\alpha}$ is shifted upward. If φ reduces, the curve is shifted downward.

Since $\varphi = s + t + \pi - g - \mu$, if μ and/or g rise, the steady state will tend to fall. On the contrary, the more s and/or t and/or π rise, the more φ will rise and the curve will be shifted on the opposite direction, upward.

Similarly, a careful interpretation of increases in autonomous investments I_0 has to be made. Such increases are likely to bring the increase of I_0/K_t, which is subtracted from $\delta + \gamma + n + \gamma n$.

The neoclassical Solow's model was presented so far, due to the emphasis that it places on capital accumulation as a driving force, apart from other reasons.[8] The diminishing marginal returns reveal that growth becomes weaker and weaker over time.[9] Several other elaborations of the neoclassical model can be followed. For example savings or depreciation can be capital-dependent.

Other models, such as the AK model (where K is capital and A is human capital), assumes that output per person is proportional to the capital stock. This assumption may lead an economy to grow but may also fully destabilize it.

---

[8] For an extended analysis in Solow's model and its various developments see in Sorensen and Whitta-Jacobsen (2005).
[9] Similar implications exist for Solow's model that includes human capital.

If we assume $f(k_t) = Ak_t$, then the growth rate Eqs. (2.3) and (2.4) that was used to find out the steady state are amended as follows:

$$s(Ak_t) - (\delta + n)k_t = 0$$

$$g(k_{t+1}) = s\frac{Ak_t}{k_t} - (\delta + n) = sA - (\delta + n)$$

Eq. (2.6) shows that two possibilities exist:

i. If $sA - (\delta + n) > 0$, the capital–labor ratio expands at constant growth rate and an economy's income grows forever, even without the assumption of exogenous technological progress (or TFP).

On the contrary, in Solow's model, diminishing returns to capital lead the economy to the steady state and growth depends on exogenous technological progress (or TFP). Growth is achieved temporarily and reduces, as the economy is led to the steady state. In the endogenous growth model, savings and investment can lead to growth.

ii. On the other hand side, if the depreciation rate, δ, is higher than sA, and $sA - (\delta + n) < 0$, then the capital stock reduces and the economy falls in a poverty trap.

Taking the example of the AK model, its graphical illustration (Fig. 2.9) reveals the problem of the possible divergence in the economy. The lines sy (of gross savings) and $(\delta + n)k$ never cross each other, since it is always $sA > (\delta + n)$.

Thus, while the AK model does not take into account technological progress (TFP) and attempts to explain the economic forces behind technological progress, the neoclassical growth model considers technology (or TFP) as the engine of growth.

The AK model is an endogenous growth model that is based on human capital theory. It is worth considering in the case of countries, like Greece, that have invested substantial amounts of funds on human capital. The theory suggests that

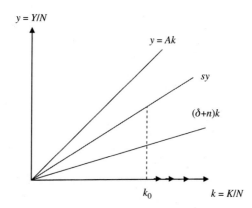

Figure 2.9 Graphical illustration of the AK model.

building on the AK model of growth is likely to lead an economy to a strong divergence path and destabilize it.

The analysis so far has revealed that the distinction between autonomous and induced investment should be considered more carefully and incorporated in growth models. As discussed, the neoclassical growth model emphasizes technological progress (or TFP) that it assumed to be exogenous but has not incorporated sufficiently the type of investment that it was treated uniformly, irrespectively of whether it is autonomous or induced. Furthermore, induced investment in not endogenous, in the vast majority of models that have historically been developed.

The neoclassical growth model has received a very strong critique from various angles. It has been considered to rely solely on the rationality of *homo economicus* who takes decisions purely on financial or economic grounds. *Homo economics* and his rationality have been contradicted to *homo socialis*, the example of a man that can take decisions by using not only financial but also social and other criteria and values.

The proliferation of critiques against the neoclassical model gave birth to numerous other models, most of them incorporating particular factors and acknowledging their significance. Examples of such factors are human capital, knowledge, R&D, learning, social and cultural factors. Endogenous growth theory aimed at endogenizing such growth factors in growth equations. The list of theoretically developed models is extended. Apart from the AK model, other models developed are Arrow's model that viewed learning-by-doing as endogenous to growth, one of its extensions designed by the Levhari−Sheshinksi model that emphasized knowledge and learning-by-doing, the King−Robson model, Romer's model on learning by investment or models that incorporate R&D and innovation (e.g., the Schumpeterian model), the models by Uzawa (1965) on human capital accumulation and by Lucas (1988), the Mankiw−Romer−Weil (1992) model, the product variety model, and various new growth theory models, for instance those taking into account social factors (Carillo, 2003) (for a description of several of these models see Aghion and Howitt, 2009; Salvadori, 2003).

New paths in economic thought were also opened by New Growth Theory, which questioned the sufficiency of the neoclassical growth equation. It investigated the prospect of noncompetitive markets, of a production function with increasing returns to scale, of externalities in the microunits, and of endogenous innovation (Hulten, 2001).

For some economists, the development of endogenous growth theory and its models has revealed the continuity and superiority of the neoclassical model against its rivals (Pomini, 2003).

The widely emphasized shift of economic growth theory and modeling toward endogenous growth theory and new growth theory was spurred by the dissatisfaction from the neoclassical growth model and the search for a credible explanation of the Solow's residual. The latter is the part of the neoclassical growth equation that remains unexplained and which has also been termed "TFP" or "multifactor productivity." It was attributed by Solow to technological change and progress (Solow, 1957). Denison (1972, 1979) and Jorgensen and Griliches (1967) debated on how much output can be explained by TFP and how much by capital formation (see in Denison, 1979; and Hulten, 2001).

Generations of economists have made extensive efforts to provide a plausible explanation of the Solow's residual. A voluminous literature was developed on its explanation, significance, usefulness, reconsideration, its association to capital or labor and other aspects related to it. Different causes of the TFP were suggested.

This discussion was spurred by the low levels of productivity in the more advanced states. A "worldwide productivity slowdown" was observed by several economists since the late 1970's. Solow's growth accounting framework was employed to calculate growth levels and it helped to realise that the levels of TFP kept falling (Valdés, 1999).

The speed of changes in technology during the last few decades and various difficulties encountered in measuring it, made difficult to analyze the contribution of Solow's residual. Certainly, part of Solow's residual should be attributed to technology, robotics, and organizational changes. Economic integration of states, and their participation in some forms of economic integration, might have also played a vital role. But would that be all? For Mankiw (1989) "Solow's residual need not be interpreted as evidence regarding exogenous technological disturbances."

From the present analysis and the evidence provided that follows, it is highly likely that a part of Solow's residual may be due to autonomous investments and the ignorance of the distinction between autonomous and induced investments. In the light of this finding, the whole critique on neoclassical theory (as well as the AK model) should be reconsidered, if not treated with skepticism.

Other economists suggested that TFP is not a theoretical concept per se (Hulten, 2001) and that, precisely as Abramovitz (1956) has argued, it is a "measure of our ignorance"; one that refers to our inability to fully understand and predict growth, at least through equations and quantitative terms only. Since economic phenomena are humane and subject to human action and choice, they may not be fully rationalized and explained by quantitative equations. A stochastic part of it may remain unexplained.

The measurement of TFP through Solow's residual have made economists all over the world sensitive in the question of the productivity of economies. A special emphasis was given in studying how economies will remain competitive, giving birth to a whole new debate on the concept of national competitiveness.

Another criticism is that the rationality of *homo economicus* is in reality bounded and his decisions actually constrained. Bounded rationality was espoused by behavioral approaches used in economics that place behaviorism and behavioral imitation above economic freedom and other forces driving economic growth and development. In societies, people are influenced by each other and behavior spreads, for instance consumer behavior and consumerism.

Institutions, networks, social norms, the social and cultural capital have all been considered to exercise substantial influence on growth, at a large extent (see for example Carillo, 2003).

2.1.6   On the theory and policy of competitiveness

2.1.6.1   Competitiveness: concept, measurement, and main challenges to consider

The word "competitiveness" derives from the word "competitive" that, according to Webster's Dictionary, means "of or involving competition; based on or determined by competition" (Webster's New World Dictionary, 1957). The noun-forming suffix of the English grammar "-ness" means "1. condition, quality, a state of being" or "2. a single instance of such as state, condition, quality or state" (Webster's New World Dictionary, 1957). Competitiveness is a recently created, thus a technical word, used mainly when referring to economies or businesses, mostly found in economic and business policy lexicons.

Existing literature on competitiveness forms around several themes. The most important are definitional issues, the question on which factors form, sustain, and improve competitiveness, its measurement, the building of relevant indexes, the policies associated with it, and the validity and usefulness of the concept.

Competitiveness is a concept with a relative meaning. It does not stand alone but always in relation to another (at least one) part(s) or component(s). For example the competitiveness of a national economy is related to and measured against that of other economies. Similarly the competitiveness of firms within an economy, national or regional, is related to and measured against that of other firms found in that economy (or another economy). The two (or more) parts or components have to be in some form of relation or state of competition. Hence, "competitiveness" refers to the degree or capacity of an—economic—partner to participate in a competitive environment with other, similar (and comparable) partners, which attributes to every partner a relevant state, condition, or quality of competitiveness. If he or she is not that competitive, his or her competitiveness is lower compared to that of others. Furthermore, there is no negative competitiveness, though it can be considered that a partner forced to exit a relation or state of competition has no competitiveness with regard to this state of competition. Hence, competitiveness is strictly a concept with a positive meaning, taking only positive values when measured (or in the worst case scenario a zero value).

The concept of competitiveness has been relatively recently theorized in economics. Its development aimed—among other reasons—at explaining how economies compete. For numerous reasons, economic theory has always been concerned and placed emphasis on the concept of competition that it is derived from. Similarly economics have always been concerned with the production of wealth in nations and their economic relations with other nations. Many studies and microeconomic theory itself have explained firm behavior, placed within the context of various forms of competition. However, such developments in the discipline of economics were made at business level and a gap was soon identified by economists and business theorists that was worth considering on what drives the capacity of states to compete, not only that of the firms contained in them.

The concept's continuous change over time appears to follow the great interest of some national economies for sustaining a growth impetus and their prospects of development. For example in the United States, where a Council of Competitiveness was created, composed of subcouncils focusing on particular themes regarding competitiveness, the concept was associated with productivity, the reduction of national trade deficits, the capacity of large US corporations to remain at the top of the list of business world-class leaders, and the rising or sustaining of high standards of living for its population.

In the prolific debate about the meaning of national competitiveness, some definitions were reached. Few of these were selected by Waheeduzzaman and Ryans (1996) as the most critical to consider. Competitiveness was identified as "the degree to which a nation can, under free and fair market conditions, produce goods and services that meet the tests of international markets while simultaneously maintaining or expanding real incomes of its citizens." It was therefore related to the international positioning of a nation (Report of the President's Commission on Industrial Competitiveness, 1985). Other definitions in the 1980s emphasized a country's "ability to create, produce, distribute and/or service products in international trade while earning rising returns on its resources" (Scott and Lodge, 1985: 3; see Waheeduzzaman and Ryans, 1996: 8). Others referred to a broader ability to "realize central economic policy goals, especially growth in income and employment, without running into balance of payments difficulties" (Faberger, 1988: 355). In the UK's policy view it was associated with the ability of a country's producers to "compete successfully in world markets and with imports in its own domestic market" (His Majesty's Treasury, 1983: 1, see Waheeduzzaman and Ryans, 1996: 8).

2.1.6.2 Competitiveness and international trade

National competitiveness was associated in the past mainly with exports and international trade (McGreehan, 1968). The removal of trade barriers over the last 30 years, through consecutive agreements on international trade progressively building a new system of free international trade and the global expansion of trade promoted through many changes across the international environment, has exposed domestic firms to international competition, enhancing their vulnerability and the levels of domestic competition in most states. Many concerns have been raised on the state's self-sufficient production, i.e., their actual capacity to produce goods and services and not to leave ample room for imports to cover their production needs. These concerns were also spurred by the increasing generation of new technologies, R&D research, their spillovers, and other technological advances that have driven growth and the restructuring of many economies and technological products, as well as by the advent of an age associated—more than any other before—with the use of information and communication technologies. Nation states are all now burdened with the need to cope with such changes and keep or enhance their capacity to produce across a range of industries, to sustain or increase their productivity and export their products, without at the same time undermining their standards of living nor worsen their terms of trade.

The relationship between competitiveness and trade varies, and various trade theories or views have been suggested that relate trade to the capacity of state to compete and sustain their competitiveness (Krugman, 1996). In the classic— Ricardian—view, states gain a comparative advantage when offering products and services that they produce using the factors of production offered in lower costs. The principal factor of production tested in the Ricardian model is labor. The lower labor costs, especially salaries, act as opportunity costs, moving production from one state to another, through trade (Krugman and Obstfeld, 2000). The states with lower labor costs in the production of particular goods and services gain a comparative advantage in this particular production. Trade leads nations to their production specialization, as labor used in domestic production moves from those industries where it is less productive to those where it is comparatively more productive (Krugman and Obstfeld, 2000). This process brings an industrial restructuring inside states. But it is not certain whether states will manage to achieve industrial specialization in a new industry. Removing industrial specialization from one industry does not necessarily bring industrial specialization in another. Several conditions should be first met, such as for example the creation of institutions supporting firms in one new, infant industry and providing information on production (as discussed in Best, 1990). In the Heckscher—Ohlin view it is the analogy of factors of production available and employed in states that drives trade. But the Leontief paradox proved that US's exports had a lower analogy of capital to labor than its imports, emphasizing the priority of labor costs, as in the Ricardian view, apart from the role of protection (more present at the time). This seeming paradox could also relate to the economies of scale created among domestic industries, forming an aggregate advantage of economies that are turned to a comparative advantage (Krugman and Obstfeld, 2000).

In general a larger, positive balance of trade is likely to indicate roughly a state's capacity to compete, the more it is extended on time.

However, trade is subject to exchange rates and associated with competition in price terms. Undermining the value of a currency is a temporary, technical reason for the creation of trade surpluses. Even though a large trade deficit could signal an economy's vulnerability, it could also derive from large foreign direct investments (Candace and Singh, 2000). Similarly, the case of Mexico in the 1980s that was forced to run large trade surpluses to repay the interests for its loans is an example of the limitation of the use of trade as a competitiveness indicator (Krugman, 1994). Trade balances can reveal export performance. This however is subject to trade barriers and decisions on supporting strategic trade, which are not uniform all around the world. Hence they may not reveal well the comparative state performance in trade. For all these reasons trade balances alone may be "inappropriate" for measuring state's competitiveness (Krugman, 1994).

Trade surpluses are not only subject to costs and prices, as Kaldor's empirical paradox has revealed. According to this paradox, Germany and Japan improved their world trade in the 1960s and early 1970s, while their prices and costs rose rather than decreased, as opposed to the United States and the United Kingdom that deteriorated their position while their prices and costs decreased (Kaldor, 1978).

The relation of trade with competitiveness depends on whether trade is a zero-sum or a positive-sum game. In the former case that is less accepted nowadays, states increasing trade surpluses achieve it against other states and so their relative competitiveness would be higher. But if trade is a positive-sum game (as pertained in Krugman, 1994; Krugman and Obstfeld, 2000; and many others), a good trade record of a state does not necessarily reflect the weaknesses of another, especially in families of nations, such as the EU is considered.

The Balassa–Samuelson theorem, which states that productivity growth varies more by country in the traded goods sector (rather than in the nontraded goods sector), relates state-level competitiveness, measured through productivity, back again to traded goods and state's international trade. Integrating the nontradable goods sector in international comparisons on competitiveness helps to move away from static analyses on competitiveness based on trade only and to view the broader picture of an economy.

Both the Balassa–Samuelson theorem and the emphasis placed on the role of labor by trade theory highlight the significance of labor and its productivity.

2.1.6.3   Competitiveness and industrial change

The discussion on competitiveness has developed in the last 30 years, simultaneously with the remarkable changes occurring in the private sector and its restructuring across the world. The latter relates to increasing globalization and international trade, the negative effects of a de-industrialization process and a global production shift transforming the world economy, in particular industries, with a parallel internationalization in services. The debate on competitiveness is influenced by the particular structure of economies.

Part of the competitiveness literature focuses on industrial competitiveness.

Since the 1980s the fall in growth rates of the most advanced economies, as opposed to those in emerging economies, raised a concern for the progressive loss of their capacity to compete and doubts over whether they remained capable of selling their products in international markets. New managerial, organizational, administrative, and other business principles, enhanced by the support of state-level authorities facilitating and catalyzing industrial change, were believed to have the power to reshape the geography of international production to the benefit of states promoting such changes and the resulting industrial restructuring (Best, 1990; Auerbach, 1988). A new form of competition was argued to emerge (Best, 1990), against which industrial growth ought to be an answer, at least for industries where states kept an international lead (Dertouzos et al., 1989).

The theme of new competition was also referred to the need to reorganize production, introduce bottom-up managerial techniques, new organizational values and principles, and a regulatory framework that would help the transition from massive production and the paradigm of Fordism to new, softer forms of support and regulatory frameworks that reduce wages and enhance productivity (Best, 1990).

De-industrialization and the reduced significance of some industries made the question of industrial growth very relevant to national economic performance. To various views, competitiveness became synonymous with industrial competitiveness, i.e., the capacity of specific industries to compete, especially in manufacturing and services. This capacity could be enhanced through industrial policies. It necessitated the spread of competition and rivalry, the opening of markets, the provision of incentives, the development of regulatory authorities and specific institutions supporting growth (Best, 1990; Porter, 1998). The industrial structure of the economy could affect competitiveness. A clearer distinction between competitiveness and industrial policies and a more concrete turn to the latter could have helped to improve the former (Agraa, 1997).

On the other hand side, competitiveness was associated with the role of larger firms (Chesnais, 1986), especially those having exporting activity. Such firms having to compete on the international scene have also to enhance their competing capacity. Their structure, organization, strategies could affect the growth of larger firms and that of a nation (Porter, 1998). The changing international environment that constantly exposes domestic firms to international competition and enhances the levels of domestic competition, raises a debate on which factors are necessary for firms to become or remain competitive on the international scene and which industrial changes are needed to sustain or create a national advantage in producing and selling products, while keeping up with changes all over the world (Auerbach, 1988; Best, 1990).

Even if many studies have explained before firm competitiveness and behavior from a microeconomic point of view, the microeconomic concept does not suffice to explain why and how the entire economies of states compete, not to mention their collaboration tendency. State-level competitiveness is argued to be different from that of competitiveness for nations (Krugman, 1994; Candace and Singh, 2000; and others). The Coke−Pepsi rivalry is different from the competition among any two nations, where various forms of competition and collaboration are formed (Krugman, 1994). Thus, a microeconomic approach on competitiveness differs from an approach focusing exclusively on macroeconomic factors.

2.1.6.4 More complex views on competitiveness

The term "national competitiveness" is constantly changing meanings and adjusting over time. In the past it was mostly associated with trade, the balance of payments, price competition, the costs of domestic labor, those of production, as well as with nonprice factors (McGreenan, 1968). But this concept appeared to have changed and theorized.

A prolific academic debate has recently emerged on the significance of competitiveness and the related policy prescription. Several disagreements were expressed between proponents of competitiveness and its theorization on the one side, and those arguing its ambiguity or evasiveness on the other (see for example the dialog between Burton, 1994 or Preeg, 1994 and Krugman, 1994, respectively). For some academics, even though larger nations compete for getting larger shares in both national and international markets (Thurow, 1992), they also seek to create various forms of collaboration and association, which are a valuable asset at the international economy (Krugman, 1994).

One outcome of this academic debate was to relate competitiveness with economic development and changes occurring in state economies and at the international level. Though plenty of views have been expressed, we can consider a side of proponents to have suggested that competitiveness relates to economic growth, development, and the standards of living in a certain economy, at a certain period of time (Aigigner, 2006a, b; Grilo and Koopman, 2006). This view had brought a more enriched view in the analysis on economic competitiveness. Indeed, more modern international comparisons among states incorporate such aspects as the role of institutions, infrastructure, health and primary education, macroeconomic environment, higher education and training, goods market efficiency, labor market efficiency, financial market development, technological readiness, market size, business sophistication, and innovation (Schawb, 2011).

More complex views on competitiveness attempt to incorporate various aspects of the economy when analyzing the concept. In Porter's view competitiveness is composed of several aspects, forming the sides of a diamond (Porter, 1998). These sides are the factor conditions, the demand conditions, the firm strategy, structure, and rivalry, and the related and supported industries. This is an attempt to synthesize within the same framework the microeconomic with the macroeconomic factors influencing competitiveness. Despite taking this more complex view, Porter highlights the value of productivity (Porter, 1998).

Competitiveness has been associated with productivity. On the one hand lie those views suggesting productivity to be one important—but a single—factor affecting competitiveness, even at the business level (Dertouzos et al., 1989). Other views argue that national competitiveness relates to productivity (Porter, 1998; Krugman, 1994; Dollar and Wolf, 1993) or that it is even a "poetic" way to emphasize productivity and highlight its significance, at least in the cases of reduced trade (Krugman, 1996). Competitiveness is also associated with TFP, by the use of relevant indexes (Dollar and Wolf, 1993). This reminds one of the emphasis placed by the neoclassic analysis on the significance of TFP. Several empirical works agree that state-level competitiveness is achieved by enhancing productivity (Dollar and Wolf, 1993; Dertouzos et al., 1989; Durand and Giorno, 1987) or increasing investing capacity (Oughton, 1997). Yet, the competitive advantage of an industry depends not only on productivity but on domestic labor costs and salaries (Krugman and Obstfeld, 2000). This association between competitiveness and productivity is generally captured through unit labor cost indexes.

2.1.6.5 Measuring competitiveness: the use of indicators and relevant problems

Historically, various indicators have been used for measuring competitiveness. Durand and Giorno (1987) enumerate several of these: producer or wholesale prices, consumer prices, GDP deflators, export prices, unit labor costs and exchange rates. They also discuss their drawbacks (Durand and Giorno, 1987). Such drawbacks relate to the lack of comparable data, their reference to goods and services which are not subject to international competition, a limited conceptualization of firm profits,

Measures of competitiveness should meet some criteria. They should be constructed by data that allow international comparisons and cover all sectors and markets exposed to competition (Durand and Giorno, 1987).

Two different institutions provide a methodology for calculating national competitiveness. These are the WEF and the International Institute of Management Development. The WEF progressively enriched its view on competitiveness, as found in a series of consecutive Global Competitiveness Reports. In the earliest versions,[10] these reports identified competitiveness in relation to eight major factors: domestic economic strength, internationalization, government, finance, infrastructure, management, science and technology, and people (Oral and Chabchoub, 1996; Waheeduzzaman, 2002). The WEF gave later more emphasis to openness, institutions, and labor as competitiveness factors (Waheeduzzaman, 2002).[11] The most recent WEF's report, developed by a group of world known economists, incorporated 12 "pillars": institutions, infrastructure, health and primary education, macroeconomic environment, higher education and training, goods market efficiency, labor market efficiency, financial market development, technological readiness, market size, business sophistication, and innovation (Schawb, 2011).

By constantly changing over time the calculation method of competitiveness indexes, these reports make very difficult any comparisons in international competitiveness levels over the years. Within a few years the countries included in the list of international competitiveness reposition themselves at 10 or 20 positions below their initial, without domestic or peripheral economic changes to excuse such significant replacements. Similarly, the inclusion of countries in the list (not included before for various reasons) creates another comparability problem. For example, when comparing the list of competitiveness index between 2003−2004 and 2011−2012 we identify cases such as Ghana falling from 71st to 114th position or Paraguay falling from 95th to 122nd position. This means that, practically, every 3 years these countries fall 10 different positions, while we should rather expect the competitive position of a country to remain similar over a shorter period of time.

Furthermore, problems can be raised with the significance attributed to particular factors. The horizontal weighting of factors or "pillars" (all having an equal weight) does not create any particular hierarchy of competitiveness factors. The significance of labor is practically undermined, by introducing other factors, largely discussed in economic theory to relate to economic growth. Similarly, exchange rates and the particular role of public administration and bureaucracy are ignored, despite their effects upon growth and trade.

The competitiveness index is also sensitive on personal opinions and statements, as collected in surveys addressed to business managers and analysts in the countries

---

[10] These reports were first developed in collaboration by these two institutions, WEF and IMD.
[11] The factors remained the same in the World Competitiveness Yearbook (WCY) produced by the IMD.

themselves that are used to build some of the competitiveness factors. Even though weights are applied, a significant level of subjectivity is associated with their statements. Similarly, the choice of weights used is arbitrary and could provide a different outcome, if changed.

While these indexes exploit the surveys to business managers, they do not make use of any financial or employment growth measures at the micro/firm level, for example, with regard to SMEs or larger firms. The latter, by taking into account that competitiveness relates to businesses and their internationalization, is a more objective measure to be considered. This could have been the case at least for the industries where an industrial competitive index is absent.

Moreover, building the index is subject to the accuracy of data provided by national authorities.

Hence, the following conclusions are reached with regard to these competitiveness indexes: despite efforts made and the improvements achieved over time, they remain a subjective measure of ambiguous value that, most importantly, create ambiguity for the concept of competitiveness itself. Even though enriched to incorporate various aspects of the economy that are important for its growth and development, they do not offer an hierarchy of factors, avoid the weighting among their components, create a misleading hierarchy of countries in a ranking relation (two countries that differ one position from each other may have remarkably different standards of living), and are generally sensitive to various choices concerning the factors composing them. Changes made in the measurement methods over time undermine comparability efforts, while similarly this is made with the inclusion of new countries leading to re-rankings.

Measuring competitiveness with unit labor costs, real or nominal exchange rates would have brought a ranking of countries with poorer countries (having lower unit labor costs for example) in better positions than wealthier.

These issues highlight further the ambiguity of the concept of competitiveness.

2.1.7 Investment under EU Cohesion and Agricultural Policy

Greece's crisis helps to raise several doubts whether past and present investment policies, both at EU and the country level, have managed to bring its sustainable growth and development sufficed and to enhance the competitiveness of the Greek economy. Before analysis the the policies followed, one needs to understand few basic points for the context of EU Cohesion Policy and its associated EU agricultural policy.

2.1.7.1 EU Cohesion Policy

In the EU, investment planning and strategy is subject to a variety of common regulations and various planning requirements. In less advanced spaces, common regional and cohesion policies are pursued that allow development and resource reallocation, based on the use and exploitation of common budget funds. These funds are matched with domestic, public or private, funds, acting in essence as foreign investments.

In states undergoing structural change in the EU, domestic investments are framed by three main aspects: the structuring of common EU budget and availability of funds, various EU-wide promoted policy priorities and agendas, and domestic, state-level policy priorities. The common EU budget acts as an EU-wide financial and fiscal instrument. It is an instrument for implementing EU level resource exploitation, allocation, and redistribution both in geographical and sectoral priorities, in policy areas such as transport, energy, communication, environmental protection, agriculture, competitiveness, science, research, and territorial cohesion. It is scheduled on the basis of multiannual financial frameworks and comprises funds devoted to each of the common economic policies followed. These funds are allocated to each state. Each state has the obligation to provide revenues toward the budget. The balance of payments minus receipts for each state provides its net contribution.

The design of common EU policy priorities, historically influenced by various factors, aims at facing contemporary challenges in every historical and programming period. The origins of EU Cohesion and Regional Policy date back to 1975, to the first concrete effort to implement regional policies at the common EC level, through the creation of the European Regional Development Fund (ERDF). In the 1980s, the rather premature integration phase was associated with a shift from traditional regional support schemes of national origin that emphasized single programs until 1984 (funded by Community Funds), to the building-up of the Integrated Mediterranean Programmes (IMPs or MIPs), from 1984 to 1988. Their necessity sprung out of the blooming prospect for already integrated regions in the Mediterranean area (in France, Italy, and Greece) and the urgent need to compete in the integrated, common space, especially after the prospective enlargement toward the Iberian peninsula.

The contribution of MIP was twofold. On the one hand, they promoted further the scope of the CAP and, on the other, they provided an understanding that a more integrated framework is required for intervention, made at the regional and peripheral level; one that takes into account various integration targets and is extended beyond the strict level of nation states (since both Italy and France were beneficiaries of MIP). Greece's accession at first and that of Spain and Portugal, secondly, have raised regional disparities. As a response, both the Commission's 1985 White Paper, which first emphasized the need and tools for completing market integration, and the 1986 Single European Act, have paved the ground for the first major Reform of the Structural Funds (ERDF, ESF, and FEOGA-G), in 1989, by allocating 68 BECUs from the EU budget (Inforegio, 2016; Maraveyas, 1994).[12]

---

[12] At the time, Jacques Delors, an insightful French politician at the Commission's presidency, realized what has become a general thread lying behind common EU policies later, the need to provide common solutions to common problems.

Signed in 1986, the Single European Act referred to article 130A for the promotion of "harmonious development" and "economic and social cohesion" in the Community. This decision signaled the end of a long period of ignorance for the need to correct territorial imbalances and the beginning of a new era of integration for the EC.[13]

Five main targets were introduced in EU Regional and Cohesion Policy, the primary of which was the promotion of development and structural adjustment of the less advanced regions.[14] Fund allocation per target and program was decided, as well as the basic principles for the selection of regions (75% of average GDP of the Community), the limits of community support per target were set and specific programming principles were imposed.[15] Hence, significant amounts were directed to the least advanced regions and geographical concentration of interventions was promoted. It was also decided that the strength of financial support should double by the end of the first programming period, in 1993. Co-funding structural actions by adding the Community's funds to national funds was agreed, in partnership with states (Andreou and Maraveyas, 2007). The new integrated programming logic emphasized a horizontal approach, the principles of multiannual planning and a theoretical approach of endogenous development (Andreou and Maraveyas, 2007).

All least advanced countries had to strictly conform to this particular programming logic and to identify financial resources and programs that could promote their economic and social restructuring. This medium-term programming logic has excluded a possible reallocation of resources toward other directions throughout each period, which would have benefited different stakeholders (e.g., supporting firms in particular sectors). It has also excluded the chance to quickly reschedule and readjust policies in times of crisis. Despite these points, it was later assessed to bring added value in policy and programming on a regional level, effectiveness and improved governance of the delivering system, as well as the strengthening of management structures and their accountability (Mairate, 2006).

In the 1990s, the interest to lay down more solid foundations for deeper integration and for the common currency union was associated with strengthening structural and cohesion policy by devoting 200 BECUs via Structural Funds in nation states.[16] The Edinburgh Council decided to add new points to the previous

---

[13] In the 1988 Cecchini Report, Delors referred also to the promotion of actions targeting at economic and social cohesion and the development of less developed regions to an extent comparable to that of the Marshall plan.

[14] The rest of the targets were: (2) Converting regions, border regions or part of regions seriously affected by industrial decline (including employment areas and urban communities), (3) combating long-term unemployment, (4) facilitating the integration of young people, (5a) speeding up the adjustment of agricultural structuring and (5b) promoting development of rural areas.

[15] These principles were (1) concentration (the actions had to concentrate on a limited number of targets), (2) partnership (all stages of programming had to take place in close collaboration and partnership among the Commission, national, regional, and local authorities), (3) programming (single programs are avoided and multiannual frameworks should be followed) and (4) the additionality (Structural Funds are not substituting national funds but adding to them) (Andreou and Maraveyas, 2007).

[16] An initial amount of BECUs 168 decided in December 1992, by the European Council.

programming experience in target setting, the expansion of the programming period (from 5 to 6 years), the introduction of compulsory ex ante and ex post assessments, changes in the selection procedures for targets 2 and 5b, expansion of targets 5a to fisheries with the creation of the Financial Instrument for Fisheries Guidance, the upgrading of Community Initiatives through a greater involvement of national authorities, the enhancing of partnership and the clarification of conditions for securing additionality (Andreou and Maraveyas, 2007).

Finally, the completion of the Single Market in 1993, the Treaties of Maastricht (1993) and Amsterdam (1999) reaffirmed and prioritized economic cohesion policies for less advanced areas. The Maastricht Treaty introduced the subsidiarity principle, launched the Cohesion Fund and the Committee of the Regions. It also extended the scope of the ESF.

The creation of the Cohesion Fund, whose mission was to finance major infrastructure projects that would promote market integration and projects on the environment and the SMEs (Inforegio, 2016), was the outcome of a compromise achieved between the member states and the Commission. In the early 1990s, the Spanish government had brought into negotiation in the European Council a proposal which, insightfully, diagnosed the need to relate the prospect of Monetary and Political unification with further enhancing solidarity in public finance and recommended the creation of an Interstate Compensation Fund to promote such a direction by focusing on the creation of physical and human resources necessary for achieving cohesion. The Commission and the governments of France and Germany realized the necessity of an additional support mechanism and agreed to introduce the Cohesion Fund, geographically more extended, since it would support areas whose GDP per head was at 90% of the EC average, leaving however aside a potential enrichment of its role (Andreou and Maraveyas, 2007).

Due to fears expressed for permanent problems of instability in national economies, the 1999 Reform of Structural Funds have allocated €213 billion between 2000 and 2006 (Inforegio, 2016).

In this period, management, decentralization, and subsidiarity in programming were requested and increasing the Commission's role was limited to defining and controlling the general direction of structural policy principles, while assuming responsibility for them (Andreou and Maraveyas, 2007). In the 2000s, in view of the enlargement, the EC realized the necessity to increase the concentration of intervention of Funds, to simplify and decentralize structural programming, and to enhance cost-effectiveness, as expressed in Agenda 2000 (EC, 1997). The 2000 Lisbon agenda emphasized growth, competitiveness, and infrastructure building. In the next decade, it was followed by the "Europe 2020" strategy that prioritized smart, sustainable, and inclusive growth across the European territory, thereby emphasizing a partial shift toward energy sustainability, resource efficiency, the environment, and research and innovation. In the 2007−2013 programming period, €347.5 billion were allocated in Structural Funds for development of the least advanced regions, the highest record of resources.

2.1.7.2 EU Common Agricultural Policy

Common Agricultural Policy represents one of the oldest in operation systems of protection and regulatory intervention in the EC. It results from an understanding that agriculture is based on living organisms, is highly dependent on the environment and is characterized from extended production uncertainty and high seasonality due to the biological character of production that results in underemployment of production factors. Agricultural production can be quite idiosyncratic, being composed of many small production units, scattered around the agricultural land, with different production conditions, cost, access to information, diffusion of innovation, and coordination of the various ambitions of farmers and people occupied in it (Papageorgiou, 1995).

Originally, the Treaty of Rome (1957) set the following targets for agriculture (article 39): (1) increasing productiveness, through development of technical progress, *rational exploitation* of production and optimum use of production factors, especially of the labor force; (2) guaranteeing a sustainable standard of living for producers; (3) stabilizing markets; (4) guaranteeing the supplying; and (5) securing reasonable prices in the supply of goods to consumers.

During the 1980s, CAP was scheduled on the basis of a protection scheme offering the chance for producers to sell their own production to Community at the low level of an intervention price if prices were not improving in the market. The purpose of the scheme was to provide producers with sufficient income, avoid agricultural business failures, and also increase intracommunity trade and exchange in agricultural products. The system benefited producers, created autonomy, but also brought increasing production surpluses ("mountains of butter" or milk), as increases in consumption did not follow increases in production. Surpluses would require subsidies to be exported. Following the 1985 Green Book, and as efforts to restrain increases in institutional prices had not brought a permanent result, the CAP underwent a phase of restructuring by the late 1980s. In 1988, the Commission introduced some motives that were named as "stabilizers" for CAP, namely the set-aside, extensive farming, a shift toward other cultivations, and an early retirement.

In the early 1990s, the limited application and effect of stabilizers, the pressures exercised from international agreements reached through GATT, as well as the prospect of eastern enlargement brought some new changes (Papageorgiou, 1995). Most of the CEE countries faced strong inflationary problems and a system of income support based on prices would have accentuated the problem of inflation and finally failed to support producers (EC, 1996). The application of MIP and the introduction of structural support policies that focused also on agricultural areas provided many opportunities for enhancing and diversifying the income prospects of the farmers. The new measures decided in the Reform of CAP in May 1992 aimed at reducing prices of agricultural products, the decoupling of subsidies from production (as a way to compensate from income losses due to price reductions), and the imposition of controls in production, through compulsory set-aside, the association of the number of animals to pasture land, and through quotas (Papageorgiou, 1995; CEC, 1992).

A few main problems had to be considered: (1) The problem of small agricultural land size, which increases slowly and only after the merging of existing land and/or the abandoning of land by farmers; (2) the problem of dramatic and constant over the years reduction of agricultural labor; as well as (3) the problem of fiscal constraints and requirements within which CAP Reforms had to be placed (Fennell, 1997).

Agenda 2000 deepened the reform process and enlarged the scope of CAP toward the far-reaching aim of rural development that comprised aspects of improvement of targets beyond modernization of agricultural farms, greater sensitivity toward agro-environmental causes and policy, and changes in structural policy in rural areas (Maraveyas, 2000). The directions were to increase competitiveness in agriculture through price reductions, to increase the interest of consumers (in quality and food security terms), to place priority in total rural development through income stabilization, to increase environmental sensitivity and support of biological ways of production, and to create complementary and alternative incomes in rural areas (Maraveyas, 2007).

The midterm review of CAP in 2002 provided an orientation for CAP across the targets of a competitive agricultural sector, of production methods that would support environmentally friendly, quality products that satisfy public needs, a fair standard of living and income stability for agricultural community, diversity in various forms of agriculture promoted, the maintenance of visual amenities and support of rural communities, the simplification of policies and the sharing of responsibilities among Commission and member states, and the justification of support through the provision of services that the public expects farmers to provide (CEC, 2002: 2).

These measures were not combined with policies in support of marketing, promotion, and web advertising of products in European markets, which remained an important problem for peripheral countries like Greece (Chryssochoidis and Blouchos, 2003).

2.1.8   A few comments on EU Cohesion Policy, management, and organizational learning: a reference to Senge's theory

The EU Cohesion Policy was turned into a principal EU policy for the promotion of economic and social investments in less advanced regions and states, along with the CAP. It is however subject to changes in promoted targets, of a differential focus and structure. It is based on the structuring of the common edifice of the EU at each historical period, the degree of integration achieved, the promoted enlargements and the concerns for their potential effects, different national development priorities, various compromises achieved—especially at the EU summit level—the nature and perception about existing common problems, the advancement of new policy approaches and policies, the availability of tools and funds—including the limitations related to them. Furthermore, since it takes place within a medium-term time period, it cannot be considered to have a long-term character and perspective, as policies may differ significantly from one period to another. All these parameters create a dynamic environment of continuous change, the outcome of which, in policy terms, may not be necessarily the most desirable.

The EU Cohesion Policy has set a development paradigm, generally considered successful for its effects on regional growth and convergence, even though it is subject to institutional operation (Kehagia, 2013). Irrespective of how it is assessed, the extended in time application of EU Cohesion Policy creates self-reinforcing economic development paths that are based on national, historical processes of capital accumulation and are sustained not only by economic and financial but also by institutional, social, and technological factors. These are likely to change through "shocks" or accidents or other catalytic actions placed in operation.

Implementing the internal market and building-up monetary unification through the assistance of Cohesion and agricultural policy, while promoting competition and competitiveness policies, may encounter two types of problems and difficulties: those resulting from a fragmented policy approach of the Commission and those resulting from general factors inhibiting the development of specific Community policies (Lavdas and Mendrinou, 1995). The last category may result from efforts of the EU states to protect their own interests.

Several important policies were neglected at common state level for an extended period of time, such as policies on small businesses (Lavdas and Mendrinou, 1995). Negative externalities of the integration process have brought concerns about their absence. One may ask why ignorance about such policies has not been mixed with cautiousness?[17] For example, in the case of EU small business policies, hitherto applied in states by aiming at domestic pacification and indirect protection of larger firms (Berger and Piore, 1980, quoted in Lavdas and Mendrinou, 1995: 175), the EU Commission realized their significance only in the 1990s, while an intense process of restructuring in the SME sector was already taking place in some of the most integrated states. Furthermore, in the late 1990s, the Commission, rather than promoting further national industrial policies by building on common industrial policies elements, decided to emphasize state-level competition and competitiveness policies. Such a shift was theoretically informed by a respective shift in academic literature,[18] as similarly this was the case with a more recent shift toward sustainability, green engineering, and smart policies, without an element of differentiation for economies with more elementary development needs. One could wonder if "dressing" the "costume" of policies with the

---

[17] As discussed, the OECD now emphasizes more the need to apply small business policies along with infrastructure policies.

[18] Spurred by the works of Best, M., 1990. The New Competition: Institutions of Industrial Restructuring. Harvard University Press, Harvard. and Porter, M., 1990. The Competitive Advantage of Nations: Creating and Sustaining Superior Performance. The Free Press, New York, and the prolific academic debate on competitiveness.

most updated theories and theoretical debates suffices to promote development in states of different stages of economic development and integration, without considering all the necessary aspects of planning and programming requirements. The uniformity of development direction is likely to lead to a reform "fatigue," forming "states-laboratories" that simply experiment in the application of new policies: Is the continuous organizational rescheduling of policies a feasible and viable development direction?

The management of EU cohesion policies requires not just economic programming but also the application of the remaining managerial principles, namely organization, control, and leadership.

Expanding a learning capacity is required for organizations involved in implementing EU Cohesion Policy. However, as Senge (1990) explains for the learning ability of organizations in general, every organization learns through team learning, the sharing of a common vision in the members involved in it, as well as a systematic element in the operation of its projects and programs. According to Senge (1990) employees should also have the opportunity to reach a "personal mastery." This is not advanced though in state-level organizations involved in EU Cohesion Policy, when continuous organizational amendments and constant replacements of executives and employees in charge of its application take place. If most of these conditions (the "disciplines" discussed in Senge's theory) are not met, organizational learning, which in this case refers to the capacity of whole states to apply a range of policies, often quite complex, is not advanced and aims are not reached. What is more organizational learning is significantly undermined by subcontracting substantial organizational work, required in the learning process, in external consulting.

At the top of all these, ex post assessments at program and state-level mysteriously disappeared after 1999. This was made at a time when they were mostly needed, since the setting-up of the monetary union required the effective and judicious correction of significant programming and organizational mistakes. As far as leadership is concerned (which is a last discipline in Senge's analysis), this is not by definition always present, as it relates to political power and its use. Leaders could have helped to integrate the outcome of various assessments and create the more general picture of problems and mistakes, to implement various controls required, identify where programs become the object of exploitation, and to take decisions about adjusting to organizational weaknesses.

Finally, the allocation of great amounts of funds is bound to cause political conflicts for these amounts, expressed through politics, political instability, division, and enmity. It is important to be aware of this eroding power of resources, especially occurring for resources not produced domestically, and which may require a series of institutional arrangements, such as regulatory authorities or the setting-up of ad hoc institutions, and independent authorities.

Analysis of the deeper causes of the Greek crisis

3

3 The allocation of EU Funds in Greece

3.1 Amounts and levels of invested expenditure

Greece is an EU state that kept its structural support status over the decades. From 1989 until 2013, four programming periods took place under EU Regional and Cohesion policy support and guidance: the first (1989—94), known as the 1st Community Support Framework; the second, of the 2nd C.S.F. (1994—99); the third, of the 3rd C.S.F. (2000—06); and the fourth, of the 2007—13 National Strategic Reference Framework (N.S.R.F.), when a part of its territory was structurally supported. The last programming period is the current one (2014—20). During all these periods, EU funds were matched with Greek national expenditure—together composing public expenditure—and with private expenditure.

The Community's contribution remained the most important component of total and public expenditure over these years (Fig. 3.1). More than half of the funds invested from 1989 until 2013 (54.2 out of €100.1 billion) were provided by the EU. National expenditure was less than half of that amount (€23.9 billion), approximately €1.5 billion more than total private (€22.04 billion). For the 1989—2013 period alone, the total expenditure of €100.1 billion is proportionately divided into 23.9% of national expenditure, 54.1% community expenditure, and 22% of private sector contribution. Public sector expenditure accounts for 78% of total expenditure.

From 1989 to 2006, the Community's expenditure more than doubled in every programming period, reaching almost €23.8 billion in the 2007—13 period in Fig. 3.1.[1] This does not reflect simply the determination, willingness, and efforts made by the Community to support the Greek economy but also the association of financial support to each state's economic performance. This is also illustrated in the next programming period, when the Community expenditure falls because the Greek GDP reduces.

Public expenditure represented more than 91% in the 1989—93 programming period. It then fell approximately to 71% in the following period and increased afterwards to 76% and 81% in the 2000—06 and 2007—13 periods, respectively. On the other hand side, the private sector contributed with less than one-fourth of funds in all but the second programming period, when it reached its highest contribution at 29%.

From 1989 to 2013, the EU invested €2.2 billion per year, Greece invested €957.5 million per year and the private sector barely exceeded a contribution

---

[1] Deflated prices as explained in **Figure**.

Funding the Greek Crisis. DOI: https://doi.org/10.1016/B978-0-12-814566-1.00003-3

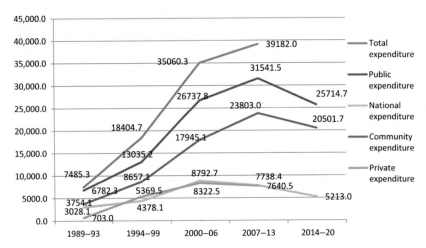

Figure 3.1 Levels of total, public, national, community, and private expenditure in five
programming periods (1989−93, 1994−99, 2000−06, 2007−13 and 2014−20).
Source: Data for the four programming periods were extracted from Oikonomou et al., 2010:
241 and originally processed by the Ministry of Finance and Economics. For the 2014−20
period, data were collected from www.espa.gr and are not final. *Other notes*: (1) After 1989,
the Mediterranean Integrated Programmes (implemented in the second half of 1980s) were
integrated in the 1st C.S.F. (2) In the 3rd C.S.F., the financing of €3.3 billion from the
Cohesion Fund and Community Initiatives (current prices) were not included (also excluded
in the original dataset). (3) Prices in original dataset were turned to constant, using the
harmonized consumer price index (AMECO series ZCPIH, 2015 = 100), BECUs in the 1st
and 2nd C.S.F., B€ in the 3rd, 4th and 5th (1 ECU = 1 Euro). The base years selected were
1994 (for 1989−93, in the absence of data before 1994), and for the rest of the programming
periods a yearly average was created for the consumer price index for each programming
period (61.93 for 1994−99 period, 79.03 for 2000−06, 97.96 for 2007−13 and an average of
100.59 for the 2014−17 part of for the 2014−20 period). *Note that sums are lower if
calculated by using HCPI for the initial year of each period.*

of €881 million per year. Total expenditure was €4 billion per annum, almost multiplied five times from the first to the last period.

For the full period 1989−2020, the amount contributed by the Community
reaches €74.6 billion, national expenditure is at €29.2 billion, and public expenditure, taken together, is at €103.8 billion. Annually these amounts are €2.4 billion of
community contribution, €940 millions of national contribution, and an overall
€3.35 billion of public expenditure (for the 2014−2020 period sums are estimates).

If the amounts were not deflated as previously, for the 1989−2013 period total
expenditure is €127.7 billion, the Community's contribution is €68 billion, national
expenditure is €30.4 billion, and private sector expenditure is €28.3 billion.
Annually, the respective sums are €4.8 billion of total expenditure, €2.6 billion of
Community's contribution, €1.2 billion of national expenditure, and €1 billion of
private expenditure.

Measured as a percentage of GDP until the crisis erupts (Table 3.1), both the EU
and national expenditure are reduced, an outcome which should relate to GDP rising

Table 3.1 Breakup of total expenditure as % of GDP

	Total expenditure (V = III + IV)	Public expenditure (III = I + II)	Community's contribution (I)	National contribution (II)	Private contribution (IV)
1st C.S.F. (1989−93)	6.25%	5.74%	3.26%	2.48%	0.50%
2nd C.S.F. (1994−99)	6.36%	5.07%	3.44%	1.63%	1.29%
3rd C.S.F. (2000−06)	4.41%	3.48%	2.40%	1.08%	0.93%
3rd C.S.F. (2000−06)[a]	4.32%	3.31%	2.19%	1.12%	1.01%

Note:
[a]November 2005, after revision by the Greek Ministry of Finance.
Source: Giannitsis (2005), p. 293.

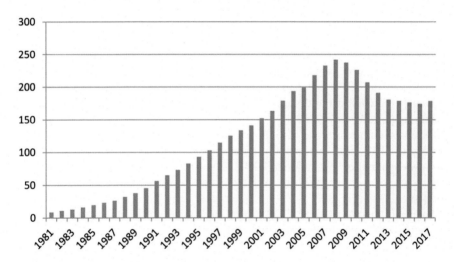

Figure 3.2 Greek GDP, market prices, 1981−2017.
Source: Hellenic Statistical Authority, www.statistics.gr.

(see Fig. 3.2). The EU's contribution as GDP percent increased in the 2nd C.S.F. but fell afterwards. National contribution fell in every period. In the 2nd C.S.F. they both accounted for a fall in public expenditure. As private contribution increased in the 2nd C.S.F., the levels of total contribution, as % GDP, finally increased.

In the 3rd C.S.F., the Community's contribution fell by more than 1% of Greek GDP. As Greek national expenditure fell by half a percent, public expenditure was also reduced by almost 1.5% of GDP. Due to the fall in private expenditure, the total expenditure fell by almost 2% of GDP.

A significant increase in private expenditure, as % GDP, occurred in the 2nd C. S.F, partially accounting for the total expenditure increases.

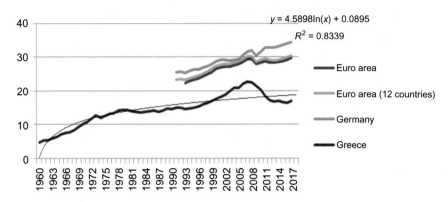

Figure 3.3 GDP per head in Greece, comparison to Germany, EA and EA12.
Source: AMECO series, variable RVGDP, at 2010 reference levels. *Note*: Data were available for Euro area of 12 countries (founding member-states and Germany from 1991 onwards and for the (current) Euro area from 1993 onwards. The dark line projects the trend for Greece's rise in GDP per head. The regression refers to Greece.

The rise in GDP, especially after the first programming period (1989−93) and in particular after 2000, is very high (Fig. 3.2), thus accounting for a large part of the reduction in the EU's and national expenditure measured as proportion of GDP. Obviously the GDP is multiplied within a few years and in particular in the 3rd programming period (up to 2008).

A substantial rising trend of GDP per head is also achieved since 1960. Greece's per capita GDP rises substantially from 1960 until 1972, it stabilizes after and increases again after 1993 and until 2008. The clear picture of a cycle for the Greek economy appears after 1993 for over two consecutive periods, taking a downward trend after 2008 (Fig. 3.3).

Seen as a long-term trend, GDP growth rates generally fluctuate and rise only in the 1993−2002 period, and after 2011 (Fig. 3.4).

3.2 Funding allocation and priorities

3.2.1 An imbalanced allocation of EU funds

From 1989 to 2013, a significant part of the EU expenditure allocated in Greece, approximately €30 billion, was directed to autonomous investment and infrastructure in transport, telecommunication, energy, health care, and environment (Table 3.2). Transport obtained €17.9 billion, the *lion's share* from the Community's expenditure. Proportionately, transport infrastructure represented 60.9% of the total Community's expenditure, while the proportion of total expenditure targeted at transport was even higher, at 69.2%. In other words, more than two-thirds of total funds targeted transportation. In the 1st C.S.F., transport comprised more than one-third of the Community's funds and increased to more than half in

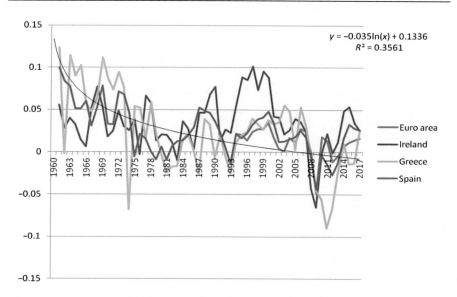

Figure 3.4 Long-term fall in GDP growth rates in Greece since 1960s, comparisons with Ireland, Spain, and the Euro area and logarithmic model fit.
Source: AMECO series, variable RVGDP, constant 2010 prices, calculated by author. *Note:* Calculations were made using the $(GDP_{t+i} - GDP_t)/GDP_t$ formula.

the 2nd C.S.F., reaching a remarkable 71.5% in the 3rd C.S.F., and falling to approximately two-thirds in the 1st N.S.R.F.

This evidence reveals an emphasis on transport infrastructure. Hard infrastructure policies were prevalent in large-scale transport projects of pan-European interest, such as the Athens METRO, the Rio–Antirrio bridge, and major highways and railways.

Greece's poor initial conditions necessitated the development of a relevant infrastructure. Basic public infrastructure was seen as a "precondition for long-term viable development" (Ministry of Finance, 2003: 6). Taking into account the increasing private sector contribution, as requested by EU Cohesion Policy, one can refer—along with other explanations—to sunk costs, invested interests in transport and construction for large Greek construction corporations, and the maturity of firms benefiting from this particular industry, which all impeded directing funds elsewhere to other industries. Some remarkable needs, whose satisfaction absorbed the major stake of funds, were not fully reduced through these efforts of Greek and EU authorities. Until today, infrastructure, again in transportation and physical environment, keeps absorbing a significant part of the investment pie.

The principal problems in implementing infrastructure policies were: (1) the lack of appropriate structures to develop projects and of managerial capacity of state authorities for large-scale projects. In every programming period, several changes in the management and operation of infrastructure programmes had to take place. Semiprivate corporations (in electricity, telecommunication, or gas) and ad-hoc

Table 3.2 Community's Funds and total expenditure in selected sectors

	1st C.S.F. (1989–93)	C.S.F. %	2nd C.S.F. (1994–99)	C.S.F. %	3rd C.S.F. (2000–06)	C.S.F.%	1st ESPA (2007–11)	ESPA %	Total	Total %
Transport	1296.6 (3542.3)	38.5% (40.25)	5394 (12,975)	53.7% (62.36)	7552.2 (17,125)	71.5% (81.05)	3700 (11,026)	67.3% (79.93)	17,942.8 (44,668.3)	60.9% (69.2)
Telecommunication	771 (1589)	22.9% (18.05)	358 (646)	3.6% (3.1)					1129 (2235)	3.8% (3.5)
Environment	163.1 (332.6)	4.8% (3.78)	2397 (2903)	23.9% (13.95)	2019.3 (2710.2)	19.1% (12.82)	1800 (2769)	32.7% (20.07)	6379.4 (8714.8)	21.6% (13.5)
Health and Care	53 (231)	1.6% (2.62)	323.4 (484.8)	3.2% (2.33)	445.4 (567)	4.2% (2.68)			821.8 (1282.8)	2.8% (2.0)
Energy	1086 (3106)	32.2% (35.29)	1235.7 (3053.8)	12.3% (14.68)					2321.7 (6159.8)	7.9% (9.5)
Culture			335.7 (742.8)	3.3% (3.57)	546.5 (736.3)	5.2% (3.48)			882.2 (1479.1)	3% (2.3)
Total	3369.7 (8800.9)	100%	10,043.8 (20,805.4)	100%	10,563.4 (21,138.5)	100%	5500 (13,795)	100%	29,477 (64,539.8)	100%

Notes:
1. 2010 prices, sums in million Euros, deflated.
2. Productive investments, human resources and agriculture are not included.
3. Total expenditure (comprising also private and national contribution) is included in parentheses (the columns with percentages also contain total expenditure percentages in parentheses).
4. 2nd and 3rd C.S.F. include funds from Community Initiatives and the Cohesion Fund but do not include Regional Operational Programmes.
5. % calculated against Community Contribution.

Source: Integrated Information System (O.P.S.), as presented in ELIAMEP (2011B: 1), adjusted by the author.

partnerships (in roads or METRO infrastructure) that were less dependent on state, were the most efficient in project implementation, absorbing more funds (ELIAMEP, 2011); (2) enhanced costs in most programmes due to voluntary over-booking and exorbitant discounts to cope with high competition (ELIAMEP, 2011; MoF, 2003); (3) the lack of a complete guide for costs to use in all projects (ELIAMEP, 2011); (4) the lack of project maturity because either the physical object was not accurately defined or not accepted by social and local actors, causing various delays. On many occasions, costs were raised because land that belonged to citizens had to be reallocated by the state and citizens had to be reimbursed, which was a time-consuming procedure (ELIAMEP, 2011); (5) problems related to studies (detective, inappropriate, scattered, geotechnical, and environmental problems) (MoF, 2003: 145); (6) expropriation problems; (7) problems related to the protection of archeological sites (and excavation rates) in a country with many such sites (MoF, 2003); (8) subsoil problems (MoF, 2003); and (9) legal difficulties (MoF, 2003).

As seen in Table 3.2, "environment" was the second funding priority until the fourth programming period, representing more than a fifth (21.6%) of Community funds. In the 1st N.S.R.F., transport and environment comprised together more than 75% of Community's contribution and an even higher percentage of total expenditure. For the whole period, these two priorities amounted to more than 80% of the Community's intervention. They included several projects funded all over the country, for improving urban and transport infrastructure, water supply, drainage, waste and sewage collection, disposal, and management, the protection of natural and human-made environment, in the urban scenery and in rural land, and the building of institutions to protect areas under protection. Large-scale projects comprised resolving the problem of limited water resources and drought episodes in Attiki, the restoration of lake Karla, and the progressive implementation of the national land and property register.

To explain the imbalanced allocation of funds, one cannot neglect the influence of Greece's physical geography and distance from EU centers, which increases costs and substitution effects from cheaper production elsewhere. For most of its integration period up to the early 2000s, Greece has also been physically isolated from the rest of EU markets. The country's peculiar landscape affects business behavior that tends to turn to monopolistic in various places where market sizes are limited and competition is difficult to advance. Whichever is the principal explanation for the reasons favoring transport and physical environment, one has to acknowledge the serious transportation needs at EU level, which is envisaged by pan-European level projects. Also, the extent of funds transferred toward transport and environmental projects may have had some crowding-out effects for firms in other industries.

3.2.2   Other priorities funded

In the policy field of energy and gas, initial planning targets were achieved up to the early crisis years (ELIAMEP, 2011). As explained in ELIAMEP (2011) this was achieved because projects: (1) have been scheduled based on one or more long-term strategic plans, backed up by major corporate "players"; and (2) were infrastructure projects of strategic importance, whose need from the side of the society was already matured.

Similarly successful were the policies focusing on culture (Table 3.2). They have focused on construction and the improvement of hard infrastructure, such as museums or theaters. However, approximately 70% of them were concentrated in the main urban areas, especially Athens and Thessaloniki (ELIAMEP, 2011).

Health and Care attracted more than €820 million from 1981 to 2011 (Table 3.2). Many of the related projects aimed at improving related infrastructure at the Greek periphery, especially through building hospitals and increasing the health sector personnel. Significant capacity was built in emergency help, centers for education, social support and formation of persons with special needs, and significant national-scale infrastructure projects in Greek hospitals were also advanced, strengthening the national health system. These investments had many delays, budgetary and programme deviations that revealed a lack of programming capacity and readiness in the sector (ELIAMEP, 2011).

The number and importance of social solidarity programmes increased (ELIAMEP, 2011). They appeared in the 2nd C.S.F. and continued thereafter. They helped to open various debates on supporting socially vulnerable groups and minorities, opening new policy paths for social policies. This is the case of clinics for persons having psychiatric and psychological needs or home support for the elderly, in the 2nd, 3rd, and 4th programming periods. Such social, health, and care infrastructure was also associated with high operational costs, not taken into account in planning and in times of crisis (ELIAMEP, 2011).

Numerous primary schools and kindergartens were created out of EU funding in social care, to reconciliate work with family life. Many projects were implemented by the General Secretary of Equality and the Centre for Research in Equality Issues, as well as the application of EC initiative EQUAL that all promoted equality, in collaboration with various NGOs and the social economy, especially in the N.S.R.F. (ELIAMEP, 2011), including integration of immigrants, refugees, gypsies, and other minorities.

Most of the Greek Universities were equipped with new and improved infrastructure, created new labs and spaces, restructured and improved their syllabuses, mechanized their administrative and academic operations, managed to increase their operating capacity and their postgraduate programmes. The Hellenic Open University was also created and all universities made steps toward open and distance learning.

3.2.3 Human capital policies

A great portion of funds was allocated to human capital policies. Their allocation should be read simultaneously with unemployment rates at the same period (Table 3.3 and Fig. 3.5). The amounts for human capital have not increased much throughout the different programming periods.

Table 3.3 **Human resource funds allocation**

Operational Programme	Programming periods				Total
	1st CSF	2nd CSF	3rd CSF	NSRF 2007–13	
O.P. Human Capital Exploitation	3601				3601
O.P. Education and Initial Formation		1989			1989
O.P. Continuous Formation and Promotion of Employment		1674			1674
O.P. Combating Labor Market Exclusion		274			274
O.P. Public sector modernization		320			320
O.P. Employment and Professional Formation			1890		1890
O.P. Education and Initial Professional Formation			2325		2325
O.P. Human Resource Development				2260	2260
O.P. Education and Continuing Learning				1440	1440
O.P. Administrative Reform				505	505
Totals:	3601 (6101)	4257 (6379)	4215 (5685)	4205 (5903)	16,278 (24,068)

Notes:
1. 2010 prices, sums in million Euros, deflated.
2. Total expenditure in parentheses (comprising private and national contribution).
3. Human capital is also emphasized, and, as a result, unemployment remains in low levels.
Source: Integrated Information System (O.P.S.), as presented in ELIAMEP (2011C: 7).

It is logical to assume that the emphasis placed on human capital and unemployment policies for an extended period of time had as a result the low unemployment levels, in comparison to other Cohesion states (see Fig. 3.5).

From 1989 to 2006 more than 1.6 million (450,000 unemployed[2]) obtained some type of formation through ESF programmes (ELIAMEP, 2011). However, diffusing an entrepreneurial direction in human employment policies and promoting a broad range of social targets were not well considered (ELIAMEP, 2011).

---

[2] This figure includes cases of more than one beneficiaries.

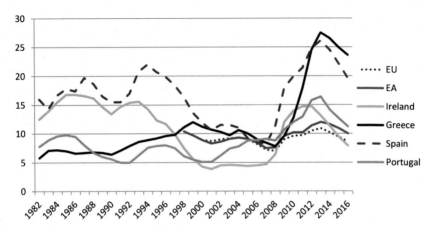

Figure 3.5 Unemployment levels in Greece, Spain, Ireland, Portugal, Euro-area (EA), and the EU (1982–2016).
Source: AMECO series, ZUTN, Eurostat, author's work. *Note:* Missing part for EU and EA is due to nonavailable data.

Table 3.4 Funding distinction between EAGGF-Guarantee and Cohesion Funds

	Total funds	EAGGF-Guarantee	%	Cohesion	%	Total %
1st C.S.F.	15,557.3	9410.2	60.5	5454.7	35.1	95.6
2nd C.S.F.	36,205.5	18,522.3	51.2	16,659.0	46.0	97.2
3rd C.S.F.	39,027.9	19,217.7	49.2	18,493.5	47.4	96.6

Source: ELIAMEP (2011A).

3.2.4   Agriculture as a principal funding priority

The Greek agricultural sector and its restructuring was a special funding priority since 1981 (Table 3.4). This is due to the significance of the sector for the Greek economy that was historically based on agriculture and the general context of Common Agricultural Policy. According to ELIAMEP (2011), from 1989 to 2006 (during the first three programming periods) the EU invested more than €47,150.2 million. The EAGGF-Guarantee fund has absorbed in the first three programming periods more than 50% of all EU funds (Table 3.4). This results in a picture of funds allocation that emphasizes the expenditure on agriculture and appears to be different from the aforementioned.

Significant economies of scale were created and capacity was built in several firms, giving rise to the Greek agro-industrial sector, one of the few sectors thriving in the Greek economy until now.

However, most of the principal problems in the Greek agriculture were not resolved, despite the plethora of measures targeted at them. This indicates simply that the size and intensity of investments are not their most important aspects. Other aspects, such as the philosophy of the Common Agricultural Policy (C.A.P.) are important too. The size of Greek agriculture land remained small and fragmented over the years, the costs of production remained high and have not fallen due to energy costs, the common currency has not reduced the intensity of competition from abroad and the economies of scale remained limited. The modernization of the Greek agricultural holdings has taken place only in some cases, agricultural infrastructure has not improved much despite the creation of several institutions, and the use of natural and human resources was far from optimum.

Many other problems remained over the years. These are the (1) reckless use and overconsumption of fertilizers and pesticides due to the limited knowledge of farmers; (2) lack of technical in-the-field knowledge of farmers; (3) high irrigation costs because waters were collected from sources deep inside the land that required the use of energy; (4) higher costs of borrowing for the Greek farmers in comparison to other European or non-European farmers; (5) inefficient structures of trade and distribution of products that kept a large price divide between producer's and retailer's prices; (6) bad production structure (i.e., high plant and low animal production and a lack of their combination); (7) inefficient use of water and irrigation that worsened problems, given Greece's irrigation problems in summers; (8) lack of labor mobility in the agricultural sector due to transportation problems, lack of information, and lack of transparency; (9) very limited possibility to become an entrepreneur with a very limited size of agricultural land; (10) lack of a clear distinction between agricultural land and forests; (11) desertification of agricultural land; (12) pollution and soil erosion; (13) lack of controls for waste; (14) high levels of agricultural imports and (15) the renaming of foreign products into Greek.

Institutional building in agriculture has not aimed at resolving these particular problems but emphasized payments, subsidies, certification, education, and formation. Technical, field-based support and applied research across the Greek territory, in collaboration with Universities or technical institutions, has never been prioritized in policies. Very limited amounts were left in Universities specializing in agriculture out of a very large part of the pie of funds offered to the sector. The emphasis, on the contrary, was placed on income support and the support of several products over the years.

Structural support has gained more importance, e.g., in the 2nd and 3rd programming periods (Fig. 3.6), with measures comprising investments in agricultural holdings, support of most deprived areas, incentives for new entrepreneurs, the resting of agricultural land, and early pension support.[3] The market price support system

---

[3] In a broader perspective, one has to judge agricultural policies in the EU with more sympathy, and acknowledge their value in sustaining strong interests in agricultural production, in food security and autonomy in EU markets, significant cohesion effects, taking into account the more general protective character of a sector that extends beyond strict national and EU borders and receives strong competitive pressure from the rest of the world. Besides, changes advanced to common agricultural policy have never been pursued from a single-nation perspective only.

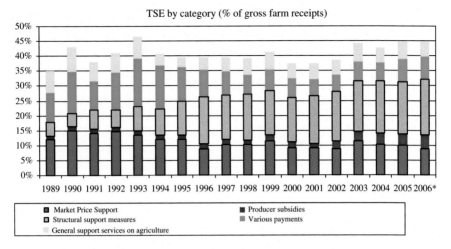

Figure 3.6 Types of support in Greek agricultural sector, 1989–2006 (as % gross farm receipts). *Source*: ELIAMEP (2011A), provided by Karanikolas et al. (2008).

has become less significant after the 2nd programming period, because of the consecutive changes in C.A.P.

The emphasis placed on income support and subsidies, especially in the 1980s and 1990s, had several negative implications: It created (1) a "funding culture" amongst people working in agriculture; (2) the favoring of subsidies in the most fertile areas, of products with greater subsidies, and larger in size producers; (3) various distortions in production (e.g., the reckless expansion of cotton production) that substituted the production of various nutritious agricultural products; and (4) an overuse of water and other physical resources. The state has overemphasized in the targeting of its policies the need to maximize public benefit and has not managed to offer a solution to the rise in production prices.

Some positive effects took place, such as the stabilization and increase of income of farmers and of the agricultural population, reversing the rural flight that had been occurring in Greece since the 1950s. Production was significantly mechanized and both biological and organic agriculture were promoted. The level of production also increased, due to the use of fertilizers, machines, and the development of market and distribution chains.

The overabundance of financial resources replaced the use of agricultural planning; the technical and agricultural experience of agricultural planners was abandoned and replaced by the shallow knowledge of agricultural economists. Fights over various responsibilities, mixed duties, and dispersed authority impeded rescheduling the Ministry's general authority and powers. Various problems appeared, such as budget deviations, corruption, untruth statements about agricultural property, and shadow business practices to gain from subsidies and the protectionist environment, constant attempts to bypass, neglect, or even to bribe authorities, tax-evasion malpractices, misleading calculations of agricultural holdings intended to absorb more income support from the declared amount of kilos, and, of course, the resulting punishments from the EC authorities (ELIAMEP, 2011).[4] Many of these problems appeared due to the absence of controls from the EU Commission, which were intensified after the year 2000, brining many penalties for Greece (subscribed in its national agricultural bank and the state's budget).

All these points have brought a loss of a developmental direction, limiting the scope of spreading a healthy entrepreneurial model. The hard-working ethos and spirit that historically characterizes people working in the agriculture sector was over-shadowed by this funding culture and its consequences. A combination of low educational levels, the average lifetime of farmers, and liquidity constraints may have contributed toward this direction. The agricultural strategies followed, failed to properly emphasize the strengths and to exploit the various opportunities opened for the Greek agriculture sector, given the intensification of international and European competition. Short-term interests, narrow perceptions and perspectives, and a continuous focus on absorbing funds and subsidies have won a historical battle over long-term planning and restructuring of land, the use of innovations and new technologies, the application of research and new techniques, new instruments and institutions related to their application (such as stock markets for agricultural products).

3.2.5   Private investments

Policies on private investments have centered around resolving liquidity constraints. An important component of these policies was the Greek investment law that was cofunded by the EU, in the various forms it took over the years. From 1989 to 2010, a range of policies were pursued on private investments, introducing new elements missing in the private sector, such as leasing, factoring, credit, and other financial support techniques and schemes. Policy novelties concerned mostly the financial domain, but the question of quality was also raised, especially in manufacturing and the agro-industry. Private sector investments were not sufficiently engaged with the softer aspects of business development, such as the need to improve management and business administration. They neglected important components of controls in the allocation of funds and the research required for their efficacy that was practically inexistent. Notable shifts should be underlined between the 1st C.S.F., when loose business support policies pursued mostly the support of semipublic companies; the 2nd C.S.F., promoting more enhanced and concrete forms of manufacturing policies through the Operational Programme for manufacturing and the implementation of sustainable business support mechanisms; and the 3rd C.S.F. and 1st N.S.R.F. that aimed at promoting the context of competitiveness through scattered institutional building, pilot initiatives, and support schemes but without any concrete and coherent, background plan for business and SME support.

3.2.5.1   The invisible target of Competitiveness

The economy's integration process arrived at a crossroad when Greece joined the Eurozone, in 2002. At this very critical moment, the 2000−06 Competitiveness programme was prepared in a wrong manner. First a series of sectoral operational

---

[4] Such problems have been associated with C.A.P. in many other places in Europe and should be seen as side effects of both a protectionist form and the large amounts offered.

programmes were produced for Manufacturing, Tourism, Energy, and Research and Development, and then, these programmes were bound and presented as a collection, under the unifying umbrella-concept of competitiveness. Policies for strengthening the Greek manufacturing sector in the 1994—99 period, which required strong organizational efforts and the creation of a special office by the Prime Minister's office, were no longer considered necessary in the subsequent programming period. Partly this is due to the fact that manufacturing policies were no longer emphasized in EU policies at the dawn of the new millennium. On the contrary, after 2000, manufacturing policies were bypassed and used simply to emphasize what was claimed to be of outmost significance, advancing competitiveness. Manufacturing problems were dealt within the context of competitiveness policies.

In funding terms, the 2000—06 Competitiveness Programme was again less significant, if compared against transport (Table 3.5). Competitiveness was allocated almost half of the funds that were directed to transport. What is more, half of these funds (49.8%) were directed to the private investments law (known also as Development Law) (Table 3.6). This is a rather fixed, historical instrument, with its core philosophy remaining intact until now. It is not necessarily promoting induced investment nor supporting innovation but it rather emphasizes subsidies and direct capital transfers to businesses and for a long period of time without any distinctions or groupings of businesses in size terms. Only 8.7% of the 2000—2006 Competitiveness programme was directed to technology and innovation. 16.9% out of it, was devoted to energy and 65.3% directed toward enterprises (priority axes 1—3), of which only 15.5% went to actions supporting enterprises beyond the Development Law (Table 3.6). Hence, it becomes evident that entrepreneurship, the setting-up of business, and small- and medium-sized enterprise policies were never a priority of the structural policies, as applied in Greece.

Similar conclusions on the significant misallocation of funds are reached when comparing the annual average of funds for basic infrastructure against those in productive environment, both for 2000—06 and 2007—13 (Tables 3.7).

Table 3.8 shows the initial resource allocation for the critical third programming period (2000—06), by strategic objective. Agriculture is included as part of the competitiveness strategic objective, without which the amounts devoted on entrepreneurship and the private sector are limited, when compared against the first and second strategic objectives (infrastructure and living conditions, respectively).

Table 3.9 illustrates the misprioritization of entrepreneurship policies for the 2007—13 period in funding terms and, among them, of research and innovation policies. Only €192 million of Community funds were directed to research (economy of knowledge), representing 14.88% of the total in the Programme, while less than half a billion were directed at the main axis to support Greek enterprises (priority axis 2). When the part that refers to energy policy (and sustainability) is removed, the Community contributes less than €1 billion in competeiveness and entrepreneurship for the whole period (out of many billions offered in the Greek economy). Clearly both the designers of the Programme and its funders had neither had in mind as a target the development of the Greek production nor realized the extent of problems appearing in postcrisis Greece. Hardly can one consider that the

Table 3.5 **Distributed financial resources, 3rd programming period, 2000–2006**

Priority axes	Public expenditure	Public expenditure %	Private contribution	Private contribution %	Total cost	Total cost %
Development of Human Resources	4,744,685,251	14.6	59,264,451	0.6	4,803,949,702	11.5
Transport	8,716,772,598	26.9	2,996,495,691	31.4	11,713,268,289	27.9
Competitiveness (Manufacturing, Tourism, Energy, Research and Development)	3,018,451,757	9.3	3,032,066,603	31.8	6,050,518,360	14.4
Rural Development and Fisheries	2,366,445,185	7.3	1,313,575,951	13.8	3,680,021,136	8.8
Improvement of Quality of Life (Environment, Culture, Health Care)	1,669,067,878	5.1		0	1,669,067,878	4
Information Society	2,167,474,859	6.7	508,500,000	5.3	2,675,974,859	6.4
Regional Development	9,620,137,733	29.7	1,622,805,056	17	11,242,942,789	26.8
Technical Assistance	114,996,704	0.4		0	114,996,704	0.3
Total	32,418,031,965	100	9,532,707,752	100	41,950,739,717	100

Source: Ministry of Economics and Finance, http://www.hellaskps.gr/2000-2006.htm, revision of C.S.F., December 2006, Euros.

Table 3.6 Allocation of funds per priority axis, for the Operational Programme "Competitiveness" 2000–06

No priority axis	Priority axis (title)	Measures	Actions	Planned total contribution (net figures and %)	Total public contribution (net figures and %)
1	**Improving the entrepreneurial environment**	1.1. Industrial, Technological and entrepreneurial infrastructure	1.1.1. Projects of improvement of interventions of protection for the environment in selective industrial areas ("BI.ITE.") of national scope of ETVA	167,707 (2.6%)	
			1.1.2. Projects of expansion, completion and improvement of existing industrial areas ("BI.ITE.") of national scope, where private and public-private agencies are created	117,400 (3.6%)	
			1.1.3. Projects of improvement of derelict industrial buildings and their reuse for industrial purposes		
			1.1.4. Creation of industrial areas ("BI.IIE.") of national scope		
			1.1.5. Amelioration of infrastructure of the Greek Institute for Health and Safety		
			1.1.6. Land sanitation for Technological Park in Lavrion		
			1.1.7. Orientation/guidance Study for Actions 1.1.1.–1.1.4		
		1.2. National System of Quality	1.2.1. Standardization		
			1.2.2. Certification	44,015 (0.7%)	
			1.2.3. Accreditation		
			1.2.4. Metrology	44,015 (1.4%)	
			1.2.5. Surveillance and market control		

	1.3. Simplification of Entrepreneurial Environment	1.2.6. New techniques and tools for managing quality	
		1.2.7. Information and public awareness	
		1.3.1. Simplification of administrative processes for investments in energy	15,886 (0.3%)
		1.3.2. Simplification of entrepreneurial environment	
		1.3.3. Centers for Welcoming Investments (one stop shop)	
		1.3.4. Information applications	15,886 (0.5%)
		1.3.5. General Trade Register	
	1.4. Structures of SME support	1.4.1. Development of Network of Structures of SME support	43,643 (0.7%)
		1.4.2. National Observatory for SMEs	43,643 (1.4%)
		1.4.3. Council for Competitiveness	271,251 (4.3%)
1 Total			220,944 (6.9%) 122,080 (1.8%)
2 Encouraging the entrepreneurial spirit	2.1. Support of investments in coproduction energy systems, environmental Renewable Energy Sources and saving of energy	2.1.1. Information, Support, Promotion and Diffusion of Coproduction of energy, Renewable Energy Sources and saving energy	1,072,006 (16.9%)
		2.1.2. Expansion of infrastructure technical support in coproduction, Renewable Energy Sources and saving of energy	382,170 (11.9%)
		2.1.3. Financial incentives in support of individual private energy investments	
	2.2. Upgrade of accommodation and support of tourist SMEs	2.2.1. Qualitative modernization of hotels and campings C and higher, based on (Development) Law 2601/98	358,812 (5.7%)

(Continued)

Table 3.6 (Continued)

No priority axis	Priority axis (title)	Measures	Actions	Planned total contribution (net figures and %)	Total public contribution (net figures and %)
			2.2.2. Qualitative modernizations of hotels, campings, and rooms to let, rooms with furniture and houses, according to Law 2601/98	116,818 (3.6%)	
			2.2.3. Entrepreneurial plans for SMEs in all tourist industries		
		2.3. Support of private investments of Law 2601/98	2.3.1. Support of private investments of Law 2601/98	405,514 (6.4%) 160,303 (49.8%)	
		2.4. Completion of investments of Law 2601/98	2.4.1. Completion of investments of 4 projects (103,000)	541,775 (8.6%)	
			2.4.2. Completion of investment of 2 projects (263,000)	205,857 (6.4%)	
		2.5. Technological Modernization of Enterprises	2.5.1. Technological Modernization of Enterprises	279,161 (4.4%)	
			2.5.2. Organizational Modernization of SMEs	192,723 (6.0%)	
		2.6. Financial Support of SMEs & micro firms	2.6.1. Financial Support of SMEs and micro firms	89,689 (1.4%) 44,016 (1.4%)	
		2.7. Improvement of Competitiveness in SMEs and micro firms	2.7.1. Business Plans in SMEs and micro firms	318,453 (5.0%)	
			2.7.2. Promotion of networking of SMEs (clustering)	132,123 (4.1%)	
		2.8. Encouraging Entrepreneurship in groups of population	2.8.1. Promotion of youth entrepreneurship	117,258 (1.9%)	
			2.8.2. Promotion of female entrepreneurship		

		2.8.3. Promotion of entrepreneurship of people with special needs	58,361 (1.8%)	
	2.9. Support of entrepreneurship in the sector of environment	2.9.1. Industrial Policy for Sustainable Development	146,754 (2.3%)	
		2.9.2. Support of Environmental Plans		
		2.9.3. Support of Environmental Cooperations	58,707 (1.8%)	
		2.9.4. Support of Unit for Management and Exploitation of Sewage		
		2.9.5. Support of SMEs for their Investments toward the prevention and facing of Industrial accidents of Big Scale		
	2.10. Founding and Operation of Guarantee Fund for the SMEs and micro firms "TEMIIME"	2.10.1. Founding and Operation of Guarantee Fund for the SMEs and micro firms "TEMIIME"	102,715 (1.6%) 102,715 (3.2%)	
2 Total			3,423,117 (54.1%) 1,364,391 (42.4%)	4,169,147 (62.5%)
3	Promotion of excellence			
	3.1. Promotion of Entrepreneurial Excellence in the Sector of Energy	3.1.1. Application of projects that demonstrate innovative technology	7714 (0.1%)	
		3.1.2. Defining credibility & efficiency of energy infrastructure & energy products	5400 (0.2%)	
	3.2. Promotion of Entrepreneurial Excellence in manufacturing and tourist enterprises	3.2.1. Organization and Functioning of National Prize of Quality		
		3.2.2. Support and reward of enterprises adopting the European Model of entrepreneurial excellence or the national prize of quality or for developing systems of entrepreneurial excellence	20,214 (0.3%) 9214 (0.3%)	
	3.3. Promotion of Excellence for technological development and research	3.3.1. Excellence of Research Institutions, under the aegis of the General Secretary of Research	16,000 (0.3%)	

(Continued)

Table 3.6 (Continued)

No priority axis	Priority axis (title)	Measures	Actions	Planned total contribution (net figures and %)	Total public contribution (net figures and %)
			3.3.2. Excellence of Higher Education Institutions – Universities	13,300 (0.4%)	
			3.3.3. Excellence in Firms	43,928 (0.7%)	
3 Total					68,728,284 (1.0%)
4	**Technological innovation and research**	4.1. Support of Research Units for standardization and commercial exploitation of research results. Identification and Use of research results with the creation of new enterprises—technological spin-offs	4.1.1. Support of Research Units for standardization and commercial exploitation of research results. Identification and Use of research results with the creation of new enterprises—technological spin-offs	27,914 (0.9%) 67,452 (1.1%) 36,000 (1.1%)	
		4.2. Incubation of new knowledge-intensive enterprises in scientific and technological parks and research centers with the participation of enterprises	4.2.1. Incubation of new knowledge-intensive enterprises in scientific and technological parks and research centers with the participation of enterprises	123,000 (1.9%)	
			4.2.2. Funding support for public research centers and labs ("AKMΩN")	71,000 (2.2%)	
			4.2.3. Intermediation Bureaus (in Universities and public research centers, for professional and careers purposes)		
		4.3. Encouraging of research, transfer and diffusion of technology in enterprises, support of activity of international scientific and technological cooperation and transfer of technology	4.3.1. Projects of industrial research for old enterprises ("ΠABET")	138,687 (2.2%)	
			4.3.2. Projects of industrial research in new enterprises, under the support law 760/00 ("ΠABET-NE")	82,576 (2.6%)	

	4.3.3. Promotion of projects of demonstration and innovation for enterprises under the law 545/01	
	4.3.4. Support of firms in technology, under the law 70/2001	
	4.3.5. Support in participation of SMEs in international R&D programmes	
	4.3.6. International scientific and technological cooperation	
	4.3.6.1. Project Funding of international cooperation	
	4.3.6.2. Project Funding of international cooperation in industrial research	
	4.3.6.3. Project Funding of international cooperation for space research	
	4.3.6.4. Cooperation with International Organizations	
4.4. Public awareness of common and new technologies, Support and Shaping of Research and Technology Policy, Management of Information in Research and Technology	4.4.1. Development of two museums in Athens and Thessaloniki	32,992 (0.5%)
	4.4.2. Creation of a network among museums	
	4.4.3. Support actions in learning in Higher Education Technological Institutes ("Τεχνομ άθεια")	28,909 (0.9%)
	4.4.4. Project "Hydropolis" (suspended)	
	4.4.5. Project "Hermes" (research, technology and the human)	
	4.4.6. Public awareness, information and acquaintance in industrial property matters	
	4.4.7. Management of scientific and technological information	

(Continued)

Table 3.6 (Continued)

No priority axis	Priority axis (title)	Measures	Actions	Planned total contribution (net figures and %)	Total public contribution (net figures and %)
			4.4.8. Project for orientation of research until 2020 ("Foresight")		
			4.4.9. Policy support in R&D with statistical data and indexes		
			4.4.10. Public awareness and information in Science and Technology matters		
		4.5. Research and Technology Development Complexes in Sectors of National priority	4.5.1. Promotion of cooperation between productive and research agencies in projects of research and technological development of long-term scope, with the purpose to produce innovative products or services and to cover social and cultural needs that affect the competitiveness of the Greek economy	134,978 (2.1%) 82,980 (2.6%)	
4 Total				497,108 (7.9%) 301,465 (9.4%)	577,247 (8.7%)
5	Transformation of the tourism product and promotion of tourism	5.1. Support of special tourism infrastructure (Provision of Integrated Tourist Infrastructure-"ΠΟΤΑ")	5.1.1. Provision of Integrated Tourist Infrastructure-"ΠΟΤΑ"	123,408 (1.9%)	
			5.1.2. Private investments in special tourism infrastructure	45,661 (1.4%)	
		5.2. Integrated actions for alternative tourism and tourist "ΑΓΚΥΡΟΒΟΛΙΑ"	5.2.1. Creation of networks of cultural elements and journeys of cultural tourism	49,039 (0.8%)	
			5.2.2. Interventions for supporting enterprises in tourist sector and exploitation of cultural stock	45,829 (1.4%)	

			5.2.3. Building of tourism "ΑΙΚΥΡΟΒΟΛΙΑ"	
			5.2.4. Actions for the development of ecotourism	
		5.3. Tourist promotion—reduction of seasonality	5.3.1. Plans for tourist promotion of the Greek National Tourism Organization ("EOT"), in synergy with respective plans of the private sector	13,962 (0.2%)
			5.3.2. Plans for reducing seasonality through actions that attract demand beyond the tourist period, in areas having the appropriate tourist product	13,962 (0.4%)
5 Total				268,671 (4.0%)
6	Energy supply security and the continued liberalization of the energy market	6.1. Access in alternative sources of supply of natural gas	6.1.1. Connection of the Greek system of transport of energy with the Italian	186,402 (2.9%)
			6.1.2. Connection of the Greek system of transport of energy with the Asean	105,452 (3.3%) 523,333 (8.3%)
				303,500 (9.4%)
		6.2. Promotion of Flexibility, Stability and Credibility of the Systems of Supply of Natural Gas	6.2.1. Station of Liquidified Natural Gas at Revithoussa	172,747 (2.7%)
			6.2.2. Creation of underground deposit of natural gas in the area of South Kavala	77,720 (2.4%)
			6.2.3. Installation of stations of compression of high-pressure conductors	
		6.3. Special Energy Infrastructure in the islands and promotion of renewable energy sources	6.3.1. Submarine connections of high and average voltage	317,468 (5.0%)
			6.3.1.1. Submarine connections of average voltage	
			6.3.1.2. Submarine connection of high voltage	158,734 (4.9%)

(Continued)

Table 3.6 (Continued)

No priority axis	Priority axis (title)	Measures	Actions	Planned total contribution (net figures and %)	Total public contribution (net figures and %)
			6.3.2. Projects of innovative solutions (inactive action)		
			6.3.3. Projects to improve the system of transportation and projects of expansion and enhancement of the distribution network in the islands		
			6.3.4. Projects of expansion and enhancement of already connected system of transport and distribution		
			6.3.5. Identification of geothermal potential in Lesvos		
		6.4. Operation of liberalized energy market	6.4.1. Projects of the Manager of Greek Systems of transport of Electric Energy ("ΔΕΔΜΗΕ")	125,500 (2.0%)	
			6.4.2. Projects of Accounting separation and Decentralization of Accounting and Financial Systems of the Greek Energy Provided ("ΔΕΗ"), based on the Law 96/92	121,600 (3.8%)	
			6.4.3. Projects of Organization and Operation of the Greek Regulation Authority ("PAE") and projects for the liberation of the market of Natural Gas		
6 Total				1,139, 048 (18.0%) 661554 (20.6%)	724,526 (10.9%)

7	Energy and sustainable development	7.1. Penetration of Natural Gas in households and the service sector, in new industrial consumers and the sector of transport	7.1.1. Penetration of Natural Gas in households and the service sector	310,973 (4.9%)
			7.1.2. Penetration of Natural Gas in new industrial consumers	129,030 (4.0%)
			7.1.3. Penetration of Natural Gas in the sector of transport	91,399 (1.4%)
		7.2. Safety Infrastructure for storage and transportation of Petroleum products	7.2.1. Transport and underground installations for storage of fuel	26,360 (0.8%)
			7.2.2. Promotion of the Public Safety for storage and transportation of Petroleum products	
		7.3. Use of natural resources and support in keeping environmental commitments	7.3.1. Studies of distribution, evaluation and, technological and financial assessment and use of mineral raw materials and geothermal energy	62,702 (1.0%)
			7.3.2. Distribution and Assessment of water resources	
			7.3.3. Project of Technical Support of the 2 previous actions	61,760(1.9%)
			7.3.4. Development and promotion of new materials, new technologies and new uses of mineral raw materials	
			7.3.5. Projects and activities to support water resource policy	
			7.3.6. Support of Technical Environmental Commitments	
7 Total				465,074 (7.3%)
8	Human resources	8.1. Education and Training in the Sector of Tourism	8.1.1. Action Plan, studies and researches for restructuring and upgrading of tourist education and training	217,150 (6.7%) 46,327 (0.7%)
			8.1.2. Development of network of national and international cooperations	
			8.1.3. Change and improvement of programmes of study in tourist education and training, pilot policies	43,733 (1.4%)

396,760 (6.0%)

(Continued)

Table 3.6 (Continued)

No priority axis	Priority axis (title)	Measures	Actions	Planned total contribution (net figures and %)	Total public contribution (net figures and %)
			8.1.4. Connection of education to production		
			8.1.5. Programmes of training in the context of integrated plans supporting the targets of tourist policy, as addressed in the Competitiveness Programme		
			8.1.6. Training of workers in the enterprises of the tourist sector		
			8.1.7. Public awareness activities		
		8.2. Human resources in manufacturing and services	8.2.1. Training of human resources in enterprises that will receive support by Measure 2.5	65,155 (1.0%)	
			8.2.2. Training for starting entrepreneurial activity in Measure 2.8		
			8.2.3. Training of employees in General Secretaries of Industry and of Trade and their supervised agencies (and employees working in Measures 1.2, 1.3, 1.4 and 2.9)	48,866 (1.5%)	
			8.2.4. Training targeted in the needs of SMEs and micro firms		
			8.2.5. Training in the context of programme "Connected" ("ΔΙΚΤΥΩΘΕΙΤΕ")		
		8.3. Human Research and Technology Resources and Potential	8.3.1. Education and training of new research potential ("ΠΕΝΕΔ")		

	8.3.2. Incentives to support development & diffusion of research activities ("HPΩN")	129,364 (2.0%)	
	8.3.3. Subsidies for employment of research and technology employees in public research centers	100,400(3.1%)	
	8.3.4. Observatory of Research and Development needs in labor markets		
	8.3.5. Education and management of research and Technology		
	8.3.6. Special Technological Matters		
9.1. Technical Assistance	9.1.1. Technical Assistance		
8 Total		240,848 (3.8%)	236,107 (3.5%)
9 Total **Technical assistance**		193,000 (6.0%)	103,344 (1.6%)
All Total		125,548 (2.0%)	6,666,610 (100%)
		125,548 (3.9%) (100%)	
		6,329,333 (100%)	
		3,217,421 (100%)	

Note: Amounts in thousands of Euros.
Source: Interim Report of Competitiveness 2000–2006, p. 96 and EC (2016).

Table 3.7 Annual mean expenditure, 2000–06 and 2007–13 periods

	Real annual mean of 2000–06 period						Annual mean prediction for 2007–13 period					
	Total public expenditure	Of which public enterprises	C.S.F.		Outside C.S.F.	Total	Total public expenditure	Of which public enterprises	National Strategic Reference Framework		Outside C.S.F	Total
	National and EU^a	National and EU	EU	National	National	National	National and EU^a	National and EU	EU	National	National	National
	$2 = 4 + 5 + 6$	3	4	5	6	$7 = 5 + 6$ $= 2 - 4$	$8 = 10 + 11 + 12$	9	10	11	12	$13 = 11 + 12 = 8 - 10$
Basic infrastructure	5172 (53.1)	1380	731	525	3916	4491	5649 (53)	1522	1146	579	3923	4503
Transport	3699 (38)	723	558	440	2699	3139	3764 (35.3)	796	623	315	2825	3141
Telecommunication and information society	73 (0.7)	64	19	7	48	55	345 (3.2)	70	154	78	113	191
Energy	552 (5.7)	467	56	36	460	496	608 (5.7)	515	59	30	520	550
Environment and waters	526 (5.4)	49	41	18	466	485	577 (5.4)	54	256	129	192	321
Health	323 (3.3)	79	57	23	244	267	355 (3.3)	87	54	27	274	301
Human resources	2425 (24.9)	144	403	147	1875	2023	2696 (25.3)	159	551	279	1867	2145
Education	1837 (18.9)	0	239	86	1511	1597	1923 (18)	0	242	122	1560	1682
Formation	347 (3.6)	144	141	48	158	206	509 (4.8)	159	238	120	151	271
Research and technology	241 (2.5)	0	21	13	206	219	264 (2.5)	0	72	36	156	192
Productive environment	683 (7.0)	19	194	96	392	489	721 (6.8)	21	172	87	463	549
Manufacturing	384 (3.9)	16	75	40	269	309	353 (3.3)	18	92	46	215	262
Services	68 (0.7)	3	1	7	47	55	62 (0.6)	3	16	8	38	46
Tourism	231 (2.4)	0	106	49	75	125	305 (2.9)	0	64	32	209	242
Other	1462 (15.0)	0	75	31	1355	1387	1602 (15)	0	138	69	1394	1464
Total	9742 (100)	1543	1403	799	7539	8339	10,667 (100)	1702	2007	1014	7464	8661

^{a}For total public expenditure, percentages of the total are indicated in parenthesis.
Source: MoF (2007), p. 133, M€, rounded.

Table 3.8 Initial Recourse Allocation, 3rd programming period, 2000–06, expenditure by strategic objective, category and EU Fund, public, national, and private

	Total	Total public expenditure	Public expenditure						Total national expenditure	Private expenditure
			Contribution of Structural Funds							
			Total	ERDF	ESF	EAGGF	FIFG			
	1 = 2 + 9	2 = 3 + 8	3	4	5	6	7		8	9
Strategic objective 1: Infrastructure	**6,410,878**	**4923.293**	**2810.247**	**2769.274**	**40.973**	**0**	**0**		**2113.046**	**1487.585**
1. Road axes and accessibility	3467.861	2410.852	1446.468	1446.468	0	0	0		964.385	1057.009
2. Railways	534.062	534.062	320.481	320.481	0	0	0		213.581	0
3. Telecommunications	478.328	474.696	273.188	232.215	40.973	0	0		201.508	3.632
4. Energy	1031.189	689.677	383.703	383.703	0	0	0		305.974	341.512
5. Natural gas	899.438	814.006	386.408	386.408	0	0	0		427.598	85.432
Strategic objective 2: Living conditions	**2553.587**	**2553.587**	**1458.207**	**1436.413**	**21.794**	**0**	**0**		**1095.381**	**0**
i. Urban development	1706.470	1706.470	853.235	853.235	0	0	0		853.235	0
ii. Health and social welfare	369.432	369.432	246.708	224.914	21.794	0	0		122.724	0
iii. Environment	477.685	477.685	358.264	358.264	0	0	0		119.421	0
Strategic objective 3: Competitiveness	**7888.300**	**4403.480**	**3022.172**	**1192.916**	**81.836**	**1605.758**	**141.661**		**1381.307**	**3484.820**
9. Industry and services	3060.847	1294.858	784.584	746.445	38.140	0	0		510.274	1765.990
10. R&D	615.157	443.868	344.563	311.763	32.800	0	0		99.304	171.289
11. Tourism and culture	564.469	219.830	123.812	112.915	10.897	0	0		96.018	344.639
12. Agriculture	3308.199	2226.984	1605.758	0	0	1,605.758	0		62.226	1081.215
13. Fisheries	339.628	217.940	163.455	21.794	0	0	141.661		54.485	121.688
Strategic objective 4: Human resources	**4097.273**	**3797.605**	**2781.241**	**406.458**	**2374.783**	**0**	**0**		**1016.363**	**299.668**
14. Education and initial training	2008.971	2008.971	1505.638	236.465	1269.174	0	0		503.332	0
15. Continuous training and employment promotion	1398.086	1098.418	823.813	27.351	796.462	0	0		274.604	299.668

(Continued)

Table 3.8 (Continued)

	Total		Public expenditure							Private expenditure
		Total public expenditure	Total public expenditure	Contribution of Structural Funds					Total national expenditure	
				Total	ERDF	ESF	EAGGF	FIFG		
	1 = 2 + 9	2 = 3 + 8	2 = 3 + 8	3	4	5	6	7	8	9
16. Combating exclusion from the labor market	357.422	357.422		268.066	10.897	257.169	0	0	89.355	0
17. Modernization of Public administration	332.794	332.794		183.723	131.745	51.979	0	0	149.071	0
Strategic objective 5: Reducing regional disparities	7259.566	6578.492		4934.455	4101.909	253.914	578.632	0	1644.037	681.073
Total C.S.F.	28,209.605	22,256.457		15,006.322	9906.971	2773.301	2184.390	141.661	7250.134	5953.147

Note: ERDF, ESF, EAGGF, and FIFG are initial for EU Structural Funds, €.
Source: EEO (2003), M€, constant 1999 prices.

Table 3.9 Allocation of funds in Priority axis of the Operational programme Competitiveness and Entrepreneurship, 2007–13

Priority axis	Community Funding	Participation in the axis %
Axis 1: Accelerating the economy's transition in the economy of knowledge	192,083,000	14.88
Axis 2: Enhancing entrepreneurship and outward looking, upgrade of productive tissue of the country	466,020,000	36.10
Axis 3: Strengthening of entrepreneurial environment—enhancing competition and consumer's protection	272,907,000	21.14
Axis 4: Completion of energy system and support of sustainability	330,990,000	25.64
Axis 5: Technical support	29,000,000	2.25
Total	**1,291,000,000**	**100**

Note: In Euros, €.
Source: MoF (2007b:153).

Community has contributed in enhancing Greece's competitiveness and entrepreneurship, at a time when problems for the Greek economy were culminating.

Needless to argue that the state's contribution from resource reallocation might have been greater, if the Community had exempted from getting involved in funding such policies. In practice, one can refer more to an invisible target of competitiveness, whose extent and scope is significantly low and misprioritized.

A similar conclusion is reached from Table 3.10 that refers to initial and final allocation of Community funds in the 2007–13 period and the amounts transferred from a category to another (net shift). Table 3.10 shows the limited importance of entrepreneurship in funding terms, initially planned to represent only 1.1% of all financial aid and finally obtaining 4.2%. On the other hand, road transportation finally accounted for 29% of all aid, and together with energy and other social and cultural infrastructure accounted for 52.8% of all Community funds. The substantial net shifts of amounts, revealing programming weaknesses, do not alter this picture (Tables 3.11 and 3.12).

3.3 Comparing the allocation of funds in Greece and other Cohesion countries

When compared against the other three states that started to obtain EU Cohesion Policy funds over the same period as Greece, namely Spain, Portugal, and Ireland,[5] several conclusions can be reached. For instance, the distribution of Cohesion support in Greece in the 2nd C.S.F. emphasized infrastructure and human resources rather than productive investments (Table 3.13). This has not been the case in

[5] All less advanced and known as "Cohesion 4" in the 1990s.

Table 3.10 The allocation of Community funds in the 2007–13 period, by category, initial (2007) and last (April 2016), and shift between categories (measured as difference between added and deducted amounts)

	2007	2016	Added	Deducted	Net shift	% Total 2007	% Total 2016
Innovation and RTD	11,921	1287.4	457.7	− 362.5	95.3	7.5	8.1
Entrepreneurship	182	660.8	478.8	–	478.8	1.1	4.2
Other investment in enterprise	498	1039.7	689.6	− 147.9	541.7	3.1	6.6
ICT for citizens and business	1345.9	737.8	48.4	− 656.4	− 608	8.5	4.7
Environment	2716.1	2057	141.8	− 800.8	− 659	17.1	13
Energy	625.2	861.3	596.7	− 360.5	236.1	3.9	5.4
Broadband	210.9	87.4	–	− 123.4	− 123.4	1.3	0.6
Road	3672.4	4603	1811.8	− 881.2	930.6	23.2	29
Rail	810.7	530.6	–	− 280.1	− 280.1	5.1	3.3
Other transport	1574.4	1096.8	304.2	− 781.9	− 477.7	9.9	6.9
Human capital	–	–	–	–	–	–	–
Labor market	96.4	0.2	–	− 96.3	− 96.3	0.6	0.0
Culture and social infrastructure	1888.2	1713.5	176.9	− 351.6	− 174.7	11.9	10.8
Social inclusion	–	–	–	–	–	–	–
Territorial dimension	602.1	665.5	159.5	− 96.2	63.4	3.8	4.2
Capacity building	25.1	6.2	3	− 21.9	− 18.9	0.2	0.0
Technical assistance	407	499.3	145	− 52.7	92.3	2.6	3.2
Total	15,846.5	15,846.5	5013.4	− 5013.4	–	100.0	100.0

Note: "Added" is the sum of additions made to resources in OPs where there was a net increase in the funding going to the category. "Deducted" is the sum of deductions made to resources in OPs where there was a net reduction in funding. "Social inclusion" includes measures to assist disadvantaged groups and migrants. "Territorial dimension" includes support for urban and rural regeneration and tourist services and measures to compensate for climate conditions. The sums are in thousands of Euros.
Source: EC, 2016b, original source DG Regional and Urban Policy, Inforegio database, April 2016.

Table 3.11 Community fund allocation (scheduled) in the priority axes of the 2014−20 programming period

	Total amounts
Competitiveness, entrepreneurship, and innovation	3,646,378,290.48
Transport infrastructure, environment, and sustainable development	4,333,917,413.04
Human resource development, education, and long-life learning	1,933,409,508.56
Initiative for youth employment	171,517,029.00
Public sector reforms	377,228,417.18
Regional Operational Programmes	4,495,184,442.57
Agricultural development	4,223,960,793.00
Technical Support	317,612,062.97
Total	19,499,207,956.80

Source: Ministry of Finance and Competitiveness (2014: 139).

Table 3.12 Community fund allocation (scheduled) per thematic target, in 2014−20 programming period

Thematic targets	Amounts scheduled
Support of research, technological advancement, and innovation	1,286,693,707.58
Improvement of access to ICT, their use, and quality	826,739,456.56
Improvement of competitiveness of SMEs, including agricultural sector (FEOGA) and fisheries	2,420,967,802.22
Support of transition in a low carbon emission economy in all industries	1,614,846,358.72
Promotion of necessary adjustments to climatic change and risk precaution	776,602,898.48
Sustainability and protection of environment and promotion of efficient use of resources	3,714,794,842.02
Promotion of sustainable transports and removal of obstacles for basic infrastructure in networks	3,202,735,447.68
Promotion of sustainable and qualitative employment and support of labor mobility	1,926,199,580.44
Promotion of social inclusion and combating of poverty and any prejudice	1,303,336,729.60
Investment in education and formation for skills acquisition and long-life learning	1,304,175,573.92
Support of institutional capacity of public services and agencies, and of efficient public administration	281,126,069.76
Technical support	669,472,460.40
Total	19,327,690,928.00

Source: Ministry of Finance and Competitiveness (2013: 122−123).

Table 3.13 Distribution of Structural Fund and Cohesion Funds expenditure in "Cohesion 4," 2nd C.S.F., 1994−99 (as %)

Type of expenditure	Greece	Spain	Ireland	Portugal
Structural Fund expenditure				
Infrastructure	45.9	40.4	19.7	29.7
Human resources	24.6	28.4	43.9	29.4
Productive investments	27.8	30.5	36.2	35.7
Cohesion Fund expenditure[a]				
Transport infrastructure	51.2	49.7	50.0	48.1
Environment	48.8	50.3	50.0	51.9

Note:
[a]Cohesion Fund expenditure refers to the period 1993−99.
Source: European Commission.

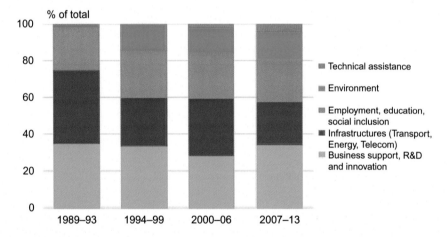

Figure 3.7 Distribution of Cohesion Policy Investments in less developed regions, 1989−2013, different programming periods.
Source: DG REGIO (as it appears in EC, 2014: xix).

Ireland that emphasized human resources and productive investments in structural support at the critical time when the bases were laid for an entrepreneurial, self-reinforced economy. Similarly, in the rest of these Cohesion supported states, other priorities were made.

From 1989 to 2013, the allocation of Cohesion Funds for all less developed regions (Fig. 3.7) offers clearly a different picture from that of Greece, as they emphasize business support, R&D, and innovation. Infrastructure was the principal policy priority for the European Communities in the 1989−93 period.

This picture for the EU as a whole reverses when one examines Fig. 3.8A and 3.8B. Proportionately to the total EU Cohesion Funds received (100%), Greece obtained substantial amounts for agriculture and fisheries and both ERDF structural

(A)

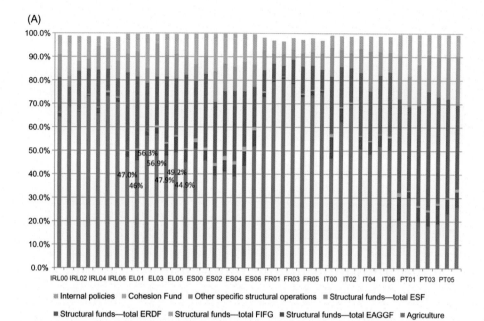

Figure 3.8A Expenditure breakdown in Agricultural, Structural Funds support (per Structural Fund) and internal policies, 2000−06.
Source: EU, ec.europa.eu, accessed the 16/5/2016 from ec.europa.eu/budget/library/biblio/ .../2014/Internet%20tables%202000-2014.xls, data processed by the author. *Note*: The rest of financial support includes the following categories: external actions, administration, reserves, preaccession countries, compensations. IRL: Ireland, EL: Greece, ES: Spain, FR: France, IT: Italy, PT: Portugal.

actions in the 2000−06 period, and actions in the Convergence Objective in the 2007−13 period arrive second. Since the latter priorities include also investments in transport, energy, and telecommunication, we identify again the lack of focus on the business and competitiveness sector in Greece and a misallocation that opposes the European example (in Fig. 3.7). This picture is for example far from that of Portugal.

3.4 The programming of Cohesion policy in Greece

The programming of EU cofunded policies from 1989 to 2020 is seen in the following, extended in size, Tables (Tables. 3.14, 3.15, 3.16, 3.17. and 3.18) that include the principal institutions involved, their actions and aims promoted. The main priorities, tools, and incentives selected by the Greek state (in agreement with the EU authorities) are presented for the different economic sectors and programmes (for Sectoral Operational Programmes and Regional Operational Programmes), in different programming periods. The Tables also provide the series of institutions involved in the implementation of EU Cohesion Policy, mostly Ministries and their surrounding institutions, as well as the new institutions created by EU Cohesion Policy.

(B)

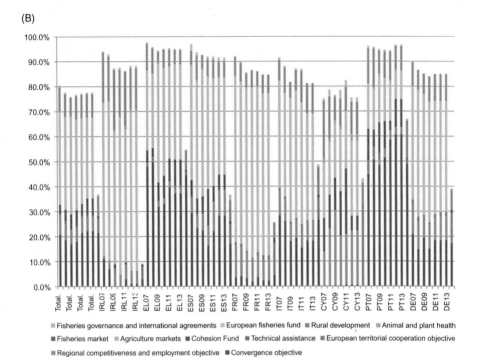

Figure 3.8B Expenditure breakdown in Agricultural, Structural Funds support (per Structural Fund), and internal policies, 2007–13.
Source: EU, ec.europa.eu, accessed the 16/5/2016 from ec.europa.eu/budget/library/biblio/ .../2014/Internet%20tables%202000-2014.xls, data processed by the author. *Note*: The above mentioned categories represent the most important categories (but not all categories) out of the three main priorities at the 2007–13 programming period, which were (1) sustainable growth, (2) preservation and management of natural resources, and (3) citizenship, freedom, security and justice). Three more priorities were included in the original dataset (4) "the EU as a global partner," (5) administration, and (6) compensation. These priorities and the rest of categories not included in the figure add up to the total of 100% in the table.

The 1989–93 is a period of intense development needs, where whole sectors such as telecommunications are underdeveloped and many services were insufficiently provided, for example in banking, insurance, electricity, etc. Economic programming was centered around covering the relevant needs and providing the necessary infrastructure (Table 3.14).

In the 1994–99 C.S.F. (Table 3.15, pp. 162–176), the strategic targets were five: infrastructure; improving living conditions; competitiveness; human potential and; the reduction of regional imbalances. Infrastructure was allocated 46% of total expenditure, of which 28.6% was used for transport infrastructure; 23.5% was used for human capital expenditure, of which 13.5% for education; 30.2% was directed to production, of which 15.6% was for agriculture (MoF, 2003).

In the 2000–06 period (Table 3.16, pp. 177–191), the strategy centered around supporting human resources, transport, competitiveness, agricultural development, fisheries, quality of life, information society, and regional development.

Table 3.14 National and regional economic and social programming, 1989–93

Axis of Priority: ENERGY

	Reduction of petrol dependence (creation and development of Public Gas Enterprise ("Δημόσια Επιχείρηση Αερίου," "Δ.Ε.Π. Α."))	Exploitation of domestic energy sources-	Intensive research in Greek physical space for identification of new energy deposits	Economizing energy	Promotion of renewable energy sources	Increase of share of Greek enterprises in investments in the energy sector
Principal institution Involved	Public Enterprise of Electricity ("Δημόσια Επιχείρηση Ηλεκτρικού," "Δ.Ε.Η.")					
Aims of institution	Optimal development of electrical system, securing of long-term base of electric energy for the country's needs, improvement of energy balance					
Actions to be taken	Development of new sources, such as lignite mines, thermoelectric power stations, hydroelectric power stations, thermal power stations Exploitation of renewable energy sources Transport and distribution infrastructure projects					

TELECOMMUNICATIONS

	Development of radio-electrical networks, mobile and wireless telephony	Expansion and modernization of conventional circuits and introduction of new technologies (cellular, optical fiber, etc.) with the purpose to cover a great part of existing demand in the whole of country's territory, especially in deprived regions and areas	Development of multiplex cellular systems and centers of cellular technology	Development and expansion of faxing, of network of data transmission	Satellite communications and satellite stations	Construction of buildings
Principal institution Involved	Greek Organization of Telecommunication ("Οργανισμός Τηλεπικοινωνιών Ελλάδος, "O.T.E.")					
Aims of institution **Actions to be taken**	Network of optical fibers and cables, domestic, and international connection					

Table 3.14 (Continued)

		(HELLASPAC), and provision of new services (VIDEO, TELETEX, TELEFAX, VIDEO CONFERENCE etc.)	(INMARSAT, EUTELSAT etc.)
TRANSPORT			
Principal institution Involved	Organization of Greek Railways ("Οργανισμός Σιδηροδρόμων Ελλάδος," "Ο.Σ.Ε."), Olympic Airways ("Ολυμπιακή Αεροπορία," "Ο.Α.")		
Aims of institution			
Actions to be taken	Creation of a national railway axis of high quality of provided services, connected with European railways of equal quality	Improvement of regional networks that will empower the basic axis along Athens, Thessaloniki, and Eidomeni	expansion of aviation network and improvement of level of services with renewing and organization of fleet, with concrete actions for creation of freight stations, city terminals, creation of centers for training all types of airplane employees, and the expansion and modernization of Olympic Airways's infrastructure in the Athens Airport	New Athens Airport in Spata
MANUFACTURING			
ECONOMIC INFRASTRUCTURE & SERVICES	Economic infrastructure and services for the support and modernization of industries in manufacturing and SMEs		
Principal institution Involved	Greek Bank of Industrial Development ("Ελληνική Τράπεζα Βιομηχανικής Ανάπτυξης," "ΕΤΒΑ")		
	Greek Organization for small and medium-sized enterprises and craftsmanship ("Ελληνικός Οργανισμός Μικρομεσαίων Επιχειρήσεων," "ΕΟΜΜΕΧ")		

Aims of institution	In "ETBA": Organization and equipment of industrial areas, provision of financial consultant services, loan or equity participation in productive investments		
	In "EOMMEX": Support in business start-ups, improvement of organization methods, Support of export activity, computerization and technical installation and equipment		
Actions to be taken			

INDUSTRIAL LAW 1262/82

SPECIAL PROGRAM FOR DEVELOPMENT of LOCAL GOVERNMENT ("ΕΠΤΑ")

	Modernization of organizational and functional structures of local government	Organizational connection of agencies with maximum achieved development effort	Creation of preconditions for endogenous local growth
Principal institution Involved	Local government organizations ("Οργανισμοί Τοπικής Αυτοεδιοίκησης," "O.T.A."), in collaboration with the Ministry of Internal Affairs		
Aims of institution	Infrastructure improvements	Startup of private and semipublic enterprises that expand the entrepreneurship horizon	Improvement of quality of life at local level	Training and improvement of human resources	Organizational and economic support of information, programming, publicity, and encouragement
Actions to be taken			

Axis of Priority: METRO ATHENS

RESEARCH & TECHNOLOGY

Principal institution Involved	General Secretary of Research		
Aims of institution			
Actions to be taken	Connecting research and production, by financially	Transfer and diffusion of technology,	Financial and organizational support for basic	Improvement of buildings and mechanical equipment of the General Secretary of Research	Actions of the Hellenic Organization for

(Continued)

Table 3.14 (Continued)

Standardization for the creation of certification centers for products and materials and the Hellenic Statistical Services for development of statistical infrastructure adjusted in the needs of an integrated European System of Statistical database	research, with the support of human, scientific potential and research cooperations. Priority is given to industries in informatics/ telecommunications, chemical technology, biotechnology, energy, health and in studies for physical environment	through the National Documentation Center ("Εθνικό Κέντρο Τεκμηρίωσης"), libraries, databases etc.	supporting intrafirm research and research of specific industrial research firms, through important contribution of technology parks in Patras, Thessaloniki and Herakleion		
ENVIRONMENT					
PROFESSIONAL TRAINING & EMPLOYMENT					
Training of already employed in new technologies, in products, management, organization, and business transformation	Training of newcomers in labor market and adjustment of their qualifications to technological change	Subsidy of employment for reducing unemployment			
Principal institution Involved — Undertaken by many institutions, across transport, energy, telecommunication, banking, insurance, private and public enterprises, health					
Principal institution Involved (cont.)					
In Transport:	*In Energy:*	*In Telecommunications:*	*In Banking - Insurance:*	*In Research:*	*In Health:*
Olympic Airways, Olympic Aviation ("Ολυμπιακή")	Public Power Corporation S.A. ("Δ.Ε.Η.") Public		Banks	General Secretary of Research and Technology,	Ministry of Health, National Health

	In Transport:	In Energy:	In Telecommunications:	In Banking - Insurance:	In Research:	In Health:
	Αεροπλοϊα"), Organization of Greek Railways ("Ο.Σ.Ε."), Ministry of Mercantile Marine	Corporation of Petroleum ("Δ.Ε.Π."), Hellenic Aspropyrgos Refinery ("Διυλιστήρια Ασπροπύργου"), ΕΚΟ			Hellenic Pasteur Institute, Research Center of Crete	System, Public hospitals
Aims of institution	To serve the broader efforts for the modernization and rational organization of the system of transportation	Support the restructuring and modernization programme of Public Power Corporation S.A. ("Δ.Ε.Η."), for projects of introduction, transport and distribution of natural gas, and exploitation of new resources	Adjustment of labor force in technological changes in the industry (cellular technology, optical fiber, information technology, etc.)	Deregulation of banking market, consolidation and improvement of effectiveness of financial and insurance industry that requires a flexible human resource with broader capacity in planning and study of new banking activities and the exploitation of new technologies in banking and insurance industry		Adjustment of nursing personnel in needs created from introducing new technologies in health industry, adjustment of professional qualifications of nursing personnel from needs created out the expansion and improvement of services of the national health system
Actions to be taken	Improvement of basic training for	Improvement of basic training for	Improvement of basic training for	A progressive change to a new training	Personnel training and executive	Training actions

(Continued)

Table 3.14 (Continued)

	newcomers in the industry, continuous improvement of already employed for adjustment in technological change, acquisition of relevant professional experience in the context of secondary and tertiary professional education, and employment subsidies for increasing of new job positions	newcomers in the industry, continuous improvement of already employed, and employment subsidies	newcomers in the industry and employment subsidies of new job positions	model of seminars in high quality structured training and employment subsidies of new job positions	specialization in new technology sectors
Principal institution Involved (cont.)	*In Secondary Education:* Ministry of Education		*In technical support:*	*In private enterprises:*	*For collective needs:* Ministry of Education, Ministry of Culture, Manpower Employment Organization ("Οργανισμός Απασχόλησης Εργατικού Δυναμικού," "Ο.Α.Ε.Δ.")
Aims of institutions (cont.)	*In Secondary Education:* Adjustment in labor market, expansion and improvement of the whole system of technical		*In technical support:* Specific studies, programmes and	*In private enterprises:* To cope with the significant	*For collective needs:* Easing of employment of

Actions to be taken (cont.)				
	professional training, with parallel reduction of general education	assessment of educational programmes are required to develop and extensive knowledge that improves the effectiveness of educational programmes, in relation to labor market needs	problems in the system of intrafirm training, so that human potential and resources are accurately employed	long-term unemployed that allows gaining complementary training and professional experience
	In Secondary Education:	*In technical support:*	*In private enterprises:*	*For collective needs:*
	New specializations are added, as requested in regional labor markets and, simultaneously, improvements are offered in training to cover needs from the introduction of new technologies in education, improvement in the methodology and organization of professional training, and the change in structures adjusted to needs and technological changes in labor markets	Actions at the national level, at the level of each operational programme, as well as innovative actions and social dialog. New measures, such as exchange of experience, transfer of technological knowledge, experimentation in new professions, as well as developmental actions in the context of social dialog	Along with encouraging private investments through the Industrial Law, actions are promoted to encourage productivity and competitiveness of enterprises and the sustaining and creation of new job positions Actions addressed at types of employees: Training of already employed in new technologies, new products, management, organization and	Actions included in a specific operational programme

Table 3.14 (Continued)

ANIMAL-HUSBANDRY				
Principal institution Involved	Ministry of Agriculture			
Aims of institution	*In agriculture:* Adjustment of imbalances in markets of agricultural products	*In Forests:* To turn forests to a basic developmental factor that substantially improves incomes in mountainous areas, keeps populations in those areas and sustains and improves the physical environment	*In Fisheries:* To cover the maximum possible needs in consumption in fishery products for increasing income of employees in the industry and promote the scope of a development policy in the industry	business transformation Training of financial executives and managerial personnel Training of newcomers in labor market Subsidy of newcomers in public and semi-public sector enterprises

Actions to be taken	*In agriculture:*
	Imbalances and chronic surpluses will be tackled through:
	1. Restructuring of cultivation
	   Higher quality production
	   Price and subsidy policies
		In Forests:
		Protection of forests and physical environment from various dangers (fires, deforestations, land abuses, and various other interventions against forest wealth)
		Increase in the surface of forest land, through reforestations in burnt and degraded forest
			In Fisheries:
			Protection and rational management in domestic fisheries wealth and expansion of activity in new fishery fields, Greek and foreign
			Improvement of physical conditions and management methods of fish farms and	

2. Improvement of adjustment and structures of agricultural sector through many interventions to modernize structures, improve the supply of services to farmers, improvement of training and agricultural training of agricultural population, modernization of agricultural land, infrastructure improvement, etc.

- lands, as well as various improvements in the composition and shape of existing forests through agile forestry manipulations
- Improvement of forest production by 10%—15% annually, especially in industrial timber and timber for construction, to increase autonomy in timber items
- Increase in production of various other products and services that come out of the forest through the development of basic infrastructure that will make them more accessible to the society

- exploitation of the rest of internal waters, to the extent that economically viable products are produced
- Development of water cultivation in sustainable units
- Increase of productivity in fishery units and improvement of safety and living of employees working on them
- Improvement of conditions of trade of fishing products and promotion of exporting and manufacturing activity
- Promotion of organization of producers in cooperations and associations of producers for increasing their intervention in the exploitation and distribution of production
- Development and organization of supporting activities in the industry, such as research, education, credit in fisheries, technical support, production inflows in the industry, etc.

REGIONAL OPERATIONAL PROGRAMMES

Principal institutions Involved	State and Regional authorities
Aims of institution	Separate strategy at regional level
Actions to be taken	Regional Operational Programmes, actions differ at regional level, for each region: ROP Eastern Macedonia and Thrace, ROP Central Macedonia, ROP Western Macedonia, ROP Epirus, ROP Thessaly, ROP Ionian Islands, ROP Western Greece, ROP Central Greece (Sterea Ellada), ROP Attica, ROP Peloponnesus, ROP Northern Aegean, ROP Southern Aegean, ROP Crete

Table 3.15 **National and regional economic and social programming, 1994–99**

Axis 1: Reduction of Peripheral Character of Country and Promotion of Internal Integration Through Development Of Large-Scale Infrastructure Networks					
	1.1. Accessibility and road axes (highways, ports, airports)	1.2. Railway network	1.3. Telecommunication	1.4. Energy	1.5. Natural gas
Principal institution Involved	Ministry of Environment, Planning and Public Works (former "ΥΠΕΧΩΔΕ")	Greek Railways ("Οργανισμός Σιδηροδρόμων Ελλάδος" or "Ο.Σ.Ε.")	Telecommunication service provider, in particular Greek Organisation of Telecommunication ("Οργανισμός Τηλεπικοινωνιών Ελλάδος," or "Ο.Τ.Ε."), Greek postal services ("Ελληνικά Ταχυδρομεία" or "ΕΛΤΑ")	Public Enterprise of Electricity ("Δημόσια Επιχείρηση Ηλεκτρικού," or "Δ.Ε.Η.")	
Aims of institutions	Priority in axes linking to Trans European Networks (TENs) or forming part of it Doubling the length of Greek highways Increase expenditure per GDP in TENs Reducing deaths by accident in highways by half Reducing time distance (Athens to Patras by 30' and Athens to Thessaloniki by 60')	In Athens-Thessaloniki line: increase the speed of trains up to 200 km/h reduction of time distance by (from 6&15' in 1993 to 4&20' by year 2000) increase in two- sided part of the line (both directions), at 88% Study of the Eleusina-Corinthe axis and its financing Raise the length of railway network from 2484 to 2588 km, of unidirectional line from 8.5% to 13.3%, of electric power movement	*In telecommunications:* Improving quality of provided services and efficacy in the sector Provide the capacity to provide services on a commercial basis (including the creation and pursuing of a long- term business plan) Business plan of the Greek Organisation of	Improving performance through an operational plan for the industry Saving energy, rational management and promotion of renewable resources Increase in consumption as % of GDP from 440KGOE/TECU92 in 1992 to 452 in 1999 and in industry consumption from 742 in 1992 to 760 in 1999	Continuation of the project to introduce natural gas (that started with 1st C.S.F. and REGEN Community Initiative) 4% of households using natural gas by 1999 Increase in natural gas production from 0% to 12% in 1999

	Increasing connectivity to Italy (from ports) Increasing connection to Balkan countries Improving capacity and functionality of Greek airports Helipad network that satisfies social needs (passenger transfer, supplies, etc.) and reduces isolation in isolated areas	from 3% to 21.2%, of network exceeding 140 km/h from 0.6% to 13.3%	Telecommunication ("O.T.E.") *In postal services*: Business plan of the Greek postal services ("Ελληνικά Ταχυδρομεία" or "EATA")	Increase in production capacity from 9.1 MW in 1993 to 11.5 in 1999 Reduction in conventional thermal station electrical production from 92.6% to 88.3% in total production Renewable energy sources from 7.4% in 1993 to 11.7% in 1999 Fall in SO_2 emission from 11.8 in 1993 to 8.9 tonnes in 1999. Fall in COs emissions from 1.12 tonnes in 1993 in 984 tonnes in 1999	Use of INTEREG Community Initiative to continue the natural gas project Regulatory work needed that includes technical and security guidelines, as well as operational rules for low pressure networks in urban areas
Actions to be taken	*In roads*: Axis Patras-Athens-Thessaloniki Egnatia Road ("Εγνατία Οδός") Rio–Antirrio bridge-Peripheral Athens road Few parts of Ioannina-Antirio road	Creating a business plan for the Organization of Greek Railways ("Οργανισμός Σιδηροδρόμων Ελλάδος," "Ο.Σ.Ε."), Creating a railway connection among Patras, Athens and Thessaloniki (a Trans European Network) Creating a new railway line Eleusina-Corinthe and its connection to Thessaloniki Modernization of Corinthe-Patras railway line	*In telecommunications*: Securing service provision in areas with relatively high cost through improving access in the network Introduction of new technology in distant and geographically inaccessible areas Accelerating and improving the	Operational plan for the industry that includes aspects of production capacity for lignite and natural gas Creation of an effective management structure that will allow assessing the real effect of implemented actions	

(Continued)

Table 3.15 (Continued)

Axis 1: Reduction of Peripheral Character of Country and Promotion of Internal Integration Through Development Of Large-Scale Infrastructure Networks			
Few parts of Thessaloniki—borders with Bulgaria Northern part of Crete *In ports:* Western part of the country —"western gate," increasing connectivity to Italy Modernization of Igoumenitsa and Patras ports Actions for Corfu port Development projects in 3 principal ports in Eastern shore (Alexandroupoli, Kavala, Volos), to increase freight transportation and connection with Balkan *countries* *In airports:* Emphasis in international	Supply of railway line material/ equipment Improvements in the rest of the country, connection with Kavala airport, horizontal actions, technical support, operational plan	provision of new, advanced and commercially viable in groups of users important for the economy Public sector administration modernization and development of rural, border and island areas Training measures for introducing new technologies and modern methods of management *In postal services:* Modernization of the Greek postal services ("EATA") through a business plan that requires its organizational planning, the use of its resources, their relation to productivity and effectiveness, cost and price policies, definition of	

airport of Athens, relocation to SPATA Modernization projects in airports of Thessaloniki, Herakleion, Corfu, Rhodes Creation of a network of helipads	minimum provision requirements and basic services as a social service provider	2.3. Environment Ministry of Environment, Planning and Public Works Effective, active and energetic prevention Combating pollution at its source Implementation of the "polluter pays principle" Environmental sustainability Precautionary principle, if needed

Axis 2: Improvement of Living Conditions

	2.1. Urban Development (Athens Metro and Thessaloniki Metro)	2.2. Health and Social Protection	
Principal institution Involved	State, regional and local authorities, METRO S.A.	Ministry of Health, Health institutions of the National System of Health	
Aims of institution	Modernization of public infrastructure in historical neighborhoods Management of obsolete industrial spaces and areas, in downgraded environment Continuation of METRO of Athens and METRO of Thessaloniki to reduce important circulation problems and pollution of the city of Athens	Improvement of quality of provided health services Reduction of regional inequalities (reducing by 50% between less favored areas and urban centers) Improvement of organizational and managerial health services and the efficacy of its personnel Increasing effectiveness Continuation of the restructuring process in the psychiatric sector (based on Community Regulation) Improving and framing of social security policy on the basis of Structural Funds, its needs (for infrastructure, organization, human labor shortage) and its finance	

(Continued)

Table 3.15 (Continued)

Axis 1: Reduction of Peripheral Character of Country and Promotion of Internal Integration Through Development Of Large-Scale Infrastructure Networks		
Actions to be taken	Interventions through Regional Operational Programmes for urban development in greater Greek cities URBAN Community Initiative Completion of Athens METRO, as programmed through the 1st C.S.F. by constructing line 2 (Sepolia-Dafni) along North-South axis (9.2 km), with 12 stations and line 3 (Keramikos–Ethniki Amyna) along East-West axis (8.4 km), 12 stations Following the 1993 international procurement competition for Thessaloniki METRO, the 25 stations and 9.5 km project has been planned and private sector contribution needs to be secured	Modernization of infrastructure and equipment with scientific labor of health institutions with needs (Centres of Health, hospitals, National Centre of First Aid, telemedicine) Some of these actions conducted through the Regional Operational Programmes Integrated actions of modernization of management of hospitals and other services, including development of informatics Vocational training of nurses, which comprises basic professional training and continuous training and retraining of existing personnel Formation, launch and operation of National Blood Donation Centres Actions compatible with Structural Funds and their regulations and study of additional actions of complementary character, especially for combating unemployment and exclusion from labor market	Launch of surveillance mechanisms of environmental factors (in collaboration with European Environment Agency), improvement environmental impact assessment Creation of mechanisms for environmental controls in primary and secondary sector activities, especially in public works Support of activities targeting at conforming with EU regulations for environmental protection, especially for polluted waters, waste, toxic waste and drinking water, land protection, soil protection and air quality (especially in Athens) Support of actions to enhance knowledge in planning, and forest and natural reserve protection Management of household and toxic waste, through sanitation of public spaces, creation of waste disposal spaces, creation of centers for recycling, adoption of rational management processes and techniques Management of public dangers Actions to reduce sound pollution Actions for the management of physical environment, such as protection of the seas and natural reserves, biodiversity, soil protection, protection of 10 main sea areas, actions for species in extinction, 100 natural reserve places and 300 places of natural beauty, as well as ecosystems

Axis 3: Development and Competitiveness of the Economic Tissue

	3.1. Manufacturing and Services	3.2. Research and Technology	3.3. Tourism and Culture	3.4. Agriculture (Targets 1 & 5a)	3.5. Fisheries (Targets 1 and 5 a)
Principal institution Involved	Ministry of Development	General Secretary of Research	Ministry of Tourism and Culture	Ministry of Agriculture	Ministry of Agriculture
Aims of institution	Supporting firm start-ups and industrial tissue modernization Improvement of business environment and business infrastructure Improving competitiveness of small and medium-sized enterprises (SMEs) Creation of new implementation mechanism, acquisition of knowledge, simplification of procedures Radical change of the Greek Development Law Cofunding and support of manufacturing actions included in regional operational programmes (service provision for the SMEs, manufacturing	Support of technical and economic human labor, so as to attract productive investments Massive introduction of R&D and innovation in all productive mechanisms to advance competitiveness To increase human research potential, by 60%	Improvement of quality in provided tourist services to enhance international competitiveness Preservation and exploitation of culture and civilization, in particular as a tourist attraction instrument Effective cooperation among involved institutions and agencies Private sector participation and involvement Integrated interventions, not scattered	Improving competitiveness through Structural adjustment in production Improvement of conditions of manufacturing, trade and marketing of agricultural and forestry products Adjustment of agricultural land units that support vegetable production, meat production support, emphasis in quality and product diversity Improvement, technological support, specialization of various agencies of the agricultural sector Modernization of agricultural land units and infrastructure via Reallocation of agricultural land units	Adjustment of the fisheries sector Modernization and improvement of fleet Protection and improvement of fishing ports and infrastructure

(Continued)

Table 3.15 (Continued)

Axis 1: Reduction of Peripheral Character of Country and Promotion of Internal Integration Through Development Of Large-Scale Infrastructure Networks			
and industrial parks, regional support schemes, integrated actions for restructuring of deindustrialized areas)		Rational use of water resources Improvement of agricultural infrastructure Increase of % of youth in agricultural population Rural development Maintenance of rural population through alternative job generation and incomes Revitalization and removal of isolation of rural land, improvement of living conditions Protection and exploitation of physical resources, including forests	

Actions to be taken				
Supporting firm start-ups and industrial tissue modernization with: creation of systems of support, ad-hoc adjusted in the needs of domestic and foreign investors finance of activities in business plans, for firms that can compete internationally regional support system, of limited fund availability Creation of "One-stop-shop" agency Improvement of business environment and business infrastructure with: creation of a high quality standardization system progressive transfer of management in industrial and manufacturing spaces in specialized agencies, including private sector creation of private utilities, especially in Northern Greece	Productive sector cooperation of scientific and technological institutions in sectors of interest (new materials, biotechnology, environment) Creation of mechanisms for technology transfers and innovation, the exploitation of four existing technological parks, and those newly created, and improvement of information networks. Integrated actions for exploitation of innovativeness Reorientation and expansion of existing R&D infrastructure and its rational organization and use New infrastructure building Renewal of human labor potential, with greater emphasis in the acquiring extra knowledge by researchers, the training of young researchers, in updated technologies, especially in training techniques and management of R&D and innovation	Modernization of tourist firms, through business plans proving effectiveness from private and public enterprises through financing of market studies, vocational training, leisure equipment, innovative services, intra-firm networks and cooperation Common infrastructure funding in areas of sufficient tourist capacity, such as marines, golf fields or conference centers, based on effectiveness studies Balanced development of a limited number of tourist poles. Development of infrastructure, hotel infrastructure, leisure equipment, transport, human labor etc. Integrated approach based on feasibility studies Local actions of limited funding that will differentiate supply of the tourist product, e.g., through ecological,	Structural adjustments, including implementation of all regulations relevant to 5a target Actions improving initial manufacturing and trade of agricultural products and forestry products (target 5a) Actions for vegetable production, such as improving control systems for plants, including relevant checks, the creation of integrated systems of cultivation and vegetable protection, and continuation of actions for restructuring of vineyards. Actions in meat production, for the expansion of meat capital, its health and protection, the organization of meat production in space, the creation of infrastructure for genetic, health and qualitative checks, increase in meat production per meat	Adjustment of fishery activity Reduction of fleet Renewal and modernization of fleet Increase in water cultivation, through modernization or removal of existing firms Fish products adjustment to market requirements Protection of sea zones Equipment of fishing ports Manufacturing and trade of products Product promotion Infrastructure of ports and sea-ports Research in the fisheries sector Vocational training and social support Technical support

(Continued)

Table 3.15 (Continued)

Axis 1: Reduction of Peripheral Character of Country and Promotion of Internal Integration Through Development Of Large-Scale Infrastructure Networks		
(intrafirm communication networks, logistics, storage and freezing facilities, etc.) incentives/measures for the protection of environment, and business relocation outside urban environments-integrated actions for deindustrialized areas Improving competitiveness of small and medium-sized enterprises finance of business services for the modernization of SMEs, a competitive system based on the demand for SMEs measures for the accessibility of SMEs in financial markets, using modern financial techniques Vocational training to finance business plans prepared by firms. Actions for certification in the national system of vocational training	cultural or mountainous tourism Funding of vocational training actions incorporated in business plans Management of historical centers, modernization of museums, renovation and conservation of monuments, recording of monuments and sites	head. Priority of complementary interventions of vertical integration in sectors Rational management of water sources, with such actions as hydraulic measures for water storage and provision, protection of waters and lands, improvement of quality of irrigation waters Forrest protection measures, forest development and complementary measures (such as recording, mapping, equipment, studies etc.) Actions that improve the terms of agricultural research, promotion of products and their exporting, promotion and increase of information Technical support

Axis 4: Development of Human Potential and Promotion of Employment

Principal institution Involved				
Aims of institution				
Actions to be taken	Actions to improve the capacity to access and to improve the quality of systems of elementary education and professional training. Both qualitative and quantitative enforcement of various existing structures requires: more flexible systems, open to the world of labor with the aim to guarantee a greater mobility of specialized labor force and improve its capacity to new technologies and improve knowledge transfer in economic activities Improvement of competitiveness through supporting adjustment of employees in the evolution of systems of production. The principal weight to be given in a systematic approach in the organization of activities of continuous formation and continuous education, in the context of business and labor market demand Improvement of employment opportunities, through implementing a series of coherent measures against unemployment and nonprivileged and in favor of other categories endangered with exclusion from labor market. The principal weight to be given in enhancing employment organizations and promotion of special actions in matters of professional orientation, consulting, professional training and employment enhancement. Support and investigation of the modernization effort of public administration. The principal weight to be given in the exploitation of human force, with the support of measures of initial and continuous professional training of high quality.			
	4.1. Education and initial professional training	4.2. Continuous training and promotion of employment	4.3. Combating exclusion from labor markets	4.4. Modernization of public administration
Principal institution Involved				
Aims of institution	Guaranteeing, based on the White Paper "Growth, Competitiveness and Employment" for all young people below 20 years old access to a recognized form of education or professional training that includes schooling or other forms connecting work with professional training. The creation of Institutes of Professional Training ("IEK") in the 1st CSF is a basis upon which new propositions toward this direction. Enriching and enhancing national schooling system, especially with respect to organization and practice and job experience gained	Development of an effective system of continuous training that would respond in priorities created in the demand of economies. Emphasis is given in the creation, especially during the first phase, in the development of	Measures will concern disadvantaged people, people with body or mental problems, immigrants, refugees, as well as drug addicts, single-parented families, people released from prison, and other	Undertaking a complete action for improving management of human resources and increasing productivity and efficacy of public sector employees

(Continued)

Table 3.15 (Continued)

Axis 1: Reduction of Peripheral Character of Country and Promotion of Internal Integration Through Development Of Large-Scale Infrastructure Networks			
Enhancing secondary education, after compulsory education, and making it more attractive and adjusted in the needs of labor markets. Modernization, enrichment and adjustment of educational programmes and programmes of study (e.g., introduction and/or expansion of new technologies, foreign languages, professional orientation, supportive and special modules, and measures in favor of school leavers, weak students and minorities, environmental education etc.), precautionary measures with the aim to reduce early school leaving, and low performance. As far as infrastructure is concerned, and after taking into account demographic changes, a selective approach adopted: priority given in educational equipment matters, abolishing of double-shifts in secondary education, the improvement of school infrastructure and libraries	basic structures that would guarantee qualitative upgrade and the opportunity to respond to economic changes. Greece has a critical number of centers of professional training developed in the 1st CSF (under regulation 815/84)	population groups facing the danger of exclusion	
	A. Continuous formation for employees	Basic research to trace better social target groups, their problems and needs, the number of people, their geographical distribution, and assessment of existing system of service provision. Setting in operation mechanisms for constant tracing of needs and priorities	This leads in the formation of public sector employees, especially in issues concerning the introduction of new technologies, as well as better preparation of new employees for their entrance in the public sector
Training of school teachers, educators, school principals, educational consultants and the rest of personnel, as a primary concern to guarantee educational adjustments	Development of special requirements for centers of professional training, educational material and the educational personnel, exploring the	Enhancing and improving existing structures and, if needed, creating new structures, including hard infrastructure. This	Continuous formation of middle and higher executives in public

	human resources of educational institutions and institutions of professional training, the requirements of professional training and the practices of advanced businesses in every industry, as well as experience in other member-states	leads to actions such as training of trainers, provision of same reception opportunities, adjustment of infrastructure projects to offer more opportunities for education/professional training and employment to people in need	Improvements of structural character, such as the creation of mechanisms for tracing educational needs, processing formation programmes adjusted in business operational needs, training of trainers, transfer of know-how and educational equipment, the creation and/or expansion educational infrastructure, depending on needs
Development and improvement of higher education, given its prime role in competitiveness. Improvement in the management of programmes of university education, in order to take into account more the current needs of market, promotion of short in size postgraduate modules oriented toward the market. Organization of postgraduate modules containing a research component, as well as development of libraries and development and improvement of infrastructure and equipment	Development of mechanisms (including observatories) for accelerating industrial change, especially its effects upon employment and the organization of work as well as the performance of information systems in (with the creation of information services in basic urban centers and information actions) for entrepreneurs and managers	Developing the service provision for combating exclusion from labor market and removing obstacles for economic and social inclusion and reinclusion. Funding of preliminary professional training, service provision, psychological support, provisional housing provision, upgrade of basic professional qualifications, help in job search process and support inside the job	Institutionalization of a system of assessment that will secure that measures taken respond to real needs of formation
Linking all degrees of educational system more with real economic activity and improving the response capacity of the educational system and the educational system of initial professional training, to ease the access of youth in labor market and adjust studies in the needs of markets. Obstacles separating the educational system from economic activity	Provision of support to assess educational needs of enterprises (especially of the SMEs) from specified experts. Strong links		

(Continued)

Table 3.15 (Continued)

Axis 1: Reduction of Peripheral Character of Country and Promotion of Internal Integration Through Development Of Large-Scale Infrastructure Networks		
should be removed and communication improved. This is achieved through the development of networks, the creation of job search offices, exchange between educational institutions and businesses, further development and improvement of the institution where students gain experience in businesses	among observatories, design services and educational centers	Identifying problems of legal and administrative character, defining solutions at the organizational level from a great administrative unit (including of regional and local level), implement measures that will provide such solutions, including experimental applications, structural interventions, assessment and diffusion of results
Public administration modernization and that of central and regional authorities of the Ministry of Education, with the purpose to investigate and support the reform and to upgrade the educational system. The importance of development and upgrade of educational design is critical in all educational degrees, as well as the assessment and revision of educational measures based on a systematic research, along with the development of mechanisms and processes for the implementation of the programme	Development of special actions for professional training for trainers of business personnel	
	Guaranteeing necessary coordination with the actions undertaken by the Ministry of Education, to connect higher education the business activity Ex-post assessment that will become the basis for future adjustments B. *Professional Training and efforts to*	

guarantee employment to the unemployees

The systems supporting employment have to be completed with a broader and consistent approach that comprises:

Development of organizations of employment and job search occupied with professional training and with advice provision to unemployees in their efforts to find job and development of information and awareness mechanisms

Special measures that include subsidies for start-ups and professional training with the aim to promote the creation of enterprises and self-employment

Special emphasis in applying policies in equal opportunities between men and women, inclusion and reinclusion of women in labor markets, special priority in youth and long-term unemployed, combating exclusion from labor markets

Table 3.15 (Continued)

Axis 1: Reduction of Peripheral Character of Country and Promotion of Internal Integration Through Development Of Large-Scale Infrastructure Networks	
Actions to be taken	
Axis 5: Reduction of Regional Inequalities and Removal of Isolation in Island Areas (Regional Operational Programmes)	
Principal institutions Involved	State and Regional authorities
Aims of institution	13 separate strategies at regional level, but with common elements, through exploiting special characteristics and limiting disadvantages at regional level
	Each regional operational programme will contain:
	A subprogramme containing actions for local development, based on the directions of the Special Programme for Local Authorities ("EAIITA"). Special emphasis in sustainable actions (especially the creation of infrastructure) on behalf of local administration agencies and actions among local organization authorities
	A subprogramme containing actions for human potential that will comprise measures in the fields of education, training, as well as actions of continuous professional training and combating exclusion from labor markets that can be linked to actions of other thematical subprogrammes of the regional operational programme
	A low-budget subprogramme containing actions to complete unfinished actions of previous 1st CSF
	A subprogramme for agricultural development, including fisheries, in coherence and agreement with central planning in agriculture and the respective sectoral programme
	Apart from actions for "EAIITA" the rest of actions center around projects of large scale with real effect on the economy (more than 1 MEcus and for EAIITA more than 300.000 Ecus)
Actions to be taken	Regional Operational Programmes, actions differ at regional level, for each region:
	ROP Eastern Macedonia and Thrace, ROP Central Macedonia, ROP Western Macedonia, ROP Epirus, ROP Thessaly, ROP Ionian Islands, ROP Western Greece, ROP Central Greece (Sterea Ellada), ROP Attica, ROP Peloponnesus, ROP Northern Aegean, ROP Southern Aegean, ROP Crete

Source: E(94)1716.

Table 3.16 National and regional economic and social programming, 2000–06

Axis 1: Development of Human Resources and Promotion of Employment

Principal institution Involved	Ministry of Education, Ministry of Culture	Manpower Employment Organisation ("Οργανισμός Απασχόλησης Εργατικού Δυναμικού" or "Ο.Α.Ε.Δ.")	Public Employment Services (Δημόσιες Υπηρεσίες Απασχόλησης) including Centres for promotion of employment ("Κέντρα Προώθησης Απασχόλησης")	National Observatory for Employment ("Εθνικό Παρατηρητήριο Απασχόλησης") National Institute of Employment ("Εθνικό Ινστιτούτο Εργασίας")	Private Employment Services involvement
Aims of institution	Improvement of competitiveness of Greek economy through development of its human resources Improvement and adjusting of employability of persons through enhancing systems of education and professional formation, of the upgrade of prototype. development of lifelong learning and support of continuous formation Concise adoption and implementation of energetic, precautionary and individualized approach in the battle against unemployment, especially youth and female unemployment, as well as long-term youth and adult unemployment Modernization and development of employment support public services Increase in the participation rate of employed, especially female employees, so as to reach EU averages More effective connecting of initial education and systems of formation to the system of continuous formation, as well as the needs of labor markets and country's economic development Human labor support in the research sector, its connection to the business area, and promotion of innovation of SMEs—modernization of labor market with the introduction of flexibility and adjusting capacity Promotion of entrepreneurship Support of efforts that aim to public sector modernization Development of a society of information in selected sectors of the Greek economy of great economic and social importance Promotion of equal opportunities for all, especially for nonprivileged groups threatened from social exclusion and improvement of their employability Promotion of equal opportunities between men and women Support of local initiatives and local employment agreements Support of implementation of concrete actions in programmes cofunded by other Structural Funds				
Actions to be taken	*Policy field 1:* • Precautionary approach actions, following Guidelines 1 &2 of European Employment Strategy	*Policy field 2:* • Favor job finding and repeated job finding for people in social exclusion • Securing of better access in basic services, such	*Policy field 3:* • Upgrading and expanding initial professional training, when levels are very low. • Preparation of strategy for rationalization of system and improvement of its effectiveness • Continuation and substantial improvement of education of the educators, centered around	*Policy field 4:* • Improvement and adjustment of skills of employees in SMEs, • Formation of public sector employees in significant issues, e.g.,	*Policy field 5:* • Development of special services- provision of consulting and individualized support, so as to ease accession and reaccession of

(Continued)

Table 3.16 (Continued)

• Repressive approach actions • Improvement and increase of adjustment of Public Employment Services and other structures of labor markets comprising: A Master plan of the Manpower Employment Organization that includes new structures, equipment and operations Actions for improving and effectively using existing structures (e.g., Centers for Promotion of Employment, National Observatory of Employment, National Institute of Employment) to study and analyze systematically new directions and needs in labor market, to prepare and assess integrated employment national strategies and policies, as well as monitoring and	as in education, formation, lifelong learning, professional orientation, consulting, employment promotion, introduction of required adjustments as to cover concrete needs of socially excluded people • special measures that support people in need, special measures to support people threatened by social exclusion, such as actions tackling illiteracy, foreign language learning, actions that improve basic skills, supportive actions (e.g., orientation, consulting, support in job search, support in first employment phase, psychological support etc.) • In case people with special needs: individualized approach that takes into account special conditions, type and seriousness of their needs, long-term approaches through integrated measures,	obtaining ICT and technological knowledge, rationalization and better organization of related actions • Enhancing access to third-degree education in sectors related to labor markets • Creation of sustainable postgraduate degrees in sectors related to market needs • Concrete measures to easy transition from school to work • Better connecting educational system and initial formation to labor market needs through programmes • Connection of education and initial formation with continuous and lifelong formation (the creation of unified system of certification for structures, educators, as well as for programmes and professional qualifications) • Expansion of the use of ICT in all levels of educational system • Development and expansion of systemic intervention for human resources for environmental and cultural matters • Upgrading and modernization of school and educational infrastructure	issues for economic and social cohesion • Promotion of entrepreneurship to ease creation of job opportunities (regulatory, taxing, reducing bureaucracy measures) • Adoption of flexibility actions in labor markets (partial, nonpermanent employment) • Development of human capital skills in research, technology and innovation, promotion of research in SMEs • Encouraging an approach based on partnership and the promotion of commitments on behalf of social partners in all appropriate level for improving modernization in the organization of labor	women in labor markets, including accession in job positions, and the promotion of female entrepreneurship, self-employment and the creation of their own enterprises • Improving capacity and of the quality of services for care and support of children, elderly, people with special needs, at the municipal and community level, as well as in the professional field, to reconciliate family to professional life. Funding of all-day schools to reduce school attrition in less-favored areas and to remove barriers in women occupation • Improvement of conditions of work and of prospects of career development, supporting higher participation rates of women in decision-

			• making, including in science • Improving information and awareness of public opinion in equality of two sexes, promotion of networking in female organization, in rendering sensitive policies in private and public sector in gender matters
cooperation of the National Action Plan for Employment, links to Information Society	• Securing of better access of the nonprivileged of the society of information, promotion of the social economy, local economic development and employment • Combating direct and indirect discriminations that are faced by nonprivileged groups in labor markets through a coherent set of actions to resolve the problem, including legal measures • Actions centered in children in primary school age with cultural and linguistic difficulties, such as schools of Greek expatriates, immigrants, Muslim families, to integrate them in education system and the society		

Axis 2: Transport

Principal institution Involved	Ministry of Environment, Planning and Public Works (former "ΥΠΕΧΩΔΕ")	Greek Railways "ΟΣΕ"	Organisation of Urban Transport in Attiki "ΟΑΣΑ"	Athens METRO

(Continued)

Table 3.16 (Continued)

Aims of institution	In roads:	In railways:	In airports:	In ports:	In urban infrastructure: Athens METRO:	Horizontal aims:
	Secure the continuation and completion of basic infrastructure network cofunded in the previous C.S.F., which comprises the Axis Patras-Athens-Thessaloniki—Euzonoi ("ΠΑΘΕ"), Egnatia Road and vertical connections with the rest of Balkan countries. These axes are part of Trans-European Networks. It also includes the Western axis (Ionian Road, from Antirio to Ioannina)	To complete the Operational Plan of "ΟΣΕ"	Secure continuation and completion of basic infrastructure network cofunded in the previous C. S.F., which comprises basic airports	Secure continuation and completion of basic infrastructure networks in ports, as cofunded in the previous C.S.F.		Taking into account all environmental regulation, environmental impact assessment studies and the EU laws for the protection of environment, including the of NATURA areas
	Improvement of accessibility of all regions in mainland Greece (especially those not served by "ΠΑΘΕ" & Egnatia Road), the Aegean and Ionian islands, and combating traffic problems in greater urban centers	To improve connection to EU and the rest of Europe, especially in the node of Thessaloniki	Effectively challenge the expected passenger and freight movement among great urban centers in Greece (Athens, Thessaloniki, Patras) through basic airports (SPATA and Thessaloniki)	Improving the country's connection to the rest of Europe, through building main road axes connecting basic ports (Athens, Thessaloniki, Piraeus, Patra, Igoumenitsa, Alexandroupoli), main emphasis in the country's gates to the rest of Europe	Project implementation and completion	
	Improving the country's connection to the rest of Europe, through building main road axes that have	To complete infrastructure from previous C.S.F.	Modernization and automatization of air traffic system	Challenge effectively the expected passenger and freight movement	Connectivity	

been included in Trans-European networks and in Pan-European transport corridors, the development of systems of integrated transports in key nodal points of the Greek road network			among great urban centers in Greece (Athens, Thessaloniki, Patras) through connection to central ports (Patras, Thessaloniki, Piraeus, Igoumenitsa, Alexandroupoli)	*Thessaloniki METRO:*
Challenge effectively the expected passenger and freight movement among great urban centers in Greece (Athens, Thessaloniki, Patras) mainly via completing ΠΑΘΕ, Egnatia and Ionian Road	To improve domestic connectivity, in nodes and with other means of transportation	Airport infrastructure development funding through special airport fees applied for this purpose, apart from Herakleion and Thessaloniki airport	Promote integrated network of ports to support balanced development in islands, funded by ROPs	
Managerial and administrational changes & improvements	To increase the speed of railway			Construction of Thessaloniki METRO, creation of stations for passengers transfers in buses and parking places, possibly through transferring the appropriation of property right
Improving road safety National pricing policy for tolls, to increase private sector participation and the rise of private contribution	*In suburban railways:* Completion of operational programmes for "ΟΑΣΑ" (Athens)			

(Continued)

Table 3.16 (Continued)

Actions to be taken	In roads:	In railways:	In airports:	In ports:	In urban infrastructure: Athens METRO:
	Axis Patras–Athens–Thessaloniki–Euzonoi ("ΠΑΘΕ"),	Operational Plan of 'ΟΣΕ and its investments	Infrastructure building, especially in Herakleion and Thessaloniki airport	Development of ports in Piraeus, Patras, Thessaloniki, Alexendroupoli	Completion of basic project of 18 km, as well as expansion of new lines (2&3) cofunded by C.S.F.
	Egnatia Road and vertical connections with the rest of Balkan countries	Improving railway connection to EU and the rest of Europe, through interventions in Greek parts of Trans-European and Pan-European railways and the creation of networks of integrated transports, especially in the node of Thessaloniki	Modernization of the electronic system of air traffic across the country and application of an automatic airport control system	Completion of port infrastructure in Igoumenitsa and Herakleion	Implementation of part of operational plan that refers to building stations with parking places, through transferring the appropriation of relevant rights
	Western axis (Ionian Road)	Completion of infrastructure that has started in the previous C.S.F. Put in operation of the new electrical line in "ΠΑΘΕ"	Preparation of a Vessel Traffic System (VTIMS)	Funding of an integrated network of ports	Financing and completion of the connection of the METRO with new Athens Airport
	Improvement of accessibility of all regions in mainland Greece (especially those not served by "ΠΑΘΕ" & Egnatia Road), the Aegean and Ionian islands,	Improving connection to other means of transportation, through improving integrated networks in ports, airports and other passenger and freight transportation nodes, especially in Athens and Thessaloniki		Emphasis in integrated freight centers in Piraeus (in «Θριάσιο Πεδίο») and in Thessaloniki	
	Transfer of management of vertical axes in Egnatia Road to Egnatia S.A.	Completion and operation of high speed trains along the Corinth, Athens and			Thessaloniki METRO:

Integration of management consultants in the implementation of "ΕΥΔΕ ΠΑΕ" and "ΕΥΔΕ ΜΕΔΕ"	Thessaloniki axis, especially in important and difficult parts (e.g., in Domokos tunnel)		property right	
Creation and organization of companies for: • the METRO Thessaloniki • the Athens Peripheral Ring (ΕΑΕΣΣΥ) • the Rio—Antirrio bridge (already signed)	Connecting the railway axis to "ΠΑΘΕ"		Creation of a company that will undertake all relevant procedures on behalf of public sector	
Creation and support of ΕΥΔΕ (founding companies) for every big road project axis, such as in South Peloponnese and North Crete, as well as integration of management consultants				
Action plan for road safety to suggest interventions in specific spots and specific improvements				

(Continued)

Table 3.16 (Continued)

Axis 3: Competitiveness			
		See Table 3.6	
Axis 4: Rural Development and Fisheries			
Principal institution Involved	Ministry of Agriculture		
Aims of institution	**Aim no 1: Improvement of competitiveness of the Greek agriculture to face challenges in international competitive environment**	**Aim no 2: Sustainable and integrated development of agricultural areas, to increase competitiveness and attractiveness and to regain economic and social operation**	**Aim no 3: Sustaining and improving of environment, natural resources, and land of agricultural areas**	**Aim no 4: Fisheries**
	Improvement of product quality in primary production and in manufactured products, to achieve balance between demand and supply and increase in efficacy of production in markets, including exports	Renewal and boosting of active agricultural population in agricultural areas	Protection, development and rational exploitation of natural resources and the environment, including woodland resources	Based on the IV and V multiannual programmes
	Product diversification and production of products offering new market opportunities	Creation of complementary or alternative activities in the framework of integrated local development interventions	Preservation of cultural heritage and traditions of the agricultural world	Avoid distortions
	Improvement of technical support and technical knowledge and know-how of agencies in the agricultural sector, including the	Removal of isolation of agricultural areas and improvement of basic services for the economy and the agricultural population	Prevention and upgrade of agricultural or woodland potential that has been harmed by fires or other natural disasters	Avoid aging of fishing fleet

organization and provision of formation tools, information and raising awareness Creation of preconditions for the improvement of attractiveness of agricultural jobs toward young people, with the aim to accelerate the renewal and boosting of active agricultural population, especially in areas presenting an inverse pyramid structure Improvement and upgrade of inflows in agricultural production Mitigation of deficiencies of rural structures & holdings (size and chopping)	Improvement of operations of local economies in mountainous and island areas Promotion of the appearance of agricultural areas, their advantages, and their natural wealth		Improve technological progress in fishing fleet Encourage the use of selected tools and methods of fishing Improve quality of products fished ad conserved in boats Improvement of conditions of work and security Actions of collective interest that favor interests in the whole fishery sector Combating of negative environmental externalities and improvement of the quality of products, even the disposal of surplus of some types of fishes Developing demand-based production in sea bass/ gilt-head brims

(Continued)

Table 3.16 (Continued)

Actions to be taken	Integrated interventions at the level of agricultural holdings Interventions at the level of manufacturing and trade of agricultural and woodland products Improvement of age composition of active agricultural population Improvement of mechanisms of support and information Interventions at the level of agricultural product Protection and development of natural resources and the environment Integrated programmes of rural development At each regional operation programme, special actions for agriculture are clearly proclaimed in relation to exploitation of natural resources, rural structures (including land-redistribution), the local utilization of products with emphasis in quality and its special characteristics, differentiation in agricultural cultivations, development of traditional sectors and introduction of new activities, protection and development of forest and natural resources through precautionary and restitutions measures, integrated complementary development and development of alternative activity, provision of services and structures in agricultural populations, clustering of agricultural enterprises, preservation of natural environment, of land, and heritage of the agricultural land In fisheries Adjustment of fishing activity Renewal and modernization of fishing fleet Protection and development of water resources, aquaculture, equipment of fishing ports, manufacturing and trade, and fishing in domestic waters Other measures Technical support Measures funded by other Structural Funds within the framework of the Operational Programme

Axis 5 Improved Quality of Life	Environment and Natural Heritage	Culture	Health
Principal institution Involved	Ministry of Public Works	Ministry of Culture, museums	Ministry of Health & hospitals
Aims of institution	Infrastructure creation and improvements Collection and processing of waste Promotion of biological wastewater treatment Harmonization of water policy with the EU Promotion of water policy that will encourage its sustainable use	Protection and exploitation of cultural heritage Development of contemporary civilization Development of sector of civilization in the framework of society of information Enhancing and specialization o human resources Balanced regional development, in supply and demand conditions for cultural goods and services, taking into account special characteristics and special needs	To promote all axes of the new strategy and reform in health, promoted by a new law Operation of all supportive mechanisms to promote the new strategy Introduction of new integrated systems of information and telemedicine Enhancing of further development of primary services in health care in urban centers Reduction of geographical inequalities in access of citizens in the Health system

Actions to be taken		
Actions for raising awareness in environmental matters Units of industrial cleaning Use of appropriate technically and financially rational techniques Biological wastewater treatment units Actions/initiatives for harmonizing water pricing Merge of smaller businesses in water to encourage better management participation of private sector Water policy comprising management actions and plans (the setting of a national network for the monitoring of the quality of water) Adoption of Water Framework Direction Priority actions for de-hydrated areas across the Greek territory Actions for appropriate management of protected areas Special actions of air and sound pollution	Actions to improve infrastructure in museums, services provided by them, as well as exploitation of museums, and archeological sites **In museums:** Improvement of technological equipment, Construction of new ones, raising of their educational dimension Inclusion in ordinary civilization life in the country Improvement of their communication policy Promotion of a network of production and trade of high quality copies and objects of high quality **In monuments and archeological sites:** Protection and exploitation Creation of modern and well organized spaces of reception Promotion of wider cultural paths Organization of modern actions of civilization in some monuments Raising education dimension Use of new technologies for information of public and promotion of cultural goods at international level Enhancing institutions and networks of cooperation with European partners Promotion of great communication events	Improvement of efficiency and effectiveness of hospitals by reducing their burden Promotion of prevention Actions for functional integration National Center for Emergency ("EKAB") and training **Mental Health** Actions to promote reform in mental health (based on EC 815/84) Enhancing of actions for deinstitutionalization of long-term patient in large mental health hospitals and for avoiding chronic hospitalization Development of an effective sectoral network of units of mental health, at local level, for precaution and immediate intervention, consulting and care, as well as of structures easing transition in socioeconomic inclusion (and reinclusion) **Care** Move away from traditional approach of protectionism toward an approach based on rights and equal opportunities Actions of description of extent and contribution of services of social care including qualitative and quantitative assessment of existing personnel Rationalization in organization, management, control of services of care, including their functional modernization and their connection to health and mental health services, to allow equal access of citizens, social inclusion, combat discriminations and reintegration in labor market, at local level (and potential creation of new structures serving these goals)

(Continued)

Table 3.16 (Continued)

Axis 6: Information Society				
Principal institution				
Involved				
Aims of institution	**In Education and Culture**	**In public administration and quality of life 1st priority**	**Employment and social inclusion**	**Digital Economy**
	Adjustment of the educational system in the requirements of digital age, to become characterized by an increased use of new technologies in networking in school, university and academic communities (including administrative services), from well trained teachers and students, development of digital educational material	The creation of open and effective public administration, with better services for citizens and enterprises, in an environment of transparency and increased accessibility in public information	Basic training in computers and informatics for broader groups of population that will bridge the gap between professional qualifications and needs in professions related to ICT	Use of ICT in SMEs and the three sectors of economy to increase productivity and competitiveness
	ICT to promote Greek spirit and civilization, through the documentation of cultural heritage and the protection of Greek language	Exploitation of ICT in domains such as in health, care, environment protection and transports, to improve quality of life of citizens	Special educational programmes and multimedia material in Greek language	Use applied electronic commerce, so that Greek firms adopt electronic
	Access in public spaces in less favored areas	Use ICT to improve service provided at national, local, and regional level	Adoption of flexible processes to exploit more appropriately libraries, municipal centers and other infrastructure. This action could combine with other concerning the reentry in the labor market	forms of entrepreneurial actions, in national and international level
	Train teachers individually or not, in the use of Internet and multimedia tools	Development on-line applications (including processes of public procurement)	Special action for the promotion of understanding and use of applications in CSF and Internet among women, elderly and socially disadvantaged groups of population	Creation of a legal framework that will ease the electronic implementation of

Turn by 2003 all graduates of compulsory education to digital literate	Use of ICT to simplify and redefine processes and communication in and among public administration, in all public sector, especially in fiscal and financial sector, social security, the justice sector, regional development and administration, as well as in emergency services Completion of actions from previous CSF Support in the reorganization of services of the labor market **2nd priority** Support in management of resources from Structural Funds and transition to Euro for every level of public administration **3rd priority** Exploitation of ICT for the support of a broader strategy of provision of improved services of health and care for all citizens and reorganization of public administration and budget in the health system Connection of scientific and administrative personnel in health with infrastructure in telemedicine in precaution, diagnoses, and treatment	Energetic support of actions in labor market through ICT	transactions in an environment that will secure the protection of private life and trust of consumers Enforcement of infrastructure necessary to operate electronic businesses Introduction of electronic processes for procurement Development of manufacturing with digital content Creation of high-technology SMEs Use of ICS applications in businesses for energy and environmental protection Systems of tele-work Applications for businesses in distant and island regions Collaborations among enterprises and with academic and research institutions for development and productive use of technologies and ICTs, digital learning environments, alternative

(Continued)

Table 3.16 (Continued)

organizational environments, knowledge-intense work, enterprise networking, and "smart cards" Upgrading high speed national research network and telematic services and ICT infrastructure in research centers Development and diffusion of content and information in digital platform for the research community, education and training of young researchers	Connection of regional and local health centers (including centers in distant, island, or mountainous regions) **4th priority** Adoption of a system of subsidies for funding innovative pilot actions, where public administration services, local and regional, are involved **5th priority** Adoption and support of geographical and environmental information and managerial systems, linking central to regional and local administration **6th priority** "Smart transports" through adoption of telematic applications, in collaboration and coordination with management authority (effective use of ICT in road transports, development and support of electronic systems of circulation in air transports, as well as systems of management of urgent

Actions to be taken

Axis 7: Regional Development

	Regional Development		
Principal institution Involved	Regional Authorities		
Aims of institution	Regional Operational Programmes, actions differ at regional level, for each region: The Attiki ROP, the Central Macedonia ROP, the Eastern Macedonia and Thrace ROP, the Western Macedonia ROP, the Epirus ROP, the Crete ROP, the Northern Aegean ROP, the Southern Aegean ROP, the Central Greece ROP, the Western Greece ROP, the Thessaly ROP, the Peloponnese ROP, the Ionian Island ROP		

Actions to be taken	*The key aims/objectives are as follows:*
	• Interventions which strengthen the international competitiveness of the regional economies, identify advantages and promote extroversion
	• Implementation of a strategy to disseminate innovation, equal opportunities in having access to research and technology, and upgrading of human resources
	• Interventions to relieve isolation
	• Interventions to protect and promote cultural and environmental resources in each Region
	The programmes include the following types of actions:
	• Development of the spirit of innovation in the Regions
	  ○ Development of urban programmes—Urban development
	  ○ Local development and rural development
	
	Human resource actions include, among others:
	• Local Employment Pacts and other initiatives to promote employment
	• Day care services for children and senior citizens, and promotion of equal opportunities
	Local authorities are in charge of preparing the integrated urban programmes in small scale local zones
	Actions for rural development will focus on two basic types of rural areas:
	• Areas that have been (or are expected to be) affected to a greater extent by the Common Agricultural Policy
	Disadvantaged areas, and areas with specific development problems		

Source: EC (2000).

In the 2007–13 period (Table 3.17 that follows), the strategy focused on (1) investments in the production sector; (3) the society of knowledge and innovation; (3) employment and social cohesion; (4) the institutional environment; and (5) the attractiveness of Greece and its regions as a place of investment, employment, and living.

Finally, in the 2014–20 period (Table 3.18), strategy is influenced by the "Europe 2020" strategy that focuses on smart, inclusive, and sustainable growth and centers around (1) competitiveness and entrepreneurship; (2) human resources; (3) environmental protection and the development of an environmental friendly economy; (4) modernization of transportation and energy infrastructure; and (5) institutional competence of the public Administration.

What the Tables cannot show is that whenever existing or new institutions, large-scale businesses (domestic or foreign, public, semipublic, or private), and stronger and mature interests are involved in the design and implementation of policies, then more funds are requested and finally allocated to these policies.

3.5 Regulation and competition

Greece witnessed a transition of its economic model during the study period. The general view held during the 1980s was that the state has to deliberately espouse the necessity of the public sector and put large enterprises under its authorship, by retaining the monopoly in most utilities and the provision of natural resources (such as energy, water, etc.). This view progressively changed during the 1990s, when the significance of regulation and that of strengthening competition was espoused (Vaitsos et al., 1994). A large part of the Greek society had to be convinced of this shift. Hence, academic debates were held toward this direction and the necessity of privatization (Vaitsos et al., 1994). In the meantime, significant amounts were transferred to state-owned enterprises and public-sector monopolies. The availability of Cohesion funds and the protectionist character of the Common Agricultural Policy has not helped to change this direction easily.

Throughout the 1990s and 2000s, following a number of EU policies, an effort was taken to introduce regulatory processes, far from the central authority and services and to launch a number of institutions less vulnerable to bureaucracy and state arbitrariness that would also produce competition in some industries. These were the Greek National Council for Radio and Television (NCRTV) (created in 1989), the Supreme Council for Civil Personnel Selection (in 1994), the Hellenic Competition Commission (in 1995), the Hellenic Telecommunications and Post Commission (in 1992 that undertook the surveillance and regulation of posts in 1998), the Greek Ombudsman (in 1997), the Hellenic Data Protection Authority (in 1997), the Regulatory Authority for Energy (in 1999), and the Hellenic Authority for Communication Security and Privacy (in 2003) (Papoulias, 2011; Kalogirou, 1994).

3.6 Critical issues: the use and absorption of funds and programming failures

The use of funds differs from their allocation. Despite limited amounts being directed to competitiveness, some of them were invested in public or semipublic

Table 3.17 2007−2013 National Strategic Reference Framework: strategic aims, general targets, their specialisation and focus.

Strategic aims	General target	Target specialization	Focus on (specific targets)
Production investments	**Rise of export—orientation and FDI inflows**	Target-oriented investment attraction	Improvement of institutions and supportive structure, infrastructure, and mechanisms and tools for entrepreneurship, connection to international integrated systems of production and location of permanent cooperation of Greek and international enterprises
			Development and attraction of high added-value activities in high technology industries, with increasing demand of scientific human capital
		Improvement of the export-oriented character of the Greek production system.	Support of productive investments for reducing import penetration and increasing the presence of Greek firms in local and international markets
		Exploitation of the country's geographical advantage as a gate to South Eastern European Countries in the field of entrepreneurship	Reinforcing the role of trade, tourism and their accompanying services in the production system, in order to increase the presence and marketing of Greek business and their products in international markets
		Turning the country an international business and economic center	Developing targeted promotion programme for investments via international and regional communication channels, to attract foreign prospective investors
	Development of entrepreneurship and the rise of productivity	Supporting predilection for entrepreneurship	Development of a rational system of support structure for entrepreneurship, upgrade and simplify entrepreneurship environment, obstacle removal in the development of SMEs and creation of friendly administrative and regulatory environment

(Continued)

Table 3.17 (**Continued**)

Strategic aims	General target	Target specialization	Focus on (specific targets)
		Shift from needs-driven entrepreneurship to corporate	Reorientation of governmental subsidies to the benefit of qualitative and specialized entrepreneurship, development of communication plan and entrepreneurship education
		Entrepreneurship of higher potential	Improvement of coastal connection mainly for social purposes, promotion of sustainable and secured mobility, improvement of services provided in ports, in order to become factors that attract activities and investments
		Supporting of innovative entrepreneurship in sectors with competitive advantage	
		Promotion of entrepreneurial dimensions in protection and management of environment	
	Differentiation of touristic product	Enrichment of tourism and its product	Exploitation of natural and cultural deposit for expansion of touristic season
			Dynamic development of special and alternative forms of tourism via integrated and innovative acts that aim at modernizing tourism.
			Completing and upgrading infrastructure for developing traditional, special and alternative forms of tourism
		Promotion of touristic product	Exploitation of knowledge society's achievements and tools and modem information and communication technology

(*Continued*)

Table 3.17 (Continued)

Strategic aims	General target	Target specialization	Focus on (specific targets)
Society of Knowledge and Innovation	Improvement of quality and intensity of investments in human capital, to upgrade the educational system	Investment in future, promotion of reforms in educational system and improvement of access and level of basic skills for all	Reshaping educational programmes/curricula, acceleration of introduction of new technologies in education and systematic measurement of progress achieved through (1) development of an evaluation system for primary, secondary education and early career formation, (2) development of national evaluation system that ensures the quality and documentation for HEI
			Improvement of conditions and levels of education for people with special needs and disabilities, and reinforcement of decentralization in administrative organization and function of an educational system
		Support of Lifelong Learning	Widening lifelong learning, with development of a system of appropriate motivation (especially for low-skilled people, elderly, school-leavers)
		Facing early school leaving by fighting against school failure and drop out	
		Improvement of quality and attractiveness of professional education and formation	Reforming the structure and connection of the specialization of educational programmes/curricula in the field of initial professional formation, defining professional rights and institutionalizing of systems that acknowledge formal educational certification, at the level of European framework of professional qualifications

(Continued)

Table 3.17 (Continued)

Strategic aims	General target	Target specialization	Focus on (specific targets)
	Support of Research, Technology and promotion of Innovation in all industries as basic factor of restructuring of the Greek economy and transition in the knowledge economy	Production of new knowledge in priority fields for the production tissue that serve applied policies	Creation of networked centers of excellence and their connection to partners from abroad. Improving competitiveness and exporting capacity of businesses and restructuring of the Greek economy through a shift toward the production of products and provision of high technology and added-value services, cooperation with other business and/or agencies of research and technological development (RTD), creation of national industrial poles of research and technology development in sectors of major significance, creation of centers of excellence and their connection to foreign
		Converting knowledge to innovative products, services and processes, aiding knowledge and technology transfer toward businesses and SMEs	Innovation programs, integrated strategic actions for innovation at regional level, support intermediate public and private agencies, creating spin-off, support of new, innovative and/or high technology SMEs and groups of SMEs (clusters)
		Promotion of export orientation through international cooperation in RTD	Support in participation of Community Programs and intergovernmental organizations, support of cooperation actions in the 7th Framework Programme in RTD and on Competitiveness and Innovation Framework Programme, support of activity cooperation in RTD, programmes and infrastructure in the context of European Programmes with third countries (Western Balkans, Black Sea) with European intergovernmental organizations in the context of creation of European Research Area

Table 3.17 (Continued)

Strategic aims	General target	Target specialization	Focus on (specific targets)
		Horizontal actions for human capital in Research, technology and innovation	Reinforcement of human capital, mobility, through RTD and production agencies in national and international level and integration of highly educated personnel in businesses
			Research activities that improve human research potential
			Support for basic research in the context of reform and unification of the institutional framework that transcends the organization and operation of Master's Degrees and Research
	Nation's Digital Convergence with integration and systematic use of ICT in Sectors of Economic and Social activity	Productivity improvement through the use of ICT	Use of ICT and provision of digital services toward firms, support of the contribution of ICT industry in the Greek economy, promotion of entrepreneurship in sectors that exploit new technologies and promote further a modern environment of electronic and broadband infrastructure that twill improve significantly Greece's "network readiness," as well as institutional interventions that will speed up the transition to digital broadcast
		Improving quality of life through the use of ICT	Exploitation of new technologies in informatics and electronic communication in sectors that improve everyday life of citizens, supporting in parallel equal access to new technologies. Focus on development of digital services in serving citizens and promoting access of citizens in broadband and innovative services

(Continued)

Table 3.17 (Continued)

Strategic aims	General target	Target specialization	Focus on (specific targets)
Employment and Social Cohesion	**Support adaptability of employees and businesses**	Implementation of a National system linking Professional Education and Formation with Employment	Ex ante tracing of needs and changes in employment market and development of an Integrated System of Research of Employment Needs
			Establishment of a common system of certification of supplied initial and continuous professional formation
			Defining standards of recognized initial learning of people
			Completion and application of institutional framework for the provision of programmes of continuous formation
			Reform of the system of employee formation
			Development of a system of provision of necessary motives for the participation of people in actions of lifelong learning
			Development of services of lifelong consulting and professional orientation and support of participation of self-employed in programmes for upgrading skills
		Improving labor quality and productivity	Introduction of new and innovative methods and forms of employment, with emphasis in policies that will seek the flexibility, in conditions of security for the employees
			Emphasis in the support of the role of social partners, the promotion of satisfying conditions of security and hygiene at work, encouragement of active participation of labor force of the elderly in facing collective losses of jobs

(Continued)

Table 3.17 (Continued)

Strategic aims	General target	Target specialization	Focus on (specific targets)
		Support adaptability of businesses (especially of the SMEs)	Motives for investments in improving skills of employees and developing a learning culture
			Employee formation and promotion of new techniques for lifelong learning in businesses (including formation and diffusion of ICT, continuous formation of low-skilled employees and employees of high/technical specialization, women formation and elderly and support of relevant initiatives by social partners
			Promoting of Corporate Responsibility in businesses
			Promoting and rewarding of new structure and methods of organization of businesses and work in relation innovation integration, personalized actions for long life learning of the self-employed
			Double approach: facilitating self-employment and small business start-ups and growth enhancement of the SMEs
	Facilitating access in employment	Widening, restructuring and improvement of effectiveness of active policies in the labor market	Increase of financing efforts until 2013
		Support of female employment and promotion of equal access and development in the job market	Continuation of investments aiming to women availability without obstacles for employment, in order to combine their career and family responsibilities

(Continued)

Table 3.17 (Continued)

Strategic aims	General target	Target specialization	Focus on (specific targets)
			Measures reducing wage divergence, concentration and segmentation of labor market, related to gender discrimination
			Creation of measures of support of single-parented families
	Support of youth employment	Creation of opportunities for studying, working, and for complementary formation, acquisition of job experience or employment in every early school leaver that is unemployed. Reduction of transitory period between graduation and the active professional life
			Offering opportunities of participation to active employment policies, before the completion of 12 months of unemployment
	Activating at least 25% of long-term unemployed and reduction of long-term unemployment inflows	
	Increase of sustainable, newly created businesses from self-employed, especially new unemployed	
	Modernization and upgrading of the structure and systems of labor market that serve the citizen (including intervention of systemic character)	Continuous improvement, upgrading and converting the Center for Promotion of Employment of the (Greek) Manpower Agency of Greece into one-stop shops, offering individualized services that integrate three basic operations: information, career-orientation, job placement, in cooperation of the actions of the network with the Ministry of Employment and Social Protection
			Development of a framework for linking labor

(*Continued*)

Table 3.17 (Continued)

Strategic aims	General target	Target specialization	Focus on (specific targets)
			supply and demand with the participation of public and private sector agencies, local administration, tertiary education and social partners as well as development of an integrated network of an integrated service provision for employment with certified structures of public and private sector
			Redefinition and upgrade of the role and operation of an observatory for Employment and Computer Research.
		Fighting undeclared work and nonregistered unemployment	Upgrading of mechanisms of the job market surveillance, increasing the sensitivity of employers at local scale, the support of interventions of the Hellenic Labor Inspectorate, implementation of existing legislation for undeclared work and the regulation of (future) migration flows
		Implementing of integrated policies for active ageing of the labor force	Increase of chances for employment and formation for the elderly that participate in labor force, combating age discrimination, improving labor market demand projections, withdraw motives for early retirement
		Systematic registration and prediction of changes in the local labor markets due to the productive restructuring of economic activity	Upgrade of potential of existing structures ("ΣΕΙΠ," "ΟΑΕΔ," "ΠΑΕΠ," "ΕΚΕΠΣ") for early diagnosis of problems and development of quick reaction in changes
		Embodying principles of Community Initiative EQUAL in the development policy (including interventions of systemic character)	

Table 3.17 (Continued)

Strategic aims	General target	Target specialization	Focus on (specific targets)
	Promotion of social integration, to secure equal access of all in labor market and prevention of marginalization and exclusion		
	Institutionalization of an effective and financially sustainable health system that will offer qualitative and individualized services in citizens and focus on continuous upgrade of services of care and prevention	Development of network of Primary Health Care and Public Health	
		Improving responsiveness and secondary health care (hospitals) and the quality of provided services	
		Promotion of Informatics Technology and e-services for health and social Solidarity - Completion of policy for the introduction of digital technology	
		Reforms in the field of mental health and development of rehabilitation policies	
	Highlight economic, social and developmental character of gender equality issues, correlating them with main national policy priorities (Development- Employment- Social Cohesion)	Promoting of specified targeted measures for female support	
		More effective adjustment of gender dimension in sectorial and regional policies of all priorities of NSRF policies	
		Support female employment and promotion of equal access and development in the labor market	

(Continued)

Table 3.17 (Continued)

Strategic aims	General target	Target specialization	Focus on (specific targets)
		Reintegration in labor market after long term absence	
		Support of women entrepreneurship	
		Securing of accessible units for child care units and people in need	
		Facing violence against women	
Institutional environment	Improving the quality of public policies and their effective implementation for upgrading the quality of life and facilitating entrepreneurial action	Improving the quality of the public policies and support open governance	Improving the quality and mechanisms of design and implementation of public policies, by prioritizing policies in specific sectors of public activity, especially of horizontal character, in combination with modernization of structures and processes of operation in public services in respective fields and the education of personnel
			Support of transparency and accountability of the action of public principles, the promotion of active participation of the citizen and of social consensus and the securing of fair and equal treatment of citizens and the businesses
		Modernization of institutional context of regulation of public action and the structures and operational procedures of public services	Support of entrepreneurship with removal of bureaucratic obstacles imposed in the normative framework and out of organizational practices and operations in public services, minimization of public sector costs from the adjustment of enterprises in existing regulations, modernization of processes of procurement of goods and services by the public sector
			Reinforcing the efficiency and effectiveness of the operation of public administration and

(Continued)

Table 3.17 (Continued)

Strategic aims	General target	Target specialization	Focus on (specific targets)
			improvement of the quality of the work and services produces in critical sectors of public action
			Orientation of labor organization and the practices of public services toward the needs of users of public goods and the development of simple and flexible infrastructure for public sector action
			Use of new technologies in support of the achievement of strategic goals public agencies, in the context of general entrepreneurial restructuring and empowerment. Special mechanisms will be created for this purpose, time scheduling of respective actions and synergy and complementary actions that will secure the successful integration of ICT in public services
		Development of human force in the public administration	Modernization of the institutional framework of personnel management in the public sector, by emphasizing its rational utilization, through mobility, the development of modern public administration structures for the personnel of the public sector agencies, the empowerment of skills and technical knowledge, in association with participation motives for their training and certification
			Reinforcing responsibility of the personnel of the public administration, creation of more productive attitudes and behavior oriented toward the values of efficient, effective, open and fair public administration and the

Table 3.17 (Continued)

Strategic aims	General target	Target specialization	Focus on (specific targets)
			improvement of quality of the working life of the personnel
		Creation of mechanisms to support implementation	Securing the necessary political and technical support for the successful implementation of actions and the systematic documentation, analysis and assessment of the state of the country, by exploiting the use of European and international experience.
Attractiveness of Greece and its regions as a place for investments, labor, & living	**Development and modernization of natural infrastructure and their coherent services in transportation systems**	Facing lack of continuity in Trans-European transportation networks	Completion of the country's road and railroad network, the country's Trans-European Road Network, with emphasis placed in the road network and the principal connections with neighboring countries, as well as completion of basic railroad network (PAThE)
		Development combined transports and reinforcing intermodality of transport systems	Connection of infrastructure with the Trans-European transport networks
		Connection of areas across the land with Trans-European transportation networks	Connection of urban centers, productive areas and main tourist destinations of the country with the Trans-European networks
		Developing and expanding urban transportation	Support of infrastructure for Public Transportation Means in urban centers, to reduce circulation problems
		Upgrading the infrastructure	Modernization of road, railroads, ports and airports, to increase the quality of services and security of users

(Continued)

Table 3.17 (Continued)

Strategic aims	General target	Target specialization	Focus on (specific targets)
	Safe and sustainable supply of energy	Promotion of institutional and organizational interventions	Improve the effectiveness and efficiency of the system of production of projects and services
		Completing and modernizing the electricity network	Connection of the country with TEN-E (trans-European networks in Energy)
			Support and modernization of the national interconnected system of energy transport, including the connection of islands with the mainland, and the increase of its capacity for location of stations of renewable energies
		Reducing the dependence on oil, in a more environmental friendly manner	Promoting the penetration of renewable energy sources and natural gas in the country's energy balance
			Improving the energy effectiveness, research and development of innovative energy technologies and the rational management of mineral sources
	Sustainable environmental management	Rational management of land systems	Integrated management for solid and hazardous waste and protection from soil erosion, degradation, desertification and pollution, completion of the implementation of infrastructure projects for the management of solid and hazardous waste, to achieve targets set through national and community legislation
		Management of water sources and protection of sea environment	Achieving and maintaining the good condition in all water systems, the withdrawal of degradation of surface, underground, seawater systems and the sustainable management of water sources
			Management of urban waste, with priority given on covering the needs of Directive 92/271

(Continued)

Table 3.17 (Continued)

Strategic aims	General target	Target specialization	Focus on (specific targets)
			and to conform with national and European legislation, the provision of drinking water in adequate quantities and good quality and the maintenance and restitution of good quality of swimming waters (in implementing Directive 2000/60) for the provision of good condition of surface and under-surface waters and border cooperation for the good management of intraborder water catchment areas and the implementation of international conventions for the protection of sea environment
		Securing and maintaining the quality of atmosphere and hearing environment	Achieving and maintaining the quality level of the atmosphere and its environment, strategic reduction of gas emissions and other particles by the industry, fall of levels of noise in urban centers and sensitive in noise areas or areas of special uses and management of gas emissions
		Facing climatic change	Achieving the Kioto's Protocol Agreement for CO_2 levels and other gas emissions
		Risk management	Integrated national network of civil protection and upgrade of all services for civil protection and the facing of physical and technological destruction, the coordination of restitution, infrastructure for civil protection, development and modernization of mechanisms, their tools

(Continued)

Table 3.17 (Continued)

Strategic aims	General target	Target specialization	Focus on (specific targets)
			and the equipment for simultaneous use of synergies in interstate and interborder level
		Sustainable management of natural environment	Creation of a connected, organized and functional networks of protected areas of biodiversity, improvement of the state of maintenance of habitats and the populations of endangered species and areas of ecological interest, the maintenance and revealing of natural landscapes of high esthetic value, the integrated developmental and environmental design of protected areas and their incorporation in participatory processes in the design and management of protected areas
	Implementing of effective environmental policies	Improving planning and the implementation of environmental policy	Creating mechanisms and means and supporting agencies and institutions for control and exercise of environmental policies, by developing financial tools, promoting financial means of application of environmental policies, and the credible environmental information and evaluation of effects of programmes and projects
		Civil society for environmental protection issues	Stimulating citizens, establishing democratic and participative forms of public consultation between the State and the Civil Society, in designing environmental policies and programmes, in developing skills of all employees in protection and management of environment and environmental education

(Continued)

Table 3.17 (Continued)

Strategic aims	General target	Target specialization	Focus on (specific targets)
	Revealing Culture as a critical factor for the country's economic development	Support of Cultural Infrastructure in the country	Developing infrastructure of Modern Civilization in urban centers and rural areas
			Creating cultural infrastructure and services in islands, mountainous areas and across important road axes and seaways
		Boosting demand for culture	Developing quality services for cultural institutions of European and/or international scope

Table 3.18 Strategic Vision of the 2014–2020 National Strategic Reference Framework

1. Competitiveness—Entrepreneurship

Basic Sectors:

- Energy
- Agro-food industry & Blue Growth
- ICT (Information & Communication technologies)
- Environment
- Pharmaceutical Products
- Health
- Transportation & Logistics
- Culture & Tourism

Emphasis in:

- Creation of business-friendly environment which attracts investments
- Smart Specialization, Innovation, Research & Technology
- Regional Priorities & Strengths
- Competitive advantage of country/region
- Supportive Entrepreneurship Structures
- Orientation toward exports
- Access to finance
- Development of entrepreneurship cooperative culture
- Added-value domestic production
- Expansion to new markets & enrichment of the offered touristic product
- New generation of investment at ICT
- Promotion & utilization of the cultural heritage, the creative industry, and of the modern cultural creation

2. Human Resources

Health

- Rearrangement of the existing model of the health provision services in order to improve the cost-efficiency
- Access to high quality health infrastructure for all
- Primary care
- Focus on those threatened by exclusion

Social Inclusion

- Targeted intervention to combat the crises consequences
- Strengthen of public prevention policy / combat poverty and social exclusion
- Interventions for the traditional team-goals of the welfare politics, but also for the other teams threatened by exclusion from the labor market
- Connection with civil society
- Migration

Employment, Education & Resources

- Facilitate the entrance to the labor market and ensure the first occupation
- Connection between education and employment-guided by the capability demand
- Mobility-employment upgrade
- Employment Subsidization
- Actions for the integration of the youth and the long run unemployed people to the labor market

(Continued)

Table 3.18 (Continued)

		• High collaboration for the "guarantee for the youth" initiative • Utilization of the Social Economy • Redefinition of the Hellenic Manpower Employment Organization operational model and rearrangement of it • Combat undeclared work • Effectiveness improvement of the Greek educational system • Lifelong learning

3. Environmental Protection—Environmentally-Friendly Economy

- Efficient use of resources and low carbon dioxide emissions
- Effective waste management ("acquis communautaire")—Recycling
- Entrepreneurial opportunities in developing sectors
- Energy Saving—Energy Efficiency
- Renewable Energy Sources
- Danger management and prevention from climate change
- Protection and designation of biodiversity and natural landscape
- Cultural Environment Protection
- Complete urban development—Clean transportation

4. Development—Modernization of the Transportation and Energy Infrastructure

Transportation
- Completion of the national network (basic trans-European transport network)
- Development of networks for the reinforcement of Entrepreneurship
- Forward combined transportations/ Junctions logistics
- Upgrade of ports

Energy
- Modernization and expansion of the transportation and distribution networks of electric energy and natural gas
- Creation of competitive market's requirements

(Continued)

Table 3.18 (Continued)

5. Institutional Competence of the Public Administration		
Management & Control System of the NSRF (National Strategic Reference Framework) • National Level • Regional Level • Local Level • Simplification of Management System • Support of the Beneficiaries	Public Administration Horizontal Intervention • Simplification/Law • Codification • Human Resources Development • Educated and efficient human capital • E-Governance	Public Administration Sectorial Intervention • Business Friendly Environment • Justice • Health • Fiscal/Taxation Reforms • Targeting projects of the support programme

Source: Ministry of Finance and Competitiveness (2014 :70).

Table 3.19 Indicative actual spending of Community Funds, 1st C.S.F. (1989–1994) in Greece

	Expenditure in training–restructuring			Investment expenditure				Total expenditure
	Public	Rest of institutions	Total	Public	Semipublic Enterprises ("ΔEKO")	Private	Total	
Billion Euros	2.73	1.38	4.11	5.58	3.52	3.23	12.33	16.4
%	66	34	100	45	29	26	100	100

Source: Regional Development Plan, 1989–1993, p. 26.

companies that later became privatized. In the 1st C.S.F., less than a third of funds allocated to the competitiveness programme went to the private sector, while significant expenditure was directed to public enterprises (Table 3.19), and inelastic expenses, such as wages and salaries. At the time, the national telecommunication company obtained substantial funds which continued over the years, aiming at the sector's restructuring, even though it was later purchased by another European telecommunication company. Thus, in retrospect, it is difficult to judge EU and Greek redistribution policies purely in funding allocation terms.[6]

Data from each operational programme should be read cautiously, taking into account the structure of each programme. For example, the 1989–93 competitiveness programme reveals an emphasis placed on training rather than on enterprises (Table 3.20). In this program, only 37% was devoted to enterprises support, of which the Community contributed 27%. Infrastructure support for competitiveness represented 17% of total funds originally planned, 60% of which were offered by the Community. At the same time, in proportional terms the Community has over-emphasized support for training than for other targets. One can see in Table 3.20 that the contribution of the private sector for enterprise support, training of employees and in total was scheduled to be more extended than that made by the Community.

Concerning the use of EU funds, a large part was directed to nonemployment intensive policies. This is the case of the environmental and green engineering policies promoted by the 2000–06 C.S.F., and of the capital-intensive policies of the 2004 Greek Development Law,[7] advanced at a difficult time in the Greek economy.

---

[6] A special research is required to find out what part of EU funding and value added finally remained in domestic economies or transferred elsewhere, to the macroeconomic and microeconomic benefit of other economies. It is the author's view that the Greek economy would have ranked as one of the most harmed, in terms of capital invested by Government and the EU that leaked away, to the benefit of other neighboring economies. The other side of this negative outcome is a contribution of less developed countries, such as Albania (where significant amounts were transferred) and the diffusion of development efforts across the European space.

[7] The Greek Private Investments Law is referred here as Development Law, its most popular name.

Table 3.20 1989−93: The limited contribution of Community to enterprise support

	Total		Type of expenditure		
	Amounts	%	Community %	National %	Private %
Enterprise support	254,168	37	27	9	64
Infrastructure support	114,071	17	60	37	3
Training of employees in private sector	259,680	38	37.5	12.5	50
Training of employees in public sector	61,044	9	75	25	–
Implementation	2000	0	–	–	–
Total	690,963		40.6	16.4	43

Source: CEE, 1992, in constant 1992 prices, millions ECUs.

Problems with the absorption of EU Cohesion Funds are also important. For instance during the 2000−06 period, no Operational Program absorbed more than half of its funds before September 2005 (Table 3.21). Five years elapsed to reach half of the financial absorption targets. The average per Operational Program absorption was at 13.2% in September 2003 and 31.2% in September 2005. Programs that were very critical for the future of the Greek economy, such as that on competitiveness, were at a remarkable low ranking position in absorption terms, as only 28.61% of funds were absorbed by September 2005. This was at a very significant time in modern economic history, only a few years before the global crisis erupted. This bad performance should account, at least partially, for the substantial loss in the competitiveness of the Greek economy in the first half of the last decade, exposing the economy even more to the crisis. Fund absorption is of course a matter of experienced managerial and political personnel, and of organisational preconditions, as rising absorption figures reveal after 2005.

One can extract some additional conclusions from Table 3.21. It is no coincidence that all island regions (South Aegean, Ionian islands, Northern Aegean), as well as the less advanced regions of Epirus have a difficulty in absorbing funds (and are placed at the bottom of the list for September 2005). These are the most geographically isolated Greek regions, suffering from long-term administration problems, and lacking the capacity to implement programmes, as well as lacking the required human resources for their implementation. Furthermore, one cannot see as a coincidence that the newest operational programme of "Information Society" (first time applied in Greece) lies at the very bottom of the list.

The 2003 interim report[8] of the 2000−06 C.S.F. questioned its efficacy. It identified that few amongst the Operational Programs were significantly lagging behind in implementation terms. Principal problems for their relatively weak performance

---

[8] Submitted in October 2003 and based on the interim reports in 24 operational programmes of C.S.F., the exploitation of data from the Greek Integrated Information System, and primary data collection.

Table 3.21 Absorption of EU funds for all programs in the 2000−06 period

Sectoral Operational Programs (S.O.P.) and Regional Operational Programs (R.O.P.)	% Absorption	
	September 2003	September 2005
Employment and Professional Formation	20.00	43.87
ROP Attica	21.78	42.59
Road and Marine Transport Infrastructure and Urban Development ("OAAAA")	37.02	41.42
Education and Initial Formation ("EΠEAEK")	22.05	40.81
ROP Western Greece	19.24	38.36
ROP Crete	12.31	38.06
Culture	20.32	37.54
Fisheries	15.56	36.94
Agricultural development	19.23	32.04
Railways, Airports, Urban transports ("ΣAAΣ")	12.43	31.36
ROP Western Macedonia	9.47	31.21
Health and Care	6.97	30.95
ROP Thessaly	7.04	30.05
ROP Central Macedonia	10.70	29.19
ROP Eastern Macedonia and Thrace	10.96	28.84
Competitiveness	7.95	28.61
Environment	12.39	27.48
ROP South Aegean	10.10	26.15
ROP Peloponnese	6.79	24.01
ROP Ionian Islands	9.17	23.17
ROP Central Greece	5.93	22.77
ROP Epirus	5.90	22.29
ROP Northern Aegean	5.36	21.13
Information Society	8.09	20.88
Average per Operational Program	13.2	31.24

Source: MoF (2003).

were found to be: (1) a large component of innovative or simply new actions; (2) a very wide and varied spectrum of actions; (3) aspects of planning and the readiness of projects; (4) failure to correctly anticipate demand, on behalf of prospective beneficiaries; (5) inadequacies in the performance of implementing authorities and final beneficiaries; and (6) unforeseen difficulties beyond the control of competent authorities (MoF, 2003: 17). It emphasized that conditions external to Greece's economic environment, especially participation in the common currency zone, the EU enlargement, and the slowdown of growth rates in the EU and globally, appeared to have some effect upon the C.S.F. performance.

However, the report diagnosed that the acceleration of the private and public sector investments until that moment significantly contributed to the relatively high ratios of investments to GDP (MoF, 2003: 13). Thus, it is not strange that its principal suggestion, to partially redistribute the pie of resources, failed to empha-size the specific need to enhance the amounts directed to the private sector and the supportive mechanisms needed.

Furthermore, in its compulsory ex-ante assessment (derived from article 41 of EC regulation 1260/99), the 2000—06 Regional Development Program indicated that, with respect to programming experience, the Greek state has faced significant difficulties in preparing, implementing, and monitoring programmes, which leads to partial application of programming (EC, 2000: 20).

One can identify several programming weaknesses. For instance, in the 2000—06 program on competitiveness, the SWOT analysis was implemented sepa-rately for each of the four sectors that originally composed the program, which were simply united to form the general SWOT analysis on competitiveness, without considering further aspects and a more general strategy (MoF, 2003: 3). Furthermore consecutive SWOT analyses had referred neither to previous SWOT analyses nor to any available scientific and research work and analyses. The latter were needed to strengthen not only the organizational and planning elements but also the strategic, long-term development choices and policies followed, at least for sectoral-level programs. The use of more robust analysis was not promoted (nor requested). For example, none of the EU-funded programs—and especially the Competitiveness program—had made use of econometric techniques for studying effects and impact, both ex-ante and ex-post.[9] Applied in certain cases, economet-rics would have helped to investigate which factors influence or associate more with a successful or unsuccessful outcome of projects and actions (such as the application of business support policies and funds).[10] After the completion of the 2nd C.S.F., the scientific background of implemented policies was substantially weakened and not taken seriously into account. Choices were rather transferred from institutions specialized in economic planning and research and other relevant think tanks (such as the Greek Regional Development Institute and the Greek Center of Planning and Economic Research) to several poorly informed and inade-quately equipped consultancies and their associated consultants of low scientific and academic credentials. At the time, the EU regulations requested the spread of knowledge in planning economic policies across the private sector, through the growing involvement of consultancies, since many newer member-states had not any prior experience in planning and needed support from international consultan-cies. Within this context, the Greek state was forced to give up and waste all the precious planning knowledge and experience, acquired by specific people and insti-tutions throughout consecutive programming periods. It is not strange that after the

---

[9] Models were used to study ex-ante the effects of the economy as a whole (e.g., by Christodoulakis and Kalyvitis (1993) Likely Effects of C.S.F. 1994—1999 on the Greek Economy: An Ex-Ante Assessment using an Annual Four-Sector Macroeconometric Model, KEPE, Discussion Papers, no 46, or the HERMIN model).

[10] One can refer to many such studies that use econometrics to investigate small- and medium-sized enterprise policies, policies on competitiveness, and the operation of support to the private sector insti-tutions. For example in the United Kingdom, one can refer to extended assessments conducted by Professors Bennett, R.J. and Robson, P.J.A. on Business Links.

1994–99 period, not a single preparatory study nor an operational program is signed by a University Professor or a team of Professors that would have undertaken the full responsibility for their suggestions.

The 2000–06 competitiveness program contained significant planning weaknesses and problems that impeded the programs efficiency and effectiveness. As discussed in the ongoing evaluation of the 3rd C.S.F., these comprised too general targets that allowed various interpretations and serious misjudgments in quantification terms, the use of inappropriate base values for these targets, or the preference or use of unofficial data. Other targets were not accurately related to effects, overlapped with each other, or were set beyond expectations for demand and related projections (MoF, 2003).

The interim evaluation of the 2000–06 C.S.F. emphasized the following planning design failures: (1) many delays in the specification of program; (2) legal entanglements with national and community laws; (3) multiplication and extension of selection processes for projects and subprojects; (4) extremely intensive monitoring work; (5) difficulty of final recipients to participate and to be included within the new and demanding procedures; (6) multiplication of dangers during controls; (7) difficulty to secure synergies; (8) saturation of potential final recipients from the extent of offered products; and (9) inability to accurately define and synthesize the effects and impact of the program (MoF, 2003: 105). Too many new and innovative actions were introduced, of "incomplete design" (MoF, 2003: 105).[11]

Furthermore, the 3rd C.S.F. failed to incorporate dynamic elements related to the creation of the monetary zone, which are necessary to analyze a small open economy. The target of enhancing interindustry flows was not seen within the common currency area and the common market. Several targets were static and were not built around the country's dynamic comparative advantage (MoF, 2003). Significant exogenous factors, such as inflation, the common currency's exchange rate, collective bargaining, and the costs of production, were not taken into account in target setting for manufacturing (MoF, 2003). Nor were suitable competitiveness indexes (such as nominal unit labor costs, NULCs) employed to indicate the state's competitiveness and to project trends (instead the exports to imports ratio was used).

Overall, the credibility of the 2000–06 Competitiveness Program was low (MoF, 2003a,b). The program was prepared at the sector level. It lacked a more general overview of the competitiveness across all industries. It failed to pinpoint clearly and concisely the internal and external causes of limitations in competitiveness, and lacked analytical power in the explanation of strengths, weaknesses, opportunities, and threats for the Greek economy, neglecting many aspects. For example, the common currency zone was not envisaged through the lenses of a potential threat for domestic production and small businesses. It made a rather superficial use of some indexes (a complete range of which was not used), and did not focus on the implications upon the trade balance deficit from joining the currency union. On the contrary, it emphasized an overwhelmingly positive

---

[11] It is no coincidence that three separate revisions of the whole 2000–06 C.S.F. took place.

expectation approach on the evolution of the international macroeconomic environment (which, only few years after, resulted in a global crisis), as well as a rather optimistic view (as a few years of positive results beforehand were enough to create positive expectations and neglect any reference to negative scenarios). Most likely it was trapped in index analyses, without looking at the deeper causes of the negative effects on the state's competitiveness after abandoning a currency and associated stability mechanisms, at least upon the Greek manufacturing. One can hardly argue that the program's strategy focused on resolving the real problems of the Greek economy. It had poorly defined the necessary development priorities for the new era of globalization and monetary zone. Rather it can be considered, as MoF (2003) has put it, as a sum of best practices, fixed targets, and of experimenting in the use of newer European tools. Besides, this is a period when most macroeconomic indexes improved, as Greece was preparing to join the Eurozone and infrastructure projects were implemented to prepare for the Olympic Games, which absorbed a great deal of policy concerns. On the contrary, the microeconomic level and the actual effects upon firms of various sizes were disregarded, or, at best, seen as part of a restructuring process.

However, even on the occasion that the programme had been fully successful, it remains questionable whether and how the path toward loosening competitiveness could have ever been changed. The interim report of the 2000—06 Competitiveness Program clearly stated that "the reduction in the relative significance of manufacturing is a 'time bomb' in the foundations of competitiveness" (MoF, 2003b: 27) and indicated the three main reasons for this: (1) the Greek economy's long-term dependence on exogenous factors; (2) the lack of fast adjustment capacity that is considered to lie beyond the capacity of the Greek economy to cope with such exogenous factors and successfully react to them; and (3) the continuous reproduction of a traditional model for the Greek economy that covers its trade deficit through invisible resources, ever since the 1950s (MoF, 2003b: 27).

The interim report of the Competitiveness 2000—06 programme was clearly and concisely explaining the problems of the operational program. It identified that the Program was limited in scope and that competitiveness was not really strategically prioritized in financial terms (MoF, 2003b: 34). This "strategic deficiency was reflected in the financial scheme[12] of the C.S.F." (MoF, 2003b: 34). As explained in the text, "productive environment was absorbing 22% of total EU contribution in the total of C.S.F., as opposed to 30.5% in the respective Spanish C.S.F. and 48.5% in the Italian (for South Italy)." This contribution was "even lower if the share of agricultural sector was removed" (MoF, 2003b: 34). Furthermore, the C.S.F. comprised a lower share in human resources (19% in Greece, as opposed to 29.6% in East Germany and 27% in Ireland). As underlined in the text, "from the already low community contribution in the 'productive environment,' only 9.8% is attributed to the sectors of manufacturing, tourism, and research and technology (with only 2% attributed to infrastructure in energy that according to C.S.F. is introduced in the axis of

---

[12] The word "scheme" is used in this context to explain the underfunding of the Program in comparison to other Program. All translations by the MoF (2003b) document are made by the author.

competitiveness and integrated in the actions of the Competitiveness Program)."[13] The report referred to the following data, from an EU Commission analysis, clearly indicating other priorities with respect to funds allocation and productive environment for the rest of regions under support and other for Greece (Table 3.22).

The interim report states that "the key to understand this 'unclear strategy' lies in the respective strategy that has been defined in the Regional Development Plan 2000−2006" (MoF, 2003b: 37), where a total strategy is missing and there is great distance between much ballyhooed, excessively grand targets and the actual effects of actions that ought to be expected (MoF, 2003b).

As opposed to the strategy followed by Ireland, the Greek Competitiveness Program had not organized specific interventions to attract Foreign Direct Investments (a problem stated also in its critique, in MoF, 2003b: 37). Nor has it investigated the prospect of attracting synergies between Greek and foreign enterprises (MoF, 2003b: 37). The role of a special institution ("Invest in Greece"), created in 1996 (through Law 2372/1996) in order to attract FDI, was not given special attention and, as a result, it was replaced during the crisis by "Enterprise Greece" (Law 3894/2010), a new institution that incorporated a much older institution for export promotion (the Hellenic Export Promotion Organization, created in 1977). Thus, it is no coincidence that the amounts of FDIs in Greece were kept in low levels in comparison to other states.

Furthermore, the interim report on the 2000−06 competitiveness program underlines that the targets originally set in C.S.F. had not paid attention to several points made in its SWOT analysis and that several important measures were neglected that should have been taken. These comprise measures with respect to manufacturing and other types of enterprises supported -that had not focused on the broader group of small and medium-sized firms-, the support of firm clustering and regional production and regional innovation systems, the raising of funding for basic research, and the multiplying effects of C.S.F. (MoF, 2003b: 35). All these were factors that impeded the strengthening of competitiveness of the Greek economy and were sufficient enough to harm it, at a very critical point in time, during its transition to the Eurozone. It is important to underline that the consultants spent time and efforts to organize matrices of relevance of measures and policy priorities and of synergies (which are of minor importance) but, at the same time, neglected the more central, in planning, question of how many funds will be proportionately allocated to which priorities.

It is difficult to provide a good reason why the "signal" sent by the Greek authorities was never taken into account. One should consider this to be as one of the most significant points. This "death rattle" concerning numerous failures in the competitiveness programme and their particular nature, which managed to absorb only 28.6% of initially allocated funds by September 2005, points out that specific institutions were necessary to implement the proposed actions. The responsibility for resolving these

---

[13] A point of objection is raised here by the author of the document, whether energy should be considered as part of a Competitiveness Program. One should be aware than it is mostly in the long run, after the completion of energy projects and the provision of low-cost energy that one should consider a Programme on energy to contribute on the competitiveness of an economy.

Table 3.22 Community intervention/funds per priority (2000–06)

	Productive environment		Human resources		Basic infrastructure		Miscellaneous		Total
	Net	%	Net	%	Net	%	Net	%	
East Germany[a]	8583	41.7	6102	29.6	5553	27.0	364	1.8	20,602
Greece	4662	21.9	4100	19.2	11,837	55.5	722	3.4	21,321
Ireland	939	30.6	824	26.9	1288	42.0	15	0.5	3066
Mezzogiorno[b]	10,428	48.5	4137	19.2	6294	29.3	657	3.1	21,516
Portugal	6415	33.4	3894	20.3	8507	44.4	363	1.9	19,179
Spain	11,525	30.3	8867	23.3	17,442	45.8	209	0.5	38,043
Total	42,551	34.4	27,924	22.6	50,922	41.2	2330	1.9	123,726

Notes:
[a]Brandenburg, Mecklenburg-Western Pomerania, Saxony, Saxony-Anhalt, Thuringia, East Berlin.
[b]Campania, Apulia, Basilicata, Calabria, Sicily, Sardinia.
Source: EC, Directorate-General Regional Policies, Brussels 2002 (as it appears in Beutel, J. (2002) The Economic Impact of Objective 1 interventions for the period 2000–2006, Final Report to the DG for Regional Policies, May 2002).

problems (that appeared in later 2003) was not easy to undertake in the middle of a programming period and was not taken into account by the European Commission authorities, which had not drafted a single document highlighting such problems.

Furthermore, in planning terms, not only ex-post assessments are no longer a requirement but most of the 2007−13 Operational Programmes do not contain or contain very limited information on the previous results achieved at the Operational level, as well as previous programming experience, which is not considered a pre-requisite in programming terms.

Only in the 2007−13 C.S.F. programme is it realized that threats for the Greek economy derive from: (1) enlargement and introduction of new member-states with low employment cost, high productivity, and competitiveness; (2) outflow of funds in other countries, shrinking of the manufacturing sector due to migration to countries of low costs; (3) high level of sensitivity for micro- and small- and medium-sized enter-prises; (4) difficult environment for start-ups; (5) multiple laws, bureaucracy, and many functions; (6) acquisitions of Greek firms by foreign companies; (7) deficiencies in transport infrastructure; (8) increase of highly educated brain-drain; (9) rapid devel-opment of technologies that devaluates quickly infrastructure in R&D; (x) high com-petition in manufacturing from neighboring countries (who benefit more from Greek transport infrastructure); and (9) structures of oligopsony in the tourist sector with few tourist operators (MoF, 2007b: 48). A few of these problems were identified several years ago, in the ex-ante assessment of the Competitiveness Programme of the previ-ous programming period (2000−06). Most of them appeared out of the blue.[14] Similarly the ex-ante assessment of the 2007−13 Competitiveness Programme failed to diagnose the underfunding of competitiveness and the potential problem—if not threat—of the inadequacy of resources devoted to competitiveness that were not underlined in the specific section that existed in the assessment, a few years before one of the worst economic crises in history erupted (MoF, 2007b: 95−98).

While the Ministries were in charge of the programming, management, and implementation of programmes, the latter have also been conducted throughout the years by many different institutions that were continuously restructuring.

For instance, in the 2000−06 period, new mechanisms of management, control, and implementation were put in place. Concerning management, four new institu-tions were created from scratch: (1) a new Management Authority of the C.S.F.; (2) a new Payment Authority; (3) new Managerial Authorities, for each Operational Programme; and (4) a Fiscal Control Committee of the Ministry of Finance (Greek Law, 2860/00[15]). For each of the Programmes, numerous organizational and institu-tional changes had to be enforced by various administrative guidelines, delaying the implementation phase by 1 or 2 years (e.g., MTC, 2001[16]). During this period, the transition to the currency zone was achieved and implementation of operational

---

[14] The underfunding of competitiveness programs was also not diagnosed in the specific section for the strength of interventions.

[15] Greek Law 2860/00, Management, monitoring and control of the Community Support Framework, Official Government Gazette of the Hellenic Republic, Issue 251/A/14-11-00.

[16] Ministry of Transports and Communication (2001) Administrative Guideline, Framework of Management of the 3rd C.S.F., Athens, May 2001.

mechanisms was required to be carried out on time. Their delay coincides with a proportional fall in funds allocated in the productive environment (as one may see by comparing across Tables 3.6—3.9). This is also the period emphasizing construction of infrastructure projects for the Olympic Games.

Over the years, many institutions were created not only for organizing and implementing the planned policies but also for regulatory purposes and application of authority, for extending their scope, preparing their long-term embedding, supporting relevant actions, and introducing new instruments and schemes. For example this was the case with financial institutions such as the "Enterprise Greece", the New Economy Development Fund ("TANEO"), the guarantee fund for SMEs ("TEMΠME"), the incubator-cluster "Corallia," human capital institutions such as the "National Observatory for Employment," the "National Institute for Employment," the "Center for Promotion of Employment," national Health institutions such as the "National Center of First Aid," and institutions for agriculture, such as the "Payment and Control Agency for Guidance and Guarantee Community Aid."

Several of these were built for a single programming period and incorporated in the rest of ministerial functions or merged with other institutions within Ministries, for instance the Competitiveness Council. EU funds were used to finance their building, elastic and inelastic expenses. Many existing and new institutions have made use of the financial sources available, such as the Manpower Employment Organization or the National Tourist Organization. Finally, a range of institutions may have been required to implement policies, e.g., a broader range of business support institutions.

3.7   Output produced

Several of the results and outputs of the application of the programmes have already been discussed. In the present section, a few of the rare officially documented outputs, as collected from available sources, are provided. Table 3.23 refers to all outputs gained in the 1994—99 C.S.F. and problems identified in this programming phase.[17] For each of the interventions assessed, the Table presents also the problems discussed in the original document (EEO, 2003). Similarly, Table 3.24 refers to the 2007—13 programming period and provides the results on core indicator values of its ex-post assessment.

3.8   Greece's Balance with the EU: A country progressively assuming its responsibilities

Until 2013, approximately 95% of Greece's funding via the Community's budget was obtained from Cohesion and Common Agriculture Policy (ELIAMEP, 2014: 38).

---

[17] It is unique of its kind, as no other such **Table** has been produced after the 1994—1999 period in ex-ante or other assessments.

Table 3.23 Output per sector, problems and obstacles, 1994–99 C.S.F.

	Education & training

Output	**Secondary education (General and technical)**
	- Reform of the curricula with the production of 234 new books (with 13 CD-ROMs for specific courses)
	- Innovative school activities with the participation of 600 schools, 6500 teachers and 70,000 students
	- Pilot introduction of IT technologies in school. In particular 14 schools were networked, 13 educational software packages were developed and teachers from 60 schools gained basic ICT skills
	- Formation of 6 Centres of European Languages
	- Pilot and general implementation of remedial training for 10,300 students from 102 schools
	- Introduction of professional guidance with the development of 68 Professional Guidance Centres and training of 600 teachers and executives
	- Introduction of environmental education with the formation of 10 Environmental Education Centres
	- Introduction of new courses such as Health Education and Consumers Education
	- Education of people with special needs (training of 3,500 teachers for students with special needs)
	- Innovative actions like the second chance schools and the all day kindergarten
	  - Training of 200,000 teachers
	  - Development or upgrading of 450 school libraries and 41 mobile libraries
	  - Laboratories (IT and physics) for students in almost all school units
	
	Vocational Training
	- Support of 136 Institutes of Vocational Training with 40,000 students
	- Other secondary vocational education
	- Other secondary vocational training establishments
	
	Tertiary Education
	- Reform of the curricula for 131 undergraduate courses
	- Establishment of a network for all 32 tertiary level establishments in the country along with the support of their libraries
	- Development and support of 124 postgraduate studies in 17 Universities
	- Enhancement of scholarships and research
	- Formation and support of 33 career offices

(Continued)

Table 3.23 **(Continued)**

	Education & training
	- Infrastructure support (new buildings, expansions etc.) in 13 Universities and in Technical Education Institutes - Open University - Distance learning
Problems & obstacles	Effectiveness and efficiency were influenced by delays in the beginning of OP, which suppressed actual implementation time and urged on the procedures. Overall effectiveness approximately 90%
Output	**Employment and Continuous Training** The total number of beneficiaries 648,000 people: - 165,000 unemployed attended a continuous training course (49,000 unemployed trained by relevant activities of ROPs) - 260,000 employees trained (21,000 trained in telecommunications through the relevant OP) - 192,000 unemployed placed in jobs under employment subsidization programmes - 25,000 benefited by activities of OP "Combating Exclusion from the Labor Market" - Creation and Operation of National Accreditation Center, which certified approximately 400 Centers for Vocational Training and became eligible to implement training funded by ESF
Problems & obstacles	The National Accreditation Center was established in 1995 but faced a series of problems that caused a suspension of all training activities for 2 years. In 1998 it was reestablished with a better organizational structure and presented important work in the continuous training activities. All supporting mechanisms (Programme Manager Evaluator, M.O.U., etc.) were introduced at a late stage and results appeared after 1998
Output	**Transport** **Road Axes** - 55% achieved of a total network of 919 km of road axes, all considered part of Trans European Networks (TEN): - PATHE highway (Patras, Athens, Thessaloniki, Euzonoi) - Egnatia highway, part of which has been implemented in order to link eastern and western Greece with the northern part - Rio−Antirrio bridge linking southern and northern part of Western Greece - Northwest Road Axis of Crete **Ports** - Improvements a series of ports, except for the Port of Patras and Thessaloniki

(Continued)

Table 3.23 (Continued)

	Education & training
Problems & obstacles	- Few projects related to airports, particularly infrastructure for the new Athens airport at Spata **(the airport was not funded by the C.S.F.)** and 4 terminal radars **Railways** - 75% of a double line in the Athens-Thessaloniki-Idomeni axis, without its electrification (only a part of 77 km from Thessaloniki to Idomeni was already electrified) **Urban Development** - Completion of first phase of the Athens metro (except a small part due to archeological inhibitions in city center) - Telematic project of trolley buses network - Purchase of 300 environmental friendly buses Operational Programme in Road Axes achieved 55% of its objectives. Basic implementation obstacles: - Problems related to studies (detective, inappropriate, scattered, geotechnical and environmental problems) - Expropriation problems - Problems relevant to the archeological sites protection (excavation rates) - Problems with the subsoil - Legal difficulties, exorbitant discounts of the construction firms due to high competition Delays in Thessaloniki Metro, which though initially planned has not started, due to negotiation difficulties and highly dispersed and misinterpreted auction procedures.
Output	**Environment** **Natural environment-Protection of forest ecosystems** - Implementation of Special Environmental Surveys for 20 ecosystems, 13 biosystems along with infrastructure interventions in 15 biosystems and 20 ecosystems. - Completion of 5 National Action Plans for species under threat - Awareness programs - Collaboration of central administration with local authorities and of the environmental organizations with local enterprises - Equipment purchase for the Fire Brigades in order to combat forest fires **Atmosphere-Noise-Global problems** - Formation of an Operational Center to monitor atmosphere pollution in the city of Athens - Development of a national network for the monitoring of atmosphere pollutants and emissions from central heating systems

(Continued)

Table 3.23 (Continued)

	Education & training
	- Implementation of the Attica-SOS programme focused on the reduction of fuel contribution in the atmospheric pollution - Mapping of the traffic noise in 23 urban areas - Construction of noise barriers in 6 municipalities (effectiveness 60%) - Installation of 8 noise measuring cells
	Water environment - National management plans for water resources and monitoring of the plans for 14 hydrological basins - Formation of a national network for monitoring of surface and underground waters, swimming waters, tracing toxic substances in surface waters and quality in the cross border rivers
	Soil-subsoil-solid and dangerous waste disposals - Construction of places for the sanitary burial of waste disposals, with a capacity to host 45% of the total disposals countrywide - Recycling of house disposals resulting in recycling almost 9% of rubbish - Upgrade of tourist seashores (436 km of the total 1200 km thus 36% of the needs with 100% effectiveness)
	Laws-mechanisms-administration - Formation of the autonomous National Center for the Environment and Sustainable Development - Legislation framework with specific requirements required for environmental impact studies - Creation of the National Information Network for the Environment, linking 8 prefectures with the central terminal in the Ministry of Environment - Enhancement of programs for the eco-certification (EMAS)
	Urban planning - Completion of 24 urban plans and of 82 urban reformation projects
	Land registration - 30% of initial target to map and register 35,000 m^2 of land in 700 local authorities
Problems & obstacles	Land registration project was found to have mismanagement problems (30% effectiveness by end of 1998) and was interrupted Two centers for thermal treatment of hospital disposals (in Athens & Thessaloniki) have been transferred to the next CSF
Output	**Culture** - Unification of the ancient sites in the city of Athens. This intervention included 14 projects (restoration of traditional buildings around Acropolis, conversion of the main road into a pedestrian pathway, etc.)

(Continued)

Table 3.23 (Continued)

	Education & training
	- National Cultural Network of Cities, which consisted of four projects that focused on interferences and restorations of buildings (mostly theaters and Cultural Centres) - Expansion and upgrading of museums with 10 projects - Restoration and distinction of monuments with 26 completed projects - Construction of the Cultural Convention Centres in the cities of Athens and Thessaloniki
Problems & obstacles	The Acropolis Museum was not completed, as it required unusually extended initial time phase and the Land Registry & Monument Files remained inactive
Output	**Health and Care** - Large-scale investment in biomedical technology by equipping all the hospitals, which have been built or renovated by the R.O.P.s - Development of Centres for Vocational Training in the field of health & care - Development of integrated management information systems for all the hospitals - Formation and/or support of new structures in the field of public health (e.g., National School of Public Health, Central Laboratory of Public Health, National Research Centre for Health) - Construction of buildings for the National Centre of Emergencies (in Athens and 5 other cities) - New building for the National Blood Donation Centre - Formation of the National Network of Social Support for people with special needs - Development of Physical & Social and Rehabilitation Centres for under aged and chronically ill Regional Operational Programmes Measures relevant to Health & Care: Construction of 15 new regional and prefecture hospitals Improvements, arrangements and expansions of building capacity in 26 existing hospitals Short-scale investments in high tech biomedicine equipment
Problems and obstacles	Exceptional delays in project implementation, revealing internal problems in planning and applying reform interventions. Deficient preparatory work along with underestimation of both resources and time resulted also at the noneffective implementation of interventions. Major part of planned infrastructure in health & care would become functional during the first 2 years of following programming period. Expected to accomplish partially the intermediate target of health system decentralization (EEO, 2003: 149–150)

(Continued)

Table 3.23 (Continued)

	Education & training
Output	**Tourism** - Interventions emanating from OP "Tourism & Culture" & relevant measures in ROPs **Marine tourism** - Construction of 1 yacht marine (effectiveness 25%) **Mountain, ecological, cultural, and therapeutic tourism** - 1 hydro-sanatorium (effectiveness approximately 30%) **Upgrading existing hotels** - 125 investment projects for 11,100 hotel beds and 324 traditional guest houses (effectiveness 43%) **Formation of special tourist infrastructure** - 2 thalassotherapy spa centers, 2 golf courses and 10 conference centers (effectiveness ranged between 0% and 95%) **Training in the tourist sector** - 12 continuous training courses (effectiveness 20%)
Problems & obstacles	Remarkably low effectiveness (40%). Hasty initial planning in marine tourism, inefficient planning and the weak evaluation of submitted projects in mountain, ecological, cultural, and therapeutic tourism, low effectiveness mainly attributed to legislative framework (development law) in upgrading existing hotels
Output	**Research and technology** - 16 research joint ventures in the field of environment - 32 research projects on the environment from equivalent number of enterprises - 39 research joint ventures and 24 enterprises implemented research projects on the biosciences - 40 research joint ventures and 46 enterprises implemented research projects in the field of new and advanced materials - 25 joint ventures fop research activities in the fields of culture, society and technology - 419 completed projects of industrial research - 269 research projects form the collaboration of Universities, Research Centers and Enterprises - 27 buildings for research activities (developed or upgraded), 32 equipment supply projects for R&T actions, 10 scientific libraries for Research Centers - 410 completed conferences, 36 scientific publications and 25 information bulletins
Problems & obstacles	Explicit delays in project implementation mainly attributed to prolonged planning phase Insufficient monitoring of the physical outputs of the projects **Industry** - Development laws 1892/90 and 2601/98

(Continued)

Table 3.23 **(Continued)**

	Education & training
Problems & obstacles	Implementation delays mainly attributed to nonsuitable legislative framework and the underestimation of the needed time to inform potential investors (EEO, 2003: 152)
Output	**Fisheries** - 1610 approved plans for adaptation of fishery activities (more than 90% effectiveness) - 1095 approved investment plans in renewal and modernization of fishing fleet (more than 90% effectiveness), a small portion of the Hellenic fishing fleet (70% of remaining fishing boats older than 15 years old) - 225 investment plans of aquaculture (effectiveness of 92% for shells, 100% for new sea species and 70% for the cultivation of trout). 58 existing units modernized (effectiveness more than 90%) - 113 investment plans in manufacture and commerce, which increased manufacturing capacity by −14,000 tonnes annually (80% effectiveness). 32 new fishing commercial enterprises (87% effectiveness)
Output	**Public administration** - Administration modernization - Development of integrated information systems (I.I.S.) - Training of civil servants
Problems & obstacles	Prolonged initial planning phase, absence of strategic studies identifying policy recommendations and erroneous time planning for implementation period. Limited effectiveness regarding large-scale Information Systems, while the small-scale ones have been completed, having though only limited effects
Output	**Energy** - 3 large units of electricity production (100% effectiveness) - 333 investment plans promoting energy save, electricity coproduction and use of renewable energy sources - Most targets for natural gas accomplished, particularly the high pressure transfer pipes from Greek-Bulgarian borders, the basic transfer branches to consumer centers, storing installation of liquid natural gas and 1000 km of low pressure distribution networks in three regions
Problems & obstacles	The 333 projects exhibited great delays, mostly caused by nonsuitable legislative framework, extended time required for informing investors and adapting licensing procedures. Demand for cofinancing of energy investment plans was unexpectedly high and initial targets overestimated

(Continued)

Table 3.23 (Continued)

	Education & training
Output	**Agriculture** - 33,457 improvement plans (67% effectiveness of initial targets, 112% effectiveness of updated). - 20,313 new farmers financed (145% effectiveness) - 205,325 received leveler compensation (82% effectiveness) - Capacity modernization (2,033,005 tons/year, effectiveness 91%) - New products capacity (281,470 tons/year, effectiveness 83%) - 718 agriculture enterprises have been benefited in order to improve their manufacturing and packaging (effectiveness 103%) - 4 arboriculture stations have been improved (effectiveness 100%) - 3 viticulture young plants have been upgraded (effectiveness 75%) - 9 public foundations have been funded

Source: EEO, 2003.

This funding came mostly from Cohesion Funds[18] and from the Agricultural funds. The European Regional Development Fund (ERDF) and the European Agricultural Guarantee Fund (in particular its guarantee section) were the major contributors of EU funds in Greece. The European Social Fund (ESF) is the third most important in amounts Fund, and its contribution has increased since 1997 (Fig. 3.9). The importance of the Cohesion Fund in funding terms (which has been created to promote cohesion and resolve cohesion problems) is limited, if it is compared against the three previous Funds. The importance in funding terms of the guidance section of the FEOGA, the Mediterranean Integrated Programmes, and of the Financial Instrument for Fisheries Guidance was also limited.

The proportional allocation of structural actions has increased at the expense of agricultural actions undertaken by FEOGA-Guarantee (Table 3.25).

Greece's contribution to EU revenues (as % GDP) has continuously been rising over the years (Fig. 3.10A). Progressively, the country was turned into a contributor into the EU budget. A peak was reached in 2007, followed by a fall and a subsequent rise.

On the contrary, Greece's contribution to the EU public expenditure (receipts from EU budget) as % GDP has risen, up to 1993 (Fig. 3.10B). Then, it started to fluctuate. It fell from 1993 to 1995, then it reached a peak in 1998, after which it fell again to reach 3.12% in 2003. The pattern reversed only from 2004 to 2007, reaching peaks in 2007 and 2008, like those in 1998.

Measured as a percentage of GDP, Greece's contribution to EU's net revenues (revenues minus total expenditure in the EU budget) follows a similar pattern with the one previously described. It has increased, reaching a peak in 1993 (Fig. 3.11). It has then fallen but rose again, to reach another, similar peak in 1998. Then it started to fall again until 2002, a year after which it started to rise progressively.

---

[18] Also known as European Structural and Investment Funds.

Table 3.24 Core Indicator Value (measurement unit), 2007–13— National Strategic Reference Framework, end-2014

	Greece	EU	Greece/EU
Aggregated Jobs (no.)	21,006	940,000[a]	2.2%
RTD projects (no.)	561	95,000	0.6%
Cooperation projects between enterprises and research institutions (no.)	30	33,600	0.1%
Research jobs created (no.)	1422	41,600	3.4%
SMEs supported (no.)	25,347	400,000[b]	6.3%
Start-ups supported (no.)	2611	121,400	2.2%
Jobs created in SME (gross, full time equivalent)	21,006	–	–
Additional population covered by broadband	771,851	8,200,000	9.4%
Km of new roads (no.)	144	4900	2.9%
Km of new TEN roads (no.)	144	2400	6.0%
Km of reconstructed roads (no.)	2646	28,600	9.3%
Km of new railway (no.)		1050	0.0%
Km of TEN railway (no.)	11	2600	0.4%
Km of reconstructed railway (no.)	60	3900	1.5%
Additional capacity of renewable energy production (MW)	108	3900	2.8%
Additional population served by water projects	1,455,459	5,900,000	24.7%
Additional population served by waste water projects	370,841	6,900,000	5.4%
Area rehabilitated (km^2)	57	1100	5.2%
Jobs created in tourism (no.)	13,000	16,200[b]	0.1%

Notes from EC (2016b):
Note for Greece: The figures in the table (for Greece) are those reported by MAs in Annual Implementation Reports (of Greece). Core indicators for which no data were reported by the Member State are not included. The aggregate jobs indicator is based on an examination by the Commission of all gross job creation reported for each priority axis and is regarded as the most accurate figure for the total number of gross jobs directly created as a result of funding. It tends to be higher than the sum of the figures reported by MAs for the core indicators relating to jobs created because in many cases MAs fail to report anything for these indicators. *Source*: Annual Implementation Reports, 2014 and DG Regional Policy postprocessing of these, August 2016.
Notes from EC (2016a):
[a]Now casting suggests that this was over 1 million by end-2015.
[b]** Estimate based on WP2 *Source*: DG Regional and Urban Policy, derived from 2014 AIRs.
Source: EC (2016a), EC (2016b)

Hence, with the exception of the last years of the 1st C.S.F., the 2nd period, and the early part of the last programming period, Greece's contribution to net revenues has not been high enough to be considered as a state benefiting substantially from the allocation of funds at the EU-level. In the second programming period in particular, when the Greek economy reached average annual GDP growth at approximately 3%–4%, its respective contribution reached and even exceeded these levels. Overall however, one has to mention that Greece had the greatest public benefit from the operation of common EU budget, proportional to its population (ELIAMEP, 2014: 38).

The balance (payments minus receipts from EU) was limited if one considers Greece's increasing annual contributions to the EU budget (Fig. 3.12). It has always

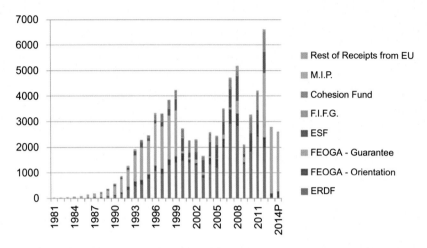

Figure 3.9 Greece's receipts from various EU Funds, 1981–2012.
Source: Ministry of Finance, Public finance relations with the EU and International
Organizations, obtained in 2014, author's work. *Note*: (1) Data are estimates for 2013, and
projections for 2014. (2) Data were deflated using a macroeconomic series for the Greek
general CPI, as provided by EL.STAT (2009 base year).

been positive, increased and fell during the early years of the crisis, then increased
again after 2010.

As GDP percent, Greece's balance with the EU has increased up to 1994 but
then started to fall significantly, reaching a low value during the crisis, in 2009.
The rise of balance has only taken place for the first programming period and since
then started to deteriorate. Despite the fact that it is positive, Greece does not have
a high balance for an extended part of the studied period, and progressively loses
out from the integration and enlargement process. The curvilinear pattern shows
clearly the change from a pure benefactor from EU Cohesion policies to a state
assuming more of its responsibilities. Had the crisis not erupted, Greece might have
become a net contributor, as a potential projection of this trend reveals.

An increasingly significant part of Greek payments to the EU is derived from its
GNI contributions (Fig. 3.13). The next significant category is VAT contributions, followed by customs and antidumping duties. These all emphasize Greece's net losses out
of the integration and enlargement processes, a larger part of which, as discussed elsewhere, is directed to its EU and Eurozone partners, and held for common EU purposes.

3.9 Long-term effects and implications from the imbalanced allocation of funds

3.9.1 Effects upon manufacturing and industrial restructuring

The numbers of small, medium, and large (SML) Greek manufacturing firms fell
substantially and progressively over the years (Fig. 3.14). One-third of them ceased

Table 3.25 Average per year receipts, for Agriculture (FEOGA-Guarantee) and Structural Actions

	Total receipt	FEOGA-Guarantee	% Contribution in total receipts	Structural actions	% Contribution in total receipts	Rest	% Contribution in total receipts
Average per year 1981–89	1566.54	1082.06	66.7	430.17	26.9	54.3	6.4
Average per year 1990–99	4724.48	2491.34	53.6	2066.60	42.8	166.5	3.6
Average per year 2000–08	6245.79	2659.71	44.9	3218.39	50.0	386.1	5.4

Note: Data in payment form. 1981–98 data in ECUs. Some deviations are found from data as they appear in the Balance of Payment of the Bank of Greece Structural Actions: FEOGA-Orientation, ERDF, ESF, FIFG and Cohesion Fund.

Source: Oikonomou et al. (2010), data extracted from Bank of Greece, based on various volumes of Annual Reports of the Court of Audit of EC, various volumes of EC's "Allocation of EU Expenditure by Member-states," various volumes of "EU Budget Financial Report."

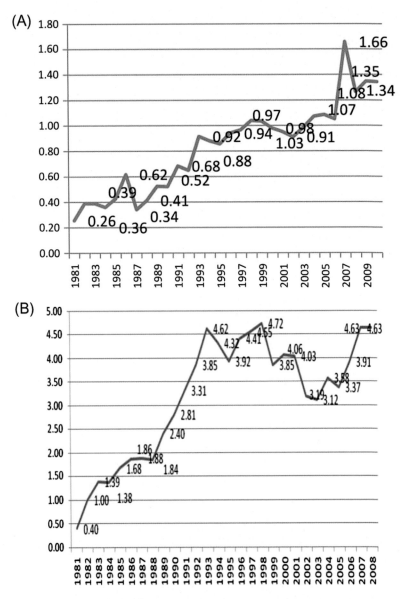

Figure 3.10 (A) Greece's contribution to EU total budget revenues, as % GDP, 1981−2010. (B) Greece's contribution in EU budget public expenditure, as % GDP, 1981−08.
Source: ELIAMEP (2013: 80).

operations from 1993 to 2009. Throughout this period, the application of two consecutive C.S.F.s targeting manufacturing support has not managed to reverse this "snowball effect" and a significant part of the competitive and productive capacity of the Greek manufacturing sector was lost. This is a trend that has been taking

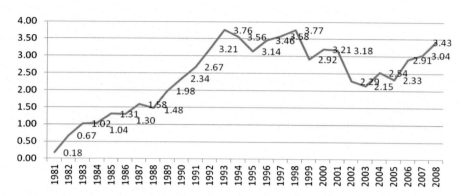

Figure 3.11 Greece's contribution in EU net revenues, as % of GDP, 1981–2008.
Source: ELIAMEP (2013: 81).

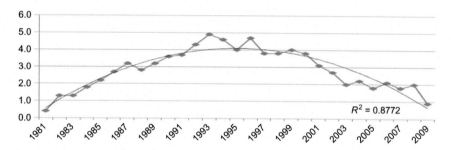

Figure 3.12 Greece's Balance with the EU (receipts minus payments at the EU budget),
current prices as % current GDP, 1981–2009.
Source: Ministry of Finance, Public finance relations with the European Union and
International Organisations, author's work.

place ever since Greece became a member of the customs union, the common market, and more recently of the Economic and Monetary Union. From 2001 to 2002, when the majority of protection barriers were removed and adjustments for the common currency culminated, 1720 manufacturing SML disappeared from PRODCOM records. In 2009, this pattern appears to reverse provisionally but it remains evident again, after 2012.

However, the value and quantity of SML sales increases during the same period (Fig. 3.15).

If such values are included, the line of the quantity of sales would have been above the one presented here. The trend of the line can be considered to be representative.

Turnover per enterprise firms has increased during the same period for SML manufacturing, both as a value and as a quantity. Most likely this indicates an increase in business sizes and market concentration processes in operation (Figs. 3.16A and 3.16B). An obvious implication of market concentration is price rising—especially if imperfect forms of competition are sustained—leading to price

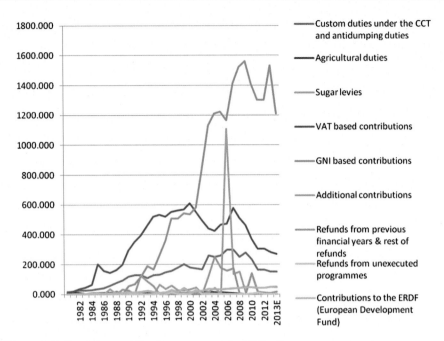

Figure 3.13 Breakdown of Greek payments to the EU budget.
Source: Ministry of Finance, Public finance relations with the European Union and International Organisations, author's work. *Note*: Data for 2013 are estimated and for 2014 projected.

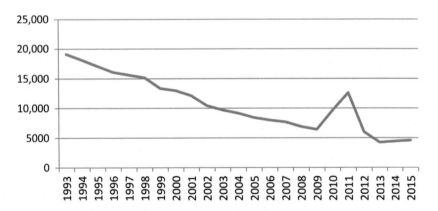

Figure 3.14 Number of small, medium, and large (SML) manufacturing firms, 1993−2015.
Source: Hellenic Statistical Services, PRODCOM, author's work.

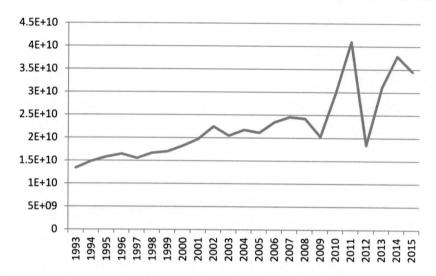

Figure 3.15 Value of Sales in small, medium, and large manufacturing firms, 1993–2015. *Source*: Hellenic Statistical Services, PRODCOM, author's work. *Note:* Greek drachmas turned to Euros, current prices.

stickiness and limited price adjustments that can become a very serious problem in times of crisis. The rise of sales per enterprise is very obvious after 2012 but in this case it is likely to be due to the continuous removal of SML firms out of the Greek market and the transfer to other countries.

This evidence unveils a process of economic restructuring, which was set in place in the Greek production long before the economy joined the Eurozone. As seen in Tables 3.26 and 3.27 (in combination), in terms of value, agricultural production, represented almost a sixth of its production in 1970, has fallen since then and reached in the early 2010s one-third of the initial 1970 levels. The secondary sector had also started shrinking its share in value terms since the 1970s, a process attributed mostly to manufacturing and only partially to construction over the course of three decades (Table 3.26).[19] After the year 2000 (Table 3.27), manufacturing reduces much less proportionately but construction is more significantly affected and shrunk. Within 14 years, only one-third remains out of the vibrant Greek construction industry, the vast part of which is lost during the years of the crisis. As one can see during the same period, notably after 2007, the real estate activities follow an exactly opposite pattern and benefit out of the crisis.

In value terms, services have expanded from more than half of Greek production (54.2%) to more than a third (72.3%), indicating a restructuring and development process favoring services across all industries, in trade, financial intermediation, real estate, public administration and security, health, and education. This is a period when new industries were created from scratch, such as ICT and software.

---

[19] This evidence explains the afore-mentioned process of significant fall in the number of manufacturing SMEs and large firms.

(A)

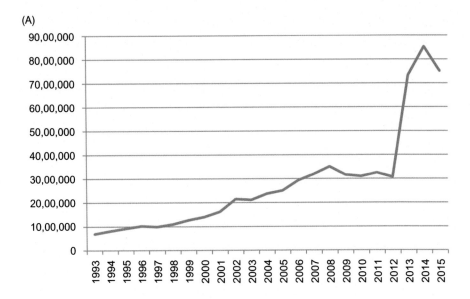

(B)

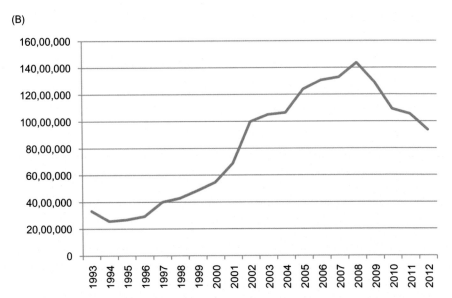

Figure 3.16A and B Value and Quantity of Sales per enterprise in small, medium, and large manufacturing firms, current prices, 1993–2015.
Source: Hellenic Statistical Services, PRODCOM, author's work. *Note:* Quantity of sales are estimates, since confidential data values are not included.

Table **3.26** **The structure of value in Greek production, current prices**

	1970	1975	1980	1985	1990	1995	2000	% Change
1st sector— Agriculture	15.8	13.9	15.1	11.8	10.6	9.9	7.3	− 53.8
2nd sector— Manufacturing	30.0	29.0	29.6	28.3	26.3	22.4	20.4	− 32.0
Mining	0.7	0.7	0.8	1.5	0.8	0.6	0.6	− 14.3
Manufacturing	17.6	18.5	17.9	17	15.2	13	11.1	− 36.9
Electricity-Gas-Water	1.9	1.5	1.5	2.5	2.6	2.4	1.8	− 5.3
Construction	9.8	8.2	9.4	7.4	8	6.4	6.9	− 29.6
3rd sector— Services	54.2	57.1	55.3	59.8	62.8	67.7	72.3	33.4
Transport-Communication	5.9	6.7	6.1	5.8	5.4	6.7	8.5	44.1
Trade	13.7	16.3	14.6	15.3	14.8	13.6	14.5	5.8
Financial Intermediation	2.9	3.6	3.2	3.2	3.4	4.2	5.5	89.7
Real estate management & related activities	13.1	11.7	10.8	10.3	11.7	17	17	29.8
Public administration & Security	4	4.7	5.3	7.3	7.7	7.2	7	75.0
Health and Education	5.9	6.4	6.7	7.8	9.2	9.7	9.9	67.8
Other economic activities	8.7	7.7	8.6	10.1	10.6	9.3	10	14.9

Source: Bryant et al. (2001), data collected from the Ministry of Finance.

The fall in transport—communication in the 1980s is regained in the 1990s. Table 3.27 reveals that the Greek crisis brings an industrial restructuring to the economy, with some industries being more hardly hit (construction, agriculture, trade) than others (real estate, tourism, accommodation and food services, and education).

3.9.2 Effects on competitiveness, exports, and the balance of payment: Greece's suffocating problem

As explained earlier, in the theoretical section, the concept of competitiveness has different meanings and connotations at the macroeconomic and at the microeconomic-firm level. The aforementioned evidence on industrial restructuring and on the substantial reduction in the numbers of SMEs and large manufacturing firms indicates a possible loss of competitiveness at the firm level.

Table 3.27 Production structure across industrial groupings, 2000–14, current prices turned to percentages

	2000	2001	2002	2003	2004	2005	2006	2007	2008	2009	2010	2011	2012	2013	2014	%
Agriculture, forestry, and fishing	6.1	5.8	5.6	5.6	4.7	4.8	3.6	3.4	3.2	3.1	3.3	3.4	3.7	3.6	3.7	−39
Mining and quarrying—	12.7	13.2	13.3	12.5	11.9	11.9	11.6	11.6	11.1	10.6	10.1	10.9	11.4	12.1	11.9	−6
Manufacturing—																
Electricity, gas, steam and air conditioning supply																
Water supply, sewerage, waste management and remediation activities	1.3	1.4	1.4	1.4	1.5	1.6	1.6	1.5	1.6	1.6	1.1	1.2	1.4	1.5	1.5	15
Construction	7.0	7.1	7.1	8.9	9.2	6.4	9.4	7.3	5.0	5.0	4.5	3.5	3.4	2.9	2.5	−64
Wholesale and retail trade, repair of motor vehicles and motorcycles	16.3	15.3	14.8	14.5	13.7	12.8	12.1	12.4	12.9	12.5	12.7	12.6	10.6	10.1	10.7	−34
Transportation and storage	6.7	5.8	5.6	6.5	7.1	7.7	7.4	8.0	8.2	7.0	7.1	7.1	6.8	6.7	7.2	7
Accommodation and food service activities	4.6	5.5	4.6	4.7	4.6	5.3	5.1	4.9	5.5	4.7	4.9	4.7	4.9	5.9	6.0	30
Information and communication	3.9	4.0	4.1	3.8	3.8	3.9	4.0	4.0	3.8	4.0	3.8	3.5	3.3	3.6	3.3	−15
Financial and insurance services	4.6	3.9	4.0	4.2	4.8	4.7	4.7	4.5	4.4	4.6	4.8	4.8	5.0	5.2	4.9	7
Real estate activities	11.0	11.0	11.5	10.6	10.3	11.6	10.4	11.8	13.2	13.9	16.8	17.2	19.1	18.9	18.3	66
Professional, scientific, and technical activities	3.0	3.1	3.4	3.4	3.6	3.6	4.2	4.3	3.8	3.9	3.7	3.7	3.7	3.4	3.4	13
Administrative and support service activities	1.8	1.8	1.8	2.1	2.1	2.1	2.1	2.2	2.6	2.4	1.6	1.6	1.5	1.4	1.4	−22
Public administration and defence—Compulsory social security	8.1	8.1	8.0	8.0	8.4	8.4	8.5	8.6	9.0	10.3	10.0	10.1	10.4	10.1	10.1	25

Industry															
Education	4.5	4.6	5.3	5.1	5.4	5.6	5.2	5.3	5.6	5.8	5.8	6.3	6.3	6.0	6.2	38
Human health and social work activities	4.5	5.4	5.2	5.0	5.0	5.5	5.8	5.8	6.0	5.9	5.8	5.8	4.6	4.4	4.6	2
Arts, entertainment, and recreation—Other service activities—Activities of households as employers; undifferentiated goods and services producing activities of households for own use	3.9	4.0	4.1	3.8	3.9	4.2	4.3	4.3	4.1	4.6	3.9	3.7	4.1	4.2	4.1	5

Source: Hellenic Statistical Services, 17/11/2017, regional dataset, extracted from dataset Value Added per industry, 2000—12, 2013, & 2014.

The most recent 2014−2020 N.S.R.F. policy document refers to a low competitiveness of the Greek firms that it attributes to the following reasons: (1) the remarkably high level of very small, small, and medium-sized enterprises, mostly of family character that operate with reduced productivity; (2) the specialization in activities of low added-value and reduced absorption of innovation; (3) institutional barriers; (4) the lack of vertical integration across the same or similar industries; (5) the deindustrialization of the Greek economy and transfer of the Greek production in neighboring countries; (6) the lack of culture of entrepreneurial cooperation among basic partners of the production systems; (7) bureaucracy and the unfriendly environment for the entrepreneur; (8) the lack of labor mobility; (9) the ineffective legal framework; (10) the lack of finance; and (11) the high energy costs (Ministry of Finance and Competitiveness, 2014: 7).

However, competitiveness at the national level should be studied more carefully across various indexes and illustrated by their use.

Starting from the study of Nominal Unit Labour Costs (NULCs), they have remarkably deteriorated during the decade of the 2000s (Fig. 3.17). Greece's position was better in comparison to Ireland's in the early 2000s. In 2006 and 2007, the Greek NULC was not very much different from that of Ireland's. It continued worsening until the crisis erupted, and started improving since 2009 and the application of IMF policies. In the year 2016, it aligns with the Eurozone and EU-28 average (Fig. 3.17).

A more careful inspection on NULCs requires studying also labor productivity. Measured in per hour worked, Greece's labor productivity levels have remained relatively low, though not as low as in Portugal or Malta (Figs. 3.18A and B). This is even more evident if compared to Ireland's labor productivity (Figs. 3.18B). It is the combination of the two different indexes, NULCs and labor productivity per hour worked, that illustrates a rather blooming picture.

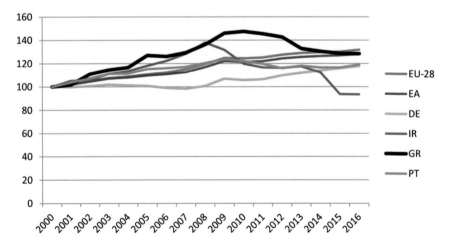

Figure 3.17 NULCs for Ireland, Greece, Portugal, Germany, EU-27, EA-17, 2000−17.
Source: AMECO series, Eurostat, author's work.

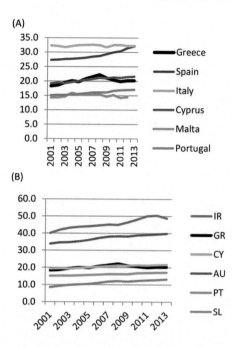

Figure 3.18 (A) Labor productivity per hour worked, Southern Eurozone's Periphery. (B) Labor productivity per hour worked, selected Eurozone states ranked top five in the years 2001 and 2011 in NULC terms.
Source: Eurostat, author's work, Eurostat, Real labor productivity per hour work (Euro per hour worked), Index, 2010 = 100, author's work, extracted 28.11.2017.

Since the Greek is not a capital-intensive economy, the particularly low levels of labor productivity per hour worked should be seen as a principal problem that takes time to be adjusted and necessitates pursuing a broad range of policies. Higher levels of labor productivity are achieved through improvements in management, organization, better forms of regulation and administration, the elimination of red-tape and bureaucracy, as well as by such aspects as industrious work, avoiding slackers, assuming working duties and responsibilities, and a socially accepted model of a hard-working ethos that fosters entrepreneurship. More organized and disciplined forms of administration and innovative forms and processes in production are required, which could overcome various problems that appear when money becomes more expensive and investments more costly than ever (with the adoption of the Euro).

Beginning in the mid-1990s and during a period that lasts almost 20 years, Greece had one of the worst export performances, compared to other European and Eurozone states (Fig. 3.19). Over an extended period, Greece's export performance resembles that of Japan and the United States, two self-sufficient and monetary independent states that have not participated in common spaces of advanced integration such as the EMU, and two European economies only, larger in size, the

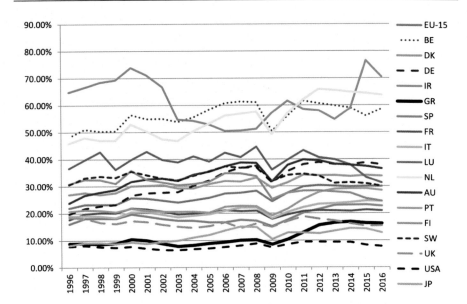

Figure 3.19 Export performance of the Greek economy, 1996−2016
Source: AMECO, using UVGD and UXGN (national accounts), author's work. *Note:* Export
performance − X/Y, where X are exports of goods and Y is GDP, in Mrd Euros, current prices.

United Kingdom and Spain (Fig. 3.19). At the opposite end lie the Benelux economies (Netherland, Belgium, and Luxembourg) and the Irish. The picture for Greece
changes after 2009 and the application of IMF policies, exceeding even that of the
United Kingdom, by 2016.

Greece's low export performance occurs despite the fact that its exports rose
over the decade (Fig. 3.20). The rise of exports is not significant, if compared
against that of other EU partners, such as Ireland or Belgium (a country of similar
population size) that offer a much better example of exporting economies
(Fig. 3.21).

Greece's import penetration on the other hand exceeds that of France, Italy, United
Kingdom, and Spain (Fig. 3.22) but does not significantly change over the years.
Greece is one of the few cases of states where import penetration ranks the country at
higher positions from export penetration, throughout the entire period studied.

Similarly, Greece's openness in international markets is the lowest amongst all
EU partners (Fig. 3.23). This behavior resembles that of the United States
and Japan, two monetary independent states, not integrated into a larger family of
states.

The Balassa indexes (for 1994, 2002, and 2006) offer a picture of Greece rather
different from the rest of EU Cohesion-4 states (Fig. 3.24). Greece appears to have
a more serious problem in the case of products of medium and high technology,
and a negative Balassa index for almost all products, irrespective of technological
degree. The Balassa indexes improve for high and medium technology products but

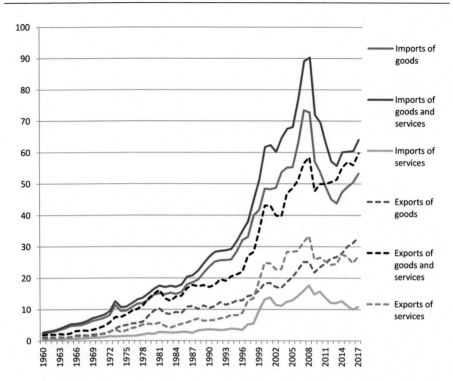

Figure 3.20 Imports and exports, goods, services, goods and services, 1960−2017.
Source: AMECO, variables used are: Imports of goods at 2010 prices (OMGN), Imports of goods and services at 2010 prices (OMGS), Imports of services at 2010 prices (OMSN), Exports of goods at 2010 prices (OXGN), Exports of goods and services at 2010 prices (OXGS), Exports of services at 2010 prices (OXSN). *Note*: Data for 2017 are estimates, variables are constant 2010 prices.

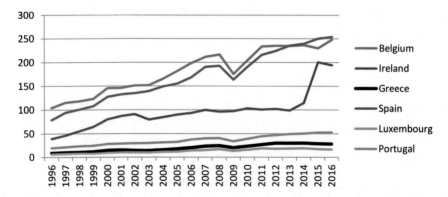

Figure 3.21 Exports of goods, current prices, selected Eurozone countries, 1996−2016.
Source: Eurostat, UXGN.

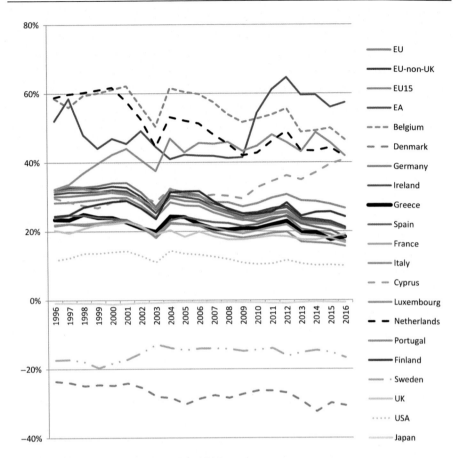

Figure 3.22 Import penetration, 1996−2016.
Source: AMECO, UMGN (imports of goods, current prices), UXGN (exports of goods, current prices), UVGD (GDP, current prices), author's work. *Note*: Import penetration: M/DD, where DD = Y + M − X is the domestic demand and X, M and Y are the exports of goods, imports of goods and GDP respectively, in Mrd Euros, current prices.

remain negative, as opposed to states like Ireland, where almost all values are positive and get higher values (Fig. 3.24).

Similarly, in the structure of Greek exports for the years 2000, 2008, and 2016 (the year before entering the Eurozone, the year before the advent of the crisis, and the most recent year of crisis, respectively), in proportional terms, most exports of the Greek state derive from primary products (Fig. 3.25). The difference between exports of primary products and exports of products of more advanced levels of technology integration is significant, much more extended than in the case of other Cohesion-4 countries. The application of IMF policies appears to benefit exports of primary goods rather than of goods of enhanced forms of technology. As such, the structure of the Greek exports is rather deteriorating in terms of degrees of

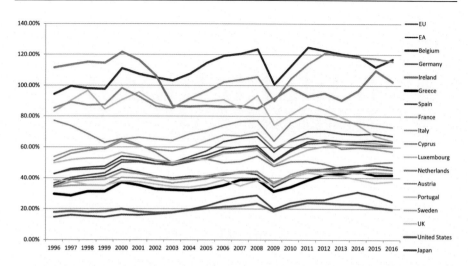

Figure 3.23 Openness in international markets of the Greek economy, 1996−2016. *Source*: AMECO data, author's work. *Note*: Openness: $(X + M)/Y$, where X, M and Y are exports of goods, imports of goods and GDP respectively, in Mrd Euros, current prices.

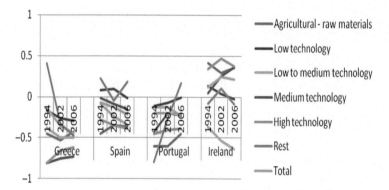

Figure 3.24 Balassa Indexes, Cohesion-4 states, 1994, 2002, and 2006, for various types of products.
Source: Data (calculated indexes) extracted from Giannitsis (2008), p. 391, author's work.

technology. It is indicative that in 2016, Greece's exports of primary products exceed by far those of all other types of products of various degrees of integrated technology. Again, this practically indicates the loss in competitiveness. The comparison with Italy, Ireland, Spain, as well as Portugal, where medium technology goods are at similar levels with primary goods reveals the problem in the Greek exports (Fig. 3.25).

By looking at Fig. 3.26, the picture for imports of goods for the three different years selected (2000, 2008, and 2016) shows that Greece's imports of primary

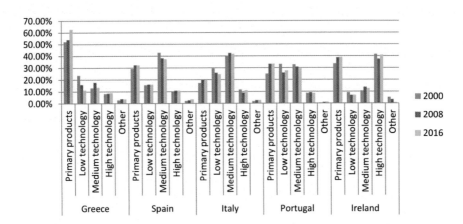

Figure 3.25 Exports of goods, Greece, Spain, Italy, and Portugal, by degree of technology integrated, 2000, 2008, and 2016.
Source: Eurostat (EU trade since 1988 by SITC), using the Standard International Trade Classification-SITC, Revision 3 (collected from UNCTAD classification, available at http://unctadstat.unctad.org/EN/Classifications.html).

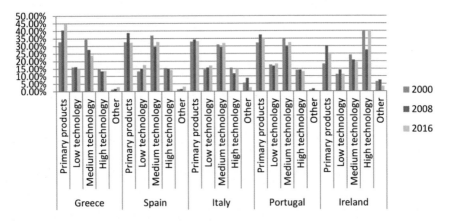

Figure 3.26 Imports of goods, Greece, Spain, Italy and Portugal, by degree of technology integrated, 2000, 2008, and 2016.
Source: Eurostat (EU trade since 1988 by SITC), using the Standard International Trade Classification -SITC, Revision 3 (collected from UNCTAD classification, available at http://unctadstat.unctad.org/EN/Classifications.html).

products have increased almost one-third from 2000 to 2016. The imports of goods of medium technology were high in the year 2000 but fell, while those of low and high technology remained at almost similar levels in the three indicative years selected. It is obvious that the years of the crisis bring a larger trade of goods in primary products, both in terms of imports and exports.

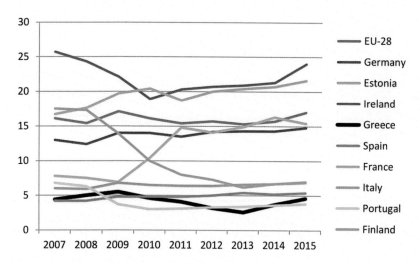

Figure 3.27 High tech exports, as % of exports.
Source: Eurostat, Code: tin00140, extracted 17.11.2017.

If Fig. 3.25 and Fig. 3.26 seen in combination, the structure of Greek imports and exports reveals the lack of technology integration in products produced in Greece. In particular Greece's high tech exports as a percentage of its total exports place the country in one of the worst positions in relation to other EU partners and the EU-28 (Fig. 3.27). Clearly the country's businesses have failed to take advantage of the years of the crisis to become an exporter of high tech products.

In Fig. 3.28, employment in high technology and medium to high technology manufacturing, as well as in knowledge-intensive services is much below the EU-28, and the levels found in Germany, Finland, Estonia, and other Southern EU states.

Similarly, in Fig. 3.29, the number of people employed in ICT as a percentage of total employment is one of the lowest in Greece and remained the same during the crisis. With fewer people working in the ICT sector, as a percentage of the total, it is natural to expect that the Greek products do not incorporate higher levels of technology and do not manage to compete with the products produced by other countries in the European and international markets.

Finally, the problem of underinvestment of activities that relate to higher technology can be traced in the limited contribution of venture capital investments, as a percentage of GDP, an index where Greece's performance is far above other European states (Fig. 3.30).

As % of GDP, Greece's balance of goods has continuously been negative (Fig. 3.31). It is the balance of services that has been positive, from an economy that progressively enhanced its service-oriented character, as explained before. The balance of goods and services though was also negative, as was the balance of current transactions and the balance of fuel (revealing the dependence of Greek production from energy imports). After the crisis, the picture is slightly changing, with

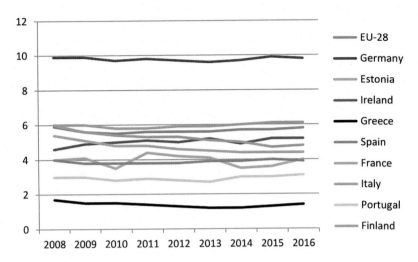

Figure 3.28 Employment in high- and medium−high-technology manufacturing and knowledge-intensive services, as % of total employment.
Source: Eurostat, code: tsc00011, extracted 17.11.2017.

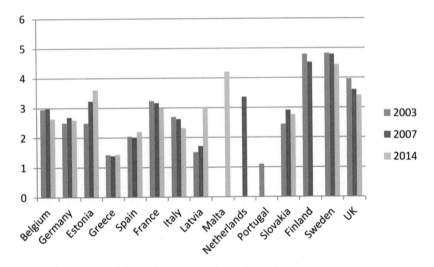

Figure 3.29 Number of people employed in ICT sector, as % of total employment.
Source: Eurostat. *Note*: Nonavailable data were either confidential or missing. The rest of values for the country can be considered as indicative of their percentage levels. For 2014 in particular, data for Greece, Spain, and France are provisional.

improvements made in the balance of goods, of current transactions, of goods and services, of services and the current account. All these changes show an improvement in the international position of the economy, although, as explained, most of

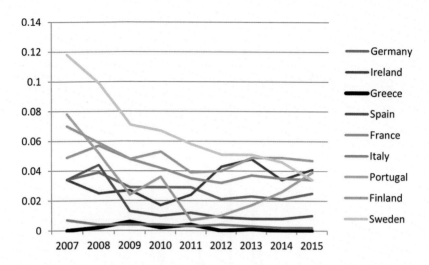

Figure 3.30 Venture capital investments, as % of GDP.
Source: Eurostat, Total Venture Capital (code: VENTURE, tin00141), extracted 11.12.2017.

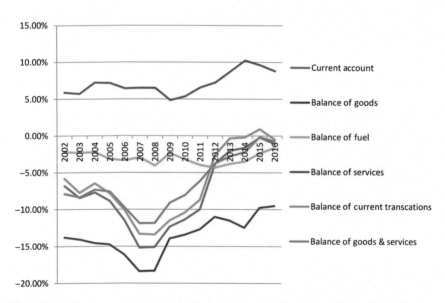

Figure 3.31 Current account Balance, Balance of Goods, balance of fuel, Balance of services, Balance of current transactions, Balance of goods and services, as % of GDP, 2002−16.
Source: Bank of Greece and Hellenic Statistical Services.

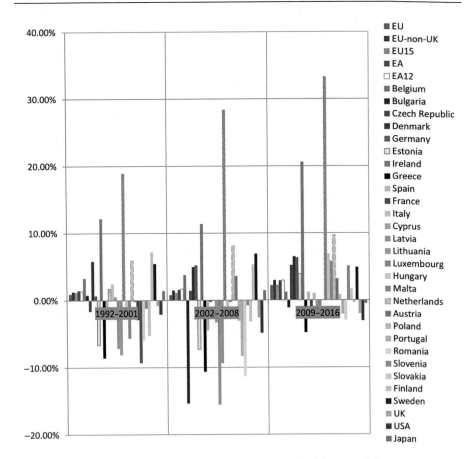

Figure 3.32 Trade Balance, as % of GDP, in EU states, United States and Japan, 1992−2001, 2002−08, 2009−16.
Source: AMECO series Gross domestic product at current prices (UVGD). *Note*: For EU, EU without United Kingdom (EU-non-UK), EA-19, Estonia and Slovakia data were available since 1993, instead of 1992. The sequence of states per period is the same with that appearing in the legend.

the exports of goods derive from primary products, of low technological integration.

In comparison to the other EU states, especially Luxembourg, Ireland, and the Netherland, the Greek economy should be grouped into those economies having negative trade balance as a percentage of their GDP (Fig. 3.32). Greece forms part of a group mostly composed of the less advanced EU states, such as Bulgaria, Estonia, Latvia, Lithuania, Romania, as well as Portugal (the United States and United Kingdom are also negative). As illustrated in Fig. 3.32, most of these states (even Bulgaria and Latvia) improve substantially their position in the postcrisis

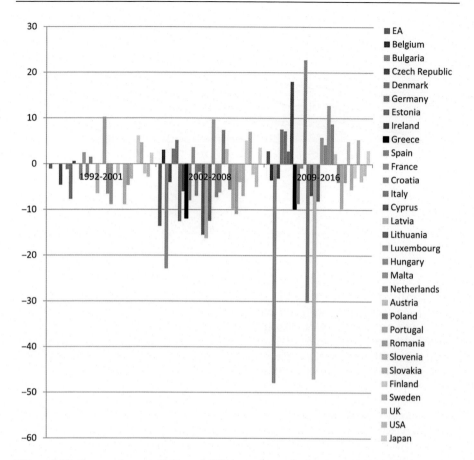

Figure 3.33 Current Account Balance in EU countries and other states, 1992−2001, 2002−08, 2009−16.
Source: AMECO series (BPM6), weighted average for the study periods, using the formula: $\left(\sum_{i=1}^{n} w_i x_i\right) / \left(\sum_{i=1}^{n} w_i\right)$, where w_i: CA in current prices and x_i: CA as % GDP. *Note*: Data for Greece were available since 2002. Data were available since 1992 only for Germany, Sweden, and United States. They started in 1993 for Czech Republic and Estonia, in 1994 for Spain, in 1995 for Italy, Luxembourg, Malta, Hungary, Austria, Finland, and Slovenia, in 1996 for Portugal and Japan, in 1997 for the United Kingdom, in 1998 for Ireland, in 1999 for EA, France, and Romania, in 2000 for Latvia and Croatia, in 2002 for Greece, in 2003 for Belgium, in 2004 for Lithuania, Netherlands, Poland, and Slovakia, in 2005 for Denmark, in 2007 for Bulgaria, in 2008 for Cyprus.

period (2009−16), while Greece, even if it has improved (as previously diagnosed), remains at the highest negative trade balance as a proportion of its GDP.

Similarly, Greece's current account balance as a percentage of its GDP has been deteriorating more than any other EU partner. It was exceeded only by Bulgaria, Latvia, and Italy and other former C.E.E. countries, especially in the 2009−16 period. Figure 3.33 illustrates a divergence between European states, with Greece being part of the group of countries that remain at a negative position.

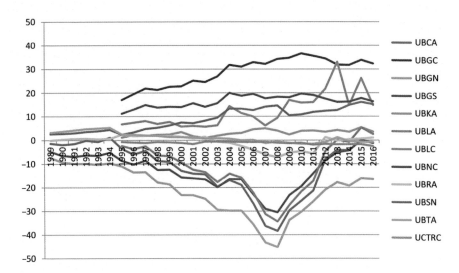

Figure 3.34 Balance of Payment variables, Greece, 1989–2016.
Source: AMECO series, Mrd EURO/EUR (2010 = 100). *Note*: UBCA: Balance on current transactions with the rest of the world (National accounts). UBGC: Gross balance of primary income, corporations. UBGN: Net exports of goods at current prices (National accounts). UBGS: Net exports of goods and services at current prices (National accounts). UBKA: Net capital transactions with the rest of the world (National accounts). UBLA: Net lending (+) or net borrowing (−): total economy. UBLC: Net lending (+) or net borrowing (−): corporations. UBNC: Net balance of primary income, corporations. UBRA: Net primary income from the rest of the world (National accounts). UBSN: Net exports of services at current prices (National accounts). UBTA: Net current transfers from the rest of the world (National accounts). UCTRC: Net current transfers received: corporations. For some variables data in AMECO series are not available for Greece for some years.

In Fig. 3.34, Greece is moving away from the horizontal axis in almost all international trade variables. The balance of current transactions with the rest of the world, gross balance of primary income (for corporations), net exports of goods, and net borrowing for the full economy, respectively, have fallen significantly after 1995 (UBCA, UBGN, UBLA, and UBGS). This illustrates Greece's problem in exports that were boosted by the increase in domestic demand (that occurs through the rise of GDP, both for consumption and investment purposes), as well as an indebtedness problem, primarily for the public sector that increases its borrowing.

3.10   Tracing the prospect of convergence; wishful thinking and reality

Convergence ought to be considered across several angles. National convergence to other state's economies differs from regional convergence among European regions or regional convergence among Greek regions only. Regional convergence has been assessed in the case of Greece at the level of 13 regions and that of 54 prefectures, which are no longer in operation as administrative units.

The crisis has hit the economy to such an extent that one observes a dichotomy of convergence processes and efforts made and advanced before and after its starting year. As national malaise spreads across the regions, at any regional levels (NUTS 1, NUTS2, or NUTS3), the effects of the crisis naturally bring divergence with other European regions, a process similar to that taking place at the national level. Thus, somehow the crisis brings a reversal of the whole academic debate on regional convergence, since the crisis period, and the associated recession and austerity, have brought the Greek regions to a similar position with that recorded much earlier in modern Greek history; as if the regional policies pursued were all conducted in vain. Fig. 3.35 illustrates the shrinking process of Greek regional GDP per capita, which in practice is a process of divergence if compared against other European regions. The geographical level selected (NUTS I) is indicative.

Fig. 3.35 shows that within a time period of two programming periods, and despite all efforts and policies implemented for the regions, the Greek macroregions have finally returned to levels similar to those found at the beginning of the 2000−07 period, i.e., their starting point when Greece joined the Eurozone. Thus, it is worth asking if policies at the geographical level have actually managed to promote and sustain regional convergence with the rest of European regions, especially at a common currency environment, or whether they are just a wishful thinking, far from the reality.

One also observes in Fig. 3.35 a few more points: While the Greek macroregions (NUTS 1) follow a trajectory of rising growth over 2000−08 similar to each other, they also all fall together, with a similar decreasing growth trajectory after 2008. It is obvious that Attiki is the wealthier region in GDP per capita terms and that a great part of the Greek territory comprising Central and Northern Greece ("Kentriki Ellada" and "Voreia Ellada") is lagging significantly behind. The two macroregions appear to converge in their shrinking pattern. What is more, GDP per capita in

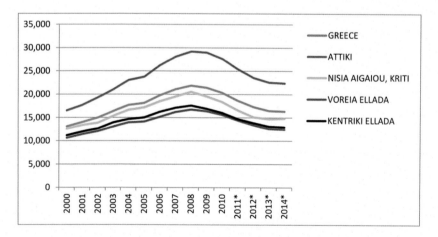

Figure 3.35 Regional GDP per capita, in Euros, current prices, macroregions (NUTS I). *Source*: Hellenic Statistical Services, 17/11/2017, regional dataset. *Note*: estimates in asterisks (regional datasets produced with significant time delays).

Aegean islands and Crete ("Nisia Aigaiou, Kriti") appear to shrink faster and diverge more than the Greek average, toward the levels of Central and Northern Greece.[20] The crisis does not alter significantly the pattern of regional divide between Attiki and the other three macroregions.

Some studies on regional convergence view the period before and after the start of the crisis as one and reach conclusions for the state of regional convergence in the Greek regions by considering a part of a postcrisis period (e.g., in Petrakos and Psycharis, 2014). Even the most recent policy documentation suggests that despite more than 30 years of application of EU Cohesion policies, Greece's distance from the European centers of economic activity and the specific geographical features of the Greek land act as market failures (Ministry of Finance and Competitiveness, 2014).

For Greek regions and prefectures that were lagging behind ever since Greece joined the EEC in 1981, a recent review of relevant literature offers a rather conclusive evidence for β-convergence but is inconclusive for σ-convergence, for different parts of the studied period (Exarchou and Chionis, 2016).[21] Benos and Karagiannis (2008) suggested β-convergence only for the Greek prefectures and not the Greek regions and no evidence of σ-convergence at both levels for the 1971−2003 period. Recent evidence for β-convergence[22] and weak σ-convergence was also provided at EU level (Petrakos and Pscycharis, 2014).[23]

In terms of regional production structure, as illustrated in Table 3.28, the vast majority of production still takes place in the region of Attiki (at NUTS 2 level). With the exception of agriculture, production in Attiki ranges from one-third of total Greek production to more than two-thirds in some services, such as ICT or financial and insurance services. Attiki benefited from a higher proportional allocation for some particular services during the crisis, e.g., for professional, scientific, and technical activities and increased its proportional allocation in agriculture, forestry, and fishing. With the notable exception of agriculture, half or more than half of the Greek production is located in two regions, Attiki and Kentriki Makedonia. A core−periphery divide remains present in production terms and has not been amended by the long-term application of EU Cohesion Policies.

Based on evidence provided through Figs. 3.36−3.38, one can hardly suggest the convergence of the Greek to the EU economy, as a whole. Ever since Greece lost its twofold capacity to apply a monetary policy and use the automatic currency

---

[20] Keep in mind data are estimates after 2011 (see Note in Fig. 3.36).

[21] See also a short review an analysis in Exarchou and Chionis (2016) The Regional Problem and Regional Disparities after the end of the 3rd CSF, 111−117 in Regional Effects of the Recession of the Greek economy and its consequences, 19th Scientific Conference of the Greek Society of Regional Scientists, 12−13 May 2016, Lamia. Also see in Lolos (2009) for 1990−2005 and Benos and Karagiannis (2007) for 1971−2003.

[22] β-Convergence relates to the neoclassical model.

[23] See in Petrakos and Pscycharis (2016) The authors, after examining data for the 1995−2010 period, have suggested that more than 40 years are needed to reduce half of the development gap between more and less advanced EU regions.

Table 3.28 Production structure across regions, 2001/2007/2014, current prices turned to percentages

		Attiki	Voreio Aigaio	Notio Aigaio	Kriti	Anatoliki Makedonia, Thraki	Kentriki Makedonia	Dytiki Makedonia	Ipeiros	Thessalia	Ionia Nisia	Dytiki Ellada	Sterea Ellada	Peloponnisos
Agriculture, forestry and fishing	2001	3.8	2.5	1.9	8.3	8.6	20.4	3.6	4.7	12.3	1.7	11.6	10.9	9.6
	2007	5.6	1.8	2.4	9.7	8.1	20.4	3.8	4.2	11.5	1.8	11.5	9.6	9.6
	2014	5.2	1.9	2.3	7.9	7.4	19.9	4.1	4.8	14.1	1.6	11.3	9.7	9.8
Mining and quarrying—Manufacturing—Electricity, gas, steam and air conditioning supply	2001	35.0	0.4	1.4	2.6	4.7	16.7	6.1	1.5	5.4	0.4	4.0	14.7	7.1
	2007	35.6	0.6	1.3	2.7	4.5	16.2	6.6	1.6	6.3	0.5	5.2	11.8	7.0
	2014	35.2	0.7	1.5	3.3	4.4	15.1	9.3	1.8	5.8	0.4	3.9	11.6	6.9
Water supply, sewerage, waste management and remediation activities	2001	50.1	0.5	3.2	3.7	4.6	17.8	1.8	3.4	4.0	1.7	3.0	4.1	2.3
	2007	50.8	1.0	3.4	3.9	4.9	15.4	1.8	3.5	4.1	1.8	3.4	3.5	2.6
	2014	46.9	1.1	3.8	4.8	4.5	14.2	2.5	2.5	6.8	1.9	3.8	3.8	3.3
Construction	2001	41.0	1.3	4.2	5.5	5.2	12.0	3.1	3.6	5.4	1.8	6.4	5.8	4.8
	2007	43.3	1.4	4.2	6.0	4.0	12.1	3.1	3.6	5.0	1.7	5.7	5.5	4.5
	2014	37.0	2.0	5.2	5.6	4.6	13.2	2.5	4.7	6.5	2.0	5.8	4.7	6.1
Wholesale and retail trade, repair of motor vehicles and motorcycles	2001	45.0	1.5	3.0	5.4	3.9	17.6	1.6	2.3	5.2	1.8	4.7	3.6	4.3
	2007	45.0	1.5	3.0	5.4	3.9	17.6	1.6	2.3	5.2	1.8	4.7	3.6	4.3
	2014	50.0	1.1	2.5	4.7	3.4	16.8	1.4	2.2	4.3	1.6	4.2	3.5	4.2
Transportation and storage	2001	51.3	1.6	8.0	5.1	3.4	7.3	0.6	1.8	3.9	3.7	6.3	4.4	2.5
	2007	51.0	1.6	7.6	5.2	3.4	8.0	0.7	1.8	3.9	3.5	6.2	4.4	2.7
	2014	54.8	1.4	6.5	4.8	3.4	8.4	0.6	1.9	3.3	3.1	5.4	4.0	2.4
Accommodation and food service activities	2001	22.5	2.9	16.4	12.1	4.5	12.4	1.4	2.8	4.3	9.1	3.2	3.6	4.8
	2007	24.4	2.6	13.0	13.3	3.8	13.8	1.3	2.7	4.9	9.0	3.6	3.4	4.3
	2014	29.4	2.1	15.2	14.0	3.2	12.2	1.1	2.3	4.0	6.6	3.1	2.9	4.0
Information and communication	2001	74.5	0.8	1.1	2.4	2.0	7.5	0.8	1.0	2.0	0.7	2.9	1.7	2.4
	2007	74.5	0.8	1.1	2.4	2.0	7.5	0.8	1.0	2.0	0.7	2.9	1.7	2.4
	2014	74.0	0.8	1.0	2.7	1.8	8.8	0.7	1.0	1.7	0.6	3.4	1.5	2.1
Financial and insurance services	2001	68.2	0.9	1.6	3.2	2.5	10.1	1.1	1.4	2.9	0.9	2.9	2.0	2.4
	2007	68.7	0.9	1.6	3.2	2.4	10.1	1.0	1.3	2.7	0.8	2.9	2.0	2.4
	2014	69.6	0.9	1.4	3.6	2.1	10.1	1.0	1.3	2.5	0.9	2.5	1.7	2.3
Real estate activities	2001	59.9	1.3	2.3	3.5	2.4	10.4	1.3	1.9	4.0	1.5	4.2	3.1	4.1
	2007	59.8	1.3	2.3	3.5	2.6	10.3	1.3	1.9	4.0	1.5	4.2	3.1	4.1
	2014	58.9	1.3	2.5	3.6	2.7	10.8	1.2	1.9	3.9	1.6	4.2	3.2	4.2

(Continued)

Table 3.28 (Continued)

		Attiki	Voreio Aigaio	Notio Aigaio	Kriti	Anatoliki Makedonia, Thraki	Kentriki Makedonia	Dytiki Makedonia	Ipeiros	Thessalia	Ionia Nisia	Dytiki Ellada	Sterea Ellada	Peloponnisos
Professional, scientific and technical activities	2001	62.3	0.7	1.5	3.8	2.9	13.4	1.1	1.4	3.9	0.9	2.8	2.4	2.8
	2007	62.6	0.7	1.5	3.8	2.9	13.0	1.2	1.4	3.9	1.0	2.8	2.3	2.8
	2014	71.4	1.6	1.3	3.0	1.5	9.4	1.2	1.2	2.0	0.9	3.3	1.6	1.7
Administrative and support service activities	2001	69.8	0.9	1.9	3.2	2.1	10.4	1.1	1.3	2.5	1.2	2.3	1.6	1.8
	2007	69.3	0.9	2.0	3.3	2.1	10.4	1.1	1.3	2.6	1.2	2.3	1.7	1.8
	2014	67.5	0.6	2.9	5.6	2.1	11.0	0.5	1.0	2.0	1.7	1.8	1.9	1.5
Public administration and defence—Compulsory social security	2001	46.6	1.8	2.7	5.1	4.5	12.4	2.1	3.0	6.3	1.7	5.3	4.0	4.4
	2007	48.6	1.7	2.7	5.1	4.4	11.7	2.1	3.0	6.0	1.6	4.7	4.0	4.3
	2014	45.6	2.9	2.8	4.0	6.4	13.5	2.1	2.4	6.5	1.2	5.0	4.0	3.8
Education	2001	42.4	1.5	2.6	4.8	6.9	16.0	2.1	2.8	6.0	1.5	6.2	3.4	3.8
	2007	40.4	1.3	2.5	4.9	7.1	17.3	2.0	2.9	6.4	1.5	6.1	3.4	4.1
	2014	40.8	1.5	2.1	4.9	6.0	18.4	2.4	3.3	6.7	1.3	5.7	3.1	3.8
Human health and social work activities	2001	48.1	1.4	2.1	3.8	4.1	17.0	1.3	3.7	6.0	1.4	4.1	3.8	3.1
	2007	49.5	1.3	1.9	3.2	4.3	15.9	1.1	4.1	5.4	1.3	4.6	3.6	3.9
	2014	47.4	1.5	1.8	4.8	4.3	14.6	1.5	2.9	7.4	1.3	5.5	2.4	4.5
Arts, entertainment and recreation-Other service activities-	2001	45.8	1.2	2.4	4.7	3.8	17.4	2.1	2.4	5.9	2.1	4.7	3.2	4.3
	2007	51.5	0.7	2.7	4.7	3.2	15.2	1.8	1.8	4.7	1.5	4.8	3.1	4.1
	2014	45.6	1.1	2.7	6.2	3.2	17.0	1.2	1.9	5.3	1.9	6.3	2.6	4.8
Activities of households as employers; undifferentiated goods and services producing activities of households for own use														
Activities of extraterritorial organizations and bodies	2001	45.4	1.3	3.4	4.9	4.2	14.0	2.3	2.4	5.3	1.9	4.9	5.5	4.5
	2007	45.3	1.3	3.3	5.0	4.1	14.1	2.3	2.4	5.3	1.9	4.9	5.4	4.5
	2014	48.3	1.4	3.4	4.9	3.9	13.3	2.4	2.2	5.1	1.7	4.6	4.4	4.3

Source: Hellenic Statistical Services, 17/11/2017, regional dataset.

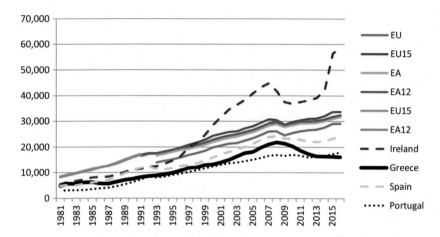

Figure 3.36 GDP per head, current prices, EU, Eurozone, Greece, and selected partners (Cohesion-4), 1981–2014 (in thousands of Euros).
Source: AMECO series, variable HVGDP. *Note*: GDP levels not adjusted for inflation, EU stands for the European Union, EA for Euro Area and EA(&L) for Euro Area plus Lithuania. EA&L are the Eurozone states including Lithuania that have recently joined.

exchange mechanism, its GDP growth rates have started to fluctuate, in the 2003–05 period, and then to fall (Fig. 3.38).

Clearly, Greece's GDP per head has risen since 1981 (Fig. 3.36). This increasing trend does not differ much from a similar trend observed both at the EU and Eurozone level. Ireland has benefited from a much stronger rise in GDP per capita. Policies implemented by the Irish state over the years. The growth model that Ireland has followed was based on private sector activity, FDI attraction and entrepreneurship and has managed to bring a distinct converging outcome. The rise of Irish GDP per capita has reached a peak in 2007, at €44,700, while Greece's peak in 2008 is at €21,600 only. This highlights a process of divergence,[24] at least between these two economies. In comparison to the Irish, the Greek economy has accelerated at a much slower pace.

The picture for GDP levels (illustrated in Fig. 3.38) is different. In all Cohesion-4 economies, GDP levels have multiplied by four times in market prices from 1981 to 2010. This emphasizes the success of EU cofunded policies to enhance GDP growth levels. However, while in the case of Spain the acceleration has been very high and abrupt, in Greece (along with Portugal) the acceleration has been more progressive until 2009. After 2009, a downward trend has appeared, where the accelerator has been dormant.

Greece's GDP growth rates have not sufficiently exceeded those of the rest of the EU (EU28 or EU27), or EU15, or those of Eurozone (EA18 or EA12) (Fig. 3.37). The picture for Greece is rather unstable and fluctuating. GDP growth

[24] That should naturally be reflected also in wages and salaries.

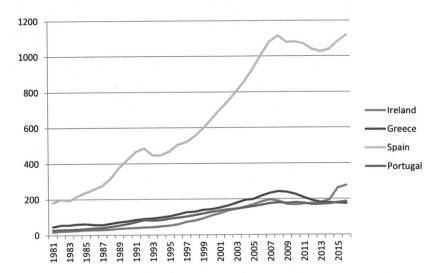

Figure 3.37 GDP at current market prices, EU, Eurozone, Greece and selected partners (Cohesion-4), 1981–2016 (in millions of €).
Source: AMECO series, variable UVGD.

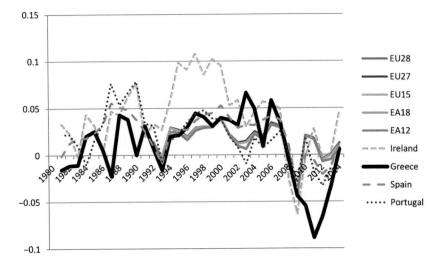

Figure 3.38 GDP growth rates, EU, Eurozone, Greece and selected partners (Cohesion-4), 1981–2014.
Source: AMECO series, variable OVGD (GDP at 2010 market prices), author's calculations.

rates were low before 1988, started to rise from 1989 to 1993, have fallen between the 1st and 2nd programming period, and the country reached a steady growth rate from 1994 to 2002. Then, they reached two separate peaks, one in 2003 (6.6%, the highest growth record in the period studied) and one in 2006 (5.8%). Growth rates have dramatically fallen after 2007 and the advent of the crisis significantly reduced the growth levels already accomplished. It is only Ireland that has achieved higher growth rates than Greece during the study period, while the rest of the Cohesion-4 countries have remained at similar levels of GDP growth rates.

In Table 3.29, the OECD national accounts database is used to compare Greece against other OECD countries over the same period. Greece has underachieved more than any other state in terms of aggregate growth rate from 1981 to 2016 (Table 3.29). During this period, its GDP has risen only by 34%. In the rest of the Cohesion-4 countries, growth rates during the study period have been higher: in Portugal 88%, in Spain 124%, and in Ireland 451%. Even large economies, such as the United Kingdom, have managed to more than double their 1981 size by the year 2016. In comparison to states having similar to Greece's initial GDP sizes in 1981, such as Austria or even Belgium, Greece's rate of GDP growth has lagged significantly behind. In comparison to other non-EU OECD countries, such as Korea, Greece has followed a very moderate trajectory, even though it started from similar levels of GDP in 1981. In comparison to Norway or Switzerland (two countries with higher levels of GDP per capita), Greece has benefited less throughout the 1980s and the 1990s, the early periods of Greece's EU membership. Table 3.29 also reveals that it is the only country that has not managed to recover after the crisis and that its high growth pace during the 2000s reached a peak in 2008.

Overall, from the comparative analysis of Table 3.29, Greece's trajectory during its EU membership (for a small, open and peripheral economy choosing the path of integration deepening), appears to bring limited benefits in comparison to other states, precisely in a period when the opposite was expected to take place, and which coincided with the transfer of many EU funds to the Greek economy.

Concerning employment, total unemployment has risen since 1981 and significantly deteriorated after the crisis erupted (Fig. 3.39). It reached a peak of 1.33 million in 2013, more than nine times higher than 1981. From 1981 to 2009, employment has significantly risen and unemployment too but at relatively lower levels in comparison to employment.

Self-employment has remained a significant part of the total employment over the years. It has followed a rather stable pattern, and has substantially fallen only after 2009. But importantly, self-employment has been reduced in comparison to total employment, since the latter rises significantly during the same period.

Thus, the growth and development model followed over the years by Greece has fueled employment, has kept self-employment relatively stable but at high levels, and has brought a rise in unemployment in net terms, although not that significant.

Stable high self-employment levels are due to the overspecialization in various jobs, across many industries and in particular in services, the pressure of the middle-class to become self-employed, as they associate professional independence solely to their own business (e.g., for doctors, lawyers, mechanical, or other engineers), a special industrial structure in employment-intensive industries like tourism or trade that is mostly composed of self-employed, the rather limited social acceptance of a good entrepreneurial model and of managerial skills, various impediments to organize firms of larger scale, various market niches opened for micro,

Table 3.29 GDP (expenditure approach), constant prices (2010), PPPs and % rate of, selected years and periods

Countries	1981	1991	2001	2011	2015	2016	% 1981–1991	% 1991–2001	% 2001–2011	% 2011–2016	% 1981–2016
Australia	375	490.8	719.3	972.7	1077.5	1103.8*	30.88	46.56	35.23	10.77	194
Austria	187.1*	242.1*	307.2	361.9	370.9	376.4	29.40	26.89	17.81	2.49	101
Belgium	244.3	304.4	376	445.1	459.4	464.9	24.60	23.52	18.38	3.21	90
Canada	682.2	837.3	1152.8	1403.9	1515.4	1537.7	22.74	37.68	21.78	7.94	125
Chile	–	116.3*	213.1	331	378	384	–	83.23	55.33	14.20	–
Czech Republic	–	178.8*	218.7	295.5	315.6	323.8	–	22.32	35.12	6.80	–
Denmark	137.4	172.4	223.2	242.2	253.1	257.4	25.47	29.47	8.51	4.50	87
Estonia	–	–	22.2	31	34.5	35.2	–	–	39.64	11.29	–
Finland	104.3	132	180.4	213.5	207.5	211.5	26.56	36.67	18.35	–2.81	103
France	1334.9	1705.7	2117.5	2391.5	2458.4**	2487.6**	27.78	24.14	12.94	2.80	86
Germany	1927.5*	2536.9	2985.1	3328.3	3485.7	3553.4	31.62	17.67	11.50	4.73	84
Greece	190.4*	213.5*	274.4	285	256**	256**	12.13	28.52	3.86	–10.18	34
Hungary	–	150.7*	182.3	218.4	235.5	240.1	–	20.97	19.80	7.83	–
Iceland	5.8*	7.3*	9.9	12	14	15	25.86	35.62	21.21	16.67	159
Ireland	53.7*	75.6*	154	203.5	281.5	296	40.78	103.70	32.14	38.33	451
Israel	65.2*	96.5*	160.8	231.1	261.2	271*	48.01	66.63	43.72	13.02	316
Italy	1361.4*	1737.8*	2051.5	2091.2	2019.3	2038.8	27.65	18.05	1.94	–3.44	50
Japan	2438.3*	3804.5*	4222.9	4476.8	4706.9	4753.9	56.03	11.00	6.01	5.14	95
Korea	207.9	550.8	1,020.7	1560.7	1745	1794.3**	–	–	–	11.81	–
Latvia	–	–	27.1	39.2	43.9	44.8	–	–	44.65	11.99	–
Luxembourg	12.1*	21.4*	34.2	44.6	50.8	52.9	76.86	59.81	30.41	13.90	337
Mexico	926.1	1,061.2	1,432.1	1798	1990.2**	2036.1	–	–	–	10.69	–
Netherlands	374*	481.4*	664.6	753.1	771.4	788.4**	28.72	38.06	13.32	2.43	111
New Zealand	68.0	75.5	107.7	139.7	155.3**	161.5*	–	–	–	11.17	–
Norway	133.3	174.4	247.9	286.7	309.5	312.8	30.83	42.14	15.65	7.95	135
Poland	–	352.8*	552.8	842.5	930.9	955.9	–	56.69	52.41	10.49	–
Portugal	149.2*	211.1*	274	284	276.2*	280.1*	41.49	29.80	3.65	–2.75	88
Slovak Republic	–	–	86.4	138.6	152.3	157.3	–	–	60.42	9.88	–

Slovenia	–	33.3*	45.1	57.3	58.1	59.9	–	35.44	27.05	1.40	–
Spain	679.5*	931.8*	1244	1474.9	1475.7**	1524**	37.13	33.51	18.56	0.05	124
Sweden	207.7*	254*	322.2	401.2	434.3	448.7	22.29	26.85	24.52	8.25	116
Switzerland	251.2	305.1	351.7	423.1	451.4	457.6	21.46	15.27	20.30	6.69	82
Turkey	375.7*	600.9*	801.4	1403.1	1779.7	1836.4	59.94	33.37	75.08	26.84	389
United Kingdom	1124.4	1496.3	1969	2277.2	2476.5	2521.3	33.08	31.59	15.65	8.75	124
United States	6,698.6	9,057.7	12,837.1	15,204	16,672.7	16,920.3	–	–	–	9.66	–
EA19	–	–	10,957.7	12,255.6	12,525.6	12,750.2	–	–	11.84	2.20	–

Note: In B$ US, estimates used for some years only, denoted by asterisks.

Source: OECD, (VPVOB).

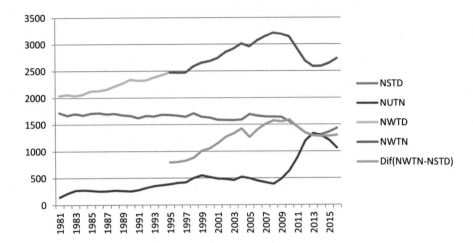

Figure 3.39 Employment and unemployment variables, Greece, 1981−2015.
Source: AMECO series, 1000 persons. Note: NSTD: Number of self-employed: total
economy; NUTN: Total unemployment; NWTD: Employess, persons: all domestic
industries; NWTN: Employees, persons: total economy Dif(NWTN-NSTD): Difference
between NWTN and NSTD.

self-employment firms, the more general working conditions, job insecurity, and
the lack of job insurance provisions by many employees.

The difference between unemployment and self-employment, which was at its
highest when Greece has joined the EU, was only but slowly reduced over the years
but violently changed after 2008, when a reversing pattern was placed in operation.
Within only a few years of crisis, self-employment has fallen and reached a size
similar to that of total unemployment, approximately 1.3 million in 2013 and 2014.

The numbers of employees rose significantly in 2009−10, both in all industries
and in total. This should relate either to an increase in average business sizes or to
average employment increases in the public sector. However, the difference
between total employees and self-employees (Dif(NWTN-NSTD)) has increased
from 1996 to 2010, showing a reversing pattern to the benefit of employees (rather
than to that of self-employees and self-employment).

3.11 Public sector expenses

Table 3.30 provides information on the annual budget and its various components
that represent main public sector expenses. The Programme of Public Investments in
particular comprises funds received from EU sources and concerns the state's main
development priorities. Total Public Expenses in pale blue the Table 3.30 are the
sum of the Regular Budget and of the Programme of Public Expenses. From 2000 to
2009, the amounts devoted to development priorities through the Programme of
Public Investments appear to follow a rather increasing pattern in net terms, though
falling proportionately to Total Public Expenses (Table 3.30). Except for the year

Table 3.30 GDP and the expenses of total annual budget, per category (and for the Programm of Public Investments), Greece, in M€, 2000–08 and 2011–16

Year	GDP	Wages	Pensions	Hospital—private care	Insurance & social protection	Financing of agencies & institutions	Consumption expenses	Interests, loans, & other expenses	Regular budget	Programme of public investments	Total of public expenses
2000	137,930	7202 (17.2%)	2910 (7.0%)	1781 (4.3%)	3669 (8.8%)	1788 (4.3%)	2108 (5.0%)	9914 (23.7%)	34,377	7421 (17.8%)	41,798
2001	146,428	7811 (17.9%)	3110 (7.1)	2054 (4.7%)	4365 (10.0%)	1640 (3.8%)	2083 (4.8%)	9711 (22.3%)	35,788	7842 (18.0%)	43,630
2002	156,615	8642 (22.5%)	3332 (8.7%)	2257 (5.9%)	4747 (12.3%)	1685 (4.4%)	2329 (6.1%)	9134 (23.8%)	37,431	8014 (20.8%)	45,445
2003	172,431	9360 (19.0%)	3523 (7.2%)	2446 (5.0%)	5993 (12.2%)	1792 (3.6%)	2316 (4.7%)	9416 (19.1%)	40,735	8435 (17.2%)	49,170
2004	185,266	10,337 (18.8%)	4065 (7.4%)	2746 (5.0%)	7236 (13.2%)	2415 (4.4%)	2291 (4.2%)	9464 (17.2%)	45,490	9522 (17.3%)	55,012
2005	195,366	10,931 (19.4%)	4211 (7.5%)	2854 (5.1%)	9073 (16.1%)	2026 (3.6%)	2351 (4.2%)	9774 (17.4%)	48,686	7524 (13.4%)	56,210
2006	211,314	11,493 (19.7%)	4576 (7.8%)	3063 (5.3%)	9381 (16.1%)	2141 (3.7%)	2396 (4.1%)	9589 (16.4%)	50,116	8184 (14.0%)	58,300
2007	227,134	12,125 (18.8%)	5052 (7.8%)	3131 (4.9%)	10,875 (16.9%)	2372 (3.7%)	3395 (5.3%)	9769 (15.1%)	55,706	8809 (13.7%)	64,515
2008	236,936	13,933 (19.6%)	5904 (8.3%)	3354 (4.7%)	13,447 (18.9%)	2606 (3.7%)	2702 (3.8%)	11,207 (15.7%)	61,642	9624 (13.5%)	71,266
2011	207,029	15,251 (19.9%)	6572 (8.6%)	1214 (1.6%)	16,502 (21.5%)	2042 (2.7%)	9981 (13.0%)	18,585 (24.2%)	70,145	6559 (8.6%)	76,705

(Continued)

Table 3.30 (Continued)

Year	GDP	Wages	Pensions	Hospital—private care	Insurance & social protection	Financing of agencies & institutions	Consumption expenses	Interests, loans, & other expenses	Regular budget	Programme of public investments	Total of public expenses
2012	191,204	13,947 (19.9%)	6564 (9.4%)	1070 (1.5%)	15,672 (22.3%)	1882 (2.7%)	8002 (11.4%)	20,476 (29.2%)	61,499	6114 (8.7%)	70,145
2013	180,654	12,572 (21.5%)	5850 (10.0%)	1721 (2.9%)	14,201 (24.3%)	1936 (3.3%)	8479 (14.5%)	7050 (12.1%)	51,809	6650 (11.4%)	58,459
2014	178,656	12,385 (22.5%)	6093 (11.1%)	1508 (2.7%)	12,913 (23.5%)	1666 (3.0%)	7707 (14.0%)	6198 (11.3%)	48,472	6592 (12.0%)	55,063
2015	176,312	12,011 (21.9%)	6348 (11.6%)	1671 (3.0%)	16,193 (29.5%)	1563 (2.8%)	7227 (13.2%)	6681 (12.2%)	48,545	6406 (11.7%)	54,951
2016	174,199	11,750 (21.3%)	6315 (11.4%)	1672 (3.0%)	12,964 (23.5%)	1442 (2.6%)	7699 (14.0%)	6054 (11.0%)	48,891	6288 (11.4%)	55,179

Note: Data corrected for 2007 in Regular Budget and Total of Public Expenses. In parentheses % of Total of Public Expenses, for each category.
Source: Data extracted from Greek government's annual report. From the 2000—08 period data were collected by Drettakis (2011: 158) from the Greek government report, as they appeal (corrected).

2002, expenses in the Programme for Public Investments have exceeded the level of 17% of Total of Public Expenses, until the year of the Olympic Games (2004). After 2004, they have risen in net terms but fell proportionally to Total of Public Expenses. This is the period when several public investments and infrastructure were implemented. In 2011 and after 2011, the levels of Programme of Public Investments appear to remain the same, both in net and proportional terms.

As illustrated in Table 3.30, the levels of the Programme of Public Investments attained in early 2000s were similar to the levels of wages, representing the second highest amount of expenses by the Greek state, for the years 2000 and 2001 (second only after the category of payments toward "interests, loans, and other expenses"). Institutional building has had an expanding cost in net terms over the years but has not changed much as proportion of Total of the Public Expenses.

What is clear from Table 3.30 is that all expenses of the Greek government have been growing from 2000 to 2008, some of them, like wages and pensions, even until 2011.

In the years of the crisis, the most significant expenses, as a proportion of Total Public Expenses are those on "insurance and social protection" and the next most significant are "wages." "Interests, loans, and other expenses" are significant in the early period, up to 2012 but the IMF-EU policies have helped to reduce their actual burden on public expenses.

3.12   The turning of an economy to consumption-based

Fig. 3.40 illustrates the consumption-based pattern developed in the Greek economy over the years. Final consumption expenditure rose from €82,400 million in 1996

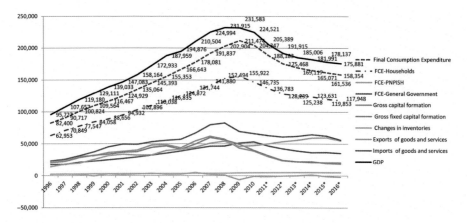

Figure 3.40 GDP and its components (expenditure approach).
Source: Hellenic Statistical Services, available on-line since 17/10/2017. *Note*: The GDP is calculated by adding Final Consumption Expenditure (FCE), Gross Capital Formation and the difference between Exports of Goods and Services and Imports of Goods and Services. GDP measured in market prices. Data have been reviewed using as a base year 2010, according to EC regulation 549/2013 (ESA 2010). Data after 2011 (in asterisks) are estimates but on several occasions such data have been calculated and provided elsewhere in the present text.

to €202,904 million in 2008, a year when GDP has reached its peak at €231,915 million. It then reached its peak a year after, in 2009, at €211,474 million.

In the consumption expenditure approach used in GDP calculations, GDP is the sum of Final Consumption Expenditure (FCE), Gross Capital Formation (GCF), and Net Exports of Goods and Services (Exports of Goods and Services minus Imports of Goods and Services). FCE is a substantial proportion of the Greek GDP. It has represented more than 80% of the GDP since 1996, fell to 82.7% in 2004 and rose again to reach levels above 90% after 2009. Three-fourths of consumption is due to household consumption.

Conclusions

4

4.1 Conclusions and final thoughts

Greece has undergone an unprecedented crisis, not only for her own history but for the modern history of nation-states, despite the policies and actions taken for her support. In 2016, Greece's economy reached its nadir because of the crisis. The shrinking of the Greek real GDP in percentage terms was greater than that of the USA in percentage terms after the 1929 crisis.

Many explanations have been offered for what has brought this great Greek crisis and its resulting recession. These can be distinguished into structural and those related to policy orientation and related errors made during the years of the crisis. Structural explanations attribute the crisis to: (i) the removal and absence of stabilizers at the national level (such as the currency exchange mechanism), the ineffective organization of the common currency zone and its "design failures", (ii) centripetal forces that accentuate core-periphery imbalances at the Eurozone level, enhanced by the speed and strength of capital mobility, a point quite evident after the crisis erupted that combines with, (iii) the intensification of globalization and over-financialization of economies (iv) the transfer of the global crisis at the Eurozone level and (v) the appearance of economic cycles, as discussed in economic theory.

Other causes identified in the specific literature developed on the Greek crisis include Greece's constant "destiny" to default (that follows the spiral of wars, civil wars and bankruptcies), the tolerance of high levels of debt for several decades, the continuous borrowing of consecutive governments to cover social needs, the mismanagement of public finances, the limited use of creative accounting to join the currency zone (if compared to the overall adjustment and preparation efforts taken), the liquidity enhancement of the Greek banks a year before the crisis that raised the country's expenses, the inability to access cheap money to repay debts after the crisis erupted, the rising cost of capital, the limited and swallow entrepreneurial opportunities and the stereotypes about entrepreneurship for many decades, the protective ideology and role of public sector syndicates, strong restrictions imposed on the productive structure, the central policy choice to limit unemployment at any (social) cost, the spread of opportunism across the society, tax evasion, the unofficial sector, corruption, the free-rider problem with public goods, limitations in the Greek cultural and social capital, the rise of political party enmity, stereotypes, of political clientelism and populism, the simultaneous rise of bureaucracy and red tape, many organizational problems such as those relating to the size of local administration and the loss of institutional memory, as well as circumstantial reasons.

Funding the Greek Crisis. DOI: https://doi.org/10.1016/B978-0-12-814566-1.00004-5

Some significant policy errors include the additional expenses made in the year 2009 by two consecutive governments in power (and especially after September 2009), the general unwillingness of all consecutive governments and finance ministers to cut expenditure during many decades, as well as the dubious methodology used to re-calculate the deficits in 2009 and the strong fears for Grexit that created an environment of uncertainty.

Policy errors were made by IMF. Having considered the Greek crisis to be a liquidity crisis and not a solvency crisis, the IMF has applied an adjustment policy without any effect upon the currency, has operated mostly in favor of Eurozone stability rather than Greece's benefit (at least in the first SBA), turning Greece into the object rather than the subject of policies on many occasions, and strongly miscalculated fiscal multipliers and overempashized debt limitation policies. It is important though to understand that Greece's economic crisis is the outcome of its economic growth model and not just a debt crisis. The rise and persistence of high levels of debt is the result of this particular growth model.

For almost two decades, the Greek state has managed to conduct numerous policies for its own development, which were deteriorated by high debt levels, above 100% of its GDP. When the global crisis erupted, its debt rose even more, while GDP started to fall. The Greek state has failed to sustain similar debt levels, as a proportion of its GDP.

The crisis appeared despite that ever since 1981, the year that it has joined the EU, Greece has gained access to an unprecedented supply of investment opportunities by the use of EU funds, both in net figures and proportionately to its GDP. The Greek state had envisaged seriously the planning of its development policies throughout consecutive programming periods. Active government intervention was applied in order to cover the growing needs of an economy at low initial levels of development, characterized by the total or partial absence of the necessary infrastructure, imperfect and unstructured in many respects markets, imperfect information, and rising negative externalities that required the provision of many public goods. Substantial developmental needs were covered, of a long-term character that have enhanced capital, labor, and other factors of production. GDP has expanded and reached unprecedented levels. The year before the crisis erupted, Greece was an equal member of the most advanced group of states in the world, being part of the Eurozone.

Overall, the EU has contributed through EU Cohesion Policy €54.2 billions out of a total of €100.1 billion invested in Greece (in constant 2015 prices) from 1989 to 2013, when the first postcrisis programming period was over. The Greek state has invested €23.9 billions and the private sector €22.4 billions. In annual terms, for the 1989−2013 period, out of a total expenditure of €4 billions, the EU has contributed €2.2 billions, the Greek state €957.7 millions, and the private sector approximately €881 millions.

The lion's share from EU funding was directed to infrastructure, mainly in transport and environment. Significant funds were also transferred for telecommunications, energy, health care, and culture. Human capital—including education—(with almost €16.3 billion) and agriculture classify also as principal policy priorities. The EU has contributed in the support of income in agriculture more than 47.1 billion

Euros within three programming periods (from 1989 to 2006) that could have been used to modernise their agricultural holdings.[1] Yet, the growing amounts of investments have not helped to resolve long-term problems in agriculture, such as high energy and irrigation costs, inefficient use of water and other irrigation problems, desertification, pollution, the reckless use of fertilizers and pesticides, the inefficient or even bad production, trade and distribution structures, the small size of agricultural land and their high borrowing costs, the re-naming of foreign products to Greek in domestic markets and the high levels of imports of agricultural goods and products.

Despite the amounts transferred to Greece, the specific allocation plan, historically, socially, politically, and spatially bound, has not helped to maximize wealth, in comparison to other EU Cohesion states and the rest of EU member-states. In collaboration with the EU authorities, the resource allocation from EU Cohesion Policy has emphasized mostly autonomous investment and infrastructure development, in the transport and physical environment, as opposed to induced investment and the support of the private sector. Throughout consecutive programming periods, and as Greece was facing new challenges and difficulties by heading toward higher stages of integration, competitiveness and the laying down of foundations for domestic business interests was turned out to—at best—a third policy priority in planning terms (if the policy axis of geographical and regional convergence is not considered as the third, separate policy axis); one that was configured around the axes of two other policy priorities: macroeconomic targeting and, as discussed, the emphasis placed on infrastructure and autonomous investment.

Infrastructure development was accelerated with the 2nd Community Support Framework (C.S.F. 1994−1999) due to the impetus for building projects for the Olympic Games, as well as to the country's strong development needs in infrastructure. This particular policy direction has not changed, due to interest groups formed in the construction sector, the building of infrastructure across consecutive programming periods, and numerous problems in infrastructure development that have appeared over the years.

Policies on entrepreneurship, small businesses and competitiveness have been clearly misprioritized in funding terms, as opposed to the example of other EU cohesion states. The 2000−06 program on Competitiveness was weakly assessed, poorly informed scientifically, and its application has encountered many problems. It is indicative that the EU has invested less than €1 billion in competitiveness and the Greek private sector in the 2007−13 programming period, when it was mostly required.

Thus, a serious misallocation of EU funds toward the provision of public sector goods, infrastructure, and what is termed in literature *autonomous investment* is diagnosed in long-term development policies and choices. Certainly, investing in infrastructure is a necessary precondition to promote development and support the transition of an economy from one stage of development to another.

---

[1] These amounts are not included in the abovementioned sum of €54.2 billion of EU's contribution through EU Cohesion Policy for the 1989−2013 period.

Overemphasizing autonomous investment though was a strategic mistake from a developmental perspective, which could have been amended in the long run. It paved the way for the expression of a long-term development problem, characterized by the significant loss of competitiveness, reduced labor productivity, trade deficits, limited technological advancement, capital widening than deepening, and a "snowball" effect upon its manufacturing small and medium-sized enterprises (SMEs), as indicated by several indexes. The signs of a "death rattle" had appeared as soon as Greece joined the Eurozone, as seen in multiple problems encountered in the implementation of 2000−2006 competitiveness program. These were suggested in the state's official policy documentation to be: (i) the outflow of funds toward other countries, (ii)the shrinking of the manufacturing sector, (iii) the strong sensitivity of SMEs and difficulties encountered for start-ups, (iv) the acquisition of Greek firms by foreign, (v) the strong competition in manufacturing from neighboring countries, and (vi) the fostering of oligopolistic structures. The shrinking of the manufacturing sector in particular was characterised as a "time bomb" for competitiveness, and the economy's dependence on exogenous factors was thought to be high, while its capacity to cope with them limited.

In the 2nd C.S.F. (1994−99), during the implementation of an active manufacturing policy that was rich in interventions in order to face significant structural problems, the Greek state had not envisaged seriously the prospect that successful economic policies were mostly the outcome of contextual amelioration of macroeconomic indexes and nominal convergence rather than of more permanent efforts to lay down foundations for competitiveness. Positive expectations and optimism from achieving most of the common currency's targets, from finally joining the currency zone and reaching an advanced stage of integration and development, had impeded realizing the strong necessity to continue making amendments in the new millennium, to improve competitiveness. The precious knowledge that real convergence is a precondition for nominal convergence was neglected. The importance of microeconomic and business foundations to achieve macroeconomic results was greater than originally appreciated both by Greek political elites and especially by EU authorities, even if they were long disregarded and left unattended. Setting the whole common currency integration planning on macroeconomic bases, instead of pursuing prudent microeconomic and business adjustments first, especially for businesss smaller in size that were unable to cope with international competition and were thus the most vulnerable, was the general EU policy direction and guidance, after the Cecchini Report was produced.[2] Greece's final results have been the product of this particular policy guidance. Laying down the foundations for promoting growth in a small open economy, where financial and monetary aspects are shared with other partners on the one hand but domestic production is not competitive and exports not promoted on the other, has acted further as a destabilizing force. The Greek state has sought to participate in European integration deepening, without considering the full extent and array of implications from not imposing early the suitable microeconomic foundations for this particular decision. In terms

---

[2] The original Cecchini report has taken into account only large-scale capital interests.

of financial, economic, and political emphasis, the state has planned in a reverse manner, following the shortest possible path of "nominal convergence" and failing to acknowledge and realize the necessity of the gap that was left behind. Like someone who cared about putting the water first but forgot to put the tea bag. Real convergence has remained a target to fulfill after joining the Eurozone, and was considered as a target possible to achieve even within 10 years (see for example in Stournaras, 2008). Clearly, Greece is responsible for not realising how important was the prospect of real convergence, letting this prospect to remain a fiction.

In reality the program for the growth of the Greek economy was demand-driven. Not until recently, has been recognized that the Greek economic problem had its roots in the lack of capacity to produce competitive products that will be offered in international markets. The Greek economy had failed to transform itself to an exporting one during its EU membership, through benefiting from the EU integration process. On the contrary, imports have rather substituted domestic production within the studied period. Weak labor markets and labor market institutions[3] had not helped to resolve unemployment and the lack of sustainable jobs. Such problems have remained, despite the significant amounts invested, multiple policies for human capital applied, and even if, starting from the mid-1990s, a policy consensus was sought among manufacturing interests, labor market representatives, and the government, as a political way to introduce and apply manufacturing policies in the long run (Pitelis, 2013).

One can argue that access to available EU resources has rather reinforced a specific growth model developed since the late 1970s. The aforementioned growth model was found in the present book to be characterized by the reduction of productive capacity, a high tendency toward imports, and a low tendency toward capital and technology accumulation, a difficulty to adjust in contemporary technological and entrepreneurial challenges, a state-centered approach of entrepreneurship influenced and reproduced by the government, as well as by serious institutional deficiencies and political anchoring in practices of the past (such points were already highlighted by Argeitis, 2011; Stasinopoulos, 2011). The Greek manufacturing has remained attached to traditional industries that have not addressed international needs and have covered domestic demand (as already suggested by Stournaras, 2008). It has been based on products of relatively low technology, while European demand required products of high or medium technology (see also Stournaras, 2008). However, building a growth and development model only around a Keynesian, demand-oriented approach and spending money on autonomous investment would naturally exhaust its limits, at some point. Significant interests were formed around autonomous investment, which have impeded the change of a traditional growth model and helped its reproduction. Apparently, it was also not realized that the domestic Greek market, whose size was expanding because of the increase of EU funds allocated and the various improvements in macroeconomic indexes, would not suffice to sustain growth in the long run. The

---

[3] Their presence is discussed in Mitsopoulos and Pelagidis (2011) and in Featherstone and Papadimitriou (2010).

Greek political system had neither acknowledged such points early (at least by the mid-2000s) nor assumed responsibility for various failures both in the design and implementation of economic programming. Overburdened with the allocation of large amounts of EU Cohesion funds, continuous organizational restructuring, and obliged to follow all the relevant EU regulations that transferred decision-making from top-down to bottom-up, it has missed several opportunities to consider how to improve a growth and development model; a model already not operating well before the eruption of the crisis.

Perhaps the most important point of criticism that can be raised against the EU Cohesion Policy, as applied in Greece, is that its application and growth results have created an illusionary view of the economy. Within few years, many significant problems were taking place in parallel, showing that the "valves" of the economy were not operating well: the 1999 Athens stock market crash, the strong liquidity constraints posed by the entry at the Eurozone and the loss of monetary independence, the collapse of competitiveness and inability to reach some average results in the 2000−2006 competitiveness program (at a time when emphasis was mostly placed in organizing the Olympic Games), and the banking liquidity problems identified in 2007. While these signals were sent, the prosperity from using EU Cohesion Funds and the achievement to share the common currency resulted in failure to realize the problems.

Over the years, the Greek state has used and experimented with various tools and incentives to promote economic development. This was a learning process for the Greek public administration, in terms of planning, organizing, and implementing all these policies, dealing with the use and allocation of extended amounts of funds and resources. A great deal of this precious learning capacity and experience was wasted, because of the outsourcing of programming and implementation work and the constant reorganizations that were required by the EU and the rearrangements imposed by consecutive governments. During the four major programming periods of EU Cohesion policy, many novelties were applied in public administration and different policies and actions were introduced, enriched by new and pilot schemes and measures, often not tested before. All these novelties required continuous public administration adjustments and their assimilation, which have pushed towards the weakening of public administration, in the long run, if not that of an organizational "dizziness" (for which the principal responsible is Greece). Many problems appeared in the absorption of funds and delays in implementation and target achievement. The organisational problems encountered were also related to legal entanglements and complications with national and community laws, the extremely intensive monitoring work that was actually required, the multiplication of selection procedures for projects and subprojects, the difficulty for the final recipients to participate and to be included within the new and demanding procedures and the inability to accurately define and synthesize the effects and impact of each program.

With the exception of infrastructure projects, where signposting was easier to organize and to present, the general impression from reading across policy documents is that it is as if EU authorities (that agreed in the plans suggested by Greece, in all consecutive programming periods) have a limited concern for expanding the work, role, and scope of existing institutions, actions, and policies already promoted. They preferred looking to build something new that will differentiate policies and actions from the past.[4] Rather than being skeptical about organizational and policy restructuring, the EU unfolded the full array of its policies, something like a "supermarket" of policies (ELIAMEP, 2011). As if growth is a matter of perpetual introduction of extra novelties rather than of pursuing critical changes needed in a whole economic trajectory. Some of these novelties were proclaimed by EU policy agendas and required updated technical and organizational proficiency from the public administration. Furthermore, administrative reorganization and the launch of new public sector institutions offered ample room for hiring new employees.

Institutional building took place, as many institutions were created over the years to promote several of the EU Cohesion policies, and others were strengthened and their role upgraded, through infrastructure building and the promotion of all necessary organizational and managerial arrangements. Few decisive steps to properly protect property rights had been taken only, since several institutions for their protection, especially the land registry, had been significantly delayed and specific interests had impeded their creation or completion. Thus, one cannot argue that all positive effects and externalities from infrastructure development were fully acquired.

If combined, increases in NULCs, low labor productivity levels, a weak export performance, and trade imbalances illustrate Greece's loss of capacity to compete, especially in the early Eurozone years. The very large numbers of self-employed may associate with problems of organizational and managerial character both for the private and public sector. These problems and the rising unemployment levels since 1981 are coupled with, if not multiplied by, the high costs of capital and the rising costs of investment.

The balance with the EU (receipts minus payments) has always been positive. Both receipts from the EU and payments to the EU have increased. Payments increased mainly due to higher GNI-based contribution. In comparison to other EU Cohesion states, Greece received a greater part of funds per capita but the GDP growth rates did not appear to increase more, proportionally to GDP payments to the EU. Needless to say that the requested national expenditure over the study period has contributed in the progressive accumulation of public debt, a process stimulated by EU Treaties and regulations making national contribution compulsory. Not to mention private sector debt accumulation due to continuous liquidity constraints. Most EU funds were obtained by ERDF and EAGGF-Guarantee, while the Cohesion Fund appears to have taken a limited, secondary role.

The balance of goods and trade deteriorated, as compared to that of most EU and Eurozone partners. The losses in competitiveness associate to the limited scope and funding in the private sector, and the substantial problems in absorbing funds. The allocation of Cohesion funds, the emphasis on infrastructure, and the limited integration of technology in products have all led to Greece's rather diverging

---

[4] There is no emphasis on what has already been achieved under the EU Cohesion Policy and how and where the achieved projects or advanced institutions could continue to implement the new policies.

pattern throughout the period joining the Eurozone, despite that GDP has progressively risen, with rates positive and sometimes high, even though fluctuating. Yet, the GDP growth rates have not been as high as in other cases of EU member-states that had joined the EU after Greece or those obtaining similar EU Cohesion support policies. In the absence of policies promoting induced investment, the economy's acceleration was limited, as opposed to other countries, and was significantly restrained during the downswing (reminding Hick's dormant accelerator).

It was thought that modernization of the Greek economy was taking place due to the increase of imports and the technology integrated in imported goods. However, the latter was not targeted and not prioritized in economic planning, even if the development of skills, human capital and, other factors increasing productivity were targeted. One can argue that Greece's integration in the EU partially substituted the necessity for technological advancements and for innovations produced by the state and domestic enterprises. This is against the teachings of widespread economic theory that technology advances growth but is expected to take place in an integrated place. Progressively, Greece was turned to a major consumer of technology. Capital widening rather than deepening took place.

Many planning failures and weaknesses have appeared during the implementation process. Among the important ones were those regarding the critical for the Greek economy, 2000−06 Competitiveness program, when the currency exchange mechanism that had been acting as a stability mechanism for competitiveness losses in the past, was neutralized. The remarkably low levels of absorption of this program are explained not only by the outcome of legal complications and bureaucratic obstacles but also by various inadequacies and failures identified in its interim report, its organizational restructuring and the negligence of many factors that have delayed its implementation.

The 2000−06 Competitiveness Program was not sufficient to restrain the process of production restructuring and the "snowball effect" observed in small, medium, and large manufacturing firms for more than two decades. The latter have paved the ground for various imbalances and market concentration processes. The ambitious target to join the common currency zone and to adjust the macroeconomic picture has not been followed by a serious consideration for its negative implications for enterprises and the strength of competitiveness pressure exercised upon the Greek firms in manufacturing and other industries. Surprisingly, implications from joining the common currency zone were restricted to only a couple of lines of comments in a Competitiveness program that aimed at Greece's long-term competitiveness, instead of being the central theme and being given special attention and treatment for the various scenarios that ought to have been examined (of inflation, of different price levels, the necessity and use of substitutes in the place of previous stabilization mechanisms, etc.). Needless to say that the prospect of global economic shock was never examined, a problem that, apart from other reasons, may of course relate to the lack of economists that would have undertaken such an effort, objectively and at the state level. Finally, a large distance was identified in almost all competitiveness actions and axes between their very ambitious titles and aims originally proclaimed and the actual results achieved.

The EU Commission has approved a series of plans, without suggesting their compulsory amendment toward a direction that would have promoted induced investment. Since 1989, four consecutive programs on "Competitiveness" have focused more on direct capital transfers through the Greek Development Law and institutional building. Even after the crisis erupted, the EU Cohesion policy continued to overemphasize this misallocation of funding and capital resources against the Greek private sector and production. From 2007 to 2013, it has allocated the predecided amount of less than €1 billion at Greek entrepreneurship policies and enterprises, during the years of the worst-than-ever crisis and of competitiveness collapse.[5] This policy guidance does not seem to change over the decades, being subject to common EU regulations and the structuring of Cohesion plans and Community Support Frameworks. As within the framework of EU Cohesion Policy, states are not allowed to act independently in development issues, one should rather acknowledge the sharing of responsibility, if not a historically unprecedented negligence of EU authorities and the Commission that supervised and agreed in all these policies. Had long-term, ex-post assessments been still compulsory, the EU Commission might have identified potential problems and prevented their expression.[6] One has to underline that some aspects, in particular the point of overemphasis in autonomous investment and the imbalanced type of investments, may have never been seen, nor clearly defined or stated in academic literature with the sufficient emphasis placed in the present text.

From an organizational point of view, the Commission could have employed more people to design, implement, and monitor different models of structural support policies between older and newer member-states, focusing more carefully upon the individual problems appearing in older member-states (especially those overemphasizing strong macroeconomic adjustments to join the common currency zone) and treating each member-state with respect to their levels of development and their integration efforts already pursued. If a more prudent, differentiated approach per nation-state was taken, the Commission could have claimed limited or even no responsibility on the problems of the Greek economy. These problems might have examined more thoroughly -and not occasionally-, their causes might have been revealed and several -more focused in the Greek case- efforts might have been taken to resolve them. On the contrary, this rather homogeneous treatment has brought a rather uniform, less robust in many respects, and organizationally weakened assessment and preparation of plans. One could ask whether it is worth spending so many funds, time, and consulting efforts in creating indexes, discovering synergies, providing matrices, and emphasizing the managerial and accounting aspects of EU Cohesion Policy, when the most critical problems cannot be properly diagnosed and identified; the latter may have lied elsewhere, for instance—as discussed here—in the misallocation of resources. More generally speaking, the value

---

[5] Approximately 250,000 businesses have ceased operations ever since the crisis erupted in 2008.

[6] One should remind that the EU Commission in its last before the crisis, 2008 fourth Cohesion Report had proudly announced the reduction of regional imbalances and the elimination of cohesion problems in the EU territory.

of a one-size-fits-all approach for EU Cohesion Policy should be reconsidered and a differential focus attributed in more and less integrated states, at least in terms of sectoral and especially competitiveness policies.

In many occasions, the aims and targets of policies proclaimed in official documents have been rather grandiose and eloquently expressed. One gets the general impression of a rather unrealistic optimism by reading the Greek economic planning documents. So many far-reaching aims would have been achieved in so much limited time. A general feeling emerges from reading carefully all the planning documents that somehow, just because funds are substantially raised, a good selection is made across a wide range of international policies and actions, more sophisticated planning is introduced, and new and innovative actions are proposed and implemented, that all these are necessary and sufficient conditions to predetermine the outcome, strengthen the economy, and bring only but positive results. This is perhaps one of the most significant mistakes of Greek planning authorities, its reduction to a self-fulfilling prophecy that has led to a self-illusionary path and vision.

From the side of the Commission, the problem relates to (i) the superficial expectations created from its policy guidance, (ii) an over-attachment to the self-fulfillment of its own theoretical and policy suggestions (imposing to the Greek authorities even to put aside, at a very critical historical moment, the rather successful 1994–99 manufacturing program, and to reschedule it), (iii) the approval of very eloquent descriptions and grandiose titles of policy targets, (iv) the inaccurate prognosis for problems emerging in the Greek economy, (v) the incapacity or indifference to study separately nation-specific problems that would have merited special attention, (vi) the promotion of continuous changes in EU Cohesion and Agricultural policies that would have naturally affected countries that have mostly participated in their application, (vii) the initial negligence for many policies required to promote integration (such as policies on SMEs), (viii) an apparent sclerosis of a programming logic (that remained unaffected even after a global crisis has erupted), and finally, (ix) the lack of a clear sight in programming matters, since technical issues, such as absorption figures, statistical indexes, and managerial processes, have outweighed critical aspects from economic theory, which could have helped to avoid a permanent damage to an economy. Thus, the Commission, apart from the aspect of policy suggestions and guidance, is responsible for focusing on the tree rather than on the forest.

The importance and role of policies supporting the economy's private sector have been rather left unattended, both by Greek and by EU authorities that were supervising, guiding, and co-funding the state's developmental priorities and planning.[7] On the contrary, significant interests were formed around autonomous investment, which have impeded the change of a traditional growth model and helped its reproduction. Seen from an EU Cohesion policy perspective, the Greek problem is essentially an overemphasis placed on autonomous investment, infrastructure, and in particular on transport and the physical environment, that while it has promoted

[7] That have witnessed the application of the much more successful short-term plan of the Irish economy.

intra-European capital and labor movements, it has left unattended an extended part of domestic production, if not exposed and weakened, while it has neglected the need to create new production. One should emphasize this to be the most cutting edge of a knife, the other side of which is the overemphasis placed on nominal convergence, public consumption, and demand-oriented policies.

The Greek case is more the case of lack of attention but primarily lack of knowledge and understanding that overemphasizing autonomous investments and infrastructure building in the resource allocation process may harm the economy in the long run, within an environment of intensive global changes and economic integration. This point and the misplacement of policy priorities are critical for the success of EU Cohesion Policy elsewhere, not just in this case. Important economies on EU and national funds can be made at least from now on, the choice of a more appropriate allocation and the targeting of only but necessary infrastructure investments, and primarily of the support of induced investments, for instance in the small- and medium-sized sector.

From a social welfare perspective, one can argue, as Rapanos (2008) had put it, that the Greek omnipresent, unselfish central planner had never actually existed. Different groups of interests, political parties, population groups, and individuals have had different individual interests that they had sought to satisfy over the decades (Rapanos, 2008). To achieve their aims, they have also sought to influence democratic procedures, exercising political and social pressure, taking advantage of various deficiencies and problems appearing in the implementation of programs, benefiting from constant outsourcing of programs, the loss of programming experience, and capacity by the state authorities, and the lowering of its academic standards. Institutional building was not sufficient to avoid the expression of such problems. Short-term individual benefits have been more important than long-term collective benefits. Information had always been imperfect, the quantity and quality of statistical data low and many economic and political decisions have been based on personal judgment and intuition rather than in-depth studies and long-term scheduling (Rapanos, 2008). Given that the income of the median voter is below that of the average voter, politicians have always been keen in promoting redistribution policies without considering their long-term implications (Rapanos, 2008). The complexity of the legal system, bureaucracy, lack of disparity and corruption, inefficiency in the mechanisms of implementation, and high implementation costs have all significantly impeded the planning process (Rapanos, 2008).

The historical coincidence of mistakes from all the different sides involved in the case of Greece should lead in promoting changes in policies that will advance its stage of development. The restructuring of the Greek economy was only but partially advanced and appears to remain largely incomplete. Using previous planning experience and achievements carefully and prudently, the Greek economy has to cross the line between an old and a new stage of development. The hierarchy of development choices and the strategy of economic development policies pursued in Greece have to change, if possible in collaboration with the EU and, in particular, the Eurozone partners. In rebuilding a coherent investment strategy, Greece, the

European Commission, and Eurozone partners have to support the restructuring of Greek production and emphasize induced investment, by attracting Foreign Direct Investments that will maximize benefits for the Greek and European production. For policy makers all over the world, it is deduced that an economy in development should not overspend available resources and funds to autonomous investments and infrastructure building that could seriously harm but should instead emphasize a better balance in favor of induced investment.

4.1.1 Projecting few conclusions in growth theory and macroeconomics

In theoretical terms, the Greek case offers some significant conclusions and a chance to rethink some points widely espoused in economic theory The first conclusion is about something already known in development theory: Countries that undergo the stages of development are often not capable to use and manage properly their resources. Their politicians do not understand which changes are required and how to select among the possible choices offered.

The evidence provided that Greece has emphasized in its development policies more autonomous than induced investment, in particular infrastructure building, throughout an extended period of time, should be given more attention in economic growth theory. It is true that the type of development historically promoted by the Greek society and consecutive Greek governments, during the period of Greece's integration to the EU (since 1981) was based on the provision of public goods and the rise of consumption. These demand-driven, Keynesian policies were rendered practically ineffective precisely when mostly required, when Greece had to cope with the effects of its own crisis. Like a patient that receives a pill so many times until he collapses and then, at the moment when this particular pill is mostly required, it is no longer effective. The Greek case therefore leads to a significant conclusion: that Keynesian policies[8] that boost consumption may be rendered ineffective if overused in periods of intensive efforts of economic integration, and that they should rather be left to be used more extensively in times of crisis or critical conjunctures of a nation's economic history.[9] Besides, Keynesian theory targets in reality at the increase of production through increases in demand. Driving demand is a mean by which production will change and become more effective. Not a way to destroy production and its structures.

Importantly though, the Greek crisis offers a base of reflection in growth theory. Not just because of its extent and size but basically because of its real causes. Many of these explanations were provided here but in terms of growth and development policies pursued, it has been stressed that its expression is due to the emphasis placed on autonomous investment and infrastructure building.

---

[8] The term Keynesian here is used in the narrow, restricted meaning that refers to demand management.
[9] As the USA have made in their 1929 crisis, a policy guidance that allowed their fast economic recovery.

Growth theory has developed over the last 60 years, across several directions. Its development was fueled by the unexplained part of neoclassical growth equation, named "Solow's residual" or total factor productivity (or "phlogiston" in the words of Romer, 2016) and the inability to explain it. Historically, there has been an extended work on Solow's residual, which has opened new paths in growth theory. Endogenous growth and new growth theory were investigated and stressed, and numerous economic growth factors have been emphasized, such as human capital, knowledge, or even institutional, cultural, or behavioral aspects and agents in the economy. As the levels of growth were rising in more advanced economies and the sizes of firms were increasing, growth modeling (that reflects at some points the efforts to explain growth and development) shifted toward the study of imperfect forms of competition, such as monopolistic competition, and espoused the view of increasing rather than of decreasing returns.

Despite its varied development, growth theory has failed to acknowledge the significance of induced investment and the distinction between autonomous and induced investments. The evidence from policies that have paved the ground to the Greek crisis shows that it is not just capital, labor, or human capital that significantly influence growth outcomes but it is also the type of investment that should be endogenous in growth equations. Induced investment or the analogy between induced and autonomous investment or -in other words- the type and proportional allocation of investment, should account for a great part of Solow's residual (at least more than initially considered), explaining Total Factor Productivity and its variation. If this conclusion has a more general value, many of the growth models have to be reviewed and their policy conclusions reconsidered.[10]

The significance of the type of investment and its contribution to capital accumulation has been discussed by many economists. It is a central theme in economic studies and a point raised also through the Cambridge controversy in capital theory. This, famous in economics, controversy has highlighted that difficulties in the measurement of capital impede the accuracy of aggregate functions and, as a result, of neoclassical theory. If, as suggested through the present evidence, the type of investment and its proportional allocation affects the process of capital accumulation and its outcome, then the view of Cambridge's economists (that have raised this controversy) at this particular point in capital theory merits even more attention.

It is also understandable that investment in infrastructure and social goods is sensitive in political terms and a matter of political ideology too.

Treating any kind of investment from a positive side, irrespective of its type or distinction, is considered to be something good after all. Why would one type of investment be different from another? Certainly, in times of crisis, such as that of the post-1929 crisis in the United States, any type of investment is necessary for economic growth and recovery.

---

[10] One has to acknowledge that all the aforementioned explanations for the Greek crisis may lead toward reducing the severity of the present finding. Furthermore this finding refers to an economy that is part of a currency zone, at a certain stage and level of development. However, it is worth considering and putting the argument in full, for future reference and research.

Another significant reason explaining why this distinction is not taken into account in growth theory relates to the rise of the subdiscipline of macroeconomics and its progressive disciplinary development. Macroeconomics were developed to explain economic phenomena at a larger, aggregate scale. They aimed at the understanding, study, prognosis, management, and reduction of fluctuations of aggregate economic variables, such as growth, unemployment, and inflation. Resource allocation and the use of policies to advance full employment of factors of production were considered important for macroeconomics. They were also occupied with the difficulty to understand whether markets are imperfect, the bridging of macroeconomic to microeconomic variables and the application of macroeconomic theory. Every time some problem appeared in macroeconomic analysis that was hard to explain (following a crisis or some other exogenous shock), new disciplinary developments were investigated to deal with their understanding, which were espoused and applied.

Despite objections raised, Keynesian views and policies focusing on effective demand have been largely acknowledged to have allowed the post-1929 US recovery. At the time, more elementary work was required to understand the macroeconomy and substantial economic recovery was prioritized. Any distinction on the type and proportional allocation of investment was not given sufficient attention because capital accumulation was the main concern.

The postwar era was associated with the suggestions of the neoclassical synthesis and the employment of the IS-LM framework. Successful efforts were made to smooth the business cycles through policies affecting IS and LM (money) markets, to such an extent that it was claimed that business cycles had become "obsolete" (Bronfenbrenner, 1969).

The rational expectations hypothesis, i.e. the idea that individuals form optimal expectations, seeking to optimize their profits, opened a path for acknowledging that predictable, systematic effects of economic policy should be finally taken into account by economic agents aiming at rationally adjusting their expectations in relation to them (Hillier, 1991). Based on the rational expectations hypothesis, the real business cycle (henceforth RBC) theory was developed (first by Kydland and Prescott, 1982) to explain growth differences and fluctuations in macroeconomic variables and short-run economic cycles. The term "real" refers to real shocks in the economy as opposed to nominal. RBC theory was developed since the 1980s, out of a growing dissatisfaction from using technology or TFP to explain observed economic fluctuations (and to allow differences in technologies to account for differentials in these fluctuations among countries) and out of the realization that fluctuations may be attributed to exogenous to economies causes, such as petroleum or energy shocks (Romer, 1996). Some of its proponents have acknowledged that technology is a cause of fluctuations and used Solow's residual as an exogenous variable explaining business cycles model, which was suggested to be a major driver of output fluctuations (Kydland and Prescott, 1982). Economic fluctuations were seen as optimal responses to technology shocks, as if recessions are periods of outright technological regress, during which firms use less efficient technologies.

A further point made in relation to expectations is that expectations and changes in beliefs or in some behavior can be self-fulfilling under certain circumstances and

affect fluctuations; once such changes take place, a series of effects are put in operation that strengthen expectations associated with them (Woodford, 1997; quoted in
Scarth, 2004). Pesaran (1987) explained further that economic agents can be
trapped in a vicious cycle of ignorance and that systemic errors made are not
resolved by rational expectations. Bryant (1991: 27; quoted in Scarth, 2004)
highlighted that, so long that there are multiple equilibria in rational expectations,
there is nothing rational in expecting one of these equilibria to be reached (since
the rational choice may be found in another equilibrium). Finally, according to
Sargent (2007), expectations errors, if they appear, can be overcome through a
learning process that might take time to advance.

The concept of rational expectations has helped to develop the *new classical
macroeconomics that* discarded the neoclassical synthesis as "flawed" (Lucas,
1972). New Keynesian macroeconomics were also developed, partly as a response
against new classical macroeconomics, by accepting rational expectations, while
insisting that markets are imperfect. They espoused the view that short-run fluctuations in output and employment are deviations from the natural rate hypothesis that
occur due to sticky prices and wages. RBC and New Keynesians both assumed that
expectations are rational and shared the view that business cycles are shaped by
long-run supply shocks. The New Keynesian models also recommended that
demand shocks are crucial too. RBC models opened also the path for the "new neoclassical synthesis," which emphasized practical macroeconomic advice, price
stickiness as a root cause of economic fluctuations, and optimization approaches to
explain macroeconomic behavior (Goodfriend and King, 1997: 231).

However, the Greek crisis questions the validity of RBC theory. To the extent
that the latter explains real cycles, as it pertains, it should also help to explain
Greece's strong contraction (and that of most of its macroeconomic aggregates), the
worst ever recorded in the history of nation-states over the last hundred years in
real terms and the second worst in nominal terms. As analyzed, the country's membership of the Eurozone has contributed to its contraction, as it did not allow the
immediate use of monetary policies. Greece's pacing during the 1990s toward
nominal convergence with the rest of EU countries has also contributed to this end.

Rational expectations are rational for individuals, since their income increases
but are not necessarily reasonable[11] for the development of an economy, if the economic regime reproduced does not follow a right direction. Multiple equilibria may
be formed from actions or inaction of this regime. Taking the example of economic
policies pursued by EU Cohesion Policy, one can argue that economic agents have
formed rational expectations with respect to the systematic elements of such policies and related policy making and have pursued their rational adjustment in
changes of the EU Cohesion Policy.[12] The similar character of policies has formed

---

[11] The word reasonable is not used here in the same way that it was used by Lucas and Prescott (1971).

[12] For example, when construction projects started to reduce, the funds invested in construction companies were turned towards energy that was turning to a key funding priority by EU Cohesion Policy and
the Europe's 2020 strategy.

Figure 4.1 Rational expectations (RE) formed by EU Cohesion Policy.

similar rational expectations from the EU Cohesion Policy for all agents involved (including political), and especially for businesses (Fig. 4.1).

As discussed, rational expectations were used by RBC theory to explain fluctuations. However, if growth and development policies advance mainly autonomous investment and infrastructure spending, failing to reach a certain critical mass of induced investment, then rational expectations naturally formed around such autonomous investments, may lead to equilibrium that traps the economy into a vicious cycle. Thus, a theory based on rational expectations—such as RBC—does not suffice to account for the downward trend in cycles but also could help to reproduce it. Certainly, the learning process of the Greek economy takes time to unfold.

Furthermore, rational expectations may not only produce or reproduce the problem but also hide its understanding, by failing to explain the root causes of macroeconomic fluctuations. RBC theory has hidden the explanation of the significance of induced investment for growth by accepting that it is technological disturbances that affect business cycles. Of course, Greece was a technology consumer but was it the only one in the Eurozone? From all the aforementioned points, a more critical path needs to be taken within the various contributions in RBC theory.

If, as pertained in the present analysis, a great part of Solow's residual can be grasped by introducing induced investment or the analogy of induced to autonomous investment in growth equations, then it is highly likely that what the RBC theory has managed to achieve was to partially trace and produce an analysis that brings investments at the forefront of the understanding of macroeconomic fluctuations.

Macroeconomic fluctuations in other places of the world are likely to be due to similar overemphasis on autonomous investments. For example, in the economy of the United States, which has been historically the major inhibitor of global crises (in 1929 and the most recent).[13] It may end up that crises like the most recent that— as discussed—is thought to derive from subprime mortgages, have been finally stimulated by such an overemphasis on autonomous investments. Of course political

---

[13] It is worth referring to evidence for numerous recessions, as for example that provided by Romer (1996:148) who suggested that during recessions, different types of investment studied (investment inventories, residential, and fixed nonresidential) and in particular investment inventories and residential investments, account for the greatest average share in GDP fall, relative to normal growth, despite their very limited contribution in the average share in GDP.

circumstances and policies followed play a significant role for the expression of such fluctuations.

If the robustness of solutions suggested by RBC theory fades away, by being wrong precisely on what it was supposed to identify better (its predictions about fluctuations and their nature), one should give more room in neoclassical synthesis and consider the return of Keynesian remedies in crisis-hit economies, even of provisional character, before economic restructuring in such demand-oriented economies takes place. Besides, the neoclassical synthesis may be more useful to study macroeconomics at the broader geographical scale of common space. Macroeconomic theory should use the full array of its tools to understand the causes of fluctuations and respond to them. In crisis-hit economies that belong to common currencies, price stickiness, the absence of a Pigou effect, and the application of macroeconomics to resolve such problems as relative poverty, price and competitiveness differences, should be given more consideration. If the present suggestions are right, the ground for New Keynesians and also for the new classical economics appears now to be more open than before.

One should consider more carefully how the Greek crisis feeds back to the theory on growth and macroeconomics as well as the interplay between common currency stability and the growth of nation-states. One way or another, Greece has several lessons to offer.

References

Abel, B.A., Bernanke, B.S., Croushore, D., 2010. Macroeconomics, sixth ed. Pearson Education, New York.

Abramovitz, M., 1956. Resource and output trends in the United States since 1870. Am. Econ. Rev. 46 (2), 5−23.

Academy of Athens, 2012. The Promotion of Reforms in the Greek Economy. Bureau of Economic Studies, Academy of Athens, Athens.

Acemoglu, D., Johnson, S., Robinson, J., 2004. Institutions as the fundamental cause of long-run growth, NBER Working Papers Series, WP 10481, May 2004.

Acemoglu, D., Johnson, S., Robinson, J., 2005. Institutions as the fundamental cause of long-run growth. In: Aghion, P., Durlauf, S.N. (Eds.), (2005) Handbook of Economic Growth. Elsevier, The Netherlands, pp. 385−472.

Afonso, A., Schuknecht, L., Tanzi, V., 2005. Public sector efficiency: an international comparison. Public Choice 123 (3−4), 321−347.

Aghion, P., Howitt, P. 2009. MIT Press. Cambridge MA.

Agraa, A.M.E., 1997. UK competitiveness policy vs Japanese industrial policy. Econ. J. 107 (444), 1504−1517.

Aiginger, K., 2006a. Revisiting an Evasive Concept: Introduction to the Special Issue on Competitiveness.

Aiginger, K., 2006b. Competitiveness: from a dangerous obsession to a welfare creating ability with positive externalities. J. Ind. Comp. Trade 6 (2), 161−177.

Allard, C., Brooks, P.K., Bluedorn, J.C., Bornhorst, F., Christopherson, K., Ohnsorge, F., et al., 2013. Toward a Fiscal Union for the Euro Area, IMF Staff Discussion Note, September 2013.

Anagnostou, S., 2017. The Nightmare of Bankruptcy and the Government of G.A. Papandreou [Ο εφιάλτης της χρεοκοπίας και η κυβέρνηση Γ.Α. Παπανδρέου]. Livanis Publications, Athens.

Andreou, G., Maraveyas, N., 2007. The Structural Policy of the European Union [Η Διαρθρωτική Πολιτική της Ευρωπαϊκής 'Ενωσης], 584−612, in Maraveyas, N. and Tsinisizelis, M. (eds) (2007) New European Union: Organisation and Policies, 50 years [Νέα Ευρωπαϊκή 'Ενωση: Οργάνωση και Πολιτικές - 50 χρόνια], Athens: «Θεμέλιο» Editions.

Anikeef, M., 2014. Infrastructure: New Real Estate Product or New Paradigm? American Real Estate Society, Annual Conference, April 4, 2014, accessed from https://www.cci-mef.org/pdf/ARES-2014-297-Infrastructure-New-Real-Estate-Product-or-New-Paradigm.pdf, (accessed 11.11.17).

Antzoulatos, A., 2017. A Brief Guide in the (very) Slippery Road to Grexit [Σύντομος Οδηγός στον Ολισθηρό(τατο) Δρόμο του Grexit]. Diplografia Editions, Athens.

Argeitis, G., 2002. Globalisation, EMU and Economic Adjustment: The Case of Greece [Παγκοσμιοποίηση, ΟΝΕ και οικονομική προσαρμογή: Η περίπτωση της Ελλάδας]. Gutenberg, Athens.

Argeitis, G., 2011. Public sector crisis in the Greek economy: failure of Greece and of the EU [Η δημοσιονομική κρίση της Ελληνικής οικονομίας: Αποτυχία της Ελλάδας και της Ευρωπαϊκής 'Ενωσης]. Greek Scientific Association of Political Economy [Επιστημονική Εταιρεία Πολιτικής Οικονομίας] (2011) Economic crisis and Greece [Οικονομική Κρίση στην Ελλάδα]. Gutenberg, Athens, pp. 180–205.

Armitage, J., Chu, B., 2015. Greek debt crisis: Goldman Sachs could be sued for helping hide debts when it joined euro, accessed from http://www.independent.co.uk/news/world/europe/greek-debt-crisis-goldman-sachs-could-be-sued-for-helping-country-hide-debts-when-it-joined-euro-10381926.html. (accessed 11.11.17)

Arndt, H.W., 1951. Mr. Hicks's Trade Cycle Theory. Can. J. Econ. Pol. Sci. 17 (3), 394–406.

Arsenis, G., 2016. Interview of Gerasimos Arsenis to Charis Mylonas, Associate Professor of Political Science and International Affairs. George Washington University. Available from: https://searchingforandreas.org/.

Auerbach, P., 1988. Competition: The Economics of Industrial Change. Basil Blackwell, Oxford.

Babson, A., 2011. Structuring a listed infrastructure portfolio, Russell Investments, Russell Research, May 2011, accessed from https://russellinvestments.com/-/media/files/au/insights/2011_june_r_rpt_res_structinfra.pdf. (accessed 11.11.17)

Balassa, B., Stoutjesdijk, A., 1975. Economic integration among developing countries. J. Common Mark. Stud. 14 (1), 37–55.

Baldwin, R., Forslid, R., Martin, P., Ottaviano, G., Robert-Nicoud, F., 2002. Economic Geography and Public Policy, Princeton: Princeton University Press.

Bank of Greece, 2009. Monetary Policy, Interim Report, October 2009, accessed from https://www.bankofgreece.gr/BogEkdoseis/monPolicyI2009.pdf. (accessed 15.09.17)

Bank of Greece, 2014. The Chronicle of the Great Crisis: The Bank of Greece 2008–2013, Athens, accessed from https://www.bankofgreece.gr/BogEkdoseis/The%20Chronicle%20Of%20The%20Great%20Crisis.pdf. (accessed 15.09.17)

Barro, R.J., 1974. Are government bonds net wealth? J. Pol. Econ. 82 (6), 1095–1117.

Barro, R.J., 1979. On the determination of public debt. J. Pol. Econ. 87 (5), 940–971.

Baumgartner, S., 2003. The Inada Conditions for Material Resource Inputs Reconsidered. University of Heidelberg, Department of Economics, Heidelberg. Discussion Paper Series, no 396, November 2003.

Baumol, W.J., 1967. Macroeconomics of unbalanced growth: the anatomy of urban crisis. Am. Econ. Rev. 3, 415–426.

Bazli, B., 2010. How Goldman Sachs Helped Greece to Mask its True Debt, Spiegel, available at http://www.spiegel.de/international/europe/greek-debt-crisis-how-goldman-sachs-helped-greece-to-mask-its-true-debt-a-676634.html, Spiegel on-line.

Benos, N., Karagiannis, S., 2007. Convergence and Economic Performance in Greece: New Evidence at Regional and Prefectural Level, vol. 95. Centre for Planning and Economic Research, Athens.

Besley, T., Ghatak, M., 2010. Property rights and economic development. In: Rodrik, D., Rosenzweig, M. (Eds.), Handbook of Development Economics, 5. Elsevier (North-Holland), The Netherlands, pp. 4525–4595.

Best, M., 1990. The New Competition: Institutions of Industrial Restructuring. Polity Press/Harvard University Press, Cambridge/Harvard.

Blanchard, O., 2015. Greece: Past Critiques and the Path Forward, accessed from https://blogs.imf.org/2015/07/09/greece-past-critiques-and-the-path-forward/ (accessed 27.12.17).

Blanchard, O., Leigh, D., 2013. Growth Forecast Errors and Fiscal Multipliers, IMF Working Papers, WP/13/1.

Bronfenbrenner, M. (Ed.), 1969. Is the Business Cycle Obsolete? Wiley, New York.

Bryant, J., 1991. A simple rational expectations Keynes-type model. In: Mankiw, N.G., Romer, D. (Eds.), New Keynesian Economics, Vol. II: Coordination Failures and Real Rigidities. MIT Press, Cambridge MA.

Bryant, R.C., Garganas, N.Ch, Tavlas, G.S., 2001. Greece's Economic Performances and Prospects. Bank of Greece and Brookings Institution, Athens.

Callaghan, M., Hubbard, P., 2016. The Asian Infrastructure Investment Bank: Multilateralism on the Silk Road. China Econ. J. 9 (2), 116−139.

Candace, H., Singh, A., 2000. Competitiveness Matters: Industry and Economic Performance in the U.S., The University of Michigan Press, Michigan.

Carillo, M.R., 2003. Human capital formation in the new growth theory: the role of 'social factors'. In: Salvadori, N. (Ed.), The Theory of Economic Growth: A 'Classical' Perspective. Elgar Edward, Cheltenham, pp. 186−204.

Case, K.E., 2008. Musgrave's vision of the public sector: the complex relationship between individual, society and state in public good theory. J. Econ. Finance 32, 348−355.

Chenery, H.B., 1952. Overcapacity and the acceleration principle. Econometrica 20, 1−28.

Chesnais, F., 1986. Science, technology and competitiveness. STI Rev. 1 (Autumn), 86−129.

Christakis, N.A., Fowler, J.H., 2009. Connected: The Surprising Power of Our Social Networks and How They Shape our Lives. Little, Brown and Company, New York.

Christodoulakis, N., 1998. The New Land of Development [Το Νέο Τοπίο της Ανάπτυξης]. Papazisis Editions, Athens.

Christodoulakis, N., 2014. Euro or Drachma? Dilemmas, Illusions and Interests [Ευρώ ή Δραχμή; Διλήμματα, Πλάνες ή Συμφέροντα]. Gutenberg, Athens.

Christodoulakis, N., Kalyvitis, S., 1993. Likely Effects of C.S.F. 1994−1999 on the Greek Economy: An Ex-Ante Assessment using an Annual Four-Sector Macroeconometric Model. KEPE, Greece. Discussion Papers.

Chryssochoidis, G., Blouchos, P., 2003. The web presence of Greek Food Firms. Agric. Econ. Rev. 4 (2), 80−92.

Cœuré, B., 2016. The importance of independent Fiscal Councils, accessed from https://www.ecb.europa.eu/press/key/date/2016/html/sp160127.en.html, (accessed 26.07.17).

Collignon, S., 2001. Economic Policy Coordination in the EMU: Institutional and Political Requirements. The European Institute, L.S.E., London.

Commission of the European Communities, 1992a. Reform of the CAP and Its Implementation, CAP Working Notes, Brussels.

Commission of the European Communities, 1992b. Community Support Framework for Greece 1989−1993, Multifund Operational Programme for Increasing Competitiveness of Enterprises, 1990−1993, ERDF No 92.08.09.002, ARINCO No 92.EL. 16.003, Luxemburg.

Commission of the European Communities, 2002. Mid-Term Review of the Common Agricultural Policy, Communication from the Commission to the Council and the European Parliament, Brussels, 10.7.2002, COM (2002) 394 final.

Commission of the European Communities, 2006. Communication from the Commission on a European Programme for Critical Infrastructure Protection, Brussels,12.12.2006, COM (2006) 786 final.

Court of Audit, 2011. Annual Report of Financial Year 2009 [Ελεγκτικό Συνέδριο, Ετήσια 'Εκθεση Οικονομικού 'Ετους 2009], Athens, 2011.

Crescezni, R., Posé – Rodriguez, A., 2012. Infrastructure and regional growth in the European Union. Pap. Reg. Sci. 91, 487–513.

Croce, R., 2011. Pension Funds Investment in Infrastructure, Policy Actions. OECD, Paris.

Dasgupta, P., Heal, G., 1979. Economic Theory and Exhaustible Resources. Cambridge University Press, Cambridge, UK.

De Grauwe, P., 2013. Design Failures in the Eurozone: Can they be fixed? LEQS Paper No 57/2103, February 2013.

De Grauwe, P., Ji, Y., 2014. The future of Eurozone. Manchester School 82, 15–34.

Denison, E.F., 1972. Some major issues in productivity analysis: an examination of estimates by Jorgenson and Griliches. Survey. Curr. Business 49 (5, part 2), 1–27.

Denison, E.F., 1979. Explanations of Declining Productivity Growth. Survey of Current Business 59 (August): 1–24.

Dertilis, G.V., 2016. Seven Wars, Four Civil Wars, Seven Bankruptcies, 1821–2016 [Επτά πόλεμοι, τέσσερις εμφύλιοι, επτά πτωχεύσεις, 1821–2016]. Polis Editions, Athens.

Dertouzos, M.L., Lester, R.K., Solow, R.M. (Eds.), 1989. Made in America. The MIT Press, Cambridge, MA.

Dicken, P., 1998. Global Shift: Transforming the World Economy. Paul Chapman Ltd, London.

Dollar, D., Wolf, E.N., 1993. Competitiveness, Convergence and International Specialisation. The MIT Press, Cambridge, MA.

Dornbusch, R., Fischer, S., 1990. Macroeconomics. McGraw-Hill, New York.

Doxiadis, A., 2015. The Unseen Rupture: Institutions and Behaviors in the Greek Economy [Το αόρατο ρήγμα: Θεσμοί και συμπεριφορές στην Ελληνική οικονομία]. Ikaros Editions, Athens.

Dracatos, C.G., 1988. The Greek Economy in Crisis. Papazisis Editions, Athens.

Drettakis, M.G., 2011. The public sector dimensions of the crisis in Greece [Οι δημοσιονομικές διαστάσεις της κρίσης στην Ελλάδα]. Greek Scientific Association of Political Economy [Επιστημονική Εταιρεία Πολιτικής Οικονομίας] (2011) Economic crisis and Greece [Οικονομική Κρίση στην Ελλάδα]. Gutenberg, Athens, pp. 143–164.

Duarte, P.G., 2015. From real business cycle and new Keynesian to DSGE Macroeconomics: facts and models in the emergence of a consensus, Department of Economics, FEA/ USP, Working Paper Series no 2015-05.

Dullen, S., Fritz, B., Muhlich, L., 2016. The IMF to the Rescue: Did the Euro Area benefit from the Fund's Experience in Crisis fighting? Freie Universitat, Berlin, School of Business and Economics. Discussion Paper, 2016/20.

Durand, M., Giorno, C., 1987. Indicators of international competitiveness: conceptual aspects and evaluation. OECD Econ. Stud. 9, 147–182. Accessed at http://www.oecd.org/ dataoecd/40/47/33841783.pdf.

Easterly, W., 2001. The Elusive Quest for Growth: Economists' Adventures and Misadventures in the Tropics. The MIT Press, Cambridge, MA.

ELIAMEP, 2011. Assessment of Effects That Have Been Exercised in (the course of) the Greek Economy From Policies Co-funded by the Budget of the European Union. ELIAMEP, [ΜΕΛΕΤΗ ΤΟΥ ΕΛΙΑΜΕΠ ΓΙΑ ΤΗΝ ΤΡΑΠΕΖΑ ΤΗΣ ΕΛΛΑΔΟΣ, ΑΞΙΟΛΟΓΗΣΗ ΤΩΝ ΕΠΙΔΡΑΣΕΩΝ ΠΟΥ ΕΧΟΥΝ ΑΣΚΗΣΕΙ ΣΤΗΝ ΠΟΡΕΙΑ ΤΗΣ ΕΛΛΗΝΙΚΗΣ ΟΙΚΟΝΟΜΙΑΣ ΟΙ ΠΟΛΙΤΙΚΕΣ ΠΟΥ ΧΡΗΜΑΤΟΔΟΤΟΥΝΤΑΙ ΑΠΟ ΤΟΝ ΠΡΟΕΥΠΟΛΟΓΙΣΜΟ ΤΗΣ ΕΥΡΩΠΑΙΚΗΣ ΕΝΩΣΗΣ], Athens, pp. 1–515.

ELIAMEP, 2011A. Assessment of Effects That Have Been Exercised in (the Course of) the Greek Economy from Policies Co-Funded by the Budget of the EU, Part (I), Athens: Bank of Greece, [Μελέτη του ΕΛΙΑΜΕΠ για την Τράπεζα της Ελλάδας, Αξιολόγηση των επιδράσεων που έχουν ασκήσει στην πορεία της Ελληνικής οικονομίας οι πολιτικές που χρηματοδοτούνται από τον προϋπολογισμό της Ευρωπαϊκής 'Ενωσης, Πρώτο]. ΜΕΡΟΣ (I), Αθ ηνα: Τρ απεζα της Ελλ αδας.

ELIAMEP, 2011B. Assessment of Effects That Have Been Exercised in (the Course of) the Greek Economy from Policies Co-Funded by the Budget of the EU, Part (II), Athens: Bank of Greece, [Μελέτη του ΕΛΙΑΜΕΠ για την Τράπεζα της Ελλάδας, Αξιολόγηση των επιδράσεων που έχουν ασκήσει στην πορεία της Ελληνικής οικονομίας οι πολιτικές που χρηματοδοτούνται από τον προϋπολογισμό της Ευρωπαϊκής 'Ενωσης, Δεύτερο Μέρος (II), Αθήνα, Τράπεζα της Ελλάδας]. ΜΕΡΟΣ (II), Αθ ηνα: Τρ απεζα της Ελλ αδας.

ELIAMEP, 2011C. Assessment of Effects that Have Been Exercised in (the Course of) the Greek economy from policies co-funded by the budget of the EU, Part (III), Athens: Bank of Greece, [Μελέτη του ΕΛΙΑΜΕΠ για την Τράπεζα της Ελλάδας, Αξιολόγηση των επιδράσεων που έχουν ασκήσει στην πορεία της Ελληνικής οικονομίας οι πολιτικές που χρηματοδοτούνται από τον προϋπολογισμό της Ευρωπαϊκής 'Ενωσης, Τρίτο Μέρος (III), Αθήνα, Τράπεζα της Ελλάδας]. ΜΕΡΟΣ (III), Αθ ηνα: Τρ απεζα της Ελλ αδας.

ELIAMEP, 2011D. Assessment of Effects That Have Been Exercised in (the Course of) the Greek Economy from Policies Co-Funded by the Budget of the EU, Part (IV), Athens: Bank of Greece, [Μελέτη του ΕΛΙΑΜΕΠ για την Τράπεζα της Ελλάδας, Αξιολόγηση των επιδράσεων που έχουν ασκήσει στην πορεία της Ελληνικής οικονομίας οι πολιτικές που χρηματοδοτούνται από τον προϋπολογισμό της Ευρωπαϊκής 'Ενωσης, Τέταρτο Μέρος (IV), Αθήνα, Τράπεζα της Ελλάδας]. ΜΕΡΟΣ (IV), Αθ ηνα: Τρ απεζα της Ελλ αδας.

ELIAMEP, 2013. Assessment of Effects Exercised in the Process of the Greek Economy of policies funded by the Budget of the European Union, Final Report, ELIAMEP, September 2003.

ELIAMEP, 2014. The Policies funded by the Community Budget and the Greek Economy, Final Report, Bank of Greece, Athens, April 2014.

Emerson, M., Giovannini, A., 2013. European Fiscal and Monetary Policy: A Chicken and Egg Dilemma. Instituto Affari Internazionali. December, 2, 2013.

Erdős, T., 1973. Investments and economic growth. Acta Oeconomica 11, 281–303.

EU Parliament, 2016. A fiscal capacity for the Euro area? Options for reforms to counter asymmetric shocks, September 2016.

European Parliament, 2018. Macro-Financial Assistance to EU Member States: State of Play - February 2018, Briefing, Economic Governance Support Unit (EGOV), DG for Internal Policies, 14 February 2018.

European Commission, 1996. The Agricultural Situation in the European Union, 1995 Report, Brussels.

European Commission, 1997. Agenda 2000: For a Stronger and Wider Union, COM (97) 2000, Luxembourg.

European Commission, 1999. Sixth Periodic Report on the Social and Economic Situation and Development of the Regions of the European Union, SEC (1999) 66 final, Brussels, 28.07.1999.

European Commission, 2000. Decision of the Committee of 28/11/2000 about the approval of the Community Support Framework for Community structural interventions in regions belonging in target no 1 in Greece [Απόφαση της Επιτροπής της 28/11/2000 σχετικά με την έγκριση του κοινοτικού πλαισίου στήριξης για τις κοινοτικές διαρθρωτικές παρεμβάσεις στις περιφέρειες που υπάγονται στον στόχο αριθ. 1 στην Ελλάδα], E (2000) 3405.

European Commission, 2010. Europe 2020: A strategy for smart, sustainable and inclusive growth, COM (2010) 2020, 3.3.2010, Brussels.

European Commission, 2011. The Urban and Regional Dimension of Europe', Seventh Progress Report on Economic, Social and Territorial Cohesion, Report from the Commission, Luxembourg, November 2011.

European Commission, 2014. Investment for Jobs and Growth: Promoting Development and Good Governance in EU Regions and Cities, Sixth Report on Economic, Social and Territorial Cohesion, Luxembourg.

European Commission, 2016a. Ex-post Evaluation of the ERDF and Cohesion Fund 2007−2013, Commission Staff Working Document, Brussels, 19.9.2016, SWD (2016) 318 final.

European Commission, 2016b. Ex post evaluation of Cohesion Policy programmes 2007−2013, focusing on the European Regional Development Fund (ERDF) and the Cohesion Fund (CF), WP1: Synthesis Report, Task 3 Country Report, Greece, September 2016.

European Commission, 2016c. Regional policy website, accessed from http://ec.europa.eu/ regional_policy/en/atlas/programmes/2000-2006/greece/competitiveness-objective-1-programme# (accessed 16.04.16).

European Economy, 2012. The Second Adjustment Programme for Greece, Fifth Review, Occasional Papers 94, March 2012.

European Economy, 2013. The Second Economic Adjustment Programme for Greece, Second Review, Occasional Papers 148, May 2013.

European Enterprise Organisation, 2003. Ex post evaluation of the Objective 1 1994−1999, National Report, Greece, Athens, March 2003.

European Investment Bank, 2010. Public and private financing of infrastructure: evolution and economics of private infrastructure finance. EIB Pap. 15 (1), 9.

Exarchou, T.R., Chionis, D., 2016. The Regional Problem and Regional Disparities after the end of the 3rd CSF [Το περιφερειακό πρόβλημα και οι περιφερειακές ανισότητες μετά το τέλος του Γ΄ ΚΠΣ], 111−117 in Regional Effects of the Recession of the Greek economy and its consequences [Οι περιφερειακές επιπτώσεις της ύφεσης της Ελληνικής Οικονομίας και οι συνέπειές τους], 19th Scientific Conference of the Greek Society of Regional Scientists, 12−13 May 2016, Lamia.

Faberger, J., 1988. International competitiveness. Econ. J. 98, 355−374.

Featherstone, K., Papadimitriou, D., 2010. The Limits of Europeanisation: Reform Capacity and Policy Conflict in Greece [Τα όρια του Εξευρωπαϊσμού: Δημόσια Πολιτική και Μεταρρυθμίσεις στην Ελλάδα]. "Okto" Editions, Athens.

Feddersen, H., unknown year. Recent Developments in Fiscal Governance in the EU; Lessons From The Crisis: From the Six-Pack to the Fiscal Compact, accessed from https://www.oecd.org/gov/budgeting/D2-AM%20-%20EU%20-%20H.%20Feddersen%20-%20EU.pdf, (accessed 26.07.17).

Fennell, R., 1997. The Common Agricultural Policy: Continuity and Change. Oxford University Press, Oxford.

Ford, R., Poret, P., 1991. Infrastructure and private-sector productivity. Econ. Stud. 17, 63−89.

Foster, V., Butterfield, W., Chen, Ch, Pushak, N., 2009. Building Bridges: China's Growing Role as Infrastructure Financier for Sub-Saharan Africa, Trends and Policy Options, no 5. The International Bank for Reconstruction and Development, The World Bank and PPIAF, Washington.

References 293

Fratesi, U., Rodriguez-Pose, A., 2016. The crisis and regional employment in Europe: what role for sheltered economies? Cambridge J. Reg. Econ. Soc. 2018 (11), 189209.
Galenianos, M. 2015 The Greek Crisis: Origins and Implications, ELIAMEP, Research Paper No 16, accessed from https://www.files.ethz.ch/isn/188283/%CE%95%CF%81%CE%B5%CF%85%CE%BD%CE%B7%CF%84%CE%B9%CE%BA%CF%8C-%CE%9A%CE%B5%CE%AF%CE%BC%CE%B5%CE%BD%CE%BF_16_Manolis-Galenianos-%CE%95%CE%9DG1.pdf, (accessed 25.01.16).
Georgakopoulos, Th. A., 1986. Greece in the EC: inter-country income transfers. J. Common Mark. Stud. XXV (2), 119–132.
Georgakopoulos, Th. A. (1997) Introduction to Public Economics [Εισαγωγή στη Δημόσια Οικονομική], Athens: Benos Editions.
Giannitsis, T. 1998. The Accession in the European Commission and Effects in Manufacturing and External Commerce [Η ένταξη στην Ευρωπαϊκή Κοινότητα και επιπτώσεις στη βιομηχανία και στο εξωτερικό εμπόριο], Institute for Mediterranean Studies, Athens.
Giannitsis, T., 2005. Greece and the Future: Pragmatism and Illusions [Η Ελλάδα και το Μέλλον: Πραγματισμός και Ψευδαισθήσεις]. Polis, Athens.
Giannitsis, T. (Ed.), 2008a. Greek Economy: Crucial Issues of Economic Policy [Ελληνική Οικονομία: Κρίσιμα Ζητήματα Οικονομικής Πολιτικής]. Alpha Bank Editions, Athens.
Giannitsis, T., 2008b. Technology and competitiveness [Τεχνολογία και Ανταγωνιστικότητα]. In: Giannitsis, T. (Ed.), (2008a) Greek Economy: Crucial Issues of Economic Policy [Ελληνική Οικονομία: Κρίσιμα Ζητήματα Οικονομικής Πολιτικής]. Alpha Bank Editions, Athens, pp. 377–400.
Giannitis, T., 2008c. In Search of a Greek Development Model [Σε αναζήτηση ενός Ελληνικού Μοντέλου Ανάπτυξης]. Papazisis Editions, Athens.
Giannitsis, T., 2013. Greece in the Crisis [Η Ελλάδα στην Κρίση]. Polis Editions, Athens.
Glencross, A., 2014. The Politics of European Integration: Political Union or a House Divided? Wiley Blackwell, Oxford.
Goodfriend, M., King, R.G., 1997. The New Neoclassical Synthesis and the Role of Monetary Policy. NBER Macroecon. Ann. 12, 231–283.
Greater London Authority, 2014. The cost of London's long-term infrastructure: Final Report. ARUP, London.
Greek Scientific Association of Political Economy, 2011. [Επιστημονική Εταιρεία Πολιτικής Οικονομίας] (2011) Economic Crisis and Greece [Οικονομική Κρίση στην Ελλάδα]. Gutenberg, Athens.
Grilo, I., Koopman, G., 2006. Productivity and microeconomic reforms: strengthening EU competitiveness. J. Ind., Comp.Trade 6 (2), 67–84.
Gropas, R., Triantafyllidou, A., 2005. Migration in Greece at a Glance. ELIAMEP, Athens.
Hamberg, D., Schultze, Ch.L., 1961. Autonomous vs induced investment: the interrelatedness of parameters in growth models. Econ. J. 71 (281), 53–65.
Harberler, G., 1968. Prosperity and Depression: A Theoretical Analysis of Cyclical Movement, fifth ed. George Allen and Unwin Ltd, London.
Hellenic Parliament Debt Truth Committee, 2015. Hellenic Parliament Debt Truth Committee, Preliminary Findings [Επιτροπή για την Αλήθεια του Δημόσιου Χρέους, Προκαταρκτική 'Εκθεση], Executive Summary of the Report, Athens: June 17 2015.
Hicks, J.R., 1952. A Contribution to the Theory of the Trade Cycle. Clarendon Press, Oxford.

Hillier, B., 1991. The Macroeconomic Debate: Models of the Closed and Open Economy. Blackwell Publishers, Oxford.

His Majesty's Treasury, 1983. International competitiveness. Econ. Prog. Report 158, 1—3.

HM Treasury, 2014. National Infrastructure Plan: Finance Update, March 2014.

Hofstede, G., 2001. Culture's Consequences — Comparing Values, Behaviours, Institutions and Organizations Among Nation, second ed. Sage, London.

House of Commons, 2015. Greek Debt Crisis: background and developments in 2015, Briefing Paper, no 7114, 13 October2015.

House of Commons, 2017. Infrastructure policies and investment, Briefing Paper, no 6594, March 2017.

Hulten, Ch.R., 2001. Total factor productivity: a short biography. In: Hulten, Ch.R., Harper, M.J. (Eds.), New Developments in Productivity Analysis. University of Chicago Press, Chicago, pp. 1—54.

Ignatiou, M., 2015. Troika: The Road to Destruction [Τρόϊκα: Ο Δρόμος προς την Καταστροφή]. Livanis Editions, Athens.

I.M.F, 2010. Staff Report on Request for Stand-By Agreement, IMF Country Report, 10/110. IMF Publication Services, Washington.

I.M.F., 2013. Greece: Ex Post Evaluation of Exceptional Access under the 2010 Stand-by Arrangement, IMF Country Report No 13/156, June 2013. IMF Publication Services, Washington.

I.M.F, 2014. Fifth Review under the Extended Arrangement under the Extended Fund Facility, and Request for Waiver of Nonobservance of Performance Criterion and Reshaping of Access; Staff Report; Press Release; And Statement by the Executive Director for Greece, IMF Country Report No. 14/151, June 2014. IMF Publication Services, Washington.

I.M.F, 2015. Greece: Preliminary Draft Debt Sustainability Analysis. IMF Publication Services, Washington.

I.M.F., 2017. Request for Stand-By Arrangement — Press Release; Staff Report; And Statement by the Executive Director for Greece, IMF Country Report no 17/229, July 2017. IMF Publication Services, Washington.

Inada, K.I., 1963. On a two-sector-model of economic growth: comments and a generalization. Rev. Econ. Stud. 30, 119—127.

Independent Evaluation Office of the International Monetary Fund, 2016. The IMF and the Crises in Greece, Ireland and Portugal: An Evaluation by the Independent Evaluation Office, July 8th 2016.

Inderst, G., 2009. Pension fund investment in infrastructure. OECD Working Papers on Insurance and Private Pensions no. 32. OECD, Paris.

Inforegio, 2016. History: The Origins of EU Cohesion and Regional Policy, http://ec.europa. eu/regional_policy/archive/policy/history/index2_el.htm (accessed 08.05.16).

Institute and Faculty of Actuaries, 2015. Infrastructure investment: policy summary, November 2015.

International Poverty Reduction Centre in China and Organisation for Economic Cooperation and Development, 2010. Infrastructure: the Foundation for Growth and Poverty Reduction, Beijing, China, 19—20 September 2010.

Ioannides, S., 2008. Entrepreneurship in Greece: four constant problems [H Ε πιχειρηματικότητα στην Ελλάδα: Τέσσερα σταθερά προβλήματα]. In: Giannitsis, T. (Ed.), In search of a Greek Growth Model [Σε αναζήτηση Ελληνικού Μοντέλου Ανάπτυξης]. Papazisis Editions, Athens, pp. 140—151.

Ioannou, D., Leblond, P., Niemman, A., 2015. European integration and the crisis: practice and theory. J. Eur. Pub. Policy. 22 (2), 155—176.

Izdorek, T., Armstrong, C., 2009. Infrastructure and Strategic Asset Allocation: Is Infrastructure an Asset Class? Ibbotson, January 2009.

Jorgenson, D.W., Griliches, Z., 1967. The explanation of productivity change. Rev. Econ. Stud. 34, 349−383.

Kaldor, N., 1939. Capital intensity and the trade cycle. Economica, February.

Kaldor, N., 1951. Mr. Hicks on the trade cycle. Econ. J. 61 (244), 833−847.

Kaldor, N., 1978. The effects of devaluation on trade in manufactures. In: Kaldor, N. (Ed.), Further Essays on Applied Economics. Duckworth, London.

Kalogirou, G., 1994. Community policies and regulatory changes in the sectors of energy, telecommunications, and of transport and their effects upon the operation of these sectors in Greece [Κοινοτικές πολιτικές και ρυθμιστικές αλλαγές στους τομείς της ενέργειας, των τηλεπικοινωνιών και των μεταφορών και επιπτώσεις στη λειτουργία των τομέων αυτών στην Ελλάδα]. In: Giannitsis, T. (Ed.), The Debate on Privatizations: Theoretical Approaches and Significance for Greece [Η προβληματική των ιδιωτικοποιήσεων: Θεωρητικές προσεγγίσεις και σημασία για την Ελλάδα]. Paratiritis, Thessaloniki, pp. 145−197.

Karanikolas, P., Bourdaras, D., Kremmydas, D., Martinos, N., 2008. Support and protection of Greek agriculture: inter-temporal developments and sectoral diversification, South-Eastern Eur. J. Econ., 2. pp. 197−212.

Karavitis, N.H., 2008. Public Debt and Deficit [Δημόσιο Χρέος και 'Ελλειμμα]. Dionikos, Athens.

Karrpi, I., 2001. Competitiveness in the Nordic Economies; Assessments and Structural Features, The Nordic Centre for Spatial Development, Nordregio Working Paper 2001: 2, Stockholm, Sweden.

Kazakos, P., 2001. Between State and Market: Economy and Economic policy in post-war Greece 1944−2000 [Ανάμεσα σε Κράτος και Αγορά: Οικονομία και Οικονομική Πολιτική στην μεταπολεμική Ελλάδα 1944−2000]. Αθήνα: Εκδόσεις Πατάκη.

Kazakos, P., 2011. After the Memorandum: Economic Policy in Greece under International Control [Μετά το «Μνημόνιο»: Οικονομική πολιτική στην Ελλάδα υπό διεθνή έλεγχο]. Papazisis Edition, Athens, pp. 381−382.

Kazakos, P., Liargovas, P., Repousis, S., 2016. The Public Debt of Greece [Το Δημόσιο Χρέος της Ελλάδας]. Papazisi Editions, Athens.

Kehagia, A., 2013. The Impact of EU's Structural and Cohesion Funds: A Literature Review, The Jean Monnet Papers on Political Economy, 6/2013. University of Peloponnese, Greece.

Kohn, L., Pease, R., Schuller, D., Pollan, L., Austin N., unknown year. Infrastructure Investing: Key Benefits and Risks, J.P. Morgan, accessed from: https://www.jpmorgan.com/jpmpdf/1158630194855.pdf. (accessed 11.11.17)

Komninos, N. 2008. In: Giannitsis, T. (Ed.), (2008a) Greek Economy: Crucial Issues of Economic Policy [Ελληνική Οικονομία: Κρίσιμα Ζητήματα Οικονομικής Πολιτικής]. Alpha Bank Editions, Athens, pp. 453−479.

Koopman, P.L., Den Hartog, D.N., Konrad, E., et al., 1999. National culture and leadership profiles in Europe: some results from the globe study,. Eur. J. Work Organ. Psychol. 8 (4), 503−520.

Korres, G.M., Chionis, D.P., 2003. Greek Economy: Economic Policy and Analysis of Basic Macroeconomic Accounts [Ελληνική Οικονομία: Οικονομική Πολιτική και Ανάλυση Βασικών Μακροοικονομικών Μεγεθών]. Stamoulis Editions, Athens.

Krugman, P., 1994. Competitiveness: a dangerous obsession. Foreign Aff. 73.

Krugman, P., 1996. Making Sense of the Competitiveness Debate. Oxford Review of Economic Policy 12 (3), 17−25.

Krugman, P., Obstfeld, M., 2000. International Economics: Theory and Policy. Pearson − Addison Wesley, Boston.

Kydland, F., Prescott, E., 1982. Time to build and aggregate fluctuations. Econometrica 50, 1345−1370.

Lamprianidis, L., 2011. Investing in Flight: the Brain Drain from Greece in the Era of Globalization [Επενδύοντας στη φυγή: Η διαρροή επιστημόνων από την Ελλάδα την εποχή της παγκοσμιοποίησης]. Kritiki editions. Athens.

Landmann, O., 2014. Short-Run Macro After the Crisis: The End of the "New" Neoclassical Synthesis? University of Freiburg, Department of International Economic Policy, Breisgau. Discussion Paper Series, Nr 27.

Lavdas, K., Mendrinou, M., 1995. Competition policy and institutional politics in the European Community: state aid control and small business promotion. Eur. J. Pol. Res. 28, 171−201.

Law No 2372/1996, Government Gazette of the Hellenic Republic Issue A 29/28.2.1996, Formation of Institutions for the Acceleration of Development Process and Other Clauses [Σύσταση φορέων για την επιτάχυνση της αναπτυξιακής διαδικασίας και άλλες διατάξεις].

Law No 2860/2000, Government Gazette of the Hellenic Republic, Issue A 251/14.11.00, Management, Monitoring and Control of the Community Support Framework and Other Clauses [Διαχείριση, Παρακολούθηση και έλεγχος Κοινοτικού Πλαισίου Στήριξης και άλλες διατάξεις].

Law No 3723/2008, Government Gazette of the Hellenic Republic Issue A 250/9.12.2008, Enhancing of liquidity of the economy for facing the consequences of international financial crises and other clauses [Ενίσχυση της ρευστότητας της οικονομίας για την αντιμετώπιση των επιπτώσεων της διεθνούς χρηματοπιστωτικής κρίσης και άλλες διατάξεις].

Law No 3894/2010, Government Gazette of the Hellenic Republic Issue A 204/2.12.2010, Acceleration and Transparency in the Implementation of Strategic Investment [Επιτάχυνση και διαφάνεια υλοποίησης Στρατηγικών Επενδύσεων].

Lolos, S.E.G., 2009. The effect of EU structural funds on regional growth: assessing the evidence from Greece, 1990−2005. Econ. Change Restruct. (2009) 42, 211−228.

Long, J.B., Plosser, Ch.I., 1983. Real business cycles. J. Pol. Econ. 91, 1345−1370.

Lucas Jr., R.E., 1972. Expectations and the neutrality of money. J. Econ. Theory 4, 103−124.

Lucas Jr., R.E., 1977. Understanding business cycles. Carnegie-Rochester Conference Series on Public Policy 5, 7−29.

Lucas Jr., R.E., 1988. On the mechanics of economic development. J. Monetary Econ. 22, 3−42.

Lucas Jr., R.E., Prescott, E.C., 1971. Investment under uncertainty. Econometrica 39, 659−681.

Magazzino, C., Giolli, L., Mele, M., 2015. Wagner's law and Peacock and Wiseman's displacement effect in European Union countries: a panel data study, Int. J. Econ. Finan. Issues, 5. pp. 812−819.

Mairate, A., 2006. The added value of the European cohesion policy. Reg. Stud. 40 (2), 167−177.

Mankiw, N.G., 1989. Real business cycles: a new keynesian perspective. J. Econ. Persp. 3 (3), 79−90.

Mankiw, N.G., 2003. Macroeconomics, fifth ed. Worth Publishers, New York.

Mankiw, N.G., Romer, D. (Eds.), 1991. New Keynesian Economics, vol. 2, Coordination Failures and Real Rigidities. MIT Press, Cambridge MA.

Mankiw, N.G., Romer, D., Weil, D.N., 1992. A contribution to the empirics of economic growth. Quar. J. Econ. 107 (2), 407–437.

Manolopoulos, J., 2011. Greece's 'Odious' Debt: The Looting of the Hellenic Republic by the Euro, the Political Elite and the Investment Community. Anthem Finance, New York.

Maraveyas, N., 1994. The Regional Policy [Η Περιφερειακή Πολιτική], 419–454, in Maraveyas, N., Tsinisizelis, M. (eds.), 1994. The Integration of the European Union: Institutional, Political and Economic Aspects [Η Ολοκλήρωση της Ευρωπαϊκής 'Ενωσης: Θεσμικές, πολιτικές και οικονομικές πτυχές]. Athens: «Θεμέλιο» Editions.

Maraveyas, N., 2000. The Reform of Common Agricultural Policy and the new enlargement of the European Union [Η Μεταρρύθμιση της Κοινής Αγροτικής Πολιτικής και η νέα διεύρυνση της Ευρωπαϊκής 'Ενωσης], 277–314, in Andrikopoulou, E., Kaukalas, G. (eds.) (2000) The New European Space: The enlargement and the geography of European Development [Ο νέος Ευρωπαϊκός χώρος: Η διεύρυνση και η γεωγραφία της Ευρωπαϊκής Ανάπτυξης]. Athens: «Θεμέλιο» Editions.

Maraveyas, N., 2007. The Common Agricultural Policy [Η Κοινή Αγροτική Πολιτική], 613–633, in Maraveyas, N., Tsinisizelis, M. (eds.) (2007) New European Union: Organisation and Policies 50 Years [Νέα Ευρωπαϊκή 'Ενωση: Οργάνωση και Πολιτικές - 50 χρόνια], Athens: «Θεμέλιο» Editions.

Mavroudeas, S.D., 2015. The Greek Saga: Completing explanations of the Greek Crisis, Kingston University, London, Economics Discussion Paper 2015-1, 10th February 2011.

McGreehan, J.M., 1968. Competitiveness: a survey of recent literature. Econ. J. 78, 243–262.

Meghir, C., Vayanos, D., Vettas, N., 2010. The Economic Crisis in Greece: A Time of Reform and Opportunity, accessed from http://www.enap.gr/attachments/article/7146/The%20economic%20crisis%20in%20Greece%20-%20A%20time%20of%20reform%20and%20opportunity.pdf (accessed 17-12-17).

Milios, Y., Oikonomakis, G., Lapatsioras, S., 2010. Introduction to Economic Analysis [Εισαγωγή στην Οικονομική Ανάλυση]. Ellinika Grammata Editions, Athens.

Ministry of Finance, 2003a. Interim Report of the 3rd Community Support Framework. Managerial Authority, Ministry of Finance, Hellenic Republic, Remaco-Eurotec.

Ministry of Finance, 2003b. Interim Report of Operational Programme Competitiveness 2000–2006, second ed. Managerial Authority, Ministry of Finance, Hellenic Republic, Remaco-Eurotec, Athens, 31.10.2003.

Ministry of Finance, 2007a. National Strategic Reference Framework. General Secretary of Investments and Development, Athens, January 2007.

Ministry of Finance, 2007b. Ex-ante Assessment of Operational Programme Competitiveness and Entrepreneurship 2007–2013, Planet S.Y. and EPISEY, Final Draft, 2/2007.

Ministry of Finance and Competitiveness, 2014. National Strategic Reference Framework 2014–2020 [Σύμφωνο Εταιρικής Σχέσης 2014–2020]. General Secretary of Public Investments, Athens, May 2014.

Ministry of Finance (2006), Revision of C.S.F., December 2006, accessed from http://www.hellaskps.gr/2000-2006.htm, the 11/10/2017.

Ministry of Transports and Communication, 2001. Administrative Guideline, Framework of Management of the 3rd C.S.F., Athens, May 2001.

Mitsopoulos, M., Pelagidis, Th, 2011. Understanding the Crisis in Greece: From Boom to Bust. Palgrave Macmillan, Basingstoke.

Morgan J.P., 2009. Infrastructure investing: Key benefits and risks, report prepared by Kohn, L., Pease, R., Schuller, D., Pollan, L. and Austin, N., J.P. Morgan Asset Management, accessed from https://www.jpmorgan.com/jpmpdf/1158630194855.pdf (accessed 11.11.17).

Morgan J.P., 2015. Infrastructure investing: Key benefits and risks, 4Q2015, accessed from: https://am.jpmorgan.com/blobcontent/1383271579721/83456/Infrastructure-Investing-Key-benefits-and-risks.pdf. (accessed 11.11.17)

Munnell, A.H., 1990. How does public infrastructure affect regional economic performance. New Eng. Econ. Rev. 11–33. Sep/Oct, Federal Reserve Bank of Boston.

Musgrave, R.A., 1959. The Theory of Public Finance: A study in Public Economy. McGraw-Hill, New York.

Neary, J.P., 2006. Measuring Competitiveness, IMF Working Paper, WP/06/209.

Nelson, R., 2017. Lessons from the IMF's Bailout of Greece, Congressional Research Service, Testimony, Statement before the Committee on Financial Services, Subcommittee on Monetary Policy and Trade, U.S. House of Representatives, USA, 7-5700, Hearing on May 18, 2017.

Nelson, R.M., Belkin, R., Mix, D.E., 2010. Greece's Debt Crisis: Overview, Policy Responses, and Implications. Congressional Research Service, 7-5700, May 10, 2010.

Nelson, R.M., Belkin, R., Mix D.E., 2011. Greece's Debt Crisis: Overview, Policy Responses, and Implications, Congressional Research Service, 7-5700, August 18, 2011.

O'Brien, P., Pike, A., 2015. City deals, decentralization and the governance of local infrastructure funding and financing in the UK. National Inst. Econ. Rev. 233 (1), R14–R26. Available from: https://doi.org/10.1177/002795011523300103.

OECD, 2007a. Infrastructure to 2030: Mapping Policy for Electricity, Water and Transport, vol. 2. OECD, Paris.

OECD, 2007b. Infrastructure to 2030, Mapping policy for electricity, water and transport, vol. 3, Paris.

OECD, 2012. Strategic Transport Infrastructure Needs to 2030. OECD, Paris, accessed from http://www.oecd.org/futures/infrastructureto2030/strategictransportinfrastructureneed-sto2030.htm (accessed 11.11.17).

OECD, 2013a. Economic Surveys: Greece, Overview, November 2013.

OECD, 2013b. The Role of Banks, Equity Markets and Institutional Investors in Long-Term Financing For Growth and Development, Report for G20 leaders, February 2013.

OECD, 2014. Annual Survey of Large Pension Funds and Public Pension Reserve Funds, Report on Pension Funds' Long-Term Investments.

OECD, 2015. Risk and Return Characteristics of Infrastructure Investment in Low Income Countries. OECD and World Bank Group, Paris, 3 September 2015.

Oikonomou, Ch, 1998. Perspectives of community agriculture and necessary adjustments of the Greek agriculture policies. In: Zioganas, Ch (Ed.). Competitiveness and Integrated Development of the Agricultural Sector: The New Challenges for Greece. "ZHTH" Editions, Thessaloniki, pp. 369–384.

Oikonomou, G., Sabethai, I., Symiyiannis, G. (Eds.), 2010. Current Account Transactions in Greece: Cause of Imbalances and Policy Suggestions [Ισοζύγιο Τρεχουσών Συναλλαγών της Ελλάδας: Αιτίες Ανισορροπιών και προτάσεις πολιτικής]. Bank of Greece, Athens, July 2010 accessed from https://www.bankofgreece.gr/BogEkdoseis/%CE%99%CF%83%CE%BF%CE%B6%CF%8D%CE%B3%CE%B9%CE%BF_%CE%A4%CF%81%CE%AD%CF%87%CE%BF%CF%85%CF%83%CF%89%CE%BD_%

CE%A3%CF%85%CE%BD%CE%B1%CE%BB%CE%BB%CE%B1%CE%B3%CF%
8E%CE%BD.pdf, the 25th of November 2015.

Oikonomou, G.E., 1992. The Greek Economy in the Prospect of 1992 [Η Ελληνική οικονομία στην προοπτική του 1992]. Institute of Economic and Industrial Research, Athens.

Oral, M., Chabchoub, H., 1996. On the methodology of the world competitiveness report. Eur. J. Oper. Res. 90, 514–535.

Oughton, C., 1997. Competitiveness policy in the 1990s. Econ. J. 107 (444), 1486–1503.

Owen, J., 2015. The Role of Investment Infrastructure in your investment portfolio, Redpoint Investment Management, accessed from http://www.redpointim.com/sites/default/files/The%20role%20of%20Infrastructure_FINAL.pdf (accessed 11.11.17).

Pagkalos, Th.G., 2012. We all ate them, together: Debt: How much? When? Whom? How? [Μαζί τα φάγαμε: Χρέος: Πόσο; Πότε; Ποιοι; Πώς;]. e-book.

Pagoulatos, G., 2008a. Public administration, political system, economy: the structural limitations [Δημόσια διοίκηση, πολιτικό σύστημα, οικονομία: Οι δομικοί περιορισμοί]. In: Giannitsis, T. (Ed.), (2008) Greek Economy: Crucial Issues of Economic Policy [Ελληνική Οικονομία: Κρίσιμα Ζητήματα Οικονομικής Πολιτικής]. Alpha Bank Editions, Athens, 211–222.

Panayiotou, A., Medda, F., 2014. Attracting private sector participation in infrastructure investment: the UK case. Public Money Manage. 34 (6), 425–431.

Papadopoulos, Th, 2016. Whom and How Have Driven us to Bankruptcy [Ποιοι και πως μας οδήγησαν στη χρεοκοπία]. Gutenberg, Athens.

Papageorgiou, C., 1995. Agricultural Policy [Η Αγροτική Πολιτική], 455–492, Maraveyas, N., Tsinisizelis, M. (1995) in Maraveyas, N, Tsinisizelis, M. (eds.) (1995) The Integration of the European Union: Institutional, Political and Economic Aspects, Athens: «Θεμέλιο» Editions.

Papathanasiou, Y., 2017. 8 Months [8 Μήνες]. Livanis Editions, Athens.

Papoulias, D., 2008a. Public policies: what impedes their implementation? [Δημόσιες πολιτικές: Τι εμποδίζει την εφαρμογή τους;]. In: Giannitsis, T. (Ed.), Greek Economy: Crucial Issues of Economic Policy [Ελληνική Οικονομία: Κρίσιμα Ζητήματα Οικονομικής Πολιτικής]. Alpha Bank Editions, Athens, pp. 185–209.

Papoulias, D., 2011. Management and Change: Simultaneously and Urgently [Διαχειρίζομαι και αλλάζω: ταυτοχρόνως και επειγόντως]. Kritiki Edition, Athens.

Pappas, T., 2015. Populism and Crisis in Greece [Λαϊκισμός και κρίση στην Ελλάδα]. Ikaros editions, Athens.

Paraskevopoulos, C.J., 2007. Social Capital and Public Policy in Greece, Hellenic observatory papers on Greece and Southeast Europe, GreeSE Pap. 9.

Peacock, A.T., Wiseman, J., 1961. The Growth of Public Expenditure in the United Kingdom. Princeton University Press, Princeton.

Peng, H.W., Newell, G., 2007. The significance of infrastructure in Australian investment portfolios. Pac. Rim Prop. Res. J. 13 (4), 423–450.

Pesaran, M.H., 1987. The Limits to Rational Expectations. Basil Blackwell, Oxford.

Petrakis, P., 2012. The Greek Economy and the Crisis: Challenges and Responses. Springer, New York.

Petrakis, P.E., 2011. The Greek Economy and the Crisis: Challenges and Opportunities [Η Ελληνική Οικονομία και η Κρίση: Προκλήσεις και Προοπτικές]. Quaestor, Athens.

Petrakos, G., Pscycharis, Y., 2016. Regional Development in Greece [Περιφερειακή Ανάπτυξη στην Ελλάδα], second ed. Kritiki Editions, Athens.

Pitelis, Ch., 2013. Developmental Manufacturing Policy in Modern Greece, 1993–2012 [Αναπτυξιακή βιομηχανική πολιτική στη σύγχρονη Ελλάδα, 1993-2012]. Gutenberg Editions, Athens.

Plosser, C.I., 1989. Understanding real business cycles. J. Econ. Persp. 3, 51–78.

Pomini, M., 2003. Endogenous growth theory as a lakatosian case study. In: Salvadori, N. (Ed.) The Theory of Economic Growth: A "Classical" Perspective. Edward Elgar, Cheltenham, 42–60.

Porter, M., 1990. The Competitive Advantage of Nations: Creating and Sustaining Superior Performance. The Free Press, New York.

Porter, M., 1998. On Competition. Harvard Business School Press, Boston.

Preeg, E.H., 1994. Krugmanian competitiveness: a dangerous obfuscation. Washington Quar. 17 (4), 111–122.

Preqin, 2017. 2017 Preqin Global Infrastructure Report, sample pages, accessed from https://www.preqin.com/docs/samples/2017-Preqin-Global-Private_Equity-and-Venture-Capital-Report-Sample-Pages.pdf (accessed 11.11.17).

PWC and GIIA, 2017. Global infrastructure investment: the role of private capital in the delivery of essential assets and services, UK, accessed from https://www.pwc.com/gx/en/industries/assets/pwc-giia-global-infrastructure-investment-2017-web.pdf (accessed 16.11.17).

Rapanos, V., 2008. Economic theory and fiscal policy: fiscal institutions in Greece [Οικονομική Θεωρία και δημοσιονομική πολιτική: οι δημοσιονομικοί θεσμοί στην Ελλάδα]. In: Giannitis, T. (Ed.) In search of a Greek development model [Σε αναζήτηση ενός Ελληνικού Μοντέλου Ανάπτυξης]. Papazisis Editions, Athens, 159–180.

Reinhart, C.M., Rogoff, K.S., 2009. This Time is Different: Eight Centuries of Financial Folly. Princeton University Press, New Jersey.

Roberts, M., Patel, J., Minella, G., 2015. Why Invest in Infrastructure? Research Report, Deutsche Asset and Wealth Management, May 2015, accessed from http://infrastructure.deutscheam.com/content/_media/Research_Deutsche_AWM_Why_Invest_in_Infrastructure_May_2015.pdf (accessed 16.11.17).

Romaios, G., 2012. Greece of Debts and Bankruptcies [Η Ελλάδα των Δανείων και των Χρεοκοπιών]. Pataki Editions, Athens.

Romer, P., 1996. Advanced Macroeconomics. McGraw-Hill, New York.

Romer, P., 2016. The Trouble with Macroeconomics, Speech Delivered on January 5th, 2016, Commons Memorial Lecture. Omicron Delta Epsilon Society, New York.

Roukanas, S.A., Sklias, P.G. (Eds.), 2014. The Greek Political Economy 2000–2010: From the EMU to the Support Mechanism [Η Ελληνική Πολιτική Οικονομία 2000–2010: Από την ΟΝΕ στον Μηχανισμό Στήριξης]. Livanis Edition, Athens.

Russ, D., Thambiah, Y., Foscari, N., 2010. Can Infrastructure Investing Enhance Portfolio Efficiency? Credit Suisse, White Paper, accessed from https://www.credit-suisse.com/pwp/am/downloads/marketing/infrastructure_ch_uk_lux_ita_scandinavia.pdf (accessed 9.11.17).

Salvadori, N. (Ed.), 2003. The Theory of Economic Growth: A "Classical" Perspective. Edward Elgar, Cheltenham.

Sargent, T., 2007. Evolution and Intelligent Design, AEA Presidential Address. New York University, New York.

Sarris, A., 2017. The Greek economic crisis: anatomy, explanation, facing and perspectives [Η Ελληνική οικονομική κρίση: Ανατομία, αιτιολογία, αντιμετώπιση και προοπτικές], Speech delivered in the Greek Scientists from Epirus, April, 26th 2017.

Scarth, M., 2004. Macroeconomics: An Introduction to Advanced Methods. MacMaster, Ontario.

Schawb, K. (Ed.), 2011. The Global Competitiveness Report 2011–2012. World Economic Forum, Geneva, Switzerland.

Scott, B.R., Lodge, G.C., 1985. U.S. Competitiveness in the World Economy. Harvard Business School Press, Boston.

Senge, P.M., 1990. The Fifth Discipline: The Art and Practice of the Learning Organisation. Currency Doubleday, New York.

Sherman, H.J., 1964. Macroeconomic Dynamics: Growth, Employment and Prices. Appleton-Century-Crofts, New York.

Simitis, C., 2005. Policy for a Creative Greece 1996–2004 [Πολιτική για μια Δημιουργική Ελλάδα]. Polis Editions, Athens.

Solow, R.M., 1957. Technical change and the aggregate production function. Rev. Econ. Stat. 39 (3), 312–320.

Solow, R.M., 1974. Intergenerational equity and exhaustible resources. Rev. Econ. Stud. 41, 29–45.

Solow, R., 2010. Building a Science of Economics for the Real World, Statement for the House Committee on Science and Technology, July 20, 2010.

Sordi, S., 2003. The interaction between growth and cycle in macrodynamic models of the economy. In: Salvadori, N. (Ed.) The Theory of Economic Growth: A "Classical" Perspective. Edward Elgar, Cheltenham, pp. 285–305.

Sorensen, P.B., Whitta-Jacobsen, H.J., 2005. Introducing Advanced Macroeconomics: Growth and Business Cycles. McGraw Hill, New York.

Spartiotis, D., Stournaras, Y., 2010. The Fundemantal Causes of Bank Bankruptcies and Financial Markets: The 2007-2008 Experience [Τα θεμελιώδη αίτια της κατάρρευσης των τραπεζών και των χρηματοπιστωτικών αγορών: Η εμπειρία 2007-2008]. Gutenberg, Athens.

Stasinopoulos, G., 2011. The crisis of economic policy in Greece, 1991–2010: in search of a new model of economic policy [Η κρίση της οικονομικής πολιτικής στην Ελλάδα, 1991–2010: Προς αναζήτηση νέου μοντέλου οικονομικής πολιτικής]. Greek Scientific Association of Political Economy ([Επιστημονική Εταιρεία Πολιτικής Οικονομίας] Economic crisis and Greece [Οικονομική Κρίση στην Ελλάδα]. Gutenberg, Athens, 165–179.

Stiglitz, J.E., 2000. The Economics of the Public Sector. W.W. Norton & Company, New York.

Stonier, A.W., Hague, D.C., 1972. A Textbook of Economic Theory. Longman, London.

Stournaras, Y., 2008. Economic Policy and Real Convergence [Οικονομική πολιτική και πραγματική σύγκλιση]. In: Giannitsis, T. (Ed.), Greek Economy: Critical Economic Policy Issues [Ελληνική οικονομία: Κρίσιμα ζητήματα οικονομικής πολιτικής]. Alpha Bank, Athens, 53–76.

Subacchi, P., Pickford, S., Tentori, D., Huang, H., 2014. Building Growth in Europe: Innovative Financing for Infrastructure. Chatham House Report, The Royal Institute of International Affairs, London.

Thurow, L., 1992. Head to Head: The Coming Economic Battle among Japan, Europe and America. Morrow, New York, NY.

Toussaint, E., 2017. The Public Debt: Its History and its Meaning at the Contemporary Crisis [Το Δημόσιο Χρέος: Η ιστορία του και η σημασία του στην σημερινή κρίση]. Redmarks Editions, Athens.

Triantafyllidou, A., 2014. Migration in Greece: Recent Developments in 2014. ELIAMEP, Athens.

Tsampra and Chatzimichalidou, 2014. The course of "expansion" of employment in the Greek public sector after the entrance in the EMU to the support mechanism [Η πορεία «διόγκωσης» της απασχόλησης στον ελληνικό δημόσιο τομέα από την ένταξη στην ΟΝΕ μέχρι το Μηχανισμό Στήριξης]. In: Roukanas, S.A., Sklias, P.G. (Eds.), The Greek Political Economy 2000−2010: From the EMU to the Support Mechanism [Η Ελληνική Πολιτική Οικονομία 2000−2010: Από την ΟΝΕ στον Μηχανισμό Στήριξης]. Livanis Edition, Athens, 268−302.

Tsatsos, N., 2001. Shadow Economy and Tax Evasion in Greece [Παραοικονομία και Φοροδιαφυγή στην Ελλάδα]. Papazisis Editions, Athens.

Tsoukalas, C., 2013. Greece of Oblivion and Truth: From Long Adolescence to Violent Adulthood [Η Ελλάδα της λήθης και της αλήθειας: Από τη μακρά εφηβεία στη βίαια ενηλικίωση]. Themelio Edition, Athens.

Tsoukas, C., 2015. The Tragedy of Commons [Η Τραγωδία των Κοινών]. Ikaros Editions, Athens.

Tzannatos, P., 2016. Greece of Memoranda 2010−2012: The Figures, the Programme and International Experience Since 1980 [Η Ελλάδα των Μνημονίων 2010−2012: Οι αριθμοί, το πρόγραμμα και η διεθνής εμπειρία από το 1980]. Gutenberg Editions, Athens.

UBS, unkown year. An introduction to infrastructure as an asset class, available on-line.

UNCTAD, 2011. Scope and Definition, UNCTAD Series on Issues in International Investment Agreements II, United Nations, New York and Geneva.

UNCTAD, 2015a. World Investment Report 2015: Reforming International Investment Governance. United Nations Publication, New York and Geneva.

UNCTAD, 2015b. Advancing the Post-2015 Development Agenda Requires a Development Policy Rethink, Policy Brief no 31, February 2015.

Uzawa, H., 1965. Optimum technical change in an aggregate model of economic growth. Inter. Econ. Rev. 6, 18−31.

Vaitsos, K., Giannitsis, T., Deniozos, D. (Eds.), 1994. The Debate on Privatizations: Theoretical Approaches and Significance for Greece [Η προβληματική των ιδιωτικοποιήσεων: Θεωρητικές προσεγγίσεις και σημασία για την Ελλάδα]. Paratiritis, Thessaloniki.

Valdés, B., 1999. Economic Growth: Theory, Empirics and Policy. Edward Elgar, Cheltenham.

Van Oorschot, W., Arts, W., Gelissen, J., 2006. Social capital in Europe: measurement and social and regional distribution of a multifaceted phenomenon. Acta Sociol. 49 (2), 149−167.

Varoufakis, Y., 2017. Ανίκητοι Ηττημένοι [Adults in the Room: My Battle with Europe's Deep Establishment]. Patakis Editions, Athens.

Venizelos, E., 2017. Myths and Realities for the Public Debt: 2012−2017 [Μύθοι και Αλήθειες για το Δημόσιο Χρέος: 2012−2017]. Epikentro Publications, Thessaloniki.

Verdum, A., 2015. A historical institutionalist explanation of the EU's responses to the euro area financial crisis. J. Eur. Pub. Pol. 22 (2), 219−237.

Vetter, S., 2013a. Do all roads lead to fiscal union? Options for deeper fiscal integration in the eurozone, Deutsche Bank, Research Briefing, EU Monitor European Integration.

Vetter, S., 2013b. The Single European Market 20 years on: achievements, unfulfilled expectations & further potential, Deutsche Bank, Research Briefing, EU Monitor European Integration.

Viera, C., Viera, I., Costa, S., 2003. Monetary and Fiscal Policies inEMU: some relevant issues, Ezoneplus WP no 17F, Jean Monnet Centre of Excellence, Freie Universitat Berlin, Germany.

Waheeduzzaman, A.N.M., 2002. Competitiveness, Human Development and Inequality: A Cross National Comparative Inquiry, CR, 12, 2, 13-29.

Waheeduzzaman, A.N.M., Ryans, J.K., 1996. Definition perspectives, and understanding of international competitiveness: a quest for common ground. CR 6 (2), 7−23.

Webster's New World Dictionary, 1957. College Edition. The World Publishing Company, Cleveland and New York.

Woodford, M., 1997. Self-fulfilling expectations and fluctuations in aggregate demand. In: Mankiw, N.G., Romer, D. (Eds.), New Keynesian Economics, Vol. II: Coordination Failures and Real Rigidities. MIT Press, Cambridge MA, pp. 77−110.

World Bank, I.M.F., O.E.C.D., 2015. Capital market instruments to mobilize institutional investors to infrastructure and SME financing in Emerging Market Economies, Report for the G20, Report no 101512, 1.12.2015.

World Economic Forum, 2016. Global Competitiveness Report 2016−2017, Insight Report. WEF, Geneva.

Xafa, M., 2017. Public Debt [Δημόσιο Χρέος]. Papadopoulos editions, Athens.

Youngson, A.J., 1956. The disaggregation of investment in the study of economic growth. Econ. J. 66 (262), 236−243.

Appendix: Additional theoretical implications

A.1 Potential theoretical implications

Autonomous investment has the capacity to generate use value and exchange value. For example infrastructure enhances the value of use and value of exchange for the products making use of this specific infrastructure. A bridge built to connect two areas, brings together firms from these areas, and helps them to progressively increase the value of use and value of exchange of their own products. But how about the bridge itself? In comparison to induced investment that enhances simultaneously the value of use and exchange of a specific goods or service provided, an infrastructure has a value of use but its exchange value is discovered only if it belongs in the private sector and can be sold and purchased for some reason. For the bridge itself, this would entail the possibility that someone purchases the state's bridge to use it for his own purpose. Thus, one can argue that its exchange value is rather limited. However, its use value is so great as long as everyone wants to use this bridge, and, at the same time, it is a producer of use value.

If the value of a good is a function of its use value and its exchange value, all possible combinations may exist: some goods may have limited exchange value and higher or no use value, some higher exchange value and limited or no use value, and some may lie in the middle, having both exchange and use value. This is illustrated schematically in Diagram 1, which indicates that infrastructure projects are characterized by an enhanced use value but their exchange value is rather limited. At the opposite end lie bonds of limited use value whose use may not be high but their exchange value is very high.

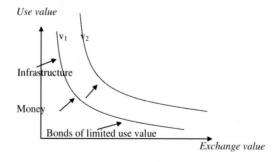

An economy that allocates its available resources to emphasize the production of goods of higher use value but of limited exchange value, not only fails to maximize the potential value of its goods but at the same time becomes subject to exchange value increases occurring in other economies. For example, this could be made by the firms of another wealthy neighboring economy that exchanges products with this particular one and would use the bridge and take advantage of both its use and its exchange value. The value levels increase as we move from curve v_1 to v_2. The higher the value levels of a product, the higher its utility.

If an economy chooses, for various reasons (whether political, social, the role of interest groups, etc.) to invest primarily in autonomous investment and infrastructure than in induced investment, we can depict two goods, one for infrastructure and one for induced investment at a diagram of indifference curves. Indifference curves can be illustrated to be quasi-linear and vertically sloped, since the economy prefers to allocate more of one good (infrastructure good) than for the other (induced).

We can illustrate the exchange patterns of two states in a common space that have opened their borders and allow free trade and exchange, by the use of an Edgeworth box that contains the indifference curves for both economies that exchange goods, from infrastructure investments and from induced investments (see Fig. A.1). Assume a home country, state H, and a foreign country, state F. State H emphasizes infrastructure and has a limited induced investment. State F follows a more balanced approach in choosing between autonomous (infrastructure) and induced investment. For products X (from infrastructure) and Y (from induced investment good), the indifference curve of state H will be vertically sloped (preferences are emphasized for infrastructure), while for state F (where infrastructure

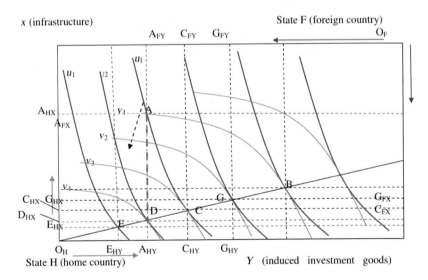

Figure A.1 Edgeworth box for two products X (infrastructure) and Y (induced investment) and two states, home country (H) and foreign country (F).

development is not overemphasized) indifference curves can be assumed to be convex (the usually illustrated curves). The vertically sloped quasi-linear preferences for state H show that if income increases, much more of the infrastructure goods will be preferred rather than induced investment goods. Fig. A.1 also illustrates the contract curve, as the locus of all contact points where the indifference curves of the home and foreign country are tangent.

State H could become better off by abandoning some of the X-products (infrastructure) that it produces and produce more of the Y-products (induced investment goods). State F on the other hand can abandon the production of some of its Y-products to produce some of its X-products.

Consider that at point A, state H has allocated its production stock into $O_H A_{HX}$ from infrastructure investment goods and $O_H A_{HY}$ from induced investment goods. A is a point of intersection between the two indifference curves of the two states. A shift could take place from A to B or C, which all belong within the same lens-shaped area (a part of this area is not illustrated in Fig. A.1 because of the shape of the quasi-linear indifference curve) and are both points of the contact line, where efficiency is maximized for both states and both goods. Infrastructure goods are sold from state H to state F and are reallocated. For example, by moving from point A to point C, both countries are better off. State H produces $O_H C_{HX}$ and $O_H C_{HY}$. In other words it improves the production of induced goods, without harming efficiency in the new allocation. An alternative path to follow is to turn to point B (within the same lens-shaped box) which is a Pareto efficient point and may improve substantially the production of induced goods in state H that has not gained at all out of this exchange process.

Hence, if an exchange is made that shifts the allocation of resources from point A to C, infrastructure goods will increase for state F from A_{FX} to C_{FX} and will reduce for state H, from A_{HX} to C_{HX}. In this case, induced investment enhances for state H, from A_{HY} to C_{HY}. The indifference curve for state F is shifted from v_1 to v_3, which shows that utility levels clearly increase for state F. For state H the indifference curve does not shift and the levels of utility do not change.

Had the indifference curve been more convex for state H, state H would have gained a greater part of the new combination of goods from infrastructure and induced investment, after a shift from A to this new combination (of more convex curves). In other words, under the present quasi-linear indifference curves, imposed by the emphasis placed on investing disproportionately more in infrastructure than in induced investment goods, state H loses in its trade and exchange with the foreign country.

The most likely and suitable allocation to occur is at point G, where a large part of infrastructure goods produced in home country H are gained by the foreign country F (the lost part is $G_{HX} - A_{HX}$), while country H now produces more out of induced investment goods, a total of G_{HY}.

However, what may take place is the following. As exchange proceeds with state F, and the economy of state H weakens even further (because of those reasons discussed in the present text) it is likely that F purchases more infrastructure goods from H and improves very much its position. This is illustrated with a shift from point A to point D, where—as seen in Fig. A.1—the indifference curve for the foreign country is shifted from v_1 to v_4 and the levels of utility are substantially improved. Again, as discussed before, had the allocation of indifference curves for state H been more convex, the loss would have been much less.

The analysis shows that a more balanced approach should be followed between autonomous and induced investment. One specification of this conclusion is that while support in infrastructure is needed for development, support in firms is also necessary, in particular firms of smaller sizes, until they turn into firms of larger or medium sizes.

Index

Note: Page numbers followed by "*f*," "*t*," and "*b*" refer to figures, tables, and boxes, respectively.

A

ABS PP. *See* Asset-Backed Securities Purchase Programme (ABS PP)
Acceleration, 81–84
  principle, 82–83
Administrative model, 70
Agricultural/agriculture
  EU Common Agricultural Policy, 104–105
  as principal funding priority, 126–129
  production, 104, 239–241
  sector, 220–221
AK model, 89–101, 99*f*
Amortization
  of private sector interest-bearing notes, 47
  of short-term bonds in European markets, 47
Aschauer hypothesis, 81
Asian Infrastructure Investment Bank, 78
Asset-Backed Securities Purchase Programme (ABS PP), 33
Autonomous investments, 82, 84, 120–121, 305
  implications from emphasizing, 84–101
    implications on balance of trade, 85–88
    implications on growth, 88–89
    implications on growth modeling and theory, 89–101
  induced investment, *vs.*, 81–84
    induced investment, acceleration, and cost of capital, 81–84

B

Balance of payments, 101, 244–255
Balance of trade, implications on, 85–88
Balassa indexes, 248, 249*f*
Balassa–Samuelson theorem, 111

Bank Recovery and Resolution Directive (BRRD), 33
Bank(ing)
  liquidity package, 44
  regulation, 33
  resolution, 33
  supervision, 33
  union pillars, 33
Borrowing, 25
"Brain drain", 53–54
Broad Economic Guidelines, 33–34
"Brownfield", 77
BRRD. *See* Bank Recovery and Resolution Directive (BRRD)
Bureaucracy, 55
"Business cycle", 35–36

C

C.A.P. *See* Common Agricultural Policy (C.A.P.)
C.S.F. *See* Community Support Framework (C.S.F.)
CA. *See* Current account (CA)
Capital (*K*), 89
  accumulation equation, 96
  cost of, 81–84
  investment theory, 36
Capital Requirements Directive (CRD), 33
Capital Requirements Regulation (CRR), 33
Capitalist crisis theory, 37
CBPP. *See* Covered Bond Purchase Programme (CBPP)
Center for Promotion of Employment, 224
Central planning, 55
Citizens' Service Centres, 55
Cohesion countries, comparing allocation of funds in Greece and, 147–151

Cohesion countries, comparing allocation of
    funds in Greece and (*Continued*)
    Distribution of Cohesion Policy
        Investments, 150*f*
    Distribution of Structural Fund and
        Cohesion Funds expenditure, 150*t*
Cohesion Fund, 103
Cohesion policy programming in Greece,
    151–194, 195*t*
    national and regional economic and social
        programming (1989–93), 153*t*
    national and regional economic and social
        programming (1994–99), 162*t*
    national and regional economic and social
        programming (2000–06), 177*t*
    strategic vision 2014–20, 212*t*
Common Agricultural Policy (C.A.P.), 102,
    104, 106, 127
Communication infrastructure assets, 77
Community, 215
    community fund allocation, 148*t*, 149*t*
    intervention/funds per priority, 222*t*
    limited contribution of community to
        enterprise support, 216*t*
Community Support Framework (C.S.F.),
    117
Competition, regulation and, 194
Competitive agricultural sector, 105
Competitiveness
    effects on, 244–255
    index, 115
    invisible target, 129–147
        allocation of funds in priority axis, 147*t*
        allocation of funds per priority axis,
            132*t*
        annual mean expenditure, 144*t*
        community fund allocation, 148*t*, 149*t*
        distributed financial resources, 131*t*
        initial recourse allocation, 145*t*
    programs, 71, 218–219
    theory and policy, 108–115
        complex views on, 113–114
        concept, measurement, and main
            challenges, 108–109
        and industrial change, 111–113
        and international trade, 110–111
        measuring, 114–115
Constant returns to scale (CRS), 90
Consumers, 74

Consumption, 92
    consumption expenditure approach, 270
    consumption-based economy, 267–270
Continuous production function, 89–90
Conventional economic approach, 60
Convergence, 255–267
    GDP (expenditure approach), constant
        prices, 264*t*
    GDP and components, 266*f*
    GDP at current market prices, 262*f*
    GDP per head, current prices, 261*f*
    production structure across regions, 259*t*
    regional GDP per capita, 257*f*
Core infrastructure projects, 80
Corruption, 59
Cost of capital, 81–84
"Costume" of policies, 106–107
Covered Bond Purchase Programme (CBPP),
    33
CRD. *See* Capital Requirements Directive
    (CRD)
Creative accounting, 42–43
Credit policy, 12
Credit rating of Greek economy, 21, 22*f*
CRR. *See* Capital Requirements Regulation
    (CRR)
CRS. *See* Constant returns to scale (CRS)
Currency value, 111
Current account (CA), 85

D
De-industrialization process, 111
Debt-to-GDP ratio, 43
    annual change of general government
        consolidated debt, 18*f*
    breakdown of consumption expenditure,
        17*f*
    credit ratings of Greek economy, 22*f*
    GDP and components, 16*f*
    general government consolidated gross
        debt of Greece, 16*f*
    net lending (+) or borrowing (−), 21*f*
    periods, 11–21
    total expenditure, total revenue and net
        borrowing of general government,
        20*f*
Debt(s), 8–11
    brakes, 34
    central government debt, 8*f*, 9*f*

to GDP and components, 66*b*
long-term government bond yields, 10*f*
long-term interest rates in Greece, 10*f*
per GDP, 69–71
points from existing theories on, 35*b*
stabilization, 27
Democratic system of representation, 1–2
'Design failures", 7
Desired investment, 83
Difference between total employees and
self-employees (Dif(NWTN-NSTD)),
267
"Disciplines", in Senge's theory, 106–107
Domestic investments, 101
"Dressing" of policies, 106–107

E
EAGGF-Guarantee fund, 126, 126*t*
EAPP. *See* Expanded Asset Purchase
Programme (EAPP)
ECB. *See* European Central Bank (ECB)
Econometrics, 218–219
Economic/economy
assessments, 71
consumption-based, 267–270
cycles, 25*b*
and explanations, 25*b*
distinction for economic growth and
development studies, 81–84
elites, 69–70
infrastructure, 77
integration process, 129–130
policies, 35, 70
primary goal, 73
programming and strategy, 75
recovery, 3
reforms, 10–11
restructuring process, 239–241
and social cohesion, 102
theory, 33, 109
stresses, 74
Economists, 74
Edgeworth box, 306–307, 306*f*
Edinburgh Council, 103
EDIS. *See* European Deposit Insurance
Scheme (EDIS)
EFSI. *See* European Fund for Strategic
Investment (EFSI)

Electricity assets, 77
Endogenous growth theory, 99
"Enterprise Greece", 224
Environment, 123
Equilibrium position, 83
ERDF. *See* European Regional Development
Fund (ERDF)
ESA95 methodology, 21
ESF. *See* European Social fund (ESF)
ESM. *See* European Stability Mechanism
(ESM)
ETBA. *See* Greek Bank of Industrial
Development (ETBA)
EU Cohesion Policy, 77–78, 86, 101–104,
121
funds, 147–150
management, and organizational learning,
106–108
EU funds allocation in Greece
amounts and levels of invested
expenditure, 117–120
comparing allocation of funds in Greece
and other Cohesion countries,
147–151
critical issues, 194–224
funding allocation and priorities, 120–147
Greece's balance with EU, 224–236
long-term effects and implications from
imbalanced allocation of funds,
237–255
output produced, 224
programming of Cohesion policy in
Greece, 151–194
public sector expenses, 267
regulation and competition, 194
tracing prospect of convergence, wishful
thinking and reality, 255–267
turning of economy to consumption-
based, 267–270
EU-wide financial and fiscal instrument, 101
EURATOM. *See* European Atomic Energy
Committee (EURATOM)
"Europe 2020" strategy, 104
European Agricultural Guarantee Fund, 232
European Atomic Energy Committee
(EURATOM), 32
European Central Bank (ECB), 7, 33–34
European Commission authorities, 221

European communities, 28−32
European Deposit Insurance Scheme (EDIS),
    33
European Financial Stability Facility, 34
European Fund for Strategic Investment
    (EFSI), 34−35
European institutional responses, 32−36
European integration process, 7
European Investment Bank, 78
European model QUEST II, 70−71
European Monetary Fund, 34−35
European Regional Development Fund
    (ERDF), 101, 232
European Semester, 34
European Social fund (ESF), 232
European Stability Mechanism (ESM),
    34−35
European Statistical Authority, 61
European Summit of Euro area leaders, 44
European telecommunication company,
    194−215
European unemployment insurance scheme,
    34−35
European Union (EU)
    EU Cohesion Funds, 216
    EU Commission analysis, 220−221
    EU Common Agricultural Policy,
        104−105
    EU Regional and Cohesion Policy, 102
    EU-funded programmes, 218−219
    funds, 215
        imbalanced allocation of, 120−123
    Greece's balance with, 224−236
    membership, 263
    policy priorities, 101
Eurozone partners, 33−34
Eurozone states, 23−24
Exogenous factors, 219
Exogenous technological disturbances,
    100
Expanded Asset Purchase Programme
    (EAPP), 33
Exports, 244−255
External balance, 61

F
FCE. See Final Consumption Expenditure
    (FCE)
FEOGA-Guarantee, 232

Final Consumption Expenditure (FCE), 17f,
    270
Financial Instrument for Fisheries Guidance,
    103
Fiscal balance, 34
Fiscal Compact, 34
Fragmented territory, 1−2
Front-loaded program, 66−67
Funding allocation and priorities
    agriculture as principal funding priority,
        126−129
    human capital policies, 124−125, 125t,
        126f
    imbalanced allocation of EU funds,
        120−123
    other priorities funded, 123−124
    private investments, 129−147
Funding culture, 128
Funds
    absorption, 194−224
    use and absorption, 194−224
        community intervention/funds per
            priority, 222t
        of EU funds, 217t
        indicative actual spending of
            community funds, 215t
        limited contribution of community to
            enterprise support, 216t

G
GCF. See Gross Capital Formation (GCF)
Global crisis, 19, 219−220
"Golden rule", 90, 92
Goods and services, 74
Greece
    balance with EU, 224−236, 237f
        average per year receipts, for
            Agriculture and Structural Actions,
            235t
        breakdown of Greek payments to EU
            budget, 238f
        contribution in EU net revenues, 237f
        contribution to EU total budget
            revenues, 236f
        core indicator value, 233t
        output per sector, problems and
            obstacles, 225t
        receipts from EU Funds, 234f
    bankruptcy, 6−7

cohesion policy programming in,
   151−194, 195t
   national and regional economic and
      social programming (1989−93), 153t
   national and regional economic and
      social programming (1994−99), 162t
   national and regional economic and
      social programming (2000−06), 177t
   strategic vision 2014−20, 212t
comparing allocation of funds, 147−151
   distribution of cohesion policy
      investments, 150f
   distribution of structural fund and
      cohesion funds expenditure, 150t
EU funds allocation in, 117−270
historical assessment of Greece's choice,
   28−32
long-term fall in GDP growth rates in,
   121f
suffocating problem, 244−255
   Balance of Payment variables, 257f
   current account balance, balance of
      goods, balance, 253f
   current account balance in EU
      countries, 256f
   employment in high-and
      medium−high-technology, 252f
   exports of goods, current prices,
      selected Eurozone countries, 247f
   high tech exports, 251f
   import penetration, 248f
   imports and exports, goods, services,
      goods and services, 247f
   imports of goods, 250f
   labor productivity per hour worked,
      245f
   number of people employed in ICT
      sector, 252f
   openness in international markets, 249f
   trade balance, 254f
   venture capital investments, 253f
Greek agricultural sector, 126
Greek Bank of Industrial Development
   (ETBA), 14−15
Greek Center of Planning and Economic
   Research, 218−219
Greek Competitiveness Programme, 221
Greek crisis, 6, 8, 61, 69

average private and public consumption
   expenditure, 41f
changes of six highest amounts of items,
   46f
consumption and investment as
   percentage of GDP, 42t
country of Greece, 1−2
   crises in history, nominal change of
      GDP, 2f
debt per GDP, 69−71
debts, interest rates and resulting political
   turmoil, 8−11
economic cycles and, 25b
extra payments, 45t
facts and figures, 2−8
   contraction and depression in Greek
      economy, 6f
   contraction results, 5t
   GDP contraction vs. GDP recovery, 4t
   Greek case, 3−8
   projection of growth trend of annual
      government gross, 19t
GDP per head and change of GDP per
   head, European OECD and OECD
   states, 29t
historical assessment of Greece's choice
   to integrate in European
   Communities, 28−32
IMF policies and mistakes, 62−69
mirror of European institutional responses,
   32−36
mistakes in predictions, 68f
periods of debt-to-GDP ratio, 11−21
policy-oriented and on-crisis policy,
   37−62
predictions and realized payments for
   2008 and 2009, 58t
repayment of Greece's loans for each
   year, 65f
significant variables of Greek economy,
   40t
six highest amounts for items of 2009
   expenses, 46f
structural and policy-oriented, 21−28
weighted and average cost/maturity of
   annual funding, 65f
yearly average annual growth rate of GDP
   and cumulative GDP change, 31t

Greek debt, 57
Greek development law, 70−71
Greek drachma, 12
Greek economy, 2, 54, 216, 233−234
  contraction and depression in, 6*f*
  credit rating of, 21
Greek National Council for Radio and
    Television (NCRTV), 194
Greek Ombudsman, 194
Greek Organization for Restructuring of
    Businesses (OAE), 14−15
Greek private sector, 50
Greek production, 241, 241*t*
Greek program, 67
Greek Regional Development Institute,
    218−219
Greek regional GDP per capita, 255
Greek society, 50
"Greenfield", 77
"Grexit", 62
Gross Capital Formation (GCF), 270
Gross domestic product (GDP), 77−78, 251
  debt per GDP, 69−71
  growth rates, 120, 262*f*, 263
  per head in Greece, 120*f*
  percentage, 118, 119*t*
  periods of debt-to-GDP ratio, 11−21
Gross policy errors, 22, 34
Growth
  equations, 99
  implications, 88−89
    on growth modeling and theory,
      89−101
  infrastructure, 77
  model, 71

H
Harmonious development, 102
Harrod−Domar model, 89−90
Health and Care, 124
Hellenic Authority for Communication
    Security and Privacy, 194
Hellenic Competition Commission, 194
Hellenic Data Protection Authority, 194
Hellenic Telecommunications and Post
    Commission, 194
Hicks' model, 82
Homo economics, 100
Homo economicus, 100−101

Homo socialis, 100
Human capital policies, 124−125, 125*t*, 126*f*

I
ICT. *See* Information & Communication
    technologies (ICT)
Imbalanced allocation
  of EU funds, 120−123
  implications from imbalanced allocation
    of funds, 237−255
IMF. *See* International Monetary Fund
    (IMF)
Immigration, 60
IMPs. *See* Integrated Mediterranean
    Programmes (IMPs)
Independent national fiscal councils, 34
Indicators, 114−115
Indifference curves, 306−307
Induced investment, 81−84, 306
Industrial change, competitiveness and,
    111−113
Industrial restructuring
  effects upon manufacturing and,
    237−243
  production structure across industrial
    groupings, 242*t*
Inelastic expenses, 194−215
Inflation, 12, 27, 39−41, 219
Information & Communication technologies
    (ICT), 258−261
"Information Society", 216
Infrastructure, 77, 79−80, 120−121, 150,
    152
  development, 77
  financialization, 79
  funding, 79
  gap, 78
  industry, 78−79
  investments, 78
    emphasizing for development purposes,
      77−81
  policies, 121−123
  transport, 120−121
Innovation theory, 37
Institutional building
  in agriculture, 127
  process, 32
Institutions, 76
"Insurance and social protection", 267

Integrated Mediterranean Programmes
    (IMPs), 101
Integration process, 73, 89
    autonomous *vs.* induced investment,
        81−84
        induced investment, acceleration, and
            cost of capital, 81−84
        emphasizing infrastructure investment for
            development purposes, 77−81
    EU Cohesion Policy, management, and
        organizational learning, 106−108
    implications from emphasizing
        autonomous investment, 84−101
        implications on balance of trade, 85−88
        implications on growth, 88−89
        implications on growth modeling and
            theory, 89−101
    investments, 74−76
        under EU Cohesion and Agricultural
            Policy, 101−105
    resource allocation, 73−74
    theory and policy of competitiveness,
        108−115
Interest rates, 8−11, 87
Interim evaluation, 219
International Institute of Management
    Development, 114
International Monetary Fund (IMF), 3−6, 8,
    10−11, 13−15, 20, 42
    policies and mistakes, 62−69
International position of economy, 251−254
International trade, 110−111
Invested expenditure, amounts and levels of,
    117−120
    breakup of total expenditure, 119*t*
    GDP per head in Greece, 120*f*
    Greek GDP, 119*f*
    levels of total, public, national,
        community, and private expenditure,
        118*f*
    long-term fall in GDP growth rates in
        Greece, 121*f*
Investment, 73−76, 86. *See also* Private
    investments
    behavior, 27
    choice, 75
    EU Cohesion Policy, 101−104
    EU Common Agricultural Policy,
        104−105

prioritization, 75
strategy, 76
supply of investment opportunities, 74
Ireland, GDP in, 28

K
King−Robson model, 99

L
Labor (*L*), 89
Law of motion of capital. *See* Capital
    accumulation equation
Lender of last resort (LOLR), 33
Lernaean Hydra of bureaucracy, 55
Levhari−Sheshinksi model, 99
LOLR. *See* Lender of last resort (LOLR)
Long-term effects and implications
    effects upon manufacturing and industrial
        restructuring, 237−243
    Greece's suffocating problem, 244−255
Long-term social choice, 52
Luxembourg, GDP in, 28

M
Maastricht Treaty, 103
Macroeconomic imbalances, 24−26
Macroeconomic theory fiscal policy, 23−24
Manpower Employment Organization, 224
Manufacturing and industrial restructuring,
    effects upon, 237−243
Marginal technical rate of substitution, 89
Market liberalization, 75−76
"Mature infrastructure", 77
Midterm review of CAP (2002), 105
MIPs. *See* Integrated Mediterranean
    Programmes (IMPs)
Modernization, 75
    of Greek agricultural holdings, 127
Monetary theory, 37
Monetary zone, 219
Multifactor productivity, 100
Myrdal's theory of cumulative causation, 24

N
N.S.R.F. *See* National Strategic Reference
    Framework (N.S.R.F.)
National Center of First Aid, 224
National competitiveness, 110, 113
National exchange rate mechanism, 7

National Health Institutions, 224
National Institute for Employment, 224
National Observatory for Employment, 224
National Strategic Reference Framework (N. S.R.F.), 117
National Tourist Organization, 224
NCRTV. *See* Greek National Council for Radio and Television (NCRTV)
Negative positioning of Commission, 13
Neoclassical growth equation, 99—100
Neoclassical model, 89—101
Net Exports of Goods and Services, 270
New Economy Development Fund (TANEO), 224
New Growth Theory, 99—100
Nominal GDP change, 2
Nominal unit labor costs (NULCs), 219, 244, 244*f*
Nonprofit institutions serving households (NPISH), 17
Nontax revenues, 57—59
NPISH. *See* Nonprofit institutions serving households (NPISH)
NSRF 2014—2020 policy document, 244
NULCs. *See* Nominal unit labor costs (NULCs)

O
OAE. *See* Greek Organization for Restructuring of Businesses (OAE)
"Odious debt", 27
OECD, 21, 80—81
  European OECD states, 29*t*
  national accounts database, 263
Olympic Games, 18, 27, 59—60, 219—220, 223—224
On-crisis policy
  errors, 22
  explanations, 37—62
Opportunistic infrastructure projects, 80
Optimal allocation, 73—74
Overemphasizing investment, 71

P
Pareto efficient point, 307
Payment and Control Agency for Guidance and Guarantee Community Aid, 224
Pensions, 87

PIGS. *See* Portugal, Ireland, Greece, and Spain (PIGS)
Policy/policies
  assessment, 69—70
  errors, 22
  indexes, 69—70
  orientation policy errors, 22
  policy-oriented explanations, 21—28, 37—62
  on private investments, 129
Political elites, 69—70
Political personnel, 62
Political turmoil, 8—11
Political—administrative mechanism, 59—60
Populism, 55—56
Portugal, Ireland, Greece, and Spain (PIGS), 23
Potential theoretical implications, 305—308
Power distribution, 76
Principal funding priority, agriculture as, 126—129
Private investments, 129—147. *See also* Investment
  invisible target of Competitiveness, 129—147
Private sector, 217—218
Private Sector Involvement (PSI), 18, 21
Production, 88—89
  cost, 74
  function, 90
  productive environment, 220—221
  rational exploitation, 104
Programme of Public Investments, 267
Programming failures, use and absorption, 194—224
  community intervention/funds per priority, 222*t*
  limited contribution of community to enterprise support, 216*t*
PSE. *See* Public Sector Efficiency (PSE)
PSI. *See* Private Sector Involvement (PSI)
PSP. *See* Public Sector Performance (PSP)
Public
  borrowing, 25
  goods production, 73—74
  loans, 25
  sector, 217—218
    expenses, 267

GDP and expenses of total annual budget, 268t
spending, 55
Public Sector Efficiency (PSE), 52
Public Sector Performance (PSP), 52
Pull factors, 59—60
Push factors, 59—60

Q
QE, 33

R
Rational exploitation of production, 104
Reform policies, 59—60
Regional Development Plan, 221
Regional production structure, 258—261
Regulatory Authority for Energy, 194
Resource allocation, 73—74
Return ratios, 81
Ricardian equilibrium, 26
Romer's model, 94

S
Salaries, 194—215
SBA. See Stand-By Arrangement (SBA)
Securities Markets Programme, 33
Self-employment, 263—266
Senge's theory, 106—108
Service-oriented character, 251—254
SGP, 34
Shrinking process, 255
Single European Act, 102
Single Resolution Fund (SRF), 33
Single Resolution Mechanism (SRM), 33
Single supervisory mechanism (SSM), 33
"Six-pack" legislation, 34
Small, medium, and large (SML), 237, 238f, 239f, 240f
SMEs, 223—224
SML. See Small, medium, and large (SML)
Snowball effect, 27
Social infrastructure assets, 77
Social needs, 1
Solow's analysis, 91
Solow's growth model. See Neoclassical model
Solow's model, 89—90
"Solow's residual", 92
Sovereign external debt crisis, 6

SRF. See Single Resolution Fund (SRF)
SRM. See Single Resolution Mechanism (SRM)
SSM. See Single supervisory mechanism (SSM)
Stability program, 13—14
Stabilizers, 23—24, 104—105
Stable high self-employment levels, 266
Stand-By Arrangement (SBA), 10—11
State-level competitiveness, 112—113
States-laboratories, 106—107
Steady state, 90—91
Stock adjustment principle, 83
Structural explanations, 21—28
Structural logic, 26
Structural weaknesses, 27—28
Substitution effects, 74
Supreme Council for Civil Personnel Selection, 55, 194
SWOT analysis, 194, 218—219

T
TANEO. See New Economy Development Fund (TANEO)
Tax revenues, 57—59
TFEU, 33
Tools and incentives, 75—76, 80—81, 151
Total factor productivity (TFP), 93, 100
Trade, 111
cycle, 35
surpluses, 111
Traditional IS-LM analysis, 25
"Tragedy of commons", 59
Transport infrastructure, 120—121
Transportation assets, 77
Treaty of Maastricht, 15
Treaty on Stability, Coordination, and Governance (TSCG), 34
"Troika", 10—11, 38
TSCG. See Treaty on Stability, Coordination, and Governance (TSCG)
Twin deficit hypothesis, 27
"Two-pack" legislation, 34

U
UBS, 79—80
Unemployment, 266
reinsurance fund, 34—35

United Kingdom, National Infrastructure
        Plan in, 77−78
Urbanization, 1−2
US Congressional Research Service, 47−48
US economy, 7

W
Wages, 87, 194−215

Walters critic, 23
War-theory, 37
Water infrastructure assets, 77
World Competitiveness Yearbook (WCY),
        115
World Economic Forum (WEF), 77, 114

Printed in the United States
By Bookmasters